ArtScroll Mesorah Series®

Rabbi Nosson Scherman / Rabbi Meir Zlotowitz

General Editors

הגדה של פסח
מנחת אשר

WEISS
ON THE
HAGGADAH

RAV ASHER

Published by

Mesorah Publications, ltd

FIRST EDITION
First Impression ... March 2008
Second Impression ... March 2022

Published and Distributed by
MESORAH PUBLICATIONS, Ltd.
313 Regina Avenue / Rahway, New Jersey 07065

Distributed in Europe by
LEHMANNS
Unit E, Viking Business Park
Rolling Mill Road
Jarrow, Tyne & Wear NE32 3DP
England

Distributed in Australia & New Zealand by
GOLDS WORLD OF JUDAICA
3-13 William Street
Balaclava, Melbourne 3183
Victoria Australia

Distributed in Israel by
SIFRIATI / A. GITLER — BOOKS
POB 2351
Bnei Brak 51122

Distributed in South Africa by
KOLLEL BOOKSHOP
Northfield Centre 17 Northfield Avenue
Glenhazel 2192, Johannesburg, South Africa

RAV ASHER WEISS ON THE HAGGADAH®
© *Copyright 2008 by* MESORAH PUBLICATIONS, Ltd.
313 Regina Avenue / Rahway, N.J. 07065 / (718) 921-9000 / www.artscroll.com

---

ISBN 10: 1-4226-0649-x / ISBN 13: 978-1-4226-0649-0
ITEM CODE: HAWH

Typography by CompuScribe at ArtScroll Studios, Ltd.
313 Regina Avenue / Rahway, N.J. 07065 / (718) 921-9000

Printed in the United States of America
Bound by Sefercraft Quality Bookbinders, Ltd., Rahway, NJ

Dedicated to
our beloved and esteemed Rav and Teacher

Maran Hagaon Rabbi Asher Weiss, shlita

for his unwavering devotion to Klal Yisrael
and for being an inspiration to us all.

In memory
of his dear young grandson

Itamar Meir Beckerman, z"l

By

Daniel and Jamie Schwartz
Teaneck, NJ

Dedicated in Honor of
The Rabbayim, Morot and Administrators
of Yeshiva Darchei Torah of Far Rockaway
and their Rosh Yeshiva,

Rav Yaakov Bender

We thank you for your
tireless dedication and devotion
in providing a Torah education
to our children and the entire
Far Rockaway — Five Towns Community.

May Hashem bless your efforts in the future

Moishe and Devora Smith

Introduction

I thank Hashem for placing my lot among those who sit and study Torah, and not among those who spend their day in idle pursuits, and who enabled me to reside in the Torah study halls throughout my life; to delight in the sweetness of the light of the Torah, and enjoy its sweet fruit.

Were our mouths as full of song as the sea, we still would not be able to thank You, Hashem, for one of the thousand thousands of thousands of favors that You performed for us.

May it be Your will that my minchah should serve as my thanksgiving offering, and may the merit of the Torah herein stand for me so that the Torah should not depart from my mouth, from my children's mouths, and from their children's mouths, forever and ever.

Asher Zelig Weiss

Table of Contents

Halachic Rulings and Practices

Halachic Rulings and Practices

৵§ Shabbos HaGadol

1. The Shabbos before Pesach is known as *Shabbos HaGadol* — the Great Shabbos — because of the great miracle that occurred then (*Shulchan Aruch* O.C. 430:1). The commentaries offer several explanations as to what this great miracle was:

    a) *Tosafos* (*Shabbos* 87b s.v. *Ve'oso*) explains that Bnei Yisrael prepared the sheep to be slaughtered for the *Korban Pesach* on *Shabbos HaGadol*. The non-Jewish firstborns gathered around and asked them what they intended to do with the sheep. The Jews answered that they were planning to offer the sheep as a sacrifice to Hashem, Who was going to slay the firstborns. The terrified firstborns entreated Pharaoh to free the Jews. When Pharaoh refused, a civil war erupted, and the firstborns slew many Egyptians. Regarding this the verse states, "To He who struck the Egyptians with their firstborn, for His kindness is eternal."

    In a slightly different vein, *Da'as Zekeinim* (*Shabbos* 87b) writes that when Bnei Yisrael prepared the sheep for slaughter, the Egyptians attacked them, since the sheep was an Egyptian deity. Hashem performed a great miracle and protected Bnei Yisrael.

    b) *Chizkuni* (*Shemos* 12:3) writes that the first mitzvah we received as a nation was to prepare the *Korban Pesach* four days before Pesach. The year of the Exodus, this day was Shabbos. The day therefore became known as *Shabbos HaGadol*.

    Similarly, *Abudraham* (p. 77a) cites from *Machzor Vitri* that the day is known as *Shabbos HaGadol* because the Jewish people entered into the covenant of mitzvos then. The *Acharonim* (*Olelos Ephraim* 31) explain that when a child turns thirteen he is considered a *gadol,* an adult, because he is now obligated to observe Torah and mitzvos. Similarly, when the Jewish people began to observe Torah and mitzvos, they became "*gadol.*" That was why the day became known as *Shabbos HaGadol.*

c) *Rashi* (*Sefer HaPardes* p. 343; *Shibolei HaLeket* 205; *Tanya Rabbasi* 42) states that on the Shabbos before Pesach, it is customary for the Rav of the community to deliver a lengthy discourse that extends into the afternoon, almost until *Minchah.* This made Shabbos seem longer than usual; hence the name "*Shabbos HaGadol.*" *Maharil* (3a) writes that Yom Kippur is known as "*Tzoma Rabbah*" — the Great Fast — because of its lengthy prayer service. Likewise, the Shabbos before Pesach is known as *Shabbos HaGadol* because of the lengthy speeches.

Alternatively, some explain that the Shabbos before Pesach is known as *Shabbos HaGadol* because a speech is delivered on that day by the Rav, who is the *gadol* — the greatest and most prominent person — in the city. *Tzeidah L'Derech* adds that a large (*gadol*) congregation of people gather to hear the extensive (*gadol*) halachos of Pesach (*Shibolei HaLeket; Pardes* ibid.).

d) *Mateh Moshe* quotes his *rebbi,* the *Maharshal,* as saying that the name *Shabbos HaGadol* is a reference to the day's Haftarah, which includes the verse, "Behold, I will send you Eliyahu HaNavi, before the coming of the great (*gadol*) and awesome day" (*Malachi* 3:23). *Maharshal* himself rejects this explanation, however. He says that if the day would be named after the Haftarah, it would have been called, "*Shabbos V'arvah,*" based on the first words of the Haftarah: "וְעָרְבָה לַה׳ מִנְחַת יְהוּדָה וִירוּשָׁלָ͏ִם" — Then the offering of Judah and Jerusalem will be pleasing to Hashem (ibid. 3:4), just as *Shabbos Nachamu* and *Shabbos Chazon* are named for the first words of their respective Haftaros.

e) *Tzafnas Panei'ach* (67d, by the *Maharit,* R' Yosef of Taroni) says in the name of his father, the *Mabit,* that when Bnei Yisrael were in Egypt, Moshe asked Pharaoh to grant them one day of rest each week. Pharaoh agreed, and Moshe chose Shabbos to be the day of rest. Each week, when

Shabbos was over, the Jews would return to their slave labor. After their last Shabbos in Egypt, however, they no longer had to perform slave labor. This Shabbos was therefore called *Shabbos HaGadol*: the great Shabbos that never ended.

f) *Shemen HaMaor* (*Yoreh De'ah* 15, quoting *Orim Gedolim*) explains the name *Shabbos HaGadol* based on the verse, "You shall count for yourselves from the morrow of the rest day (*HaShabbos*)" (*Vayikra* 23:15). Our Sages derive from this verse that the counting of the *Omer* begins on the day after the first day of Pesach, which is considered a "Shabbos" because we refrain then from work. (This is in contrast to the practice of the heretical Sadducees, who maintained that the counting of the *Omer* should always begin on a Sunday, the day after Shabbos.) The title "*Shabbos HaGadol*" was meant to distinguish the Shabbos before Pesach from the other "Shabbos" — Pesach — referred to by the Torah.

2. On *Shabbos HaGadol*, some have the custom to greet one another with the words, "*Shabbos HaGadol Hamevorach*" — a blessed *Shabbos HaGadol*, in place of the usual greeting, "*Shabbos shalom u'mevorach*" — a blessed and peaceful Shabbos (*Chida*, cited in *Kaf HaChaim* 430:2).

3. On *Shabbos HaGadol*, some recite *yotzros*,[1] additions to the Shabbos morning davening. There are those who recite *yotzros* even when *Shabbos HaGadol* occurs on Erev Pesach (*Pri Megadim, Mishbetzos Zahav* 430:1); others omit them on Shabbos Erev Pesach so they can hurry home to eat before chametz becomes forbidden (*Seder Erev Pesach She'chal B'Shabbos*, by R' Yosef Chaim Sonnenfeld; *Luach Eretz Yisrael*).

4. On *Shabbos HaGadol*, the Haftarah is read from *Sefer Malachi* (3:4), beginning with the words "וְעָרְבָה לַה' מִנְחַת יְהוּדָה וִירוּשָׁלָם" (*Siddur HaYaavetz* by R' Yaakov Emden, p. 226, 6). Some have the custom to read this Haftarah only when *Shabbos HaGadol* falls on Erev Pesach (*Ba'er Heitev* 430:1). Others have the opposite custom: they do not read this Haftarah when *Shabbos HaGadol* falls on Erev Pesach (*Aruch HaShulchan* 430:5, citing the Vilna Gaon).

5. It is customary for the Rav of the community to give a speech on *Shabbos HaGadol* about the laws of Pesach (*Magen Avraham*

---

1. See *Shulchan Aruch* O.C., *Rema* and *Mishnah Berurah* 68:1 regarding additions to prayers.

429:1). *Siddur HaYaavetz* states: "It is customary in all Jewish communities for the Rav to deliver a speech to his congregation, teaching them the laws of Pesach. He must caution them to rid their homes of actual chametz and to rid their hearts of that which chametz symbolizes: evil deeds, false ideologies, and corrupt character traits."

The central focus of the Rav's speech should be practical instruction in the relevant laws of Pesach, such as koshering dishes, ridding the home of chametz, baking matzah, etc. (*Mishnah Berurah* 429:2). If *Shabbos HaGadol* falls on Erev Pesach, the speech should be given on the previous Shabbos (*Mishnah Berurah* ibid.). Some are of the opinion that the Rav should speak even on Erev Pesach, but he should deliver his address earlier in the day (*Yaavetz* ibid.).

6. Some have the custom to recite a portion of the Haggadah, from עֲבָדִים הָיִינוּ until לְכַפֵּר עַל כָּל עֲוֹנוֹתֵינוּ, at *Minchah* time on *Shabbos HaGadol* (*Rema* 430:1). *Mishnah Berurah* (§2) explains that since *Shabbos HaGadol* marked the beginning of the Redemption and its miracles, portions of the Haggadah are recited on that day. The Vilna Gaon did not follow this practice, however, because we say in the Haggadah that the story of the Exodus should be told when matzah and maror are before us (*Be'ur HaGra* 430:3; *Maaseh Rav* 177; *Be'ur Halachah* 430).[1]

7. On *Shabbos HaGadol*, *Borchi Nafshi* is not recited (*Rema* ibid.).

8. On *Motza'ei Shabbos HaGadol*, וְאַתָּה קָדוֹשׁ and וִיהִי נֹעַם are not recited (*Rema* 295). If Pesach falls on Shabbos, וִיהִי נֹעַם and וְאַתָּה קָדוֹשׁ are recited at the conclusion of the previous Shabbos (*Mishnah Berurah* ibid. §3). Some hold, however, that וִיהִי נֹעַם and וְאַתָּה קָדוֹשׁ are not recited then either (*Shaarei Teshuvah* ibid. §2).[2]

9. When Erev Pesach falls on Shabbos, matzah is *muktzeh* and may not be moved. This is because it is forbidden to eat matzah on Erev Pesach (*Pri Megadim, Eishel Avraham* 444:1). However, young children who do not yet understand the story of the

---

1. *Shaarim HaMitzuyanim B'Halachah* on *Kitzur Shulchan Aruch* (107:5) notes that many Torah authorities recited only the first verse of עֲבָדִים הָיִינוּ, so as not to abandon the custom entirely.

2. *Luach Eretz Yisrael* writes that this is the accepted custom.

Exodus may eat matzah on Erev Pesach. For those with young children, matzos are not *muktzeh*, since they may be fed to the children (*Teshuvos Sho'el U'Meishiv Mahadura Tinyana* 2:77). If one has no other matzos [other than those to be used for the Seder], and would therefore not feed them to the children, then the matzos remain *muktzeh* (ibid.).

10. When Erev Pesach falls on Shabbos, neither the maror (*Eliyah Rabbah* 473:14) nor the charoses is *muktzeh*.

11. When Erev Pesach falls on Shabbos, some hold that *matzah ashirah* should be used for the third meal (*matzah ashirah* is matzah that contains other ingredients, such as eggs or fruit juice, and is unfit for the mitzvah of eating matzah) (*Shulchan Aruch* 444:1). However, the custom is to eat only meat, fish or fruit for the third meal, with no bread or matzah at all (*Rema* ibid., *Mishnah Berurah* §8). Some hold that one should drink a *revi'is* of wine for the third meal (*Shelah*, beginning of *Maseches Pesachim*). Some hold that the third meal can be fulfilled by discussing Torah subjects (*Magen Avraham* 444:2 citing the *Shelah*).

12. When Erev Pesach falls on Shabbos, it is proper to divide the morning Shabbos meal into two meals. One should eat, recite *Bircas HaMazon*, pause by taking a walk or the like, and then wash his hands to eat another meal (*Mishnah Berurah* 444:8). Some require a half-hour interruption between the meals (*Igros Chazon Ish* 1:188).

    Some have the custom to eat a meal of cold chametz foods immediately after davening and to eat hot, kosher-for-Pesach foods at the third meal in the afternoon (*Mishnah Berurah* ibid. §4).

13. When Erev Pesach falls on Shabbos, one should shake the crumbs off the tablecloth after eating the chametz meal (*Shulchan Aruch* 444:3). The small crumbs need not be thrown out of the house, since people walk over them and thus destroy them. It is proper to sweep the floor, however.

14. When Erev Pesach falls on Shabbos, if chametz is left over after the meal, one should either give it to a gentile as a gift, crumble it and flush it down the toilet, or feed it to a dog. If there is an *eruv*, one may relinquish ownership of the chametz and throw it into the street (*Shulchan Aruch* 444:4. *Mishnah Berurah* §16, 21; *Mishnah Berurah* 306:33).

ᴇᏰ The Search for Chametz

1. The house must be cleaned thoroughly before the night of *Bedikas Chametz*. Otherwise, it is impossible to search for chametz properly (*Rema* 433:11, *Mishnah Berurah* §46).

2. One should daven *Maariv* before beginning *Bedikas Chametz* (*Mishnah Berurah* 431:8).

3. The proper time for *Bedikas Chametz* is on the night of the fourteenth of Nissan, immediately after *tzeis hakochavim,* when it is not yet completely dark outside (*Shulchan Aruch* ibid.; *Mishnah Berurah* §1).

4. From one half-hour before the time of *Bedikas Chametz*, it is forbidden to begin any type of work or eat more than a *k'beitzah* (egg-volume) of bread. One may eat less than this amount of bread, or more than this amount of fruit (*Mishnah Berurah* §6). However, one should not eat a large amount of fruit (*Be'ur Halachah*). There is a disagreement among the *Poskim* whether one may learn Torah during this time; a halachah *shiur* that does not involve complex discussions of the subject matter is certainly permissible (*Shulchan Aruch* ibid. 2, *Mishnah Berurah* §7).

5. During *Bedikas Chametz*, one must search by candlelight in all of the places where chametz might have been brought (ibid. 2, 3).

6. It is customary to leave ten small pieces of chametz around the house before *Bedikas Chametz*. This is in order to ensure that there is chametz in the home for which to search. Otherwise, the blessing recited over *Bedikas Chametz* might be considered a *berachah l'vatalah* — an unnecessary blessing (*Rema* 432:2, *Mishnah Berurah* §13). Although some *Poskim* question the need for this practice, it would seem that nowadays it is certainly the proper procedure, since it is unlikely for chametz to be found after the house has been cleaned for Pesach. Therefore, there is a significant risk of the blessing being *l'vatalah*.

7. It is forbidden to speak between the blessing and the beginning of the search for chametz. If one spoke of matters unrelated to the search before beginning the search, his blessing is invalid and he must recite it again (*Shulchan Aruch* ibid. 1, *Mishnah Berurah* §5). Even after beginning the search, it is proper not to

discuss matters unrelated to the search until it is completed, but speaking once the search has begun does not invalidate the blessing. Once the search has begun, discussing matters related to *Bedikas Chametz* is certainly permissible (*Shulchan Aruch* ibid., *Mishnah Berurah* §7).

8. If a person begins his search for chametz before the night of the fourteenth, no blessing is recited (*Shaarei Teshuvah* §3).

ೞ§ Burning the Chametz

1. On the day of the fourteenth of Nissan, the remaining chametz must be burned until it is reduced to embers. Alternatively, it may be crumbled and thrown to the wind in such a manner that no one could benefit from it. It can also be thrown into a lake or river (*Shulchan Aruch* 445:1, *Mishnah Berurah* §1). It is customary to burn the chametz during the day, and not after *Bedikas Chametz* at night, just as the leftover meat of the *korbanos* was burned during the day. Another reason to destroy the chametz during the day is to remind people to perform another *bitul chametz* during the day (*Rema* ibid., *Mishnah Berurah* §6).

2. Chametz must be destroyed before the end of the fifth hour of the day.[1] *Bitul chametz* must be performed before the beginning of the sixth hour (*Mishnah Berurah* ibid. §7). If a person has a lulav remaining from Succos, or *aravos* remaining from Hoshana Rabbah, it is proper to use them as fuel with which to burn the chametz (ibid.).

3. One should not pour kerosene over the chametz itself to help it burn. However, he may pour kerosene around the chametz, to help fuel the fire. (By pouring kerosene over the chametz, it becomes unfit for consumption and therefore loses its status of forbidden chametz. One then loses the opportunity to destroy the chametz in the best possible manner, by burning it. Therefore, it is best to ensure that the chametz is still edible when it is burned.)

4. One should brush his teeth on Erev Pesach to ensure that no chametz remains stuck between them.

---

1. The hours referred to here are *sha'os zemaniyos*, which are calculated by dividing the actual day into 12 hours.

✎§ The Fast of the Firstborn

1. Firstborn males must fast on Erev Pesach, in commemoration of the miracle Hashem performed on Pesach night when He struck the firstborns of Egypt and spared the firstborn Jews. Whether one is the firstborn son of his father or of his mother, he must fast (*Shulchan Aruch* 470:1, citing *Maseches Sofrim*).[1]

2. Some hold that firstborn daughters must also fast (*Shulchan Aruch* ibid.). This is not the accepted custom, however, because the Torah does not give any significance to the status of a firstborn girl (*Mishnah Berurah* ibid. §4 citing the Vilna Gaon).

3. If a firstborn son is under the age of bar mitzvah, his father fasts on his behalf. If the father is also a firstborn, then according to some opinions the mother fasts on behalf of her child (*Rema* ibid. §2). According to other opinions, the father fasts for both himself and for his son (*Mishnah Berurah* ibid. §9). If a woman is pregnant or nursing, she may certainly rely on the lenient opinions and not fast. If a woman fasted once on behalf of her firstborn son, it is considered a vow, which must be annulled if she wishes to discontinue this practice (*Mishnah Berurah* ibid.). If a firstborn baby is under the age of thirty days, his father need not fast on his behalf (*Mishnah Berurah* §10).

4. If Erev Pesach falls on Shabbos, the fast is observed on the previous Thursday instead (*Shulchan Aruch, Rema* ibid.). According to some opinions, in such a case one need not fast at all. These authorities maintain that since this fast is only a custom, if it cannot be observed on its proper day, it need not be observed at all (*Mishnah Berurah* ibid. §6. See *Igros Moshe Orach Chaim* IV, 69:4).

5. In some communities it is customary for the firstborns to exempt themselves from the fast by participating in a *seudas mitzvah*, such as a *siyum* held in honor of the completion of a tractate of Talmud. Even if the firstborns did not complete the tractate themselves, it is nevertheless a *seudas mitzvah* for the person who completed it, and they may therefore join the meal. The prevalent custom is for the firstborns to be present for the

---

1. The *Beis Yosef* cites another source for this custom from the *Talmud Yerushalmi* (*Pesachim* 10:1). See *Mikra'ei Kodesh* (vol. 2, 22) for additional reasons for this practice.

conclusion of the tractate, thereby taking part in studying the final words of the tractate. They then join in the *seudah* (*Mishnah Berurah* ibid. §10). It is questionable whether this *seudah* may be made on the night of the fourteenth of Nissan in order to exempt the firstborns from the fast the next day (*Minchas Yitzchak* 8:45).

In places where it is customary not to rely on this leniency, if a firstborn wishes to participate in a *seudas mitzvah* such as a *bris milah* or *pidyon haben*, he must first perform *hataras nedarim* (*Mishnah Berurah* ibid.). Even if the *seudah* for a *bris milah*, *pidyon haben* or bar mitzvah are not held on their proper day, a firstborn may still partake, provided that he first performs *hataras nedarim*. The *mohel*, *sandek*, and father of the child (who are firstborns) may eat at the *seudah* of a *bris milah* without *hataras nedarim*, since it is considered a Yom Tov for them. However, they must fast after Pesach to compensate for the fast they missed on Erev Pesach. A person who is not a firstborn, but fasts on behalf of his son who is a firstborn, may eat at a *seudas bris*, even if he is not the *mohel*, *sandek*, or father (*Shaar HaTzion* ibid. §16).

6.   It is questionable whether the completion of a single tractate of Mishnayos warrants a *seudas mitzvah*, which would exempt firstborns from fasting. *Teshuvos Pri HaSadeh* (2:92 §2) states that no *siyum* or *seudah* should be made. However, elsewhere (3:91) he writes that if a Torah scholar knows a tractate of Mishnayos and he learns the mishnayos with the commentaries of the *Bartenura* and *Tosafos Yom Tov* and understands them well, he may make a *siyum*. *Teshuvos Pnei Meivin* (O.C. 103 s.v. *Hinei mekor*) writes that one may only make a *siyum* on the completion of all six *sedarim* (orders) of Mishnayos, or at least one entire *seder*, but not on the completion of a single tractate. *Teshuvos Binyan Shlomo* (59) writes the same. *B'Tzeil HaChochmah* (4:99) rules that if one learns an entire *seder* of mishnayos and understands what he has learned, then he may make a *siyum* which exempts firstborns from fasting. If a person learns a short *masechta* of Talmud (such as *Megillah* or *Chagigah*) quickly, he may still make a *siyum* to exempt firstborns from fasting.

7.   A *siyum masechta* made by a child under bar mitzvah age is sufficient to exempt adult firstborns from fasting.

8.   If a person completes a tractate, but not in its proper order, he

may still make a *siyum* to exempt firstborns from fasting (*Teshuvos B'Tzeil HaChochmah* 2:28).

9. If a person completes *Maseches Sofrim* or *Maseches Kallah* with its commentary, he may make a *siyum* to exempt firstborns from fasting (*Pnei Meivin* 103).

10. If a person completes a volume of *Navi* in his regular schedule of learning, then even one small volume of *Navi* is sufficient to make a *seudas mitzvah* to exempt firstborns from fasting. If he learned a volume of *Navi* with specific intent to make a meal for the *siyum*, however, it is not considered a *seudas mitzvah* (*Teshuvos Ha'Alef Lecha Shlomo* 386).

11. If a person learns a volume of *Chumash* in depth, he may make a *siyum* upon its completion (*Igros Moshe* O.C. 157). If he completes a volume of *Zohar*, it is questionable whether he may make a *siyum*, especially if he does not understand it.

12. According to some, firstborns may join in the *seudas siyum* even if they did not hear the conclusion of the *masechta* (*Teshuvos V'Hanhagos* 2:210 citing *Kehillos Yaakov*).

13. *L'chatchilah*, one should eat at the *seudas siyum* before eating at home (*Minchas Yitzchak* 9:45). Some hold that one should break his fast by eating at least a *k'koseves* (volume of a date) of food or drinking a *k'melo lugmov* (cheek full) in order to relieve his hunger. Only then is he allowed to continue eating later (*Teshuvos V'Hanhagos* ibid.).

14. Some hold that firstborns must redeem themselves on Erev Pesach (*Darkei Moshe* ibid. §2).

◆§ Matzah on Erev Pesach

1. One may not eat matzah on Erev Pesach (*Yerushalmi Pesachim* 6:1; *Rambam, Hilchos Chametz U'Matzah* 6:2). One reason for this is to show that the matzos we eat on the Seder night are eaten for the sake of the mitzvah (*Rambam* ibid.). Another reason is to ensure that the matzos are eaten enthusiastically on the Seder night (*Meiri, Pesachim* 13:1). A third reason is that matzah is compared to the *Korban Pesach*, which may not be eaten on Erev Pesach (*Rokei'ach* 280).
Some hold that the prohibition of eating matzah on Erev

Pesach is a Rabbinic prohibition (*Yitzchak Yeranen, Hilchos Pesach; Pri Chadash* 471:2). Others hold that it is a Torah prohibition (*Gilyonei HaShas, Pesachim* 99b; *Chasam Sofer, Toras Moshe, Parashas Bo*).

2. A child who is old enough to understand the story of the Exodus may not eat matzah on Erev Pesach (*Magen Avraham* 471). If he is not old enough to understand, he may be fed matzah on Erev Pesach, or on Pesach night before Kiddush (*Rema* ibid.; *Shulchan Aruch HaRav* ibid. 10).

3. Most *Poskim* agree that the prohibition against eating matzah begins the morning of Erev Pesach, not the night before (*Chok Yaakov* 471; *Chayei Adam* 129:13).[1]

4. Some have the custom not to eat matzah from Rosh Chodesh Nissan (*Chok Yaakov* ibid.). Others have the custom not to eat matzah from thirty days before Pesach.

~§ Other Foods and Drinks on Erev Pesach

1. According to some authorities, one may not eat *matzah ashirah* after midday on Erev Pesach (*Rema* 639:3, regarding Erev Succos; *Mishnah Berurah* ibid. §27). The custom, however, is to forbid *matzah ashirah* from the tenth hour of the day (*Mishnah Berurah* 471, *Shaar HaTzion* §1). If one started to eat *matzah ashirah* after that hour, he must stop (*Shulchan Aruch* 471:1, *Mishnah Berurah* §1, 2).

2. After the tenth hour of the day, it is permitted to eat fruits, vegetables, meat, fish, and eggs. However, it is best not to eat one's fill of them (*Shulchan Aruch* ibid., *Mishnah Berurah* §3, 4).

3. If a person knows that if he eats on Erev Pesach, he will be unable to eat with an appetite on the Seder night, it is proper for him to fast on Erev Pesach, in order to eat matzah with an appetite on the Seder night (*Rema* ibid.; *Shulchan Aruch* 470:3).

4. Some have the custom not to eat horseradish on Erev Pesach, or on the first day of Pesach outside of Eretz Yisrael, to ensure that

---

1. See *Tashbatz* 3:260. *Mishnah Berurah* (ibid. §12) writes that one should not eat matzah from *alos hashachar* on the fourteenth of Nissan. This implies that one may eat matzah the night before.

the maror is eaten with an appetite at the Seder (*Rema* 471). Others hold that this custom has no basis (*Mishnah Berurah* ibid. §15).

5. Some have the custom not to eat fruit on Erev Pesach, to ensure that the charoses is eaten with an appetite at the Seder (*Rema* ibid.).

6. One should not drink a small amount of wine on Erev Pesach, since wine satisfies hunger, and this will prevent him from eating matzah with an appetite. (Presumably, grape juice is included in this prohibition.) One may drink a large amount of wine, however, since this only increases one's appetite (*Shulchan Aruch* ibid.). One should not drink excessively until he is satiated, however, because it will ruin his appetite, and may also intoxicate him.[1] Similarly, one may not drink a large amount of liquor on Erev Pesach, for fear that he will become intoxicated (*Shaar HaTzion* §9).

7. The prohibition against drinking wine on Erev Pesach takes effect from the tenth hour of the day.[2]

⮜§ The Prohibition Against Working on Erev Pesach

1. It is permitted to work on the morning of Erev Pesach. In communities where it is customary to refrain from working in the morning, however, one must follow the local custom. In such a case, it is forbidden to work even in private (*Shulchan Aruch* 468:3, *Mishnah Berurah* §17).

2. On Erev Pesach in the afternoon it is forbidden to work according to all opinions (*Shulchan Aruch* ibid. 1). There is a disagreement whether work may be performed by a gentile for a Jew (ibid.).

    It is permitted to cut one's nails on Erev Pesach in the afternoon (*Mishnah Berurah* ibid. §5), but it is forbidden for a Jew to give a haircut on Erev Pesach in the afternoon, even

---

1. *Mishnah Berurah* §8. *Mishnah Berurah* rules in §6 that less than one cup, and certainly less than the majority of a cup, does not satisfy one's hunger. One may therefore drink this amount on Erev Pesach.

2. This is implied by the wording of the *Shulchan Aruch*. However, *Maharil* in *Hilchos Shabbos HaGadol* writes that the prohibition takes effect at midday.

without charge. Some authorities permit having a gentile cut a Jew's hair (*Mishnah Berurah* ibid.).

3. Activities permitted during *Chol HaMoed* are also permitted on Erev Pesach in the afternoon. One may also prepare utensils for Pesach (*Shulchan Aruch* ibid., *Mishnah Berurah* §7).

4. When Erev Pesach falls on Shabbos, it is questionable whether work is permitted on Erev Shabbos. It appears that we may be lenient in this matter (*Be'ur Halachah* ibid., s.v. *M'chatzos*).

✒ Eruv Tavshilin

1. When (at least) one of the Yom Tov days will fall on Friday, one must make an *eruv tavshilin* on Erev Yom Tov to allow food to be prepared on Yom Tov for Shabbos (*Shulchan Aruch* 527:1, 7).

2. Outside Eretz Yisrael, if the first days of Yom Tov fall on Thursday and Friday, an *eruv tavshilin* must be prepared on Wednesday to allow food to be prepared on Friday for Shabbos (*Mishnah Berurah* §1). One may not, however, cook for Shabbos on Thursday (the first day of Yom Tov), even if he has made an *eruv tavshilin* (ibid. §13).

3. An *eruv tavshilin* is made by taking a piece of bread at least the size of a *k'beitzah* (ideally, a whole loaf — *Rema* 527:2; *Mishnah Berurah* §8) and a cooked food at least the size of a *k'zayis*. The cooked food must be something normally eaten with bread, such as meat, fish or eggs (*Shulchan Aruch* ibid. 4, *Mishnah Berurah* §11). Ideally a respectable portion of meat or fish should be used (*Mishnah Berurah* §8). The cooked food may be boiled, roasted, pickled, or smoked. A food that was only salted, however — such as salted fish — cannot be used for *eruv tavshilin* (*Shulchan Aruch* ibid. 5, *Mishnah Berurah* §13).

4. If one prepared an *eruv tavshilin* using only a cooked food and no bread, it is valid *b'di'eved* (*Shulchan Aruch* 527:2).[1] If one prepared an *eruv tavshilin* using only bread, and not a cooked food, it is invalid even *b'di'eved* (*Mishnah Berurah* §6, 7).

5. When preparing an *eruv tavshilin* for Pesach, matzah is used in

---

1. *Mishnah Berurah* notes that if one remembers before nightfall on Erev Yom Tov that he did not use bread or matzah in the *eruv*, he should add it, and recite the formula, "With this *eruv*..." He should not recite a new blessing, however.

place of bread. One should not place the cooked food on top of the matzah, since this will likely ruin the matzah. Rather, he should place the cooked food on a plate (*Mishnah Berurah* 527:11).

6. The *eruv tavshilin* should be prepared before the woman of the house lights Yom Tov candles. Once she lights candles, she has already accepted Yom Tov, and the *eruv tavshilin* will no longer be effective for her (*Be'ur Halachah* 527:1, s.v. *Safek*).

7. When making an *eruv tavshilin*, a blessing is recited, followed by the declaration "Through this *eruv* may we be permitted to bake, cook, insulate, kindle flame, prepare, and do anything necessary on the Festival for the sake of Shabbos (for ourselves and for all Jews who live in this city)" (*Shulchan Aruch* 527:12). If one does not understand this declaration in its original Aramaic, he must recite it in a language that he does understand (ibid.; *Mishnah Berurah* §40).

8. If one did not recite the declaration, the *eruv* is still valid *b'di'eved*. If he remembers his omission before Yom Tov begins, he should hold the *eruv* and recite the declaration, but if he recited the blessing already, he should not recite it again. If he only recited the declaration but not the blessing, the *eruv* is valid (*Mishnah Berurah* ibid. §36, 63, 64).

9. When one prepares food on Yom Tov for Shabbos, he should be careful to complete his preparations early in the day (*Mishnah Berurah* ibid. §3).

10. Ideally, the bread used in the *eruv tavshilin* should be used as *lechem mishneh* for all three Shabbos meals and should be eaten during the third meal (*Mishnah Berurah* 527:48). Strictly speaking, however, both the bread and the cooked food may be eaten as soon as one is finished preparing the Shabbos food on Yom Tov (*Shulchan Aruch* 527:16).

◂§ Candle Lighting

1. On Erev Yom Tov, the woman of the house lights candles and recites the blessing, "Blessed are You, Hashem, Who has sanctified us with His commandments, and has commanded us to kindle the light of Yom Tov" (*Shulchan Aruch* 263:5).

2. Ideally, Yom Tov candles should be lit a short while before

sunset.[1] However, some have the custom to light candles after the men return from shul, immediately before the meal (ibid.).

3. Those who light candles after sunset on Yom Tov should be careful to melt the bottom of the wax candles to attach them to the candlesticks before Yom Tov, since it is forbidden to do so on Yom Tov (*Mishnah Berurah* 514:18; *Pri Megadim, Eishel Avraham* ibid. §6).

4. For the Seder, one should use large candles that will burn until after the *seudah* (which ends very late), since the primary purpose of Shabbos and Yom Tov candles is to illuminate the room in which we eat (*Haggadas Moadim U'Zmanim* p. 47).

5. When lighting Yom Tov candles, women should not light, cover their eyes, and then recite the blessing, as they do when lighting Shabbos candles. Rather, they should first recite the blessing and then light (the *Derishah*'s son citing his mother, in his introduction to *Tur Y.D.* vol. I; *Dagul Mei'revavah* ibid.). However, some women have the custom to light Yom Tov candles in the same manner that they light Shabbos candles (*Magen Avraham* 263:12).

6. Women should not recite *Shehecheyanu* when lighting Yom Tov candles. In places where it customary to do so, however, one should not object to the custom (*Mishnah Berurah* 263:23). If a woman recited *Shehecheyanu* when lighting candles, she should not answer "Amen" when she hears the *Shehecheyanu* blessing during Kiddush. Some hold that if she does answer "Amen," it is considered an interruption that invalidates Kiddush on her behalf (*Kaf HaChaim* 514:113; *Haggadas Moadim U'Zmanim* p. 48). It would appear, however, that this interruption does not invalidate Kiddush, since *Shehecheyanu* is part of Kiddush.

    Some hold that on the Seder night, even if she said *Shehecheyanu* when she lit candles, she should still have in mind to be exempted by the *Shehecheyanu* of Kiddush, and she should answer "Amen." Presumably, when she recited *Shehecheyanu* over the candles, she intended that her blessing apply only to the Yom Tov itself. The many mitzvos of the Seder (such as eating matzah and telling the story of the Exodus) also deserve a *Shehecheyanu*, and she is therefore still obligated in this blessing (*Mikra'ei Kodesh*, Pesach 3:38; *Luach Eretz Yisrael* by R' Y.M. Tukachinski, First Day of Succos).

---

1. See introduction of the *Derishah*'s son to *Tur Y.D.* vol. I; *Mateh Ephraim* 625:33, see *Eleph L'Mateh* §51; *Mateh Ephraim* 599:10.

❧ The Seder Plate

1. At the beginning of the Seder, a plate is brought before the head of the household containing three matzos, maror, charoses, karpas (or another vegetable), salt water, and two cooked foods, one commemorating the *Korban Pesach*, and the other commemorating the *Korban Chagigah*. It is customary to use meat and an egg (*Shulchan Aruch* 473:4).

2. The other members of the household need not have their own Seder plates; they all partake from the head of the household's plate (*Mishnah Berurah* ibid. §17).

3. When Erev Pesach falls on Shabbos, some hold that only one cooked food should be placed on the Seder plate, in commemoration of the *Korban Pesach*, since the *Korban Chagigah* was not offered on Shabbos. Others hold that two cooked foods should be used. This is the accepted custom (*Mishnah Berurah* §22).

4. According to the Vilna Gaon, two matzos should be placed in the center of the Seder plate; the maror on the top right; the charoses on the top left; and the z'roa and egg beneath them (*Maaseh Rav* 181).
    According to the Arizal, the Seder plate is arranged in the order of two inverted triangles. For the top triangle, the meat is placed on the right, the egg on the left, and the maror on the bottom. For the bottom triangle, the charoses is placed on the right, the karpas on the left, and the horseradish (for use during

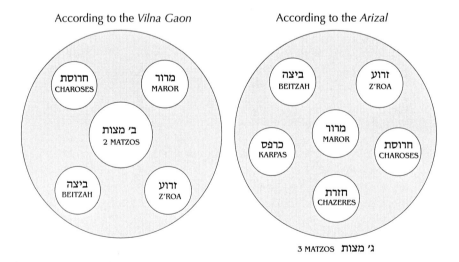

According to the *Vilna Gaon*   According to the *Arizal*

ג׳ MATZOS ג׳ מצות

Korech) on the bottom (cited in *Ba'er Heitev* 473:8).

According to the *Shulchan Aruch HaRav's* (ibid. 26) interpretation of the Arizal, the three matzos should be placed beneath the plate. According to the *Kaf HaChaim's* (ibid. §58) interpretation of the Arizal, however, the three matzos should be placed beside the plate.

5.   A beautiful plate should be used. Some have the custom to enhance the mitzvah by using a silver plate (*Seder HaYom*; *Vayaged Moshe* 2:5).

6.   There is a four-way dispute as to when the Seder plate should be arranged.
     a) On Erev Pesach (*Seder HaYom*; *Chayei Adam* 130, Laws of the Seder §1).
     b) After eating karpas, to prompt the children to ask why karpas is being eaten before the meal begins (*Shulchan Aruch HaRav* 473:20).[1]
     c) After Kiddush (*Tosafos, Pesachim* 114a s.v. *He'viu*).[2]
     d) Before Kiddush (*Abudraham*; *Pri Megadim* 486, M.Z.).

The accepted custom is to prepare it before Kiddush.

7.   It is customary to cover the matzos with a beautiful cloth (*Shulchan Aruch* 271; *Pri Megadim* ibid. M.Z. §13). The *Shulchan Aruch* and *Rambam* imply that it is not necessary to cover the matzos (*Vayaged Moshe* 12:8).

8.   Some have the custom to place cloths between the matzos, since each matzah is used for a different mitzvah, and each one has its own purpose according to *Kabbalah* (*Siddur Ha'Ari*; *Kitzur Shulchan Aruch* 118:8, *Lechem HaPanim*; *Ta'amei HaMinhagim* 520). Others hold that it is best for the matzos to touch one another (*Chayei Adam* 130, Laws of the Seder 1).[3] Some hold that no cloth should be placed between the matzos (*Vayaged Moshe* 2:9). The custom, however, is to place a cloth between them.

9.   The z'roa should be roasted before Yom Tov (*Mishnah Berurah* ibid. §33). If one forgot to do so, he may roast it at night. In such a case, however, he must be careful to eat it the next day, and not leave it for the following night (*Mishnah Berurah* ibid.). Some hold that the egg should also be cooked or roasted

---

1. However, in §25 he writes that the custom is to bring the Seder plate after Kiddush. See also *Maaseh Rav* 191.
2. This seems to be the opinion of the *Shulchan Aruch* (ibid. 1, 4).
3. He writes that separating the matzos is a practice of ignoramuses.

before Yom Tov, even though it may be eaten on the Seder night (*Vayaged Moshe* 3:10).

◆§ Preparing for the Seder Night

1. The Seder table should be set before Yom Tov, in order to begin the Seder immediately when one returns from shul, before the children fall asleep (*Shulchan Aruch* 472:1, *Mishnah Berurah* §1).

2. When Erev Pesach falls on Shabbos, the Seder table may not be set on Shabbos, since it is forbidden to prepare on Shabbos for Yom Tov. Rather, the Seder table should be set on Erev Shabbos. Similarly, outside of Eretz Yisrael where two days of Yom Tov are observed, one may not set the table on the first day of Yom Tov for the second night (*Pri Chadash* 444). Some permit having a gentile set the table on Shabbos for Yom Tov (*Maharsham, Daas Torah* 444:1, based on *Pri Megadim* 503, *Eishel Avraham* §1).

3. Some *Poskim* write that the cups used for wine should be rinsed before Yom Tov (*Chayei Adam* 130, Laws of the Seder §1). Others hold that they should be rinsed immediately before Kiddush (*Mateh Moshe* 615).[1]

4. Some hold that the seats should be prepared in a manner that will allow one to lean to the side during the Seder before Yom Tov (*Chayei Adam* ibid.; *Aruch HaShulchan* 472:3). Others hold that while the men are in shul, the family members should prepare the seats (*Misgeres HaShulchan* on *Kitzur Shulchan Aruch* 118:6).

5. As mentioned, some hold that the Seder plate should also be prepared before Yom Tov (*Kitzur Shulchan Aruch* ibid.), but the prevalent custom is to prepare it right before Kiddush (*Vayaged Moshe* 2:10).[2]

6. The Seder table should be set with beautiful utensils, to the best of one's ability. Decorative ornaments should be placed on the table, even if they are not used for eating (*Shulchan Aruch* ibid., *Kitzur Shulchan Aruch* ibid.).[3]

---

1. This also seems to be the opinion of *Shulchan Aruch HaRav* (473:39).

2. See the various opinions cited in the previous section.

3. Some hold that even ornaments taken as collateral for a gentile's loan should be placed on the table for decoration, but should not be used (*Chok Yaakov* 472:4 citing *Maharil*). This seems to be the opinion of the *Mishnah Berurah* (§6). Some hold that it is even permitted to use them (*Magen Avraham* ibid. §2; *Shulchan Aruch HaRav* ibid. §6).

7. It is a worthy custom for a person to set the Seder table himself, and not delegate this task to anyone else (*Vayaged Moshe* 1:5).

8. One should not have a gentile prepare the Pesach food and utensils on his behalf. It is preferable not to have a (Jewish) child prepare them, either (*Mishnah Berurah* 467:88).

Preparing the Salt Water and Charoses

9. The salt water used during the Seder should be prepared before Yom Tov. If one did not do so, he should prepare it before the Seder in an unusual manner (*shinui*), by first putting water in a bowl and then adding salt (*Chayei Adam* 130, 19:1). Some hold that one need do so only when Pesach falls on Shabbos (*Misgeres HaShulchan* on *Kitzur Shulchan Aruch* 118:4).

   If Pesach falls on Shabbos, and one did not prepare the salt water beforehand, he may prepare only a small amount, the bare minimum that will suffice for dipping the karpas (*Shulchan Aruch* 473, *Mishnah Berurah* §21).

10. Charoses should also be prepared before Yom Tov. If one did not do so, he should prepare it before the Seder in an unusual manner (*Pri Megadim* 444, *Mishbetzos Zahav* §2). If one does not dice the fruit for the charoses, but only cuts them into small chunks, he may do so even without a *shinui*. However, the spices may only be ground with a *shinui* (*Mishnah Berurah* 504:11, 19).

    Outside Eretz Yisrael, if one prepares charoses on the first Seder night, he may not prepare enough to use for both nights, since it is forbidden to prepare on one day of Yom Tov for the next.

    When Erev Pesach falls on Shabbos, the charoses should be prepared on Erev Shabbos (*Chok Yaakov* 444:25).

11. It is customary to make charoses using foods that symbolize the Jewish people, such as apples, pomegranates, figs, dates, nuts and almonds (*Rema* 473:5). Some hold that strictly speaking, charoses may also be made from vegetables (*Shulchan Aruch HaRav* 473:32).

    Spices such as cinnamon and ginger are added to the charoses, since they resemble the straw from which Bnei Yisrael made cement in Egypt (*Rema* ibid.). The spices should not be ground too finely, in order that they retain the appearance of straw (*Shaar HaTzion* ibid. §68). The spices should be mixed into the charoses, not sprinkled on top of it (*Vayaged Moshe* 4:3).

A small amount of wine or wine-based vinegar should be added, in order to soften the charoses and to give it the appearance of blood, representing the blood of Bnei Yisrael that was spilled in Egypt (*Rema* ibid., *Mishnah Berurah* §48). Some hold that when the charoses is first placed on the table, it should have a thick consistency. Then, immediately before dipping the maror, it should be diluted with wine or vinegar to make it fit for dipping. If one would dilute it initially, it would not resemble cement, and the symbolism of the charoses would be lost (*Chayei Adam* 130:4, 19:10).

When Pesach falls on Shabbos, wine should be added to the charoses before Shabbos, since it is forbidden to mix the wine into the charoses on Shabbos due to the prohibition against kneading (*Magen Avraham* 473:16).

If one forgot to add wine before Shabbos, some hold that it may be added on Shabbos in an unusual manner. First, wine or vinegar should be poured into a bowl, and then the other ingredients should be added. One should then mix them together using only his finger, or shake the bowl back and forth until the ingredients mix together (*Magen Avraham* ibid., *Mishnah Berurah* §67; *Shulchan Aruch* 321, *Taz* and *Mishnah Berurah* §68). If one makes them into a thin mixture, he may add the ingredients in the above order, and then mix them together normally (*Mishnah Berurah* 321:68, *Shaar HaTzion* §86).

੬ঌ Wearing a Kittel

1. It is customary to wear a white garment called a *kittel* for the Seder. Some explain that the *kittel* is a regal garment, with which one gives the impression of being a free man (*Taz* 472:3). In addition, a *kittel* resembles burial shrouds, and wearing it reminds a person not to behave frivolously on this joyous night (ibid.). Various other explanations are also offered.

2. Some hold that a mourner should not wear a *kittel* on the Seder night (*Magen Avraham* 472). This is the accepted custom. If a mourner does wear a *kittel*, however, no objection should be raised (*Mishnah Berurah* ibid. §13). Some hold that a mourner should wear a *kittel* even *l'chatchilah* (*Taz* ibid.).

3. There are various customs whether a man should wear a *kittel* on the Seder night during the first year of his marriage (*Vayaged Moshe* 12:2).

4. Some decorate the *kittel* by adding a silver *atarah* to the collar (*Mateh Ephraim* 610:11). However, one should not add an *atarah* of gold (*Eleph L'Mateh* ibid.).

✑ৡ Leaning to the Side

1. One should prepare his seat at the Seder table in such a way that he will able to lean in the manner of free men (*Shulchan Aruch* 472:2).

2. Even a poor person must lean on the Seder night.[1] A son at his father's table must lean, even if his father is also his primary *rebbi*. Although a son is obligated to revere his father and sit respectfully before him, it can be assumed that his father grants him permission to lean (*Shulchan Aruch* ibid. 5). Even if the father explicitly forbids it, some hold that his opinion is disregarded and the son may still lean (*Chok Yaakov* ibid. §9). Others hold that in such a case the son should not lean (*Pri Megadim* ibid., *Mishbetzos Zahav* §4).
   Some hold that even children under the age of bar mitzvah must lean (*Vayaged Moshe* 9:5).
   A worker who is at the Seder with his employer must lean (*Mishnah Berurah* ibid. §19).
   According to some opinions, a mourner is obligated to lean (*Mishnah Berurah* ibid. §13). However, it is proper for him not to lean on a luxurious couch. Rather, he should lean in an unusual manner: using only one cushion, or leaning on another person's lap. Even if his relative was buried on Erev Pesach and he sat shivah for only one hour before Yom Tov, he must lean (*Pri Megadim* ibid., M.Z. §3). If his relative was not yet buried, and he does not intend to have him buried that night (by gentiles), he must lean (*Siddur HaYaavetz*).
   The *Shulchan Aruch* (ibid., 4) rules that distinguished women are obligated to lean. The *Rema* (ibid.) rules that nowadays, all

---

1. If he does not have cushions on which to lean, he should lean on a chair (*Rema*). *Aruch HaShulchan* writes that he should place some sort of garment on the chair to lean on.

women are considered distinguished; nevertheless, the custom is that women do not lean. Sephardic women do lean, following the opinion of the *Shulchan Aruch*, while Ashkenazi women do not lean, following the opinion of the *Rema*. However, it is proper for the mother of the family to lean.

A person who shares the Seder with his *rebbi*, even if it is not his primary *rebbi*, may not lean without his *rebbi*'s permission (*Shulchan Aruch* ibid. 5). If his *rebbi* gives permission, then he must lean (*Mishnah Berurah* §16). Some opinions argue that even if his *rebbi* gives permission, he is not required to lean (*Aruch HaShulchan* ibid. 7). If the student eats at a different table within view of his *rebbi*, the *Poskim* dispute whether he needs his *rebbi*'s permission to lean (*Rema* ibid.; *Mishnah Berurah* §18).

A person who is exempt from leaning but leans nonetheless is considered a simpleton (*Taz* §10).[1]

3. The obligation to lean applies to the following parts of the Seder:
   - The first two *k'zeisim* of matzah (*Be'ur Halachah* 472:7, s.v. *Lo yatza*).
   - The four cups of wine (*Shulchan Aruch* 473:2; 479:1; 480:1).
   - *Korech* (ibid. 475:1).
   - *Afikoman* (ibid. 477:1).
   - *Korban Pesach*, while the Beis HaMikdash stood (*Bach* 475).[2]
   - *L'chatchilah*, one should lean during the entire meal (*Rema* 473:7).

   Instructions what to do if one did not lean for any of these parts of the Seder are found throughout the text of this Haggadah in the appropriate places.

4. One must lean to the left on a couch, or on a chair with cushions beneath his head (*Mishnah Berurah* 472:7).

   If necessary, one may also lean on another person's lap (*Mishnah Berurah* §8). However, he may not lean forward on his own knees, since this appears to be a position of distress (*Mishnah Berurah* ibid.; *Siddur HaYaavetz*; *Chida*).[3] One should not lean to the right (*Shulchan Aruch* ibid. 2). If he did so,

---

1. *Chok Yaakov* §10 is uncertain about this. See *Minchas Asher* on *Bereishis* 5.
2. *Pri Megadim* (477:1) questions this.
3. *Pesach Einayim* (5) adds that one should not place his hand over his mouth or brow for this reason.

according to some opinions he did not fulfill his obligation even *b'di'eved* (*Pri Chadash* 472:3).[1] According to other opinions, he fulfills his obligation *b'di'eved* (*Pri Megadim*, M.Z. §3).

Some hold that one may lean on another person's shoulders (*Teshuvos Torah Lishmah* 135).

If one leans on a bed or couch that is not beside the table, it is questionable whether he fulfills the mitzvah properly (*Chiddushei R' Chaim* on Shas, known as "R' Chaim stencil").

◄§ The Order of the Seder

The titles for the stages of the Seder have been accepted throughout *Klal Yisrael*. Their source is from the *Machzor Vitri*,[2] which was composed by *Rashi*. Others attribute them to R' Shmuel of Peliza, one of the authors of the *Tosafos* (*Siddur Iyun Tefillah*).

The *Sefer HaOrah* (end of *Hilchos Pesach*) writes that these titles were developed in order to organize the many laws of the Seder, and to ensure that no part of the Seder is forgotten.

Vayaged Moshe (14) adds another reason for reciting this list of titles before the Seder:

Every act of holiness requires preparation. One illustration of this principle is the custom to say "*Rabbosai nevareich*" — Gentlemen, let us bless — before *Bircas HaMazon*, based on the *Zohar* (*Parashas Devarim*; see *Magen Avraham* 192). For the Seder night, the *Rishonim* prepared a list of titles for the different mitzvos of the Seder. By reciting aloud the name of each stage of the Seder before performing it, we prepare ourselves to receive its holiness.[3]

• KADESH • URECHATZ • KARPAS • YACHATZ • MAGGID • RACHTZAH • MOTZI • MATZAH • MAROR • KORECH • SHULCHAN ORECH • TZAFUN • BARECH • HALLEL • NIRTZAH

---

1. This seems to be the opinion of the *Mishnah Berurah* (§11).

2. *Hilchos Pesach* 68, although Yachatz is absent from that version.

3. There are some mitzvos of the Seder for which no title was formulated, such as leaning, drinking the four cups, charoses, and reciting *Borei pri ha'adamah*. For each of these acts, there is a specific reason why no title was given. The *Abudraham* and *Leket Yosher* list additional titles, but these were not commonly accepted.

◈§ Kadesh

Reciting Kiddush

1. A beautiful cup should be used for Kiddush (*Shulchan Aruch*
    O.C. 472:2. *Kaf HaChaim* adds that this applies to the other three
    cups that we drink at the Seder as well). Some follow the
    Kabbalistic custom to use silver cups at the Seder (*Kaf HaChaim*
    ibid.).[1]

    R' Yaakov Emden (*Siddur Shaar HaShamayim*) writes that his
    father was careful to use a glass cup for Kiddush, based on the
    Sages' directive to use red wine, which indicates that the
    appearance of the wine is significant. The Sages also tell us that
    one should gaze at the cup while reciting Kiddush or *Bircas
    HaMazon*. (The Sages' intention was that one should gaze at the
    wine in the cup.) Therefore, it is preferable to use a glass cup, in
    which the wine can be seen.

    The *Divrei Chaim* of Sanz zt"l also used a glass cup (*Darkei
    Chaim, Hanhagos* 80; *Haggadas Divrei Chaim, Hanhagos*) as did
    his descendant, *mori v'rebbi* the Klausenberger Rebbe zt"l.[1]

2. The cups should be rinsed thoroughly inside and out (*Shulchan
    Aruch* O.C. 183:1). In principle, as long as the cup is already
    clean it need not be rinsed again before Kiddush. Unless it is
    perfectly spotless, however, it is best to rinse it anyway (*Mish-
    nah Berurah* §3). *Kaf HaChaim* (183:4; 473:1) writes that even if it
    is spotless, it should still be rinsed for the Seder, to enhance the
    mitzvah (*Pri Megadim* 486, M.Z., writes the same). The *Chok
    Yaakov* (479:1, citing *Maharshal*) writes that even if a person is
    not careful to rinse his cup before Kiddush throughout the year,
    he should rinse it for the Seder (see *Mishnah Berurah* 479:1).

3. As cited earlier, some hold that the cup may be rinsed before
    Yom Tov (*Chayei Adam* 130, Laws of the Seder). Others hold
    that it should be rinsed right before Kiddush (*Rashbatz, Maamar
    Chametz; Mateh Moshe* 615; this also seems to be the opinion
    of *Shulchan Aruch HaRav* 473:39).

---

1. Some write that according to Kabbalah, a gold cup should not be used. See *Zohar
Va'eira* 24a; *Mishpatim* 115a; *Terumah* 129b.

2. Some say that the *Divrei Chaim* used a silver cup for Kiddush, and a glass cup for
the other three cups of wine (*Darkei Chaim V'Shalom* 594. See also *Haggadas Beis
Ropshitz*, which cites a reason given by the Klausenberger Rebbe zt"l for this).

4. One need not rinse the cup again before pouring the second cup of wine, since it was already rinsed before Kiddush (*Mishnah Berurah* 473:68).

5. It is proper that the head of the household not pour the wine for himself. Instead, someone else should pour for him, in the manner of free men (*Rema* 473:2). This practice should be followed for all four cups.[1] The cup should be filled to the rim (*Shulchan Aruch* O.C. 183:2; 271:6). Ideally, one should use red wine, unless the white wine available is of higher quality.

6. The cup should be taken with both hands, and then placed onto one hand (*Shulchan Aruch* O.C. 183:4[2]). According to some opinions, a left-handed person should hold the cup in his left hand (*Shulchan Aruch* ibid. 5). Others hold that he should hold it in his right hand (*Kaf HaChaim* 29 citing the *Zohar*).

7. When reciting Kiddush, one should intend to fulfill the mitzvos of Kiddush and drinking the first of the four cups. Some add the declaration of intent, "Behold, I am prepared to recite Kiddush and fulfill the mitzvah of drinking four cups." Some use a lengthier Kabbalistic version, beginning with the words, "For the sake of the unification" (*Mishnah Berurah* 473).[3]

8. The *Rishonim* dispute whether the second cup requires a new *Borei pri hagafen* blessing or is exempted by Kiddush. The Ashkenazic custom is to recite a blessing over each of the four cups (*Rema* O.C. 474). There are two reasons for this practice: (1) One may not drink while reciting *Maggid*, and the recitation

---

1. Some hold that when the Gemara gave this instruction, it was not referring to pouring the cups of wine at the table, but rather to diluting the wine with water, as was customary then because their wines were very strong. This was considered a menial chore, which was not performed by distinguished people. According to this opinion, there is no objection against the head of the household pouring wine for himself (*Vayaged Moshe* 6:11). The *Aruch HaShulchan* (473:1) writes that today, it is not customary to have someone else pour for the head of the household. He explains that it is improper for a husband to have his wife pour for him, since this gives the appearance of arrogance. (The validity of this argument is questionable, since there is certainly good reason for the head of the household to conduct himself in the manner of free men on the Seder night, more so than the rest of the family. Besides, his children may pour for him instead of his wife.)

2. In 271:10, he writes that the halachos regarding the cup used for *Bircas HaMazon* also apply to the cup used for Kiddush and other mitzvos. However, these are only *hiddur mitzvos l'chatchilah* (*Mishnah Berurah* 183:20 citing the Vilna Gaon),

3. *Mishnah Berurah* adds that one should recite this declaration before Kiddush rather than interrupt between the blessing and drinking the wine.

therefore constitutes an interruption between the cups. (2) Because each of the four cups is a mitzvah for itself, each one deserves its own blessing (*Mishnah Berurah* §4).

To satisfy all opinions, Ashkenazic Jews should have in mind that the blessing recited over Kiddush should not exempt the second cup of wine, thus enabling himself to recite another blessing over the second cup according to all opinions (*Pri Megadim* O.C. 474, M.Z.).

The Sephardic custom is to recite a blessing only over the first cup, for Kiddush, and the third cup, for *Bircas HaMazon* (*Rosh*, *Pesachim* 10:24; *Shulchan Aruch* 474:1). Sephardic Jews should have specific intent that the blessing recited over the first cup should exempt the second, and the blessing recited over the third cup should exempt the fourth.

9. When reciting Kiddush, one should have in mind that if he wishes to drink more between the cups, he may do so. If there is any question afterward whether he fulfilled his obligation — for example, if he did not lean while drinking the cup, or if he took too long to drink the cup — he may drink another cup without making another blessing (which would give the impression that he is adding a fifth cup) (*Mishnah Berurah* 472:21).[1]

10. Kiddush should be recited with concentration, reverence, and joy (*Siddur HaYaavetz*).

11. When reciting the *Shehecheyanu* blessing, one should have in mind to exempt all the mitzvos of the night, including drinking the four cups, eating matzah, and telling the story of the Exodus (*Siddur HaYaavetz, Kadesh* 2). One should also instruct his family to have this intention.

As mentioned, even if a woman recited *Shehecheyanu* when lighting candles, she should have in mind to be exempted by her husband's *Shehecheyanu* for all the other mitzvos of the night. (Presumably, she did not have these in mind when she recited *Shehecheyanu* over the candles.)

Contemporary *Poskim* discuss whether a woman who recited *Shehecheyanu* over the Yom Tov candles should answer "Amen" after hearing *Shehecheyanu* during Kiddush. Some hold that because she is not obligated in this blessing, it is

---

1. See *Shaar HaTzion* (§32), which states that this advice is not effective between the third and fourth cups.

considered an interruption for her to answer "Amen."[1] The custom is for women to answer "Amen."

12. If one forgot to say *Shehecheyanu* during Kiddush, he may recite it any time up to the last day of Yom Tov (including the eighth day, outside of Eretz Yisrael), since the blessing applies not only to the mitzvos of the Seder night, but to the entire Yom Tov (*Mishnah Berurah* 473:1).

13. When reciting *Shehecheyanu*, the word לזמן should be recited with the vowel *chirik* beneath the *lamed*: *lizman* (*Mishnah Berurah* 676:1. See also *Mishnah Berurah* 582:16).

14. When the head of the household recites Kiddush, he should have in mind to exempt his entire family. The members of the family should have in mind to be exempted by his Kiddush and should answer "Amen" to his blessings (*Shulchan Aruch HaRav* 472:23). They should not respond "*Baruch Hu u'varuch Shemo*" when he says Hashem's Name.[2]

15. Some have the custom that every person — women included — makes his or her own Kiddush on the Seder night. Some hold that the people present at the Seder should recite the words of Kiddush along with the head of the household. Others hold that each person should recite Kiddush aloud, individually. Several explanations have been offered for these customs (*Vayaged Moshe* 15:7).

    If the people present at the Seder recite Kiddush along with the head of the household, they may not answer "Amen" to his blessings, since this would constitute an interruption of their own Kiddush.

Kiddush When Pesach Falls on Shabbos

16. When Pesach falls on Shabbos, the verses of וַיְכֻלּוּ are recited before Kiddush (*Shulchan Aruch* 473:1). If one forgot to say וַיְכֻלּוּ before Kiddush, he should hold a cup of wine and recite those verses during the meal (*Mishnah Berurah* 271:45).

17. There are various customs among Ashkenazic Jews whether *Shalom Aleichem* is recited. Our custom is not to say it.

---

1. See *Shevet HaLevi* (3:63) who holds that she may answer "Amen." *Teshuvos Har Tzvi* (O.C. 1:154) and *Mikra'ei Kodesh* (Pesach 38) write that she should not.

2. If they did, then according to *Mishnah Berurah* (124:21) they fulfill their obligation *b'di'eved* and do not need to recite another blessing. However, *Shulchan Aruch HaRav* (Ibid.) argues that if they say, "*Baruch Hu u'varuch Shemo*," then even *b'di'eved*, they do not fulfill their obligation.

Kiddush When Pesach Falls on Motza'ei Shabbos

18. When Seder night falls on *Motza'ei Shabbos*, Havdalah (וְתּוֹדִיעֵנוּ) is recited in the fourth blessing of *Shemoneh Esrei*. It is forbidden to perform *melachah* before making some sort of Havdalah. A woman who did not daven *Maariv* and wishes to perform *melachah* — such as lighting candles, cooking food, or setting the table — must first say, *"Baruch HaMavdil bein kodesh l'kodesh"* — Blessed is He Who distinguishes between holy and holy (*Mishnah Berurah* 299:36). Even if she does say these words, she may not eat until after she hears Kiddush and Havdalah recited over a cup of wine (*Mishnah Berurah*, ibid.).

   Whenever Yom Tov falls on *Motza'ei Shabbos*, Havdalah is recited as part of Kiddush (*Shulchan Aruch* 473:1). The order of the blessings is: wine, Kiddush, candle, Havdalah, *Shehecheyanu*. This is alluded to by the Hebrew acronym, יקנה"ז, which stands for יַיִן, קִידוּשׁ, נֵר, הַבְדָּלָה, זְמַן (*Shulchan Aruch* ibid., *Mishnah Berurah* §3).

19. When reciting the Havdalah blessing during Kiddush, one should pause slightly between the words, "מִשֵּׁשֶׁת יְמֵי הַמַּעֲשֶׂה" קִדַּשְׁתָּ" and "הִבְדַּלְתָּ וְקִדַּשְׁתָּ אֶת עַמְּךָ יִשְׂרָאֵל" (*Tosafos, Pesachim* 114a s.v. *Ba'ei; Tur* 473).

20. *Besamim* (fragrant spices) are not used during Havdalah when Yom Tov falls on *Motza'ei Shabbos* (*Mishnah Berurah* 473:3; 491:3). If one accidentally recited a blessing over *besamim*, this does not constitute an interruption, and he may still drink from the wine (*Chida, Machazik Berachah* O.C. 491:2.).

21. Although many have the custom to fill the Havdalah cup until the wine overflows (*Rema* O.C. 286:1), it is not customary to do so when Yom Tov falls on *Motza'ei Shabbos* and Kiddush and Havdalah are recited together. On a regular *Motza'ei Shabbos*, the wine is allowed to overflow as an auspicious sign for the beginning of the workweek. This reason is not applicable on Yom Tov, which is not a workday.

22. Some hold that when reciting Havdalah on the Seder night, one need not gaze at his fingernails as he normally does on *Motza'ei Shabbos*.[1]

---

1. *Mishnah Berurah* 298:9 cites the custom to gaze at one's fingernails during Havdalah on a regular *Motza'ei Shabbos*. See also *Chayei Adam* 130:16.

23. Although women do not normally drink from the Havdalah wine (*Mishnah Berurah* 296:6), they must drink from this Havdalah, since it is the first of the four cups.

24. Two candles should be held together, so that they may be considered a torch (*Mateh Ephraim* 600, *Eleph HaMagen* §3). Some have the custom to use two separate candles that do not touch[1] (*Minhagei Chabad*, cited at the end of *Shulchan Aruch HaRav*, vol. 3, p. 57). Others have the custom to use only one candle (*Chok L'Yisrael*, Laws of Erev Pesach that Falls on Shabbos p. 92).

25. Yom Tov candles may also be used for Havdalah, since they are meant to provide light (*Teshuvos Tzitz Eliezer* 6:10).

26. If one forgot to recite Havdalah during Kiddush and remembered after he had already begun reciting the Haggadah, he should continue reciting the Haggadah until after the blessing *Go'al Yisrael* and then recite Havdalah (*Shulchan Aruch* 473:1). *Mishnah Berurah* (§5) explains that he should first recite *Borei pri hagafen* over the second cup, then the blessing over the candle, then the Havdalah blessing, and then drink the cup.[2]

   If one realized in the middle of the meal that he did not recite Havdalah, he must stop the meal immediately and recite Havdalah over a cup of wine. In this case, he should not say *Borei pri hagafen* (*Mishnah Berurah* §5).

   If he realized immediately after the second cup that he did not recite Havdalah, he must pour another cup over which to recite Havdalah. He should not recite the *Borei pri hagafen* blessing during this Havdalah, since the wine was exempted by the *Borei pri hagafen* he recited over the second cup. If he did not intend to drink more wine during the meal, however, then he must recite another *Borei pri hagafen* for Havdalah (*Shaar HaTzion* ibid. §15).

   If he realized during *Bircas HaMazon* that he did not recite Havdalah, he should recite Havdalah over the cup used for *Bircas HaMazon* (*Mishnah Berurah* ibid.).

   If he realized his omission after he drank the cup for *Bircas HaMazon*, he should wait until after Hallel, and recite Havdalah over the fourth cup (*Mishnah Berurah* ibid.).

---

1. This is so that it should not appear as if one is extinguishing the candles when he separates them. See *Mishnah Berurah* 502:19, who states that if one's intention is to put each candle in its place, it is permitted.

2. *Mishnah Berurah* (§4) adds that even if one did not yet begin the Haggadah, once he has finished Kiddush, he must wait until *Go'al Yisrael* to say Havdalah.

If he realized after he drank the fourth cup, he should recite Havdalah over a fifth cup of wine. He must recite *Borei pri hagafen* on this cup, since he has already concluded the meal (*Mishnah Berurah* ibid.).

27. If one forgot to recite Havdalah as part of Kiddush and remembered before karpas, it is questionable whether he should eat karpas and wait until the second cup to recite Havdalah (see *Shulchan Aruch HaRav* 473:7; *Be'ur Halachah* 473:1 s.v. *Ad sheyas'chil*; *Kaf HaChaim* ibid. §28).

Drinking the Four Cups

28. The cups must contain at least a *revi'is* (quarter-*log*) of wine (*Shulchan Aruch* 472:9). *L'chatchilah*, one should drink the entire cup, even if it is very large (*Mishnah Berurah* ibid. §30), or *b'di'eved* at least the majority of it (*Mishnah Berurah* ibid.). However, if the cup contains only a *revi'is*, then one must drink the entire cup in order to be able to recite a *berachah acharonah* according to all opinions (*Mishnah Berurah* ibid.). However, one need not finish the cup down to the very last drop (*Eishel Avraham* 474). The Chazon Ish was careful to finish the first and last cups, but sufficed with drinking the majority of the second and third (*Dinim V'Hanhagos Chazon Ish* 17:36).

29. Some hold that a single cup may be used by several people, provided that it contains a *revi'is* for each person and that each person drinks the majority of one *revi'is*. Others hold that one must drink the majority of the cup, regardless of its size. According to this opinion, a single cup cannot be used by several people (*Shulchan Aruch* 473:9).[1]

30. It is proper to fill the cup to the top, even if the cup contains more than a *revi'is* (*Pri Chadash* 472:9).

31. If a person has a large face, and his cheekful is more than the majority of a *revi'is*, he must drink the equivalent of his own cheekful for each of the four cups (*Be'ur Halachah* 472:9 s.v. *V'yishteh*).

   If one has a small face, and his cheekful is less than the

---

1. *Mishnah Berurah* (§33) rules that strictly speaking, the halachah follows the first opinion. It is therefore sufficient to drink the majority of a *revi'is*, even from a very large cup. However, in deference to the second opinion, it is preferable to use a cup that contains no more than a *revi'is*, in order to be able to drink the majority of the cup.

majority of a *revi'is*, he must still drink at least the majority of a *revi'is* for each of the four cups. He may not suffice with the equivalent of his own cheek full (*Be'ur Halachah* ibid.).[1]

32. A child under bar mitzvah age may suffice with his own cheekful, even if it is less than the majority of a *revi'is* (*Mishnah Berurah* 472:47).

33. *L'chatchilah*, it is proper to drink the majority of a *revi'is* in one gulp (*Mishnah Berurah* ibid. §34).

34. If one cannot drink this amount in one gulp, he should at least finish each cup within *k'dei achilas pras* (*Rema* 472:9).[2]

35. One must lean to the left while drinking each of the four cups (*Shulchan Aruch* 473:2, 479:1, 480:1). If he did not lean, he must drink an additional cup (*Shulchan Aruch* 472:7). Some hold that the first two cups must be drunk again (without a blessing), but the last two should not (*Rema* ibid.).

    However, according to our custom not to drink between the first two cups, if one did not lean while drinking the first cup, he should not drink another cup. If he did so, he would be required to recite a new *Borei pri hagafen* blessing, which would give the impression that he is drinking an extra, obligatory cup. Instead, he may rely on the opinions that rule that the first cup is valid, even though it was drunk without leaning.

    If one did not lean while drinking the second cup, he must drink another cup. This cup would not require another blessing, since he had in mind that his blessing over the second cup should include wine that he would drink during the meal (*Mishnah Berurah* §21).

36. One should not recite a *berachah acharonah* after any of the first three cups, since they will be exempted by *Bircas HaMazon* after the meal (*Shulchan Aruch* 473:2, *Mishnah Berurah* §11), despite the fact that a significant amount of time will elapse before *Bircas HaMazon* is recited, and one will already have digested the first cups (see *Eshel Avraham* 474).

---

1. The Chazon Ish (O.C. 39:16) writes that *b'di'eved*, he fulfills his obligation with his own cheekful, even if it is less than the majority of a *revi'is*.

2. *Mishnah Berurah* (§ 34) writes that if one took longer than this to drink either of the first two cups, he must drink another cup to fulfill his obligation. However, if he took longer than this to drink either of the last two cups, he should not drink another cup.

◄§ Urechatz

Washing Hands Without a Blessing

1. After Kiddush, one washes his hands without reciting a blessing, before dipping the vegetable in salt water (*Shulchan Aruch* 473:6). Actually, one must wash his hands before eating any food dipped in liquid (*Mishnah Berurah* §51). According to the Vilna Gaon, if one eats a *k'zayis* of food dipped in liquid, he must wash his hands with a blessing, as though he was eating bread (*Mishnah Berurah* §52, *Shaar HaTzion* §70). Even those who are not careful to wash their hands prior to eating food dipped in liquid throughout the year do so on the Seder night, to encourage the children to ask questions (*Shaar HaTzion* §69).

2. When washing for Urechatz, one must adhere to all the laws of washing hands for bread (*Mishnah Berurah* 158:20).

3. Some have the custom that another person pours water over the hands of the head of the household, in the manner of free men.[1]

4. When washing hands for Urechatz, one should have in mind that he does not intend to exempt himself from the obligation to wash for the meal (*Pri Megadim* beginning of 473, M.Z.).

5. Some have the custom that only the head of the household washes his hands for Urechatz. This is my own custom, and it is the custom of Sanz and the Maharam Ash as well (as cited in *Sefer Zichron Yehudah*; see *Vayaged Moshe* 16:2).[2]

6. If one accidentally recites a blessing when washing his hands for Urechatz, he should eat a *k'zayis* of vegetable for Karpas, so that his blessing should not be in vain. However, he should not recite a *berachah acharonah* after the karpas (*Kaf HaChaim* 473:107). In order to be able to wash again with a blessing for Rachtzah, he should engage in an activity that is considered an interruption, such as walking around, or the like. Alternately, he can touch a covered part of his body (e.g., scratching his head), which would then require him to wash again with another

---

1. *Siddur Chasam Sofer* records that this was the custom of the *Chasam Sofer.*

2. *Abudraham, Mordechai,* and *Seder HaYom* imply that everyone should wash for Urchatz.

blessing (*Rivevos Ephraim* 301, citing R' Shlomo Zalman Auerbach).

7. If a person uses a fork or spoon to eat a food dipped in liquid, he usually is not obligated to wash his hands (*Mishnah Berurah* 158:26). On the Seder night, however, even if one eats karpas with a fork or spoon, he should still wash his hands for Urechatz (*Mikra'ei Kodesh* 39, based on *Chok Yaakov* 473:28).

    Similarly, a person usually needs to wash his hands only before eating foods dipped in one of the seven liquids discussed in the Torah: wine, blood, oil, milk, dew, honey, or water. However, even if he dips the karpas in lemon juice, which normally would not require him to wash his hands, he should still wash for Urechatz to encourage the children to ask questions (*Mikra'ei Kodesh* ibid.).

ᴇ᛬ Karpas

Eating a Vegetable Dipped in Salt Water

1. Our Sages instituted the practice of dipping a vegetable into liquid before beginning the meal so that the children should notice the unusual events of the night and be encouraged to ask questions, since the Haggadah is meant to be recited in the manner of question and answer (*Mishnah Berurah* 473:21). However, even if there are no children in the house, this practice must still be observed (*Shulchan Aruch HaRav* 473:15).

2. Strictly speaking, one may use for Karpas any vegetable over which *Borei pri ha'adamah* is recited, and which is not normally eaten before the meal. (Bananas, pineapples, strawberries, and the like — which are often eaten before the meal, and will not cause the children to ask questions — may not be used for Karpas.)

3. A vegetable that is usually eaten raw must be eaten raw for Karpas. A vegetable that is usually eaten cooked must be eaten cooked. Only then may *Borei pri ha'adamah* be recited (*Shulchan Aruch O.C.* 202:12, *Magen Avraham* 4). According to some opinions, the correct blessing for vegetables grown in a vessel not connected to the ground is *Shehakol*, not *Borei pri ha'adamah*. Such vegetables should therefore not be used for Karpas (*Chayei Adam* 130, Laws of the Seder 5).

4. There are varying customs as to what should be used for Karpas. Some use potato (*Aruch HaShulchan* 473:10); some use radish (*Aruch HaShulchan* ibid.; *Kitzur Shulchan Aruch* 118:2); some use onion (*Aruch HaShulchan* ibid.);[1] some use pickled cabbage (*Pri Megadim* 473 E.A. §4; *Siddur HaYaavetz*); some use celery (*Teshuvos Chasam Sofer* O.C. 136; *Kitzur Shulchan Aruch* 118:2); some use other vegetables (see *Vayaged Moshe* 17:9).

5. If one does not have a vegetable over which *Borei pri ha'adamah* may be recited, he should use a vegetable over which *Shehakol* is recited. When reciting the blessing over Karpas, one must have in mind to exempt the Maror that will be eaten after *HaMotzi*. If one recites *Shehakol* over any vegetable, he fulfills his obligation *b'di'eved*. Therefore, it is acceptable *b'dieved* to recite *Shehakol* over the Karpas and thereby exempt the vegetable used for Maror (*Pri Megadim* 486, *Mishbetzos Zahav* §1; *Shulchan Aruch HaRav* 473:18). Some hold that if one does not have a *Borei pri ha'adamah* vegetable for Karpas, he should use the same vegetable used for Maror (*Yeshuos Yaakov* 473:2).

6. Some hold that the blessing for horseradish is *Shehakol*. Others hold that the blessing is *Borei pri ha'adamah*. If one uses horseradish for Maror, he should nonetheless use for Karpas a vegetable over which *Borei pri ha'adamah* is recited (*Be'ur Halachah* 475 s.v. *Tibul rishon*).

7. Less than a *k'zayis* of karpas should be dipped in vinegar, salt water or wine (*Shulchan Aruch* 473:6, *Mishnah Berurah* §54). It should not be dipped in charoses (*Mishnah Berurah* ibid.). *Borei pri ha'adamah* is then recited over the karpas right before it is eaten.[2] When reciting the blessing over karpas, one should have in mind to exempt the maror that will be eaten later (*Mishnah Berurah* §55). Some argue that a full *k'zayis* of karpas should be eaten, since less than a *k'zayis* of food is not considered "eating" by Torah standards (*Rambam, Hilchos Chametz U'Matzah* 8:2).[3] This was the custom of the Vilna Gaon (*Maaseh Rav*), and the Brisker Rav (*Haggadah L'Beis Levi* p. 86).

---

1. However, *Eliyah Rabbah* (473:27) writes in the name of *Maharil* not to use garlic or onions for Karpas, since they cause a distasteful odor. Those who do use onions for Karpas should use green onions, which are edible raw (*Chochmas Adam* 38:15).

2. *Magen Avraham* (§19) rules that the blessing should be recited before dipping the karpas. However, *Machatzis HaShekel* argues that the blessing should be recited after dipping the karpas, and this is the common practice.

3. See *Hagahos Maimonios* (there), who writes that this ruling is a misprint.

The Brisker Rav did not recite a *berachah acharonah* after Karpas.

8. It is customary for each person to recite his own blessing over Karpas (*Rambam, Hilchos Chametz U'Matzah* 8:2).

9. No *berachah acharonah* is recited over Karpas, even if one eats a *k'zayis* or more, since it will be exempted by *Bircas HaMazon* (*Mishnah Berurah* 473:56).

10. One should instruct his family not to leave the room between Karpas and Maror, so that the *Borei pri ha'adamah* recited over the Karpas should be valid for the Maror. If one foresees a need to leave the room, he should have this in mind while reciting *Borei pri ha'adamah* (*Shulchan Aruch* O.C. 178:1; Introduction of *Mishnah Berurah*; *Be'ur Halachah* s.v. *B'vayis acher.*) *Shelah* (beginning of *Pesachim*) writes that it is proper not to interrupt between Karpas and Maror).

11. After Karpas, one may remove the vegetables and salt water from the table, since they need not be on the table for *Maggid* (*Magen Avraham* 473:2; *Shulchan Aruch HaRav* 473:25). However, a small amount of karpas should remain on the Seder plate, so that the Seder plate remains complete (*Ben Ish Chai, Parashas Tzav* 32; *Kaf HaChaim* 473:52).

12. The *Poskim* debate whether one must lean while eating Karpas. Some hold that one need not lean (*Shibolei HaLeket* 218; *Mateh Moshe* 625; *Birkei Yosef* 473:14). Others hold that one must lean (*Abudraham; Kitzur Shulchan Aruch* 119:3; *Maamar Mordechai* 473:4).[1]

   Apparently, this dispute hinges on whether Karpas serves as a commemoration of our slavery or of our salvation from the Egyptians (see *Rabbeinu Manoach, Hilchos Chametz U'Matzah* 8:2). Our custom is to lean during Karpas.

✍ Yachatz

Breaking the middle matzah

1. Before Maggid, the middle matzah is broken in half. The Torah calls matzah *"lechem oni"* — bread of poverty — and poor

---

1. *Haggadas Beis Levi* (p. 108) records that this was the custom of the Brisker Rav.

people cannot afford to eat all their bread at once, so they divide it into portions. The middle matzah is the one that is broken, because the blessing *Al achilas matzah* is recited over this matzah, while the blessing *HaMotzi lechem min ha'aretz* is recited over the top matzah (*Shulchan Aruch* 473:6, *Mishnah Berurah* §56).[1]

2. A large matzah should be used for the middle matzah, so that it may suffice to provide a *k'zayis* both for the beginning of the meal and for the afikoman (*Chok Yaakov* 475:26).

3. After the middle matzah is divided, the larger half should be given to someone else to guard for use as the afikoman. It should be wrapped in a cloth, in memory of how Bnei Yisrael left Egypt with their matzos wrapped in their pouches. Some have the custom to place the wrapped matzah over their shoulders in commemoration of this (*Shulchan Aruch* 473:6, *Mishnah Berurah* §58).[2] Our custom is for the children to hide the afikoman. The children should be cautioned not to hide it beneath a bed.

   The other half of the middle matzah should be placed between the two whole matzos (*Shulchan Aruch* ibid.).

4. If one has only two matzos, they should not be broken until after *HaMotzi* is recited, so that they remain whole for *lechem mishneh* (*Mishnah Berurah* 482:9). Some argue that on the Seder night it is not necessary to have *lechem mishneh*, since the matzah is meant to be *lechem oni* — bread of poverty. According to this opinion, a matzah should be broken before *HaMotzi* and the blessings should then be recited over one whole matzah and one broken matzah (*Chok Yaakov* 482:4).

---

1. After breaking the matzah in half, it should not be crumbled into little pieces, since it is preferable that the piece of matzah be large (*Shulchan Aruch* O.C. 168:1).

2. *Kaf HaChaim* (§123) writes that it is customary to put the afikoman on the shoulder of a child and then recite הָא לַחְמָא עַנְיָא, "This is the bread of affliction." The child then leaves the house and knocks on the door. The people ask, "Who is it?" and the child responds, "A Jew." Then they ask, "Where are you coming from?" and the child responds, "From Egypt." They ask, "Where are you going?" and the child responds, "To Yerushalayim." They ask, "What are you carrying?" and the child responds, "Matzah." The child then joins the family and recites מָה נִּשְׁתַּנָּה, "Why is this night different." The afikoman remains on his shoulder until the end of the meal, when it is eaten. *Chok Yaakov* (473:1) argues against this custom, however.

⤳ Maggid

Telling the Story of the Exodus

1. The matzos are partially uncovered (*Chok Yaakov* 473:38).[1] The Seder plate is lifted up and הָא לַחְמָא עַנְיָא, *This is the bread of affliction*, is recited loudly (*Shulchan Aruch* 473:6, *Mishnah Berurah* §61).

2. The Haggadah should not be recited while leaning, but rather while sitting erect, with awe and reverence (*Shulchan Aruch HaRav* 473:48, *Mishnah Berurah* §71). Others argue that it should be recited while leaning. However, sitting is also considered the manner of free men (*Mishnah Berurah* 480:1). One should recite the Haggadah slowly and joyously, not consider it a burden from which he hurries to be relieved (*Kav HaYashar* Ch. 4).[2]

3. One must understand what he is saying. If the family members do not understand the Haggadah in its original Hebrew, it should be read in a language that they do understand, since this is the fulfillment of the mitzvah to relate the story of the Exodus (*Rema* 473:6).

4. Women are obligated in all the mitzvos of the Seder night, including the obligation to relate the story of the Exodus (*Mishnah Berurah* ibid. §64).

5. Some hold that the family members should not recite the Haggadah, but should fulfill their obligation by listening to the head of the household recite it. It is considered a greater honor for Hashem when many people fulfill a mitzvah together (*Shulchan Aruch HaRav* 472:22, 473:24).[3] However, today it is customary for the entire family to read the Haggadah (*Aruch HaShulchan* 473:20).

6. Before beginning Maggid, one should declare, or at least have in mind, that he intends to fulfill the Torah obligation to relate the story of the Exodus on the Seder night (*Chayei Adam* 130:19 §3; *Siddur HaYaavetz*).

---

1. See *Vayaged Moshe* (22:1), who discusses whether the entire matzah must be uncovered, or if it is sufficient to uncover only part of it.

2. *Yesod V'Shoresh Ha'Avodah* (9:6) writes that the most important aspect of telling the story is the joy it inspires in a person's heart.

3. *Maaseh Rav* states that this was the custom of the Vilna Gaon.

7. It is proper for a person to read the Haggadah loudly enough to hear the words, and not just whisper the words under his breath.

8. One may not interrupt the Haggadah by eating or drinking (*Mishnah Berurah* ibid. §4).[1] Others hold that one may interrupt before he begins the blessing of אֲשֶׁר גְּאָלָנוּ — "Who has redeemed us ..." (*Shulchan Aruch HaRav* ibid. 11, *Shaar HaTzion* ibid. §9).

9. One may not interrupt between אֲשֶׁר גְּאָלָנוּ and drinking the second cup. Reciting the declaration of intent (לְשֵׁם יִחוּד) is not considered an interruption (*Vayaged Moshe* 22:29).

   It is a mitzvah to distribute nuts or sweets to the children so that they notice the unusual practices of the Seder night and ask questions (*Shulchan Aruch* 472:16). The children must be kept awake for the response to the four questions, עֲבָדִים הָיִינוּ — "We were slaves in Egypt" — so that they know about the Exodus. The main part of the mitzvah is the answer given to the child's question. This is contrary to the practice of those who keep the children up to ask the Four Questions and then put them to sleep immediately afterward, before they can hear the answer to those questions (*Mishnah Berurah* ibid. §50).

10. After הָא לַחְמָא עַנְיָא and before the Four Questions, the second cup is poured (*Shulchan Aruch* ibid.). One should not wait to pour the cup until the end of Maggid (לְפִיכָךְ), when the cup is lifted (*Mishnah Berurah* §67). The cup need not be rinsed again before pouring the second cup (*Mishnah Berurah* §68).

11. *L'chatchilah*, the child who asks the Four Questions should be young enough to really require his father's answer (*Chayei Adam* 130, Laws of the Seder 7; *Kitzur Shulchan Aruch* 119:4).[2]

12. If a person does not have sons, his daughter should ask the Four Questions (*Aruch HaShulchan* 473:21; *Kitzur Shulchan Aruch* 119:4). If one does not have a daughter either, his wife should ask (*Shulchan Aruch* 473:7). If a person conducts the Seder alone, he should ask himself (ibid.). Some hold that grandchildren ask their grandfather (*Vayaged Moshe* 21:11).

---

1. See *Be'ur Halachah* (s.v. *Ha'reshus b'yado*), where it says that even if a person just poured the second cup of wine and prepared himself to begin reciting the Haggadah, it is already forbidden to eat or drink.

2. It seems clear that one does not fulfill his obligation if the child asking is so young that he does not understand his father's answer, even if he is old enough to ask the questions.

13. Some have the custom for the father to repeat the Four Questions after the children have asked it (*Vayaged Moshe* ibid. 14).

14. The Four Questions should be recited in a pleasant tune, to give praise to Hashem (*Chok Yaakov* 473:35, citing *Maharil*).

⋖§ Rachtzah

Washing Hands with a Blessing

1. The hands are washed before eating matzah, and the blessing *Al netilas yadayim* is recited (*Shulchan Aruch* 472:1). Even though the hands were already washed before Karpas (see 473:6), Maggid and Hallel constitute a significant interruption, and it is therefore possible that the person touched something that would require him to wash again (*Mishnah Berurah* §1). If one is certain that he did not touch anything that would require him to wash, then he need not wash again. If he does wash, he may not make a blessing. It is proper in such a case to deliberately touch something that would require him to wash again, in order to be able to wash with a blessing (*Be'ur Halachah* 475 s.v. *Yitol yadav*).

2. Those who have the custom to recite the declaration of intent (לְשֵׁם יָחוּד) before eating matzah should recite it before washing their hands, so as not to interrupt between *netilas yadayim* and *HaMotzi* (*Likutei Mariach*, Customs of the First Night of Pesach: Rachtzah; *Vayaged Moshe* 24:8). Some hold that this is not considered an interruption, since it is for the sake of the meal (*Vayaged Moshe* ibid.; see also *Mishnah Berurah* 166:2). It is proper to silently contemplate the לְשֵׁם יָחוּד immediately before *HaMotzi* without actually saying the words.

3. It is customary for someone else to pour water over the hands of the head of the household, since this is the manner of free men (*Vayaged Moshe* 23:3).

4. If there are many people at the Seder and there will be a long pause between *netilas yadayim* and *HaMotzi* (more than the amount of time it takes to walk twenty-two cubits) while everyone is washing their hands, the head of the household should not wait for them (based on *Mishnah Berurah* 165:5; see *Be'ur Halachah* ibid. s.v. *V'haRosh*).

⤳ Motzi — Matzah

HaMotzi Is Recited, and the Matzah is Eaten.

1.   It is a positive Torah commandment to eat matzah on the Seder night (*Rambam, Hilchos Chametz U'Matzah* 6:1). *L'chatchilah*, one must eat two *k'zeiysim* of matzah (see below for the volume in modern measurements), one from the broken matzah and one from the whole matzah (*Shulchan Aruch* 475:1). Some hold that this is only the minimum obligation, but one fulfills a mitzvah with every additional piece of matzah that he eats (*Maharal, Gevuros Hashem* Ch. 48, cited in *Bach* 472).

2.   If one cannot eat two *k'zeiysim* at once, he should eat a *k'zayis* from the whole matzah first, and then a *k'zayis* from the broken matzah (*Shulchan Aruch* ibid.). If one only ate one *k'zayis*, whether from the whole or from the broken matzah, he fulfills his obligation *b'di'eved* (*Mishnah Berurah* §11).

   The *Acharonim* agree that even *l'chatchilah*, one need not swallow both *k'zaysim* at once. It is sufficient to put them both into the mouth at once and chew them, then swallow approximately one *k'zayis*, and then swallow the rest. We have seen that many distinguished rabbis were not scrupulous about this, however, and we see, therefore, that this is not an absolute obligation (*Chiddushei Chasam Sofer, Chullin* 103).

   B'di'eved, even if one swallowed a *k'zayis* bit by bit, he fulfills his obligation, provided that he finished an entire *k'zayis* within *k'dei achilas pras* (see below for the time limit in minutes) (*Mishnah Berurah* ibid. §9).

3.   Generally, on Shabbos and Yom Tov, it is best to use loaves that are each at least the size of a *k'zayis* (*Kaf HaChaim* 274:8; *Sdei Chemed, Maareches* 30, end of 27). *L'chatchilah*, they should also be large enough for each person at the table to receive a piece. Everyone is obligated in *lechem mishneh*, and if they eat from other bread, they do not fulfill this mitzvah.[1]

---

1. There are those who have the practice to rely on the head of the household to recite *HaMotzi* over two challos and fulfill the mitzvah of *lechem mishneh* on their behalf, and recite their their own *HaMotzi* on their portion. *Shemiras Shabbos K'Hilchasah* (Ch. 55 footnote 14) quotes R' Shlomo Zalman Auerbach as saying that those who follow this practice may also make *HaMotzi* over a different piece of matzah, if they are unable to eat from the *lechem mishneh*.

Every person at the Seder should receive at least a small piece of matzah from the *lechem mishneh*. They may then use another matzah to complete their *k'zayis* (see *Shemiras Shabbos K'Hilchasah* 55:5, footnote 15).

Some have the custom for each person at the Seder to have his own three matzos, so that everyone can recite the blessings over *lechem mishneh*, and eat the required amount from them.[1]

4. Only the person who recites the blessing over the three matzos must eat two *k'zeiysim*. Everyone else only needs to eat one *k'zayis*.

5. It is questionable whether a child should recite blessings over matzah and Maror if he cannot eat a *k'zayis* within *k'dei achilas pras*. However, if he can finish the *k'zayis* within even the most lenient estimate of *k'dei achilas pras* (9 minutes) then he should recite a blessing (R' Shlomo Zalman Auerbach *zt"l*, cited in *Shemiras Shabbos K'Hilchasah* first edition, Ch. *Chinuch HaBanim*, footnote 60).

6. Matzah must be eaten at night. Even if one accepts Yom Tov early, he does not fulfill his obligation by eating matzah before nightfall (*Tosefta Pesachim* 2:15; *Tosafos, Pesachim* 99b s.v. *Ad shetech'shach*). The matzah must be eaten before *chatzos* (halachic midnight). If one did not eat the matzah before *chatzos* then he must eat it after *chatzos*, but he may no longer recite the blessing *Al achilas matzah*, since according to some opinions he does not fulfill his obligation (*Mishnah Berurah* 477:6).[2]

7. If it is late and *chatzos* might pass before matzah is eaten, one should drink the first cup for Kiddush, wash his hands with a blessing, eat matzah and maror with blessings — all before *chatzos* — and then recite the Haggadah and eat the meal (*Mishnah Berurah* ibid. §6).

The K'zayis Measurement

8. The Talmudic measurement of a *k'zayis* literally means "the volume of an olive." According to some opinions, this equals

---

1. R' Moshe Feinstein advised that each male adult should have his own two matzos (*Shemiras Shabbos K'Hilchasah* ibid.).

2. See *Beu'r Halachah* s.v. *Viyehei zahir. Ohr Samei'ach, Hilchos Chametz U'Matzah* 6:1 argues that a blessing must be recited even after *chatzos. Mishkenos Yaakov* (157) states that there is no harm in reciting a blessing.

half the volume of an egg (*Shulchan Aruch* O.C. 486:1). According to other opinions, it equals one-third of an egg (*Pri Chadash* ibid., *Mishnah Berurah* §1). When performing a Torah commandment, such as eating matzah, one should follow the stringent opinion (*Mishnah Berurah* ibid.).

9. A sick person who has difficulty eating matzah equivalent to the volume of half an egg may rely on the lenient opinion and eat matzvah equivalent to the volume of one-third of an egg (*Mishnah Berurah* ibid.).

10. The second *k'zayis* of matzah that the head of the household eats is a Rabbinic requirement, and is not absolutely mandatory. Therefore, one may suffice with eating matzah equivalent to the volume of one-third of an egg (*Shiurei Torah* 3:13).

11. Some hold that eggs today are only half the size they were in the times of the Sages. According to this opinion, the first *k'zayis* must be the size of an entire average-sized egg (*Tz'lach, Pesachim* 167b; *Mishnah Berurah* 486:1; *Shiurin shel Torah: Shiurei Mitzvos*).[1]

    The minimum amount of matzah is calculated by volume, regardless of weight or density. Therefore, even if the matzah is soft and airy, one need not condense it before measuring its volume (*Mishnah Berurah* ibid. §3).[2]

12. The crumbs of matzah that remain stuck between one's gums are included in this minimum requirement (*Chasam Sofer* O.C. 127; *Ksav Sofer* O.C. 96). However, the crumbs stuck between one's teeth are not included. Therefore, one should add about two grams of matzah to his estimation of a *k'zayis*, in order to account for the crumbs that will get stuck between his teeth (*Minchas Chinuch* 6, 10; *Imrei Yosher* 2:183).

13. One may measure the matzos on the Seder night in order to distribute *k'zayis*-sized pieces, even if Pesach falls on Shabbos (*Shulchan Aruch* O.C. 306:7).

14. Burnt parts of a matzah are included in the minimum volume measurement, provided that they can be eaten along with the rest of the matzah.

---

1. *Chazon Ish* (*Kuntress Shiurim* 17) writes that matzah equivalent to the volume of two-thirds of an average egg is sufficient, in accordance with the Rambam, who holds that a *k'zayis* is one-third of the volume of an egg.

2. *Maharam Shick* (O.C. 264) writes that this is the opinion of the *Chasam Sofer*. See *Chazon Ish* (O.C. 39:17).

The Order of the Blessings

15. Two whole matzos are held with the broken matzah between them. *HaMotzi* is recited, the bottom matzah is put down, and *Al achilas matzah* is recited over the broken matzah (while holding it together with the top, whole matzah). Then, the top (whole) matzah and middle (broken) matzah are broken into pieces (*Shulchan Aruch* O.C. 475:1, *Mishnah Berurah* §1, 3). This procedure should be followed even when Pesach falls on Shabbos (*Magen Avraham* 475:3; *Kaf HaChaim* ibid. §10).

16. One must hold the matzos while reciting the blessings. If he did not, he still fulfills his obligation *b'di'eved* (*Mishnah Berurah* 167:22).

    When saying Hashem's Name in the *HaMotzi* blessing, one should lift the matzos (*Mishnah Berurah* 167:23).

    Although it is customary on Shabbos and Yom Tov to mark the place where the loaves will be cut before reciting the blessing (*Magen Avraham* 274:1; *Shulchan Aruch* 167:1, *Mishneh Berurah* ibid.), it is not customary to do so with matzos.[1]

17. Some have the custom that the head of the household recites the blessings of *HaMotzi* and *Al achilas matzah* and he exempts the rest of the family with his blessings (*Maggid Mishneh*, *Hilchos Chametz U'Matzah* 8:12). Others hold that each person should make these blessings for himself.[2] The custom among Chassidic Jews is for each person to recite both blessings for himself, and this is our custom.

18. When reciting *Al achilas matzah*, one should have in mind that his blessing should also exempt *Korech* and *afikoman* (*Shaar HaTzion* 477:4; *Shelah*, beginning of *Pesachim*, s.v. *V'yachzor*).

19. After reciting *Al achilas matzah*, one should not interrupt with conversation that does not pertain to eating matzah or maror until after he has eaten *Korech*. This is in order that the blessings

---

1. See *Be'ur Halachah* (167:1 s.v. *V'tzarich lach'toch*), who writes that a thin loaf of bread which can be sliced quickly need not be marked before the blessing. The same holds true for matzos, which can be broken quickly.

2. *Shulchan Aruch HaRav* (167:18) cites both opinions. See also *Aruch HaShulchan* 167:28. *Minhagei Chasam Sofer* 10:17 records that the *Chasam Sofer* would recite *HaMotzi* for everyone at the table, but each person would recite his own *Al achilas matzah*. This was also the custom of the Brisker Rav, cited in *Haggadah M'Beis Levi* (p. 193).

of *Al achilas matzah* and *Al achilas maror* also apply to the matzah and maror eaten for *Korech* (*Shulchan Aruch* 475:1). The *Shelah* is stringent, and rules that one should not speak unnecessarily until after he has eaten the *afikoman*. The *Shulchan Aruch HaRav* (475) rules leniently, however, and permits speech before eating the *afikoman*.

20. If one speaks between the blessing and the first piece of matzah (with words that are not relevant to the *seudah*), he must recite a new blessing. If he interrupts after he has begun to eat the matzah, he need not recite a new blessing (*Shulchan Aruch* 167:6, *Mishnah Berurah* §35).

21. If a person has recited *HaMotzi* and *Al achilas matzah*, but has not yet eaten the matzah, he may not answer "Amen" to another person's blessing (*Mishnah Berurah* 167:35). This halachah is especially pertinent on the Seder night, when many people eat together. If one interrupts by speaking after he has begun to chew, before swallowing, some hold that he need not recite a new *HaMotzi* blessing; others hold that he must. In practice, no new blessing should be recited (see *Mishnah Berurah* ibid. §35).

22. If there are many people at the table, it is customary for each person to receive a *k'zayis*-sized piece of matzah before *netilas yadayim*. After everyone recites the blessings and eats the matzah, the head of the household distributes small pieces of matzah from the *lechem mishneh*. This is done in order to minimize the delay between reciting the blessings and eating the matzah (see *Rema* 167:15, *Mishnah Berurah* §79).

23. According to the Ashkenazic custom, the matzah is not dipped in salt (*Rema* 475:1). Sephardic custom is to dip it in salt (*Shulchan Aruch* ibid. 1, *Kaf HaChaim* 14).

24. It is a mitzvah to eat two *k'zeisim* while leaning to the left (*Shulchan Aruch* 475:1). *B'di'eved*, one fulfills his obligation even if he eats only one *k'zayis* (*Be'ur Halachah* 472:7 s.v. *Lo yatza*). If one completed the meal, recited *Bircas HaMazon*, and then remembered that he did not lean while eating matzah, according to the *Shulchan Aruch* he must recite *HaMotzi* and *Al achilas matzah* again and eat matzah while leaning (*Be'ur Halachah*, ibid.). Others hold that he should recite *HaMotzi* and eat another *k'zayis*, but he should not recite *Al achilas matzah* (*Be'ur Halachah* ibid.; *Mishnah Berurah* §23).

25. *B'di'eved*, one fulfills his obligation using matzah soaked in water, if it is not dissolved (*Shulchan Aruch* 461:4). An old or sick person who has difficulty eating matzah may rely on this leniency even *l'chatchilah*. He may not let the matzah soak in water for twenty-four hours, however, because it renders the matzah invalid (*Mishnah Berurah* §17). An old or sick person may also use dry, ground matzah, even if has been ground to the consistency of flour. He may recite the blessings of *HaMotzi* and *Al achilas matzah* on it, but he must eat at least a *k'zayis* (*Be'ur Halachah* 461 s.v. *Yotzei adam*).

The *Poskim* dispute whether one fulfills his obligation using matzah soaked in other liquids (*Mishnah Berurah* ibid. §18). If an old or sick person cannot eat matzah soaked in water, he may soak his matzah in other liquids (*Mishnah Berurah* ibid.). This argument only pertains to *soaking* the matzah in liquids other than water; it is certainly permitted to *dip* matzah in liquid (*Mishnah Berurah* ibid.). If one soaked pieces smaller than a *k'zayis* in water, he cannot fulfill his obligation with those pieces (ibid.).

The Chassidic custom is to refrain entirely from eating soaked matzah (*gebrokts*).

26. Matzah that was cooked or soaked in hot water is invalid for the Seder (*Mishnah Berurah* 461:20).

27. Even if a person dislikes matzah, or ingesting matzah damages his health (causing him pain or a headache, but not causing him to become incapacitated), he must force himself to eat a *k'zayis* of matzah (*Maharam Shick* O.C. 260, based on *Shulchan Aruch* 472:10. See *Mishnah Berurah* 472:35).

28. If a sick person is able to eat only one *k'zayis*, or if he has only one *k'zayis* to eat, he should eat the meal without first making *HaMotzi*. After the meal he should recite *HaMotzi* and *Al achilas matzah*, and then eat the matzah with the intention that it also serve as afikoman (*Mishnah Berurah* 483:6). A person who would become dangerously sick from eating matzah may not eat it (*Maharam Shick* O.C. 260; *Teshuvos Yehudah Ya'aleh* 160; *Binyan Shlomo* 47).[1]

29. If a person eats matzah and then vomits, he has still fulfilled his obligation (*Minchas Chinuch* 10).

---

1. *Vayaged Moshe* 24:40 writes that instead he should study the laws of matzah, and he will receive credit for fulfilling those laws.

The Amount of Time in Which Matzah Must Be Eaten

30. The *k'zayis* of matzah must be eaten within *k'dei achilas pras*. This is the amount of time in which one could eat half a loaf of bread, which is considered to be enough for one meal. The exact size of this half-loaf is the subject of debate in the Mishnah (*Eruvin* 88b, see *Rashi*).

31. The opinions regarding the length of time of *k'dei achilas pras* range from two to eleven minutes:

    a) Two minutes (*Chasam Sofer* 6:16; the Steipler Gaon in *Shiurin shel Torah*, p. 67: 29, 30).

    b) Three minutes (*Sdei Chemed: Asifas Dinim, Maareches Achilah* 3).

    c) Four minutes (R' Chaim Naeh in *Shiurei Torah*; see *Shiurin shel Torah: Shiurei Mitzvos* p. 67: 30).

    d) Five minutes (*Techeiles Mordechai*, Introduction: 10, citing R' Yitzchak Elchanan Spektor).

    e) Six minutes (*Aruch HaShulchan* 618:14).

    f) Seven minutes (ibid.).

    g) Eight minutes (*Vayaged Moshe* 24:34).[1]

    h) Eight-and-a-half minutes (ibid.).

    i) Nine minutes (*Chasam Sofer* 6:16; *Mishnah Berurah* 618:21).

    j) Eleven minutes (*Sdei Chemed* ibid.).

32. *Toras Chessed* (*Teshuvos* O.C. 32) suggests that the time limit depends upon the type of food in question.[2] Similarly, *Mishnah Berurah* (618:21) rules that the time limit depends upon the individual and how long it normally takes him to eat. *Chazon Ish* (39:18) argues that the time limit is determined by the time it takes for the average person to eat (see *Minchas Asher* on *Pesachim* 74).

33. A child under bar mitzvah age may rely on the lenient opinion that *k'dei achilas pras* is nine minutes (R' Shlomo Zalman Auerbach *zt"l* cited in *Shemiras Shabbos K'Hilchasah* Ch. 54, footnote 130). Even if a child cannot eat a *k'zayis* within this time limit, he should still be given matzah to eat, to educate him in mitzvah observance.

---

1. See also *Gulos Aliyos* on *Mikvaos* 10:5, who cites a tradition from the Baal HaTanya.

2. This also seems to be the opinion of the *Mishnah Berurah* (81:3).

34. Adults should be careful to eat a *k'zayis* of matzah within four minutes. Some are stringent, and require the *k'zayis* to be eaten within two minutes *l'chatchilah*. If it takes longer than four minutes to eat the *k'zayis*, another *k'zayis* should be eaten. If the first *k'zayis* was eaten within nine minutes, however, one should not recite another blessing *Al achilas matzah* (since according to some opinions, he already fulfilled his obligation).

35. The time limit of *k'dei achilas pras* refers to the *total* amount of time in which the entire *k'zayis* must be eaten, not to the amount of time one may pause between bites (*Mishnah Berurah* 475:42, 612:10 *Be'ur Halachah* s.v. *Im*).[1]

✌ Maror

1. The Torah commandment to eat Maror is not a mitzvah for itself. Rather, it is one of the requirements of the *Korban Pesach* (*Rambam, Hilchos Chametz U'Matzah* 7:12). Some lists of the 613 mitzvos consider Maror as a mitzvah for itself (*Yerei'im HaShaleim* 94; see *Binyan Tzion*, revised edition, 38).

   Today there is no *Korban Pesach*, but the mitzvah to eat Maror is observed as a Rabbinic law (*Pesachim* 120a; *Mishnah Berurah* 473:33) in memory of the Beis Hamikdash (*Shulchan Aruch HaRav* 475:15).

2. Women are also obligated to eat Maror (*Shulchan Aruch* 472:13, *Mishnah Berurah* §44, 45). Both male and female children are obligated to eat Maror, as part of their education in mitzvah observance.

3. One should eat Maror before *chatzos*. If one did not eat it before *chatzos*, he should eat it after *chatzos*, but he may no longer recite the blessing *Al achilas maror* (*Pri Megadim* 477, *Eishel Avraham* §1; *Dagul Mei'revavah* ibid.; *Derech HaChaim* 123).

4. One must eat a *k'zayis* of Maror (*Shulchan Aruch* 473:5). When romaine lettuce is used for Maror, it must be condensed to be measured, since the space between the leaves is not included in

---

1. This is contrary to the implication of the *Mishnah Berurah* (618:21) that *k'dei achilas pras* refers to the pauses between bites. See *Teshuvos Ha'Aleph Lecha Shlomo* 323; *Minchas Chinuch* 313:6.

the measurement. One must be very careful to eat at least a *k'zayis*. Otherwise, he does not fulfill his obligation, and his blessing is in vain (*Mishnah Berurah* §41).

5. Although some hold that one fulfills his obligation with less than a *k'zayis* of maror, the accepted halachah does not follow those opinions. However, because eating maror is only a Rabbinic obligation nowadays, one may be lenient and rely on the opinion that a *k'zayis* is equivalent to one-third of an egg.

6. If only one *k'zayis* of maror is available, it should all be eaten during the Maror stage of the Seder, and none should be left over for *Korech* (*Teshuvos Ksav Sofer* 86).

7. If a person finds it difficult to eat maror, but the maror is not detrimental to his health, he should still force himself to eat it. He may use the maror that is most agreeable to his system. He may also eat it little by little within *k'dei achilas pras*, although it is preferable to eat the entire *k'zayis* at once (*Mishnah Berurah* 473:43, *Shaar HaTzion* §60, 61). One should not eat the maror together with anything else, because it masks the taste of the maror (*Shulchan Aruch* 473:3).

8. If, for health reasons, a person cannot eat a *k'zayis* of maror, he should at least eat a small amount or chew a small piece in order to remember the bitter plight of our forefathers in Egypt. However, he should not recite a blessing (*Mishnah Berurah* 473:43). Some opinions hold that in such a case, he is entirely exempt (*Divrei Chaim* 1:25).[1]

   R' Akiva Eiger writes: "I offer my assurance that anyone who performs the mitzvah with enthusiasm, thinking joyously that he is performing the will of his Creator, will not taste any bitterness at all in the maror" (*Chut HaMeshulash* p. 205).

9. Some hold that one does not fulfill his obligation with lettuce leaves that have not yet developed a bitter taste. However, one may be lenient in this matter.

10. The following vegetables are listed in the Mishnah as acceptable for use as Maror: *chazeres, ulshin, tamcha, char'chavina,* and *maror* (*Shulchan Aruch* 473:5).

    Chazeres is romaine lettuce (*Bartenura, Pesachim* 2:6; *Teshuvos Chacham Tzvi* 119; *Teshuvos Chasam Sofer* 132; *Mishnah*

---

1. See *Kaf HaChaim* 88. *Avnei Nezer* (O.C. 383) writes that he should study the laws of Maror, and he will receive credit for fulfilling those laws.

Berurah 473:34). Romaine lettuce is the preferred vegetable for Maror and should be used, if possible, even if it is slightly more expensive than other kinds of maror. It must be checked well, however, to ensure that it is not infested with worms or bugs (*Mishnah Berurah* ibid. §42). If lettuce was checked on a Seder night that fell on Shabbos, and a worm or bug was found, the piece of leaf containing the bug should be torn off, rather than removing the bug alone (due to the prohibition of *borer* — separating) (*Chazon Ish* O.C. 47:15).

11. Some hold that *l'chatchilah*, the leaves of the lettuce should be used, not the stems (*Mishnah Berurah* 473:38). The leaves should preferably be moist, and not dried out (*Mishnah Berurah* ibid.). Some have the custom to use lettuce leaves for Maror, and lettuce stems for Korech (*Magen Avraham* ibid. §13; *Taz* §5; *Chayei Adam* 130, Laws of the Seder §11).

12. Some have the custom to use *tamcha*, horseradish (*chrein*) (*Magen Avraham* 475:10; *Aruch HaShulchan* 473:13; *Mishnah Berurah* §36). Some authorities hold that one does not fulfill his obligation with grated horseradish, since it loses some of its bitter taste (*Haggadas Maaseh Nissim*, by the author of *Nesivos HaMishpat*). The majority of *Poskim* hold, however, that grated horseradish is acceptable (*Teshuvos Beis Ephraim* O.C. 43; *Chayei Adam* 130:3; *Nishmas Adam* 32; *Mishnah Berurah* 473:36, *Shaar HaTzion* §46). The Vilna Gaon would wait until he returned home from shul on the Seder night to grate the horseradish, in order to prevent it from losing its bitter taste (*Mishnah Berurah* ibid.). When Pesach falls on Shabbos, it is forbidden to grate the horseradish immediately before the Seder. Instead, the horseradish should be grated on Friday afternoon and left covered until the Seder (*Mishnah Berurah* ibid.).

13. The other three species of maror listed in the Mishnah are unknown to us. Therefore, one may only recite the blessing of *Al achilas maror* over lettuce (*chazeres*) or horseradish (*tamcha*). If these are unavailable, one should use a different bitter vegetable which fulfills the qualifications listed in the Talmud. Namely, the vegetable must be edible; it must produce a white, milky substance when cut; and its leaves must not be dark green, but rather somewhat pale (*Rema* 473:5, *Mishnah Berurah* §46). Even if a certain vegetable does fulfill these three qualifications, *Al achilas maror* may not be recited over it (*Mishnah Berurah* ibid.).

Some hold that if lettuce and horseradish are unavailable, one should instead use *la'ana* (*Rema* ibid.).[1] Others suggest using radishes (*Chochmas Shlomo*, by R' Shlomo Kluger, 473:5).[2]

One may use a mixture of two different species of maror which together equal a *k'zayis*. Since they are both bitter, we do not expect the taste of one to mask the taste of the other (*Mishnah Berurah* 473:40).

14. When Erev Pesach falls on Shabbos, the lettuce leaves should be checked for bugs on Erev Shabbos.

15. Some hold that maror may be soaked in water on Shabbos Erev Pesach to prevent it from withering (*Shulchan Aruch* 321:11).[3] Others forbid soaking the maror on Shabbos Erev Pesach, since one may not prepare on Shabbos for the following day (*Pri Megadim* 474, *Mishbetzos Zahav* §2; 473 *Eishel Avraham* §15).

16. Lettuce should not be left soaking in water for more than twenty-four hours, since this would invalidate it for use as maror. If one wishes to preserve the freshness of lettuce for more than twenty-four hours, he should wrap it in a moist cloth instead (*Sdei Chemed, Chametz U'Matzah* 15:2).

17. If the lettuce was left soaking in water from Erev Shabbos, the *Poskim* dispute whether it may be removed on Shabbos to prevent it from becoming invalid (*Shevisas Shabbos: Zorei'a* 22b; *Daas Torah* 444:1). Therefore, it should be removed by a gentile (*Daas Torah*, ibid.; *Teshuvos Chasam Sofer* Y.D. 122.) If no gentile is available to remove the maror, the *Poskim* discuss whether the lettuce may be removed in an unusual manner — see *Hisorerus HaTeshuvah* 1:17).

Eating Maror

18. After eating the required amount of matzah, one should take a *k'zayis* of maror and dip all of it into charoses. It should not be

---

1. *Be'ur Halachah* s.v. *Yikach la'ana* questions whether *la'ana* may be used, since it is not edible.

2. However, he rescinded this ruling in *Ha'Alef Lecha Shlomo* (320).

3. Although some have the custom not to eat maror on Erev Pesach, maror is not *muktzah* on Shabbos Erev Pesach because it is only a custom to refrain from eating maror, not an absolute prohibition. Furthermore, even according to this custom, maror may be fed to children on Erev Pesach. Therefore it is not *muktzeh* (*Eliyah Rabbah* 444:3, 473:14; see *Kaf HaChaim* 473:95).

left inside the charoses, so that it does not lose its bitter taste (*Shulchan Aruch* 475:1). In some communities, it is customary to dip only part of the maror into charoses (*Mishnah Berurah* §13). If one ate maror but did not dip it into charoses, according to some opinions he must dip another piece of maror into charoses and eat it (*Vayaged Moshe* 25:16). The charoses is then shaken off the maror, the blessing of *Al achilas maror* is recited, and the maror is eaten (*Shulchan Aruch* ibid.).[1] *Borei pri ha'adamah* is not recited over maror, since it was exempted by the blessing recited over karpas.

If one swallows maror without first chewing it, he does not fulfill his obligation (*Shulchan Aruch* 475:3). After chewing the maror one should *l'chatchilah* swallow it all at once (*Shaar HaTzion* 473:60). If this is difficult, one may swallow it little by little, as long as he swallows a full *k'zayis* within *k'dei achilas pras* (*Mishnah Berurah* 473:43).

19. When reciting the blessing of *Al achilas maror*, one should have in mind to exempt the maror eaten for Korech (*Pri Chadash* 475).

20. If one ate maror without intention to fulfill the mitzvah, even if he did not realize that it was maror, or did not realize that it was Pesach, according to some opinions he still fulfills his obligation (*Chok Yaakov*, cited in *Be'ur Halachah* 475 s.v. *Lo yatza*). Nevertheless, one should be stringent, and eat another *k'zayis* of maror with intention to fulfill the mitzvah, but he should not recite *Al achilas maror*.

21. Even if one recited *Borei nefashos* after eating karpas, he should not recite *Borei pri ha'adamah* over the maror (*Shulchan Aruch HaRav* 473:18).

22. One need not lean to the side while eating maror (*Shulchan Aruch* 475:1), but if he wishes to do so he may (*Mishnah Berurah* §14). Some *Poskim* write that if one leans while eating maror, he fulfills his obligation *b'di'eved*. This implies that *l'chatchilah* one may not do so (*Magen Avraham* 6; *Kaf HaChaim* 27).

---

1. This order follows the opinion of the majority of *Poskim*, who hold that the blessing *Al achilas maror* is recited after the maror is dipped. Among these *Poskim* are *Magen Avraham* (473:19), *Chok Yaakov* (475:8), *Shulchan Aruch HaRav* (472:13), and *Chayei Adam* (130, Laws of the Seder §5). They all argue against *Maharil*, who holds that the blessing is recited before the maror is dipped into charoses.

ᴥⰧ Korech

1. The third matzah is used for Korech, in order to fulfill a
    mitzvah with all three matzos. A *k'zayis* of this matzah is
    joined with a *k'zayis* of maror and dipped in charoses (*Shul-
    chan Aruch* 475:1, *Mishnah Berurah* §16). Some hold that they
    should not be dipped in charoses (*Rema* ibid.). Each person
    should act according to his custom (*Mishnah Berurah* §18).
    According to the custom to dip the Korech into charoses,
    some hold that the charoses should be shaken off before
    eating (*Mishnah Berurah* §17). Others hold that it need not be
    shaken off (*Beis Yosef* 475, citing the *Agur* in the name of
    Mahari Molin).

2. Before eating Korech, it is customary to say the paragraph that
    begins זֵכֶר לְמִקְדָּשׁ כְּהִלֵּל — "In remembrance of the Beis
    HaMikdash, according to Hillel" (*Shulchan Aruch* ibid.; *Shul-
    chan Aruch HaRav* ibid. 18; *Kitzur Shulchan Aruch* 119:7).[1]
    Some hold that reciting this paragraph is considered an inter-
    ruption between the blessings of matzah and maror and
    eating Korech. Therefore, one should say this declaration after
    eating Korech (*Be'ur Halachah* 475 s.v. *V'Omer*). However, the
    custom is to say it before eating Korech. We do not consider
    it to be an interruption, since it pertains to the food that is
    eaten.

3. Someone who is ill or finds it extremely difficult to eat maror
    may be more lenient when it comes to Korech. Nonetheless, he
    should attempt to eat a sort of maror that will not harm him as
    Korech.

4. The matzah and maror should be taken into one's mouth
    together, but they need not be swallowed together (*Mishnah
    Berurah* 475:22). However, some opinions hold that one should
    l'chatchilah swallow the *k'zayis* of matzah and *k'zayis* of maror
    together all at once (*Magen Avraham* 475:8; *Shulchan Aruch
    HaRav* ibid. 21, *Chayei Adam* 130:19). If it is difficult to swallow

---

1. According to some variations, one says: "This is what Hillel did, while the Beis
HaMikdash stood. He would combine matzah with maror and eat them together."
Other variations read: "He would combine the *Korban Pesach* with matzah and
maror" (*Mishnah Berurah* §21).

two entire *k'zeiyis*im together, one should swallow matzah and maror together in smaller pieces, until both *k'zeiysim* are finished. One should not first swallow all the matzah, and then all the maror (*Shulchan Aruch HaRav* ibid.). As discussed above, it is customary to be lenient and not attempt to swallow an entire *k'zayis* at once even when fulfilling the Torah obligation of eating matzah.

5. Korech should be eaten within *k'dei achilas pras*. Since Korech is only a Rabbinic obligation, one may rely on the more lenient measurements of *k'dei achilas pras* (*Mishnah Berurah* 613:8).[1]

6. After reciting the blessings over matzah and maror, one should not interrupt by speaking of unrelated matters, until after he has eaten Korech (*Shulchan Aruch* ibid.). *B'di'eved*, if one did speak before Korech, he should not recite another blessing (*Mishnah Berurah* §24).

7. If one accidentally ate Korech before Maror, he should eat Maror afterwards without a blessing, even if he did not recite *Al achilas maror* before eating Korech (*Maamar Mordechai* 475:2). Some hold that in this case, one should recite a blessing over the maror (*Kaf HaChaim* §26).

8. Some have the custom to use one type of maror for Maror, and a different type for Korech (*Vayaged Moshe* 26). Those who are careful not to eat *gebrokts* should not use lettuce leaves for Korech, since it is difficult to ensure that they are perfectly dry.

9. Several opinions have been offered as to how the matzah and maror are combined for Korech. Some hold that the maror should be sandwiched between two broken pieces of matzah. This is the prevalent custom (*Aruch HaShulchan* 475:7; *Kitzur Shulchan Aruch* 119:7). Some hold that the maror should be wrapped around the matzah from all sides (*Vayaged Moshe* 26:7). Others hold that the maror should be placed on the matzah, but not wrapped around it (*Vayaged Moshe* ibid.). All of these customs have ancient, authentic sources.

---

1. One should not go so far as to rely on the opinion that considers *k'dei achilas pras* to be nine minutes. This opinion is only accepted as a stringency in regard to Yom Kippur.

❧ Shulchan Orech

Eating a Festive Meal

"One should consider the Seder meal to be a meal of spirituality, similar to the delicacies that Yitzchak ate. This meal represents the feast of the Leviathan [from which we will partake after Mashiach arrives]. Therefore, one should sit with his family as if he were eating in the presence of the King. They should sit together with holiness and purity, and idle words should not be spoken. Rather, their thoughts should be directed only toward Hashem" (*Shelah*, beginning of *Pesachim*).

"One should eat and drink and behave in the manner of nobility and free men" (*Seder HaYom*).

Although this meal is indeed holy and exalted, one should ensure that it is a joyous occasion for the entire family, and not a time of harshness and solemnity.

1. *L'chatchilah* one should lean during the entire meal (*Rema* 472:7). However, if this is difficult and would detract from his enjoyment of the meal, he should not lean.

2. One should not eat excessively, since the afikoman is meant to be eaten on a full — not overstuffed — stomach. One should not drink excessively either, in order that he not become drunk and fall asleep (*Rema* 476:1).

3. Some have the custom to eat eggs as a sign of mourning over the Beis Hamikdash, since the Seder night always falls on the same night of the week as Tishah B'Av. We also remind ourselves of the destruction of the Beis Hamikdash and the consequential inability to offer the *Korban Pesach* (*Rema* 476:2). The *Poskim* discuss practical differences between these two reasons (see *Chok Yaakov* §6). The eggs should be hard boiled and cold (*Vayaged Moshe* 27:3).

    The Vilna Gaon offers an additional reason for eating eggs. Eggs correspond to the *Korban Chagigah* that was eaten before the *Korban Pesach* (*Mishnah Berurah* §11). According to this reason, one should declare, "In memory of the *Korban Chagigah*," before eating the egg (*Kaf HaChaim* 476:26). According to the explanation that eggs are eaten as a sign of mourning, however, one should not make this declaration (based on

Maaseh Rav 191). Some have the custom to dip the egg in the salt water.

According to the explanation that the egg corresponds to the *Korban Chagigah*, it should be eaten at the beginning of the meal. This is the prevalent custom (*Seder HaYom; Siddur HaYaavetz*). One should not eat a large amount of eggs (*Mishnah Berurah* §13).

4. Some have the custom not to dip any food into condiments on the Seder night, besides for the karpas that is dipped in salt water and the maror that is dipped in charoses (*Rema* ibid. 2). Korech is also dipped in charoses, but this is only done in order to fulfill the mitzvah of maror according to Hillel (*Mishnah Berurah* §14).

5. Some have the custom not to eat roasted meat on the Seder night, since this would give the impression that one is eating a *Korban Pesach* that was slaughtered outside the Beis Hamikdash (*Shulchan Aruch* 476:2). *Tur* writes that this was the Ashkenazic custom. *Magen Avraham* (§1) and *Pri Megadim* also write that this was the custom in their communities. The custom not to eat roasted meat includes sheep, goats, calves, poultry, and any other animal that requires *shechitah* (*Shulchan Aruch* ibid.). However, one may eat roasted fish (*Mishnah Berurah* §9).

On Pesach day, one may eat roasted meat, since the *Korban Pesach* was not eaten by day (*Shaarei Teshuvah* 473:10). However, some *Poskim* are stringent not to eat roasted meat even by day (*Shaarei Teshuvah* ibid., citing *Teshuvas Beis Yehudah*).

One should not even eat meat that was roasted in a pot or baking tray, even though the *Korban Pesach* was roasted only over an open fire. For the sake of a sick person, however, one may be lenient in this regard (*Mishnah Berurah* §1). Some opinions allow this kind of meat even *l'chatchilah* (*Kaf HaChaim* 476). One may not eat the roasted *z'roa* from the Seder plate on the Seder night (*Mishnah Berurah* 473:32).[1]

6. If meat was cooked in soup, even if the soup dried out completely, the meat is still considered cooked and not roasted. Therefore, it may be eaten on the Seder night (*Shaarei Teshuvah* 476:1). Fried meat has the same status as meat roasted in a pot or baking tray (*Teshuvos Pnei Meivin* 123:3, based on *Pri Megadim* Y.D. 87). Meat that was roasted and then cooked is

---

1. *Chayei Adam* 130:6 writes that it should be eaten the next day.

permitted according to some opinions (*Mishnah Berurah* §1), and forbidden according to others (*Kaf HaChaim* ibid. §4).

7. One should be careful to finish the meal early, in order to finish Hallel with its concluding blessing before *chatzos* (*Rema* 477:1). *Mishnah Berurah* (§7, *Shaar HaTzion* §6) writes that this is not an absolute obligation, but rather something one should endeavor to do *l'chatchilah*. Many of our greatest Rabbanim were accustomed to finishing Hallel even after *chatzos*.

~§ Tzafun

Eating the Afikoman

1. After the meal, the afikoman is eaten (*Shulchan Aruch* 477:1). The afikoman is taken from the middle matzah that was broken during Yachatz (*Shulchan Aruch* 473; *Mishnah Berurah* §58). *L'chatchilah*, two *k'zeiysim* of matzah should be eaten: one in memory of the *Korban Pesach*, and one in memory of the matzah that was eaten with it (*Mishnah Berurah* §1). Since the obligation to eat afikoman is only Rabbinic, one may rely on the lenient estimation of the size of a *k'zayis*, one-third of the volume of an egg (*Mishnah Berurah* 486:1). The afikoman is eaten in memory of the *Korban Pesach*, so it must be eaten on a full stomach, just like the *Korban Pesach*. Therefore, we cannot fulfill the obligation to eat afikoman with the matzah eaten at the beginning of the meal (*Mishnah Berurah* §13). Some hold that *b'di'eved* if one did not eat more matzah at the end of the meal, he fulfills his obligation with the first *k'zayis* of matzah that he ate at the beginning of the meal (see *Kaf HaChaim* 477:22).

2. Although the afikoman must be eaten on a full stomach, one should still have some appetite to eat it. If one is so full that he has no appetite left, he does not fulfill the mitzvah of afikoman in the preferred manner. If one is so full that he is disgusted by eating more food, even if he forces himself to eat the afikoman he does not fulfill his obligation at all (*Mishnah Berurah* 476:6). It is proper that the mitzvah of *afikoman* should not be viewed as a burden (*Mishnah Berurah* ibid.).

3. No blessing is recited over the mitzvah of eating afikoman,

since it is only eaten as a commemoration of the *Korban Pesach* (*Shulchan Aruch* 477:1; *Mishnah Berurah* §5).

4. If one loses the afikoman matzah, he should eat a *k'zayis* of a different piece of matzah instead (*Rema* 477:2). According to some opinions, he need not eat from another matzah, but may rely on the matzah he ate during the course of the meal (*Beis Yosef*, end of 477).

5. Some have the custom that the head of the household gives each person a small piece of the matzah stored in the cloth, and adds to that a different piece of matzah to give each person a *k'zayis* (*Vayaged Moshe* 29:9). It is proper to follow this custom.

6. Women are obligated to eat afikoman (*Mishnah Berurah* ibid. §2). Some hold that it is sufficient for women and children to eat only one *k'zayis* (*Vayaged Moshe*, ibid. 3). Similarly, a man who finds it difficult to eat two *k'zeiysim* (e.g., an old or sick person) should eat at least one *k'zayis* in order to fulfill his obligation (*Shulchan Aruch HaRav* ibid. 3).[1] When eating the afikoman, one should have in mind that he is doing so to remember the *Korban Pesach* (*Kaf HaChaim*, end of §1).

7. One should take care to eat the afikoman before *chatzos* (*Shulchan Aruch*, ibid.). *B'di'eved*, if he did not eat it before *chatzos*, he should still eat it afterward (*Mishnah Berurah* ibid. §6; *Be'ur Halachah* s.v. *V'yehei zahir*). Some authorities hold that *afikoman* may be eaten even after *chatzos* even *l'chatchilah*.[2]

8. The afikoman must be eaten within *k'dei achilas pras*. Some rule stringently, and require both *k'zeiysim* to be swallowed at once (*Vayaged Moshe* 28:7). One must eat the afikoman while leaning to the side. If one did not do so, he did not fulfill his obligation (*Mishnah Berurah* 477:4, *Shaar HaTzion* §4).

9. Pious individuals would kiss the afikoman before eating it (*Shelah*, cited in *Mishnah Berurah* 477:5).

10. It is forbidden to eat the afikoman in two different places (*Rema* 478:1). Even within one room, one should not eat it at two different tables (*Mishnah Berurah* §4). The rest of the meal may be eaten in two different places (*Mishnah Berurah* §3).

11. If a person fell asleep in the middle of eating afikoman, he

---

1. *Shulchan Aruch* in 477:1 implies that even *l'chatchilah*, one *k'zayis* is sufficient.

2. This was the custom of the Chasam Sofer, as cited in *Minhagei Chasam Sofer*.

should not continue eating it. Falling asleep is considered an interruption, and it is therefore comparable to eating the afikoman in two different places (*Shulchan Aruch* 478:2). However, if one fell asleep before beginning to eat the afikoman, he may still eat it (*Rema* ibid.). Regarding whether a new *HaMotzi* blessing must be recited, see *Shulchan Aruch* 178:7, *Mishnah Berurah* loc. cit.

12. If some of the people present fell asleep while eating afikoman but others remained awake, then the people who slept may continue eating. Since part of the group was awake, this is not considered an interruption (*Shulchan Aruch* 478:2, *Mishnah Berurah* §8). If they all fell asleep while eating afikoman, they may not continue eating when they wake up. However, if they only dozed lightly, they may continue eating (*Shulchan Aruch* ibid.; see *Be'ur Halachah* s.v. *Nisnamnu*).

13. If a person forgot to eat afikoman and remembered only after he washed his hands for *mayim acharonim* or said *Rabbosai nevareich*, he may still eat the afikoman without reciting *Ha-Motzi* again (*Shulchan Aruch* 477:2). If he remembered after *Bircas HaMazon* but before he said *Borei pri hagafen* on the third cup, then he should wash his hands again (without reciting *Al netilas yadayim*), recite *HaMotzi*, eat the afikoman, recite *Bircas HaMazon* again, and then recite *Borei pri hagafen* on the third cup and drink it (*Shulchan Aruch* ibid., *Mishnah Berurah* §9). Some hold that in such a case, one should recite the blessing of *Al netilas yadayim* (*Shaar HaTzion* ibid. §9).[1]

14. If one remembered that he did not eat afikoman only after he recited *Borei pri hagafen* over the third cup, he should not eat afikoman at all, but should rely instead on the matzah he ate during the meal (*Shulchan Aruch* ibid.). However, *Mishnah Berurah* (§11) rules that one should eat the afikoman and recite *Bircas HaMazon* again without a cup of wine.

The Prohibition Against Eating or Drinking After the Afikoman

15. After eating the afikoman one should not eat anything else, in order that the taste of the afikoman remain in his mouth (*Shulchan Aruch* 478:1, *Mishnah Berurah* §1). *B'di'eved*, if one

---

1. However, if one is certain that his hands were kept clean, then even the *Shaar HaTzion* agrees that he should not recite *Al netilas yadayim*.

ate something after the afikoman, he should eat another *k'zeiyis* of matzah as afikoman (*Mishnah Berurah* ibid.).

16. The prohibition against eating after the afikoman extends throughout the entire night, even after *chatzos* (*Milchamos Hashem, Pesachim* 119b).

17. The Talmud (*Pesachim* 120b) records a dispute between R' Elazar ben Azaryah and R' Akiva. According to R' Elazar, the *Korban Pesach* and the afikoman must be eaten before *chatzos*. According to R' Akiva, they may be eaten until the morning.

   Some *Poskim* suggest that the taste of the afikoman need only remain in one's mouth during the time that there is a mitzvah to eat it; according to R' Elazar until *chatzos*, and according to R' Akiva until the morning.

   Therefore, if a person is still in the middle of the meal, and he sees that it is almost *chatzos*, he should eat a *k'zayis* of matzah with a stipulation: if the mitzvah of afikoman extends only until *chatzos* (as per R' Elazar), then this matzah should be considered afikoman. If the mitzvah of afikoman extends throughout the night, then the matzah eaten now is not for afikoman. He should then eat the matzah, wait until after *chatzos*, continue his meal and conclude it with another *k'zayis* of matzah for afikoman (*Avnei Nezer* O.C. 388).

   L'chatchilah, one should attempt to finish the meal before *chatzos*, and not rely on this leniency.

18. The *Poskim* dispute whether one may drink after eating the afikoman. *L'chatchilah*, one should avoid drinking anything other than water. In cases of necessity, one may drink other beverages, especially on the second Seder night outside Eretz Yisrael (*Mishnah Berurah* 481:1).[1] However, one should not drink intoxicating beverages (*Mishnah Berurah* 478:5).

⇜ Barech

Reciting Bircas HaMazon

1. The third cup is poured before *Bircas HaMazon*. If the cups are not clean, they must be rinsed inside and outside (*Shulchan Aruch* 479:1; *Mishnah Berurah* §1). *Bircas HaMazon* is recited,

---

1. *Haggadas Beis HaLevi* (p. 258) records that the Brisker Rav would drink a cup of tea after the Seder.

followed by *Borei pri hagafen*. The wine is drunk while leaning to the side (*Shulchan Aruch* ibid.).

2. It is customary for someone else to pour for the head of the household, in the manner of free men (*Rema* 473:2). Before beginning *Bircas HaMazon*, the person leading *Bircas HaMazon* receives the cup with both hands, and then holds it with his right hand only. The cup is held at a height of at least one *tefach* above the table. One should fix his gaze on the cup, so that his attention does not wander from it (*Shulchan Aruch* 183:4, *Mishnah Berurah*).

3. Throughout the year, it is customary that a guest leads *Bircas HaMazon* (*Shulchan Aruch* 201:1). On the Seder night, however, the head of the household should lead (*Rema* 479:1). Nevertheless, there is no objection if he wishes to let another person lead (*Mishnah Berurah* ibid. §13).

4. Some have the custom for everyone to hold their cups during *Bircas HaMazon*, since this is one of the four cups in which everyone is obligated (*Vayaged Moshe* 29:5).

5. One should not lean while reciting *Bircas HaMazon* (*Tur*, O.C. 486).

❧ Hallel

1. Hallel with its concluding blessing should *l'chatchilah* be recited before *chatzos* (*Rema* 477:1, *Mishnah Berurah* §29, *Shaar HaTzion* §6). *Mishnah Berurah* (§7, *Shaar HaTzion* §6) writes that this is not an absolute obligation, but rather something one should try to do. Many of our greatest rabbis were accustomed to finishing Hallel even after *chatzos*.

2. Hallel is recited while sitting (*Mishnah Berurah* 480:1). No blessing is recited before it (*Mishnah Berurah* ibid.).

❧ Nirtzah

If we follow this procedure, our Seder will be favorable (*merutzeh*) before Hashem.

❧ Customs for After the Seder

1. After the Seder, we must study the laws of Pesach and discuss the miracles of the Exodus and the wonders Hashem performed

for our forefathers until we are overcome by sleep (*Shulchan Aruch* 481:2. See *Haggadah M'Beis HaLevi*, p. 24 in the name of the Brisker Rav).

2. A weak or sick person who will be unable to daven *Shacharis* properly if he stays up late should preferably go to sleep after the Seder (*Siddur HaYaavetz*; *Gevuros Hashem* 5:53; *Teshuvos Besamim Rosh* 347).

3. Some have the custom not to sleep in a bed on the Seder night, but rather to fall asleep in the place where he reclined during the Seder (*Leket Yosher*, citing the *Terumas HaDeshen*; *Chasam Sofer*, cited in *Minhagei Chasam Sofer* 10:23).

4. Some have the custom to read *Shir HaShirim* after the Seder (*Chayei Adam* 130:19:16; *Kitzur Shulchan Aruch* 119:9).[1]

5. Some have the custom to leave the door of their homes unlocked on the Seder night, since there is special Divine protection on this night. However, because there are many thieves nowadays, one should not follow this practice (*Chok Yaakov* 480:6).

6. It is customary to read only the first chapter of *Shema* before going to sleep, and not the other verses that are usually read for protection, since there is special protection from destructive forces on the Seder night (*Rema* 481:2). One must also recite the blessing of *HaMapil* (*Mishnah Berurah* §4).

7. If one davened *Maariv* and recited *Shema* before nightfall, he must say the entire *Shema* again after nightfall in order to fulfill his obligation of reciting *Shema*. It is not advisable to rely on the *Shema* that one recites before going to sleep to fulfill this obligation (*Mishnah Berurah* §4; 235:12).

The Laws of the Second Seder Night

1. Outside Eretz Yisrael, a Seder is held on the second night of Pesach, with all the same laws and customs that are practiced on the first night (*Rema* 486:2).

2. On the second night of Yom Tov, candles are lit with a blessing (*Mishnah Berurah* 514:48).

---

1. See *Haggadah M'Beis HaLevi* p. 408, which states that the Brisker Rav would read *Shir HaShirim* together with his family.

3. One may not prepare the table for the second Seder on the first day of Yom Tov (*Pri Chadash* 444).

4. If a person forgot to say *Shehecheyanu* during Kiddush on the second night (even if he did say it on the first night), he may say it any time on Pesach that he remembers — even on the eighth day, which is observed only outside Eretz Yisrael (*Mishnah Berurah* 473:1). Some hold that if one forgot to recite *Shehecheyanu* during Kiddush on the second night, he should not recite it later.[1]

5. On the second night, it is also customary to begin the Seder immediately upon returning from shul (*Vayaged Moshe* 15:1).[2]

6. Some have the custom to eat the afikoman even after *chatzos* on the second night (*Vayaged Moshe* 24:39). Some hold that if one did not eat the first *k'zayis* of matzah until after *chatzos*, he should not recite the blessing of *Al achilas matzah*. We do not follow this opinion.

7. If a person eats matzah on the second night without intention to perform a mitzvah, he does not fulfill his obligation (*Chok Yaakov* 475:19; *Be'ur Halachah* 475:4 s.v. *Lo yatza*).

8. Even on the second night, one does not fulfill his obligation with stolen matzah (*Shaagas Aryeh* 95). Some hold that on the second night, one does fulfill his obligation with stolen maror (*Aruch HaShulchan* 454:8, cited in *Kaf HaChaim* 454:29).

9. It is customary to eat eggs at the second Seder as well (*Pri Megadim* 476, E.A. §4). Some argue that eggs should not be eaten at the second Seder (*Chok Yaakov* ibid. §4).

10. In places where it is customary not to eat roasted meat on the Seder night, it is forbidden even on the second night (*Pri Megadim* 476, M.Z. §1). However, if one does eat roasted meat on the second night, he is not placed in *nidui* (excommunication) for doing so, as he would be for eating meat on the first night (ibid.).

11. When the second Seder is held on *Motza'ei Shabbos*, all agree that the phrase "from the *pesachim* and the *zevachim*" in the

---

1. *Shaar HaTzion* (§3) concludes that this matter requires further study.

2. *Vayaged Moshe* also writes that some had the custom to conduct the second Seder late at night. In 19:3, he writes that some had the custom to conduct the Seder after *chatzos* on the second night.

blessing of *Go'al Yisrael* should be substituted with "from the *zevachim* and the *pesachim*."

12. After eating the afikoman on the second night, one may drink beverages that are not intoxicating (*Mishnah Berurah* 481:1).

13. Some are lenient on the second night and do not require that one remain awake after the Seder to tell stories of the Exodus until sleep overcomes him (*Vayaged Moshe* 33:3).

14. At the end of the first Seder, the *piyut* "*Az Rov Nissim*" is recited. At the end of the second Seder, "*Ometz Gevurosecha*" is recited instead. Some have the custom to recite both *piyutim* on both nights (*Mishnah Berurah* 481:6).[1]

15. When reciting *Shema* before going to sleep, one need not add the verses recited for protection (*Pri Megadim* 481, *Eishel Avraham* §3). However, some do have the custom to recite them on the second night (*Vayaged Moshe* 33:8, 34:1).

16. On the second day of Pesach, some have the custom to add a special dish to their meal, in memory of the meal that Esther made on that day, which led to the execution of Haman (*Mishnah Berurah* 490:2).

ᥬᏙ When Erev Pesach Falls on Shabbos

1. On *Shabbos HaGadol*, the Haftarah is read from *Sefer Malachi* (3:4), beginning with the words "וְעָרְבָה לַה' מִנְחַת יְהוּדָה וִירוּשָׁלָם" (*Siddur HaYaavetz* by R' Yaakov Emden, p. 226, 6). Some have the custom to read this Haftarah only when *Shabbos HaGadol* falls on Erev Pesach (*Ba'er Heitev* 430:1). Others have the opposite custom: They do not read this Haftarah when *Shabbos HaGadol* falls on Erev Pesach (*Aruch HaShulchan* 430:5, citing the Vilna Gaon).

2. There are those who recite *yotzros* even when *Shabbos HaGadol* occurs on Erev Pesach (*Pri Megadim, Mishbetzos Zahav* 430:1); others omit them on Shabbos Erev Pesach so they can hurry home to eat before chametz becomes forbidden (*Seder Erev Pesach She'chal B'Shabbos*, by R' Yosef Chaim Sonnenfeld; *Luach Eretz Yisrael*).

---

1. See *Vayaged Moshe* 32:3, who cites various customs in this matter.

3. If *Shabbos HaGadol* falls on Erev Pesach, the speech should be given on the previous Shabbos (*Mishnah Berurah* ibid.). Some are of the opinion that the Rav should speak even on Erev Pesach, but he should deliver his address earlier in the day (*Yaavetz*, ibid.).

4. When Erev Pesach falls on Shabbos, matzah is *muktzeh* and may not be moved. This is because it is forbidden to eat matzah on Erev Pesach (*Pri Megadim, Eishel Avraham* 444:1). However, young children who do not yet understand the story of the Exodus may eat matzah on Erev Pesach. For those with young children, matzos are not *muktzeh*, since they may be fed to the children (*Teshuvos Sho'el U'Meishiv Mahadura Tinyana*, 2:77). If one has no other matzos [other than those to be used for the *Seder*], and would therefore not feed them to the children, then the matzos remain *muktzeh* (Ibid.).

5. When Erev Pesach falls on Shabbos, neither the maror (*Eliyah Rabbah* 473:14) nor the charoses is *muktzeh*.

6. When Erev Pesach falls on Shabbos, some hold that *matzah ashirah* should be used for the third meal (*matzah ashirah* is matzah that contains other ingredients, such as eggs or fruit juice, and is unfit for the mitzvah of eating matzah) (*Shulchan Aruch* 444:1). However, the custom is to eat only meat, fish or fruit for the third meal, with no bread or matzah at all (*Rema* ibid., *Mishnah Berurah* §8). Some hold that one should drink a *revi'is* of wine for the third meal (*Shelah*, beginning of *Maseches Pesachim*). Some hold that the third meal can be fulfilled by discussing Torah subjects (*Magen Avraham* 444:2 citing the *Shelah*).

7. When Erev Pesach falls on Shabbos, it is proper to divide the morning Shabbos meal into two meals. One should eat, recite *Bircas HaMazon*, pause by taking a walk or the like, and then wash his hands to eat another meal (*Mishnah Berurah* 444:8). Some require a half-hour interruption between the meals (*Igros Chazon Ish* vol. 1, 188).

    Some have the custom to eat a meal of cold chametz foods immediately after davening and to eat hot, kosher-for-Pesach foods at the third meal in the afternoon (*Mishnah Berurah* ibid., §4).

8. When Erev Pesach falls on Shabbos, one should shake the crumbs off the tablecloth after eating the chametz meal (*Shulchan Aruch* 444:3). The small crumbs need not be thrown out of

the house, since people walk over them and thus destroy them. It is proper to sweep the floor, however.

9. When Erev Pesach falls on Shabbos, if chametz is left over after the meal, one should either give it to a gentile as a gift, crumble it and flush it down the toilet, or feed it to a dog. If there is an *eruv*, one may relinquish ownership of the chametz and throw it into the street (*Shulchan Aruch* 444:4. *Mishnah Berurah* §16; 21; *Mishnah Berurah* 306:33).

10. If Erev Pesach falls on Shabbos, the fast is observed on the previous Thursday instead (*Shulchan Aruch, Rema* ibid.). According to some opinions, in such a case one need not fast at all. These authorities maintain that since this fast is only a custom, if it cannot be observed on its proper day, it need not be observed at all (*Mishnah Berurah* ibid., §6. See *Igros Moshe Orach Chaim* IV, 69:4).

11. When Erev Pesach falls on Shabbos, it is questionable whether work is permitted on Erev Shabbos in the afternoon. It appears that we may be lenient in this matter (*Be'ur Halachah* ibid., s.v. *M'chatzos*).

12. When Erev Pesach falls on Shabbos, some hold that only one cooked food should be placed on the Seder plate, in commemoration of the *Korban Pesach*, since the *Korban Chagigah* was not offered on Shabbos. Others hold that two cooked foods should be used. This is the accepted custom (*Mishnah Berurah* §22).

13. When Erev Pesach falls on Shabbos, the Seder table may not be set on Shabbos, since it is forbidden to prepare on Shabbos for Yom Tov. Rather, the Seder table should be set on Erev Shabbos. Similarly, outside of Eretz Yisrael where two days of Yom Tov are observed, one may not set the table on the first day of Yom Tov for the second night (*Pri Chadash* 444). Some permit having a gentile set the table on Shabbos for Yom Tov (*Maharsham, Daas Torah* 444:1, based on *Pri Megadim* 503, *Eishel Avraham* §1).

14. When Erev Pesach falls on Shabbos, the charoses should be prepared on Erev Shabbos (*Chok Yaakov* 444:25).

15. When Seder night falls on *Motza'ei Shabbos*, Havdalah (וְתוֹדִיעֵנוּ) is recited in the fourth blessing of *Shemoneh Esrei*. It is forbidden to perform *melachah* before making some sort of

Havdalah. A woman who did not daven *Maariv* and wishes to perform *melachah* — such as lighting candles, cooking food, or setting the table — must first say *"Baruch HaMavdil bein kodesh l'kodesh"* — Blessed is He Who distinguishes between holy and holy (*Mishnah Berurah* 299:36). Even if she does say these words, she may not eat until after she hears Kiddush and Havdalah recited over a cup of wine (*Mishnah Berurah*s ibid.).

Whenever Yom Tov falls on *Motza'ei Shabbos*, Havdalah is recited as part of Kiddush (*Shulchan Aruch* 473:1). The order of the blessings is: wine, Kiddush, candle, Havdalah, *Shehecheyanu*. This is alluded to by the Hebrew acronym, יקנה"ז, which stands for יַיִן, קִידּוּשׁ, נֵר, הַבְדָּלָה, זְמַן (*Shulchan Aruch* ibid., *Mishnah Berurah* §3).

16. When reciting the Havdalah blessing during Kiddush, one should pause slightly between the words "מִשֵּׁשֶׁת יְמֵי הַמַּעֲשֶׂה קִדַּשְׁתָּ" and "הִבְדַּלְתָּ וְקִדַּשְׁתָּ אֶת עַמְּךָ יִשְׂרָאֵל" (*Tosafos, Pesachim* 114a s.v. *Ba'e; Tur* 473).

17. *Besamim* (fragrant spices) are not used during Havdalah when Yom Tov falls on *Motza'ei Shabbos* (*Mishnah Berurah* 473:3; 491:3). If one accidentally recited a blessing over *besamim*, this does not constitute an interruption, and he may still drink from the wine (*Chidah, Machazik Berachah* O.C. 491:2.).[1]

18. Although many have the custom to fill the Havdalah cup until the wine overflows (*Rema* O.C. 286:1), it is not customary to do so when Yom Tov falls on *Motza'ei Shabbos* and Kiddush and Havdalah are recited together. On a regular *Motza'ei Shabbos*, the wine is allowed to overflow as an auspicious sign for the beginning of the workweek. This reason is not applicable on Yom Tov, which is not a workday.

19. Some hold that when reciting Havdalah on the Seder night, one need not gaze at his fingernails as he normally does on *Motza'ei Shabbos*.[2]

---

1. An objection may be raised based on *Be'ur Halachah* 298:5 s.v. *Ain*, where we find that a blessing recited over an unsuitable candle constitutes an interruption of Havdalah. However, the blessing over the unsuitable candle was a *berachah l'vatalah*, while in this case, even though the blessing over the *besamim* was unnecessary for Havdalah, it was not a *berachah l'vatalah*. Therefore, it does not invalidate Havdalah.

2. *Mishnah Berurah* 298:9 cites the custom to gaze at one's fingernails during Havdalah on a regular *Motza'ei Shabbos*. See also *Chayei Adam* 130:16.

20. Although women do not normally drink from the Havdalah wine (*Mishnah Berurah* 296:6), they must drink from this Havdalah, since it is the first of the four cups.

21. Two candles should be held together, so that they may be considered a torch (*Mateh Ephraim* 600, *Eleph HaMagen* 3). Some have the custom to use two separate candles that do not touch[1] (*Minhagei Chabad*, cited at the end of *Shulchan Aruch HaRav* vol. 3, p. 57). Others have the custom to use only one candle (*Chok L'Yisrael*, Laws of Erev Pesach that Falls on Shabbos p. 92).

22. Yom Tov candles may also be used for Havdalah, since they are meant to provide light (*Teshuvos Tzitz Eliezer* vol. 6, 10).

23. If one forgot to recite Havdalah during Kiddush and remembered after he had already begun reciting the Haggadah, he should continue reciting the Haggadah until after the blessing *Go'al Yisrael* and then recite Havdalah (*Shulchan Aruch* 473:1). *Mishnah Berurah* (§5) explains that he should first recite *Borei pri hagafen* over the second cup, then the blessing over the candle, then the Havdalah blessing, and then drink the cup.[2]

    If one realized in the middle of the meal that he did not recite Havdalah, he must stop the meal immediately and recite Havdalah over a cup of wine. In this case, he should not say *Borei pri hagafen* (*Mishnah Berurah* §5).

    If he realized immediately after the second cup that he did not recite Havdalah, he must pour another cup over which to recite Havdalah. He should not recite the *Borei pri hagafen* blessing during this Havdalah, since the wine was exempted by the *Borei pri hagafen* he recited over the second cup. However, if he did not intend to drink more wine during the meal, then he must recite another *Borei pri hagafen* for Havdalah (*Shaar HaTzion* ibid. §15).

    If he realized during *Bircas HaMazon* that he did not recite Havdalah, he should recite Havdalah over the cup used for *Bircas HaMazon* (*Mishnah Berurah* ibid.).

    If he realized his omission after he drank the cup for *Bircas*

---

1. This is so that it should not appear as if one is extinguishing the candles when he separates them. See *Mishnah Berurah* 502:19. *Mishnah Berurah* writes there that if one's intention is to put each candle in its place, this is permitted.

2. *Mishnah Berurah* (§ 4) adds that even if one did not yet begin the Haggadah, once he has finished Kiddush, he must wait until *Go'al Yisrael* to say Havdalah.

HaMazon, he should wait until after Hallel, and recite Havdalah over the fourth cup (*Mishnah Berurah* ibid.).

If he realized after he drank the fourth cup, he should recite Havdalah over a fifth cup of wine. He must recite *Borei pri hagafen* on this cup, since he has already concluded the meal (*Mishnah Berurah* ibid.).

24. If one forgot to recite Havdalah as part of Kiddush and remembered before Karpas, it is questionable whether he should eat Karpas and wait until the second cup to recite Havdalah (see *Shulchan Aruch HaRav* 473:7; *Be'ur Halachah* 473:1 s.v. *Ad sheyas'chil*; *Kaf HaChaim* ibid. §28).

25. When Erev Pesach falls on Shabbos, the lettuce leaves should be checked for bugs on Erev Shabbos.

26. Some hold that maror may be soaked in water on Shabbos Erev Pesach to prevent it from withering (*Shulchan Aruch* 321:11).[1] Others forbid soaking the maror on Shabbos Erev Pesach, since one may not prepare on Shabbos for the following day (*Pri Megadim* 474, *Mishbetzos Zahav* §2; 473, *Eishel Avraham* §15).

---

1. Although some have the custom not to eat maror on Erev Pesach, maror is not *muktzeh* on Shabbos Erev Pesach because it is only a custom to refrain from eating maror, not an absolute prohibition. Furthermore, even according to this custom, maror may be fed to children on Erev Pesach. Therefore it is not *muktzeh* (*Eliyah Rabbah* 444:3, 473:14. See *Kaf HaChaim* 473:95).

ערב פסח
EREV PESACH

בדיקת חמץ

Before beginning the search for chametz, one should wash his hands and recite the following declaration of intent:

הִנְנִי מוּכָן וּמְזוּמָּן לְקַיֵּם מִצְוַת עֲשֵׂה וְלֹא תַעֲשֶׂה שֶׁל בְּדִיקַת חָמֵץ, לְשֵׁם יִחוּד קוּדְשָׁא בְּרִיךְ הוּא וּשְׁכִינְתֵּיהּ, עַל יְדֵי הַהוּא טָמִיר וְנֶעְלָם, בְּשֵׁם כָּל יִשְׂרָאֵל: וִיהִי נֹעַם אֲדֹנָי אֱלֹהֵינוּ עָלֵינוּ, וּמַעֲשֵׂה יָדֵינוּ כּוֹנְנָה עָלֵינוּ, וּמַעֲשֵׂה יָדֵינוּ כּוֹנְנֵהוּ:

בָּרוּךְ אַתָּה יהוה אֱלֹהֵינוּ מֶלֶךְ הָעוֹלָם, אֲשֶׁר קִדְּשָׁנוּ בְּמִצְוֹתָיו, וְצִוָּנוּ עַל בִּעוּר חָמֵץ.

Upon completion of the chametz search, one must nullify the chametz he may have overlooked, by reciting the following declaration. Some have the custom to recite it three times (*Morah B'Etzba* 7:3). The declaration must be understood in order to take effect; one who does not understand the Aramaic text may recite it in English, Yiddish or any other language.

Any chametz that will be used for that evening's supper or the next day's breakfast or for any other purpose prior to the final removal of chametz the next morning is not included in this declaration.

כָּל חֲמִירָא וַחֲמִיעָא דְּאִכָּא בִרְשׁוּתִי, דְּלָא חֲמִתֵּהּ וּדְלָא בַעַרְתֵּהּ וּדְלָא יְדַעְנָא לֵהּ, לִבָּטֵל וְלֶהֱוֵי הֶפְקֵר כְּעַפְרָא דְאַרְעָא.

After reciting this declaration, some have the custom to add the following prayer (from *Avodas HaKodesh*):

יְהִי רָצוֹן מִלְּפָנֶיךָ יְהֹוָה אֱלֹהֵינוּ וֵאלֹהֵי אֲבוֹתֵינוּ, שֶׁתְּזַכֵּנוּ לָתוּר וּלְחַפֵּשׂ וּלְפַשְׁפֵּשׁ בְּנִגְעֵי בָתֵּי הַנֶּפֶשׁ אֲשֶׁר נוֹאַלְנוּ בַּעֲצַת

כָּל חֲמִירָא וַחֲמִיעָא דְּאִכָּא בִרְשׁוּתִי וכו׳ לִבָּטֵל וְלֶהֱוֵי הֶפְקֵר כְּעַפְרָא
Any chametz which is in my possession . . . shall be nullified and become ownerless, like the dust of the earth.

In *Minchas Asher* on *Pesachim* (8), we cited three approaches as to how *bitul chametz* (nullifying the chametz) circumvents the Torah prohibition against owning chametz on Pesach.

Rashi and *Ramban* hold that the Torah decrees that *bitul chametz* removes the status of chametz from the chametz. *Tosafos* (*Pesachim* 4b s.v. *Lav*), maintains that *bitul chametz* constitutes relinquishment

THE SEARCH FOR CHAMETZ

Before beginning the search for chametz, one should wash his hands
and recite the following declaration of intent:

Behold, I am prepared and ready to fulfill the positive and
prohibitive mitzvos of searching for chametz. For the sake of
the unification of the Holy One, Blessed is He, and His presence,
through Him Who is hidden and inscrutable [I pray] in the name of
all Israel. May the pleasantness of HASHEM, our God, be upon us,
and may He establish our handiwork for us; our handiwork may He
establish.

Blessed are You, HASHEM, our God, King of the
universe, Who has sanctified us with His commandments, and commanded us concerning the
removal of chametz.

Upon completion of the chametz search, one must nullify the chametz
he may have overlooked, by reciting the following declaration. Some
have the custom to recite it three times (*Morah B'Etzba* 7:3). The
declaration must be understood in order to take effect; one who does
not understand the Aramaic text may recite it in English, Yiddish or any
other language.

Any chametz that will be used for that evening's supper or the next
day's breakfast or for any other purpose prior to the final removal of
chametz the next morning is not included in this declaration.

Any chametz that is in my possession, which I did
not see, and remove, nor know about, shall be
nullified and become ownerless, like the dust of the
earth.

After reciting this declaration, some have the custom
to add the following prayer (from *Avodas HaKodesh*):

Let it be Your will, HASHEM our God and God of our fathers, that
we may be granted the merit to search and investigate the inner
recesses of our souls, which we have sullied through the designs

---

of ownership (rendering the chametz ownerless, or *hefker*). *Maharik*
(142) and other *Acharonim* write that *bitul chametz* removes the
status of food from the chametz, and it is therefore not considered
fit for consumption.

We can suggest that the text of *bitul chametz* was worded to
include all three opinions. We declare that the chametz is "nulli-

יִצְרֵנוּ הָרָע, וּתְזַכֵּנוּ לָשׁוּב בִּתְשׁוּבָה שְׁלֵמָה, וְאַתָּה בְּטוּבְךָ הַגָּדוֹל תְּרַחֵם עָלֵינוּ וּתְסַיְּיעֵנוּ וְתַעַזְרֵנוּ עַל דְּבַר כְּבוֹד שְׁמֶךָ, וְתַצִּילֵנוּ מֵאִסּוּר חָמֵץ אֲפִילוּ בְּכָל שֶׁהוּא בְּשָׁנָה זוֹ וּבְכָל שָׁנָה וְשָׁנָה כָּל יְמֵי חַיֵּינוּ, אָמֵן וְכֵן יְהִי רָצוֹן:

The chametz is wrapped well and set aside
in a safe place to be burned the next morning.

בִּיעוּר חָמֵץ

On the fourteenth of Nissan, during the fifth hour of the day, remaining chametz is burned. It is preferable that one prepare his own fire and personally burn his *chametz* (Minchas Asher).

הִנְנִי מוּכָן וּמְזוּמָּן לְקַיֵּם מִצְוַת עֲשֵׂה וְלֹא תַעֲשֶׂה שֶׁל שְׂרֵיפַת חָמֵץ לְשֵׁם יִחוּד קוּדְשָׁא בְּרִיךְ הוּא וּשְׁכִינְתֵּיה, עַל יְדֵי הַהוּא טָמִיר וְנֶעְלָם, בְּשֵׁם כָּל יִשְׂרָאֵל: וִיהִי נֹעַם אֲדֹנָי אֱלֹהֵינוּ עָלֵינוּ, וּמַעֲשֵׂה יָדֵינוּ כּוֹנְנָה עָלֵינוּ, וּמַעֲשֵׂה יָדֵינוּ כּוֹנְנֵהוּ:

While the chametz is burning,
the following declaration should be recited.

יְהִי רָצוֹן מִלְּפָנֶיךָ יְהוָה אֱלֹהֵינוּ וֵאלֹהֵי אֲבוֹתֵינוּ, כְּשֵׁם שֶׁאֲנִי מְבַעֵר חָמֵץ מִבֵּיתִי וּמֵרְשׁוּתִי, כָּךְ תְּבַעֵר אֶת כָּל הַחִיצוֹנִים וְאֶת רוּחַ הַטֻּמְאָה תְּבַעֵר מִן הָאָרֶץ, וְאֶת יִצְרֵנוּ הָרָע תְּבַעֵר מֵאִתָּנוּ וְתִתֶּן לָנוּ לֵב בָּשָׂר, וְכָל הַסִּטְרָא אַחֲרָא וְכָל הַקְּלִפּוֹת וְכָל הָרִשְׁעָה כֶּעָשָׁן תִּכְלֶה, וְתַעֲבִיר מֶמְשֶׁלֶת זָדוֹן מִן הָאָרֶץ, וְכָל הַמְעִיקִים לַשְּׁכִינָה תְּבַעֲרֵם בְּרוּחַ בָּעֵר וּבְרוּחַ מִשְׁפָּט כְּשֵׁם שֶׁבִּעַרְתָּ אֶת מִצְרַיִם וְאֶת אֱלֹהֵיהֶם בַּיָּמִים הָהֵם וּבַזְּמַן הַזֶּה:

The following declaration, which includes all chametz without exception, is to be made after the burning of leftover chametz. (Some have the custom to recite it three times.) It should be recited in a language which one understands.

When Pesach begins on *Motza'ei Shabbos,* this declaration is made on Shabbos morning. Any chametz remaining from the Shabbos morning meal, is flushed down the drain before the declaration is made.

כָּל חֲמִירָא וַחֲמִיעָא דְּאִכָּא בִרְשׁוּתִי, דַּחֲזִתֵּה וּדְלָא חֲזִתֵּה, דַּחֲמִתֵּה וּדְלָא חֲמִתֵּה, דְּבִעַרְתֵּה וּדְלָא בִעַרְתֵּה, לִבָּטֵל וְלֶהֱוֵי הֶפְקֵר כְּעַפְרָא דְאַרְעָא.

of the *yetzer hara*. Let us merit to return in perfect *teshuvah*. And may You, in Your great benevolence, have mercy on us and assist us, for the sake of the honor of Your Name. Protect us from even the slightest amount of chametz — on this year, and on every year, for all the days of our lives. Amen, may this be Your will.

The chametz is wrapped well and set aside in a safe place to be burned the next morning.

BURNING THE CHAMETZ

On the fourteenth of Nissan, during the fifth hour of the day, remaining chametz is burned. It is preferable that one prepare his own fire and personally burn his chametz (Minchas Asher).

Behold, I am prepared and ready to fulfill the positive and prohibitive mitzvos of burning chametz. For the sake of the unification of the Holy One, Blessed is He, and His presence, through Him Who is hidden and inscrutable [I pray] in the name of all Israel. May the pleasantness of HASHEM, our God, be upon us, and may He establish our handiwork for us; our handiwork may He establish.

While the chametz is burning, the following declaration should be recited.

Let it be Your will HASHEM, our God and God of our fathers, that just as I rid my home and my property of chametz, so may You rid all the *chitzonim* and the impure forces from the land, and destroy the Evil Inclination from our midst, and grant us a heart of flesh. Let all the forces of the *Sitra Achra*, and all the *klippos* and all the wickedness, disperse like smoke. Sweep the kingdom of evil away from the land, and all those who cause pain to the *Shechinah*, destroy them with a spirit of destruction and a spirit of justice, as you destroyed Egypt and its deities in those days and at this time, Amen Selah.

The following declaration, which includes all chametz without exception, is to be made after the burning of leftover chametz. (Some have the custom to recite it three times.) It should be recited in a language which one understands.

When Pesach begins on Motza'ei Shabbos, this declaration is made on Shabbos morning. Any chametz remaining from the Shabbos morning meal, is flushed down the drain before the declaration is made.

Any chametz that is in my possession, which I did or did not see, which I did or did not remove, shall be nullified and become ownerless, like the dust of the earth.

---

fied" (*Rashi* and *Ramban's* opinion); that it is "ownerless" (*Tosafos'* opinion); and that "it is like the dust of the earth" [i.e., it is no longer considered food] (*Maharik's* opinion).

יְהִי רָצוֹן מִלְּפָנֶיךָ, יהוה אֱלֹהֵינוּ וֵאלֹהֵי אֲבוֹתֵינוּ, שֶׁתְּרַחֵם עָלֵינוּ וְתַצִּילֵנוּ מֵאִסּוּר חָמֵץ אֲפִילוּ מִכָּל שֶׁהוּא, אוֹתָנוּ וְאֶת כָּל בְּנֵי בֵיתֵנוּ, וּלְכָל יִשְׂרָאֵל בְּשָׁנָה זוֹ וּבְכָל שָׁנָה וְשָׁנָה כָּל יְמֵי חַיֵּינוּ, וּכְשֵׁם שֶׁבִּעַרְנוּ הֶחָמֵץ מִבָּתֵּינוּ וּשְׂרַפְנוּהוּ, כָּךְ תְּזַכֵּנוּ לְבַעֵר אֶת הַיֵּצֶר הָרָע מִקִּרְבֵּנוּ תָּמִיד כָּל יְמֵי חַיֵּינוּ, וּתְזַכֵּנוּ לְדָבְקָ בְּךָ וּבְתוֹרָתְךָ וְאַהֲבָתְךָ וְלִדְבַק בְּיֵצֶר הַטּוֹב תָּמִיד אֲנַחְנוּ וְזַרְעֵנוּ וְזֶרַע זַרְעֵנוּ מֵעַתָּה וְעַד עוֹלָם, כֵּן יְהִי רָצוֹן, אָמֵן:

עירוב תבשילין

It is forbidden to prepare on Yom Tov for the next day even if that day is Shabbos. If, however, Shabbos preparations were started before Yom Tov began, they may be continued on Yom Tov. Eruv Tavshilin constitutes this preparation. A matzah and any cooked food (such as fish, meat, or an egg) are set aside on the day before Yom Tov to be used on Shabbos and the blessing is recited followed by the declaration [made in a language understood by the one making the Eruv].

If the first days of Pesach fall on Thursday and Friday, an Eruv Tavshilin must be made on Wednesday.

In Eretz Yisrael, where only one day Yom Tov is in effect, the Eruv is omitted.

בָּרוּךְ אַתָּה יהוה אֱלֹהֵינוּ מֶלֶךְ הָעוֹלָם, אֲשֶׁר קִדְּשָׁנוּ בְּמִצְוֹתָיו, וְצִוָּנוּ עַל מִצְוַת עֵרוּב.

בַּהֲדֵין עֵרוּבָא יְהֵא שָׁרֵא לָנָא לַאֲפוּיֵי וּלְבַשּׁוּלֵי וּלְאַצְלוּיֵי וּלְאַטְמוּנֵי וּלְאַדְלוּקֵי שְׁרָגָא וּלְתַקָּנָא וּלְמֶעְבַּד כָּל צָרְכָּנָא, מִיּוֹמָא טָבָא לְשַׁבְּתָא לָנָא וּלְכָל יִשְׂרָאֵל הַדָּרִים בָּעִיר הַזֹּאת.

May it be Your will, HASHEM, our God and the God of our forefathers, that You be merciful with us and rescue us from transgressing the prohibition of chametz even in the slightest degree — us, our entire household, and all of Israel — this year and every year, for all the days of our lives. And just as we have removed the chametz from our houses and burnt it, so may You enable us to remove the Evil Inclination from within us eternally, all the days of our lives; may You enable us to cleave to You, to Your Torah, and to Your love, and to cleave to the Good Inclination eternally — us, our children, and our children's children — from now and forever. So may it be. Amen.

ERUV TAVSHILIN

It is forbidden to prepare on Yom Tov for the next day even if that day is Shabbos. If, however, Shabbos preparations were started before Yom Tov began, they may be continued on Yom Tov. Eruv Tavshilin constitutes this preparation. A matzah and any cooked food (such as fish, meat, or an egg) are set aside on the day before Yom Tov to be used on Shabbos and the blessing is recited followed by the declaration [made in a language understood by the one making the Eruv].

If the first days of Pesach fall on Thursday and Friday,
an Eruv Tavshilin must be made on Wednesday.

In Eretz Yisrael, where only one day Yom Tov is in effect,
the Eruv is omitted.

Blessed are You, HASHEM, our God, King of the universe, Who sanctified us with His commandments and commanded us concerning the commandment of Eruv.

Through this Eruv may we be permitted to bake, cook, fry, insulate, kindle flame, prepare for, and do anything necessary on the festival for the sake of the Sabbath — for ourselves and for all Jews who live in this city.

סֵדֶר אֲמִירַת קָרְבַּן פֶּסַח

On Erev Pesach in the afternoon, after davening *Minchah*, it is customary to study how the *Korban Pesach* was offered in the Beis Hamikdash. In the generations when there is no Beis Hamikdash, learning the Torah portions concerning these offerings takes the place of actually offering them, as our Sages learn from the verse: "Let our lips substitute for bulls" (*Hosea 14:3*).

רִבּוֹן הָעוֹלָמִים, אַתָּה צִוִּיתָנוּ לְהַקְרִיב קָרְבַּן הַפֶּסַח בְּמוֹעֲדוֹ בְּאַרְבָּעָה עָשָׂר יוֹם לַחֹדֶשׁ הָרִאשׁוֹן, וְלִהְיוֹת כֹּהֲנִים בַּעֲבוֹדָתָם וּלְוִיִּים בְּדוּכָנָם וְיִשְׂרָאֵל בְּמַעֲמָדָם קוֹרְאִים אֶת הַהַלֵּל. וְעַתָּה בַּעֲוֹנוֹתֵינוּ חָרַב בֵּית הַמִּקְדָּשׁ וּבֻטַּל קָרְבַּן הַפֶּסַח, וְאֵין לָנוּ לֹא כֹהֵן בַּעֲבוֹדָתוֹ וְלֹא לֵוִי בְּדוּכָנוֹ וְלֹא יִשְׂרָאֵל בְּמַעֲמָדוֹ, וְלֹא נוּכַל לְהַקְרִיב הַיּוֹם קָרְבַּן פֶּסַח.

אֲבָל אַתָּה אָמַרְתָּ וּנְשַׁלְּמָה פָרִים שְׂפָתֵינוּ. לָכֵן יְהִי רָצוֹן מִלְּפָנֶיךָ יהוה אֱלֹהֵינוּ וֵאלֹהֵי אֲבוֹתֵינוּ שֶׁיִּהְיֶה שִׂיחַ שִׂפְתוֹתֵינוּ חָשׁוּב לְפָנֶיךָ כְּאִלּוּ הִקְרַבְנוּ אֶת הַפֶּסַח בְּמוֹעֲדוֹ וְעָמַדְנוּ עַל מַעֲמָדוֹ, וְדִבְּרוּ הַלְוִיִּים בְּשִׁיר וְהַלֵּל לְהוֹדוֹת לַיהוה. וְאַתָּה תְּכוֹנֵן מִקְדָּשְׁךָ עַל מְכוֹנוֹ, וְנַעֲשֶׂה וְנַקְרִיב לְפָנֶיךָ אֶת הַפֶּסַח בְּמוֹעֲדוֹ, כְּמוֹ שֶׁכָּתַבְתָּ עָלֵינוּ בְּתוֹרָתֶךָ עַל יְדֵי מֹשֶׁה עַבְדֶּךָ כָּאָמוּר:

שמות יב:א-יא

וַיֹּאמֶר יהוה אֶל־מֹשֶׁה וְאֶל־אַהֲרֹן בְּאֶרֶץ מִצְרַיִם לֵאמֹר: הַחֹדֶשׁ הַזֶּה לָכֶם רֹאשׁ חֳדָשִׁים רִאשׁוֹן הוּא לָכֶם לְחָדְשֵׁי הַשָּׁנָה: דַּבְּרוּ אֶל־כָּל־עֲדַת יִשְׂרָאֵל לֵאמֹר בֶּעָשֹׂר

KORBAN PESACH

On Erev Pesach in the afternoon, after davening *Minchah,* it is customary to study how the *Korban Pesach* was offered in the Beis Hamikdash.
In the generations when there is no Beis Hamikdash, learning the Torah
portions concerning these offerings takes the place of actually offering
them, as our Sages learn from the verse: "Let our lips substitute for
bulls" (*Hosea* 14:3).

Master of the universe, You have commanded
us to offer the *Korban Pesach* in its appropriate time, on the fourteenth of the first month, with
the *Kohanim* performing the Temple service,
the *Leviim* standing on their platform, and the
Yisraelim in their places reciting Hallel. Now, as a
result of our sins, the Beis Hamikdash has been
destroyed and the *Korban Pesach* is no more.
The *Kohen* does not serve; the *Levi* does not stand
on the platform, nor does the *Yisrael* stand in his
place.

You have said ... "We will offer the words of our
lips in place of the cattle offerings." Therefore, let it
be Your will, our God and God of our fathers, that the
words of our lips be deemed before You, as if we had
offered the *Korban Pesach* in its appropriate time,
and stood beside it in our places, while the *Leviim*
uttered songs and Hallel to give thanks to HASHEM.
May You establish the Beis Hamikdash on its site,
and we will ascend to offer You the *Korban Pesach*
in its appropriate time, as You have written to us in
Your Torah, through Moshe Your servant, as it is
written:

Shemos 12:1-11

And HASHEM said to Moshe and Aharon in the land
of Egypt, saying: This month shall be for you
the beginning of the months, it shall be for you
the first of the months of the year. Speak unto the
entire congregation of Israel, saying: On the tenth of

לַחֹדֶשׁ הַזֶּה וְיִקְחוּ לָהֶם אִישׁ שֶׂה לְבֵית־אָבֹת שֶׂה
לַבָּיִת: וְאִם־יִמְעַט הַבַּיִת מִהְיֹת מִשֶּׂה וְלָקַח הוּא
וּשְׁכֵנוֹ הַקָּרֹב אֶל־בֵּיתוֹ בְּמִכְסַת נְפָשֹׁת אִישׁ לְפִי
אָכְלוֹ תָּכֹסּוּ עַל־הַשֶּׂה: שֶׂה תָמִים זָכָר בֶּן־שָׁנָה
יִהְיֶה לָכֶם מִן־הַכְּבָשִׂים וּמִן־הָעִזִּים תִּקָּחוּ: וְהָיָה
לָכֶם לְמִשְׁמֶרֶת עַד אַרְבָּעָה עָשָׂר יוֹם לַחֹדֶשׁ הַזֶּה
וְשָׁחֲטוּ אֹתוֹ כֹּל קְהַל עֲדַת־יִשְׂרָאֵל בֵּין הָעַרְבָּיִם:
וְלָקְחוּ מִן־הַדָּם וְנָתְנוּ עַל־שְׁתֵּי הַמְּזוּזֹת וְעַל־
הַמַּשְׁקוֹף עַל הַבָּתִּים אֲשֶׁר־יֹאכְלוּ אֹתוֹ בָּהֶם:
וְאָכְלוּ אֶת־הַבָּשָׂר בַּלַּיְלָה הַזֶּה צְלִי־אֵשׁ וּמַצּוֹת
עַל־מְרֹרִים יֹאכְלֻהוּ: אַל־תֹּאכְלוּ מִמֶּנּוּ נָא
וּבָשֵׁל מְבֻשָּׁל בַּמָּיִם כִּי אִם־צְלִי־אֵשׁ רֹאשׁוֹ עַל־
כְּרָעָיו וְעַל־קִרְבּוֹ: וְלֹא־תוֹתִירוּ מִמֶּנּוּ עַד־בֹּקֶר
וְהַנֹּתָר מִמֶּנּוּ עַד־בֹּקֶר בָּאֵשׁ תִּשְׂרֹפוּ: וְכָכָה
תֹּאכְלוּ אֹתוֹ מָתְנֵיכֶם חֲגֻרִים נַעֲלֵיכֶם בְּרַגְלֵיכֶם
וּמַקֶּלְכֶם בְּיֶדְכֶם וַאֲכַלְתֶּם אֹתוֹ בְּחִפָּזוֹן פֶּסַח הוּא
לַיהוָה:

The following description of the *Korban Pesach*
appears in *Siddur HaYaavetz*.

כָּךְ הָיְתָה עֲבוֹדַת קָרְבַּן פֶּסַח בְּאַרְבָּעָה עָשָׂר בְּנִיסָן. אֵין
שׁוֹחֲטִין אוֹתוֹ אֶלָּא אַחַר תָּמִיד שֶׁל בֵּין הָעַרְבָּיִם, עֶרֶב
פֶּסַח בֵּין בְּחוֹל בֵּין בְּשַׁבָּת הָיָה הַתָּמִיד נִשְׁחָט בְּשֶׁבַע
וּמֶחֱצָה וְקָרֵב בִּשְׁמוֹנָה וּמֶחֱצָה. וְאִם חָל עֶרֶב פֶּסַח לִהְיוֹת
עֶרֶב שַׁבָּת, הָיוּ שׁוֹחֲטִין אוֹתוֹ בְּשֵׁשׁ וּמֶחֱצָה וְקָרֵב בְּשֶׁבַע
וּמֶחֱצָה, וְהַפֶּסַח אַחֲרָיו:

כָּל אָדָם מִיִּשְׂרָאֵל אֶחָד הָאִישׁ וְאֶחָד הָאִשָּׁה, כָּל
שֶׁיָּכוֹל לְהַגִּיעַ לִירוּשָׁלַיִם בִּשְׁעַת שְׁחִיטַת הַפֶּסַח, חַיָּיב
בְּקָרְבַּן פֶּסַח. מְבִיאוֹ מִן הַכְּבָשִׂים אוֹ מִן הָעִזִּים. זָכָר תָּמִים

this month they shall take for themselves — each man — a lamb for each family, a lamb for each household. If the household is too small to eat an entire lamb, then he shall take one together with his neighbor who lives near his house. According to the number of souls and how much they can eat, so shall they slaughter the lamb. An unblemished, male, one-year-old lamb or kid goat shall be for you; from the sheep or from the goats you shall take it. You shall guard it until the fourteenth day of this month, and the entire congregation of Israel will slaughter it in the afternoon. They shall take from the blood and place it upon the two doorposts and on the lintel of the houses in which they will eat it. They shall eat the meat on this night, roasted over fire; with matzos and bitter herbs they shall eat it. Do not eat it partially roasted or cooked in water; only roasted over fire — its head, its legs, with its innards. You shall not leave any of it until morning; anything left over until the morning, you shall burn in the fire. This is how you shall eat it: your loins girded, your feet shod, your walking staves in your hands. You shall eat it in haste; it is a *Pesach* offering to HASHEM.

The following description of the *Korban Pesach* appears in *Siddur HaYaavetz.*

This was how the *Korban Pesach* was offered on the fourteenth of Nissan. It was slaughtered only after the *Tamid shel bein Ha'Arbayim* (daily afternoon offering). When Erev Pesach occurred on a weekday or on Shabbos, the *Tamid* was slaughtered at seven and a half hours after dawn, and offered at eight and a half. If Erev Pesach occurred on Erev Shabbos, they would slaughter the *Tamid* at six and a half, and offer it at seven and a half, with the *Pesach* following it.

Every Jewish person, man or woman, who was able to come to Yerushalayim by the time the *Pesach* was slaughtered, is obligated in the mitzvah of *Korban Pesach*. It may be offered from the lambs or from the kid goats, that are male, unblemished,

בֶּן שָׁנָה. וְשׁוֹחֲטוֹ בְּכָל מָקוֹם בָּעֲזָרָה, אַחַר גְּמַר עֲבוֹדַת תָּמִיד הָעֶרֶב וְאַחַר הֲטָבַת הַנֵּרוֹת. וְאֵין שׁוֹחֲטִין הַפֶּסַח וְלֹא זוֹרְקִין הַדָּם וְלֹא מַקְטִירִין הַחֵלֶב עַל הֶחָמֵץ: שָׁחַט הַשּׁוֹחֵט וְקִבֵּל דָּמוֹ כֹּהֵן שֶׁבְּרֹאשׁ הַשּׁוּרָה בִּכְלִי שָׁרֵת וְנוֹתֵן לַחֲבֵרוֹ וַחֲבֵרוֹ לַחֲבֵרוֹ, כֹּהֵן הַקָּרוֹב אֵצֶל הַמִּזְבֵּחַ זוֹרְקוֹ זְרִיקָה אַחַת כְּנֶגֶד הַיְסוֹד. וְחוֹזֵר הַכְּלִי רֵיקָן לַחֲבֵרוֹ וַחֲבֵרוֹ לַחֲבֵרוֹ, מְקַבֵּל אֶת הַמָּלֵא וּמַחֲזִיר אֶת הָרֵיקָן. וְהָיוּ הַכֹּהֲנִים עוֹמְדִים שׁוּרוֹת וּבִידֵיהֶם בָּזִיכִין שֶׁכּוּלָּן כֶּסֶף אוֹ כּוּלָן זָהָב, וְלֹא הָיוּ מְעֹרָבִים, וְלֹא הָיוּ לַבָּזִיכִין שׁוּלַיִם שֶׁלֹּא יַנִּיחוּם וְיִקְרוֹשׁ הַדָּם: אַחַר כָּךְ תּוֹלִין אֶת הַפֶּסַח בְּאוּנְקְלִיּוֹת, וּמַפְשִׁיט אוֹתוֹ כּוּלוֹ, וְקוֹרְעִין בְּטֵנוֹ וּמוֹצִיאִים אֵימוּרִין. הַחֵלֶב שֶׁעַל הַקֶּרֶב וְיוֹתֶרֶת הַכָּבֵד וּשְׁתֵּי הַכְּלָיוֹת וְחֵלֶב שֶׁעֲלֵיהֶן וְהָאַלְיָה לְעוּמַת הֶעָצֶה, נוֹתְנָן בִּכְלִי שָׁרֵת וּמוֹלְחָן וּמַקְטִירָן הַכֹּהֵן עַל הַמַּעֲרָכָה, חֶלְבֵי כָל זֶבַח וְזֶבַח לְבַדּוֹ, בְּחוֹל בַּיּוֹם וְלֹא בַּלַּיְלָה שֶׁהוּא יוֹם טוֹב[1]. אֲבָל אִם חָל עֶרֶב פֶּסַח בְּשַׁבָּת מַקְטִירִין וְהוֹלְכִין כָּל הַלַּיְלָה[2], וּמוֹצִיא קְרָבָיו וּמְמַחֶה אוֹתָן עַד שֶׁמֵּסִיר מֵהֶן הַפֶּרֶשׁ. שְׁחִיטָתוֹ וּזְרִיקַת דָּמוֹ וּמִחוּי קְרָבָיו וְהֶקְטֵר חֲלָבָיו דּוֹחִין אֶת הַשַּׁבָּת, וּשְׁאָר עִנְיָנָיו אֵין דּוֹחִין:

בְּשָׁלֹשׁ כִּתּוֹת הַפֶּסַח נִשְׁחָט, וְאֵין כַּת פְּחוּתָה מִשְּׁלוֹשִׁים אֲנָשִׁים. נִכְנְסָה כַּת אַחַת, נִתְמַלְּאָה הָעֲזָרָה, נוֹעֲלִין אוֹתָהּ. וּבְעוֹד שֶׁהֵן שׁוֹחֲטִין וּמַקְרִיבִין וְכֹהֲנִים תּוֹקְעִין, הֶחָלִיל מַכֶּה לִפְנֵי הַמִּזְבֵּחַ. הַלְוִיִּם קוֹרִין אֶת הַהַלֵּל. אִם גָּמְרוּ קוֹדֶם שֶׁיַּקְרִיבוּ כּוּלָם, שָׁנוּ. אִם שָׁנוּ שִׁלֵּשׁוּ. עַל כָּל

---

1. On Yom Tov, one may burn the fats of offerings that were slaughtered on Yom Tov, but not of those that were slaughtered on a weekday, such as the *Korban Pesach*, which was slaughtered on Erev Pesach.

2. The fats of offerings slaughtered on Shabbos may be offered the following night, even if it is Yom Tov.

and less than one year old. It may be slaughtered anywhere in the Temple Courtyard, after the service of the afternoon *Tamid*, and after the Menorah was prepared. The *Pesach* may not be slaughtered, nor may its blood be thrown [upon the *Mizbei'ach*] nor may its fats be burnt [upon the *Mizbei'ach*], if chametz is still in one's possession.

The *shochet* slaughtered it, and the *Kohen* at the front of the line caught its blood in a sanctified vessel, and passed it to his fellow *Kohen*, who would pass it to the next, and him to the next. The *Kohen* closest to the *Mizbei'ach* would throw its blood upon the *Mizbei'ach* in one shot, above the *Yesod* (foundation of the *Mizbei'ach*). He would then return the empty vessel to his fellow *Kohen*, who would pass it to the next, and him to the next. As each *Kohen* would receive a vessel filled with blood, he would then pass back in its place an empty one. The *Kohanim* would stand in lines, some lines using only silver vessels, while other lines used only gold vessels; they did not mix [silver with gold in one line]. The vessels did not have flat bottoms, in order that they would not be put down, and the blood would then congeal.

Afterward, the *Korban Pesach* would be hung on hooks. Its entire body would be stripped of its skin, the stomach was cut open, and the *eimorin* (portions of meat for the *Mizbei'ach*) removed. The fat above the intestines, the (*yoseres hakaveid* — the diaphragm with the liver), the two kidneys and the fat above them, and the tail across from the bone, would all be placed in a sanctified vessel, salted, and a *Kohen* would offer it upon the fire [on the *Mizbei'ach*], placing the fats of each offering separately. [When Erev Pesach occurred] on a weekday, [the fats were only offered] by day and not by night, which was Yom Tov.[1] When Erev Pesach occurred on Shabbos, the fats could be offered all night long.[2] The intestines were removed, and then squeezed to remove their waste. Slaughtering [the *Korban Pesach*], throwing its blood [on the *Mizbei'ach*], squeezing out the intestines, and burning the fats all may be performed on Shabbos. The other tasks [involved in processing the *korban*] do not supersede Shabbos.

The Jewish people were divided into three groups when slaughtering their *Pesach* offerings. Each group had at least thirty people. The first group entered the Temple Courtyard until it was filled, and then the gates were shut. As they slaughtered and offered, the *Kohanim* blew upon the trumpets, a flute was played before the *Mizbei'ach*, and the *Leviim* sang Hallel. If they completed singing Hallel before everyone had a chance to offer his *korban*, they would repeat it two or three times. With every

קְרִיאָה תָּקְעוּ וְהֵרִיעוּ וְתָקְעוּ. גָּמְרָה כַּת אַחַת לְהַקְרִיב, פּוֹתְחִין הָעֲזָרָה, יָצְאָה כַּת רִאשׁוֹנָה נִכְנְסָה כַּת שְׁנִיָּה. נָעֲלוּ דַּלְתוֹת הָעֲזָרָה. גָּמְרָה, יָצְאָה שְׁנִיָּה נִכְנְסָה שְׁלִישִׁית. כְּמַעֲשֵׂה הָרִאשׁוֹנָה כָּךְ מַעֲשֵׂה הַשְּׁנִיָּה וְהַשְּׁלִישִׁית:

אַחַר שֶׁיָּצְאוּ כּוּלָּן רוֹחֲצִין הָעֲזָרָה מִלִּכְלוּכֵי הַדָּם וַאֲפִילוּ בְּשַׁבָּת. אַמַּת הַמַּיִם הָיְתָה עוֹבֶרֶת בָּעֲזָרָה, שֶׁכְּשֶׁרוֹצִין לְהָדִיחַ הָרִצְפָּה סוֹתְמִין מְקוֹם יְצִיאַת הַמַּיִם וְהִיא מִתְמַלְּאָה עַל כָּל גְּדוֹתֶיהָ, עַד שֶׁהַמַּיִם עוֹלִין וְצָפִין וּמְקַבְּצִין אֲלֵיהֶם כָּל דָּם וְלִכְלוּךְ שֶׁבָּעֲזָרָה. אַחַר כָּךְ פּוֹתְחִין הַסְּתִימָה וְיוֹצְאִין הַמַּיִם עִם הַלִּכְלוּךְ. נִמְצֵאת הָרִצְפָּה מְנוּקָה, זֶהוּ כְּבוֹד הַבַּיִת:

יָצְאוּ כָּל אֶחָד עִם פִּסְחוֹ וְצָלוּ אוֹתָם. כֵּיצַד צוֹלִין אוֹתוֹ, מְבִיאִין שַׁפּוּד שֶׁל רִימּוֹן, תּוֹחֲבוֹ מִתּוֹךְ פִּיו עַד בֵּית נְקוּבָתוֹ, וְתוֹלֵהוּ לְתוֹךְ הַתַּנּוּר וְהָאֵשׁ לְמַטָּה, וְתוֹלֶה כְּרָעָיו וּבְנֵי מֵעָיו חוּצָה לוֹ. וְאֵין מְנַקְּרִין אֶת הַפֶּסַח כִּשְׁאָר בָּשָׂר: בְּשַׁבָּת אֵינָן מוֹלִיכִין אֶת הַפֶּסַח לְבֵיתָם[1], אֶלָּא כַּת הָרִאשׁוֹנָה יוֹצְאִין בְּפִסְחֵיהֶם וְיוֹשְׁבִין בְּהַר הַבַּיִת. הַשְּׁנִיָּה יוֹצְאִין עִם פִּסְחֵיהֶן וְיוֹשְׁבִין בַּחֵיל. הַשְּׁלִישִׁית בִּמְקוֹמָהּ עוֹמֶדֶת. חָשְׁכָה יָצְאוּ וְצָלוּ אֶת פִּסְחֵיהֶן:

כְּשֶׁמַּקְרִיבִין אֶת הַפֶּסַח בָּרִאשׁוֹן, מַקְרִיבִין עִמּוֹ בְּיוֹם אַרְבָּעָה עָשָׂר זֶבַח שְׁלָמִים, מִן הַבָּקָר אוֹ מִן הַצֹּאן, גְּדוֹלִים אוֹ קְטַנִּים, זְכָרִים אוֹ נְקֵבוֹת. וְהִיא נִקְרֵאת חֲגִיגַת אַרְבָּעָה עָשָׂר. עַל זֶה נֶאֱמַר בַּתּוֹרָה "וְזָבַחְתָּ פֶּסַח לַיהוה אֱלֹהֶיךָ צֹאן וּבָקָר". וְלֹא קְבָעָהּ הַכָּתוּב חוֹבָה אֶלָּא רְשׁוּת בִּלְבָד. מִכָּל מָקוֹם הִיא כְּחוֹבָה מִדִּבְרֵי סוֹפְרִים, כְּדֵי שֶׁיְּהֵא הַפֶּסַח נֶאֱכָל עַל הַשּׂוֹבַע: אֵימָתַי מְבִיאִין עִמּוֹ חֲגִיגָה, בִּזְמַן שֶׁהוּא בָּא בְּחוֹל, בְּטָהֳרָה, וּבְמוּעָט, וְנֶאֱכֶלֶת לִשְׁנֵי יָמִים וְלַיְלָה אֶחָד. וְדִינָהּ כְּכָל תּוֹרַת זִבְחֵי הַשְּׁלָמִים, טְעוּנָה סְמִיכָה

repetition of Hallel, the trumpets were blown with *tekiah, teruah,* and *tekiah*. After the first group completed their offerings, the Courtyard was opened; the first group left and the second group entered. The gates of the Courtyard were shut. As the first group performed their offerings, so did the second and third.

After everyone had left, the Courtyard was cleansed of the filth and blood, even on Shabbos. A water canal passed through the Courtyard. When they wished to wash the floor, they would seal off its exit, and the Courtyard would fill with water. The water level would rise, and pick up all the blood and filth in the Courtyard. Then, they would open the canal, and the filthy water would stream out. Thereby, the floor was kept clean, to honor the Beis Hamikdash.

Each person would then leave with his *Korban Pesach* and roast it. How would they roast it? They would bring a spit made from the wood of a pomegranate tree, skewer it from its mouth to its bottom, and hang it in an oven with a fire beneath it. Its legs and innards would hang out of it. *Nikkur* was not performed on the *Pesach,* as is performed on other meat.

On Shabbos, they did not carry the Pesach to their homes.[1] Rather, the first group would exit the courtyard with their *Korban Pesachs,* and wait on the Temple Mount. The second group would leave with their *Korban Pesachs* and wait in the *cheil* (area surrounding the Beis Hamikdash). The third group would wait in their place [in the Beis Hamikdash]. When night fell, they would leave and roast their *Korban Pesachs.*

When the *Pesach* was offered in the first month (Nissan), they would offer together with it on the fourteenth day a *shelamim* offering, whether cattle or sheep, old or young, male or female. This was called the "*Chagigah* of the Fourteenth." In regard to this, the Torah states, "You shall slaughter a Pesach to HASHEM, your God, from sheep or cattle." The Torah does not require this, leaving it optional. Nevertheless, it was made into a Rabbinic obligation, in order that the *Korban Pesach* should be eaten afterward, on a full stomach.

When was the *Chagigah* offered with the *Korban Pesach*? When the *Korban Pesach* was brought on a weekday, in ritual purity, with insufficient meat. The *Chagigah* may be eaten for two days and one night. Its laws are the same as those of all other *shelamim* offerings. It requires *semichah* (leaning on the

---

1. Since one may not carry outside on Shabbos without an *eruv*.

וּנְסָכִים וּמַתַּן דָּמִים שְׁתַּיִם שֶׁהֵן אַרְבַּע וּשְׁפִיכַת שִׁירַיִם לַיְסוֹד:

זֶהוּ סֵדֶר עֲבוֹדַת קָרְבַּן פֶּסַח וַחֲגִיגָה שֶׁעָמּוֹ, בְּבֵית אֱלֹהֵינוּ שֶׁיִּבָּנֶה בִּמְהֵרָה בְיָמֵינוּ אָמֵן: יִהְיוּ לְרָצוֹן אִמְרֵי פִי וְהֶגְיוֹן לִבִּי לְפָנֶיךָ יהוה צוּרִי וְגוֹאֲלִי:

הדלקת נרות

On Yom Tov, the blessings are recited before the candles are lit.
When Yom Tov falls on the Sabbath, the candles are lit first, and then
the blessings are recited (with the words in parentheses added).

בָּרוּךְ אַתָּה יהוה אֱלֹהֵינוּ מֶלֶךְ הָעוֹלָם, אֲשֶׁר קִדְּשָׁנוּ בְּמִצְוֹתָיו, וְצִוָּנוּ לְהַדְלִיק נֵר שֶׁל [שַׁבָּת וְשֶׁל] יוֹם טוֹב.

בָּרוּךְ אַתָּה יהוה אֱלֹהֵינוּ מֶלֶךְ הָעוֹלָם, שֶׁהֶחֱיָנוּ וְקִיְּמָנוּ וְהִגִּיעָנוּ לַזְּמַן הַזֶּה.

It is customary for women to recite
the following prayer after lighting candles.

יְהִי רָצוֹן לְפָנֶיךָ, יהוה אֱלֹהַי וֵאלֹהֵי אֲבוֹתַי, שֶׁתְּחוֹנֵן אוֹתִי [וְאֶת אִישִׁי, וְאֶת בָּנַי, וְאֶת בְּנוֹתַי, וְאֶת אָבִי, וְאֶת אִמִּי] וְאֶת כָּל קְרוֹבַי; וְתִתֶּן לָנוּ וּלְכָל יִשְׂרָאֵל חַיִּים טוֹבִים וַאֲרוּכִים; וְתִזְכְּרֵנוּ בְּזִכְרוֹן טוֹבָה וּבְרָכָה; וְתִפְקְדֵנוּ בִּפְקֻדַּת יְשׁוּעָה וְרַחֲמִים; וּתְבָרְכֵנוּ בְּרָכוֹת גְּדוֹלוֹת; וְתַשְׁלִים בָּתֵּינוּ; וְתַשְׁכֵּן שְׁכִינָתְךָ בֵּינֵינוּ. וְזַכֵּנִי לְגַדֵּל בָּנִים וּבְנֵי בָנִים חֲכָמִים וּנְבוֹנִים, אוֹהֲבֵי יהוה, יִרְאֵי אֱלֹהִים, אַנְשֵׁי אֱמֶת, זֶרַע קֹדֶשׁ, בַּיהוה דְּבֵקִים, וּמְאִירִים אֶת הָעוֹלָם בַּתּוֹרָה וּבְמַעֲשִׂים טוֹבִים, וּבְכָל מְלֶאכֶת עֲבוֹדַת הַבּוֹרֵא. אָנָּא שְׁמַע אֶת תְּחִנָּתִי בָּעֵת הַזֹּאת, בִּזְכוּת שָׂרָה וְרִבְקָה וְרָחֵל וְלֵאָה אִמּוֹתֵינוּ, וְהָאֵר נֵרֵנוּ שֶׁלֹּא יִכְבֶּה לְעוֹלָם וָעֶד, וְהָאֵר פָּנֶיךָ וְנִוָּשֵׁעָה. אָמֵן.

korban); *nesachim* (accompanying wine libations); its blood is thrown on two corners [of the *Mizbei'ach*, spreading across] to reach all four sides; and the remaining blood is poured over the *Yesod* (foundation).

This was how the *Korban Pesach* was offered, and the *Chagigah* that accompanied it, in the House of our Lord, may it be rebuilt soon and in our days, Amen. May the words of my mouth and the thoughts of my heart be pleasing before You, HASHEM my Rock and my Redeemer.

LIGHTING THE CANDLES

On Yom Tov, the blessings are recited before the candles are lit. When Yom Tov falls on the Sabbath, the candles are lit first, and then the blessings are recited (with the words in parentheses added).

Blessed are You, HASHEM, our God, King of the universe, Who has sanctified us with His commandments, and commanded us to kindle the flame of the (Sabbath and the) festival.

Blessed are You, HASHEM, our God, King of the universe, Who has kept us alive, sustained us, and brought us to this season.

It is customary to recite the following prayer after the kindling. The words in brackets are included as they apply.

May it be Your will, HASHEM, my God and God of my forefathers, that You show favor to me [my husband, my sons, my daughters, my father, my mother] and all my relatives; and that You grant us and all Israel a good and long life; that You remember us with a beneficent memory and blessing; that You consider us with a consideration of salvation and compassion; that You bless us with great blessings; that You make our households complete; that You cause Your Presence to dwell among us. Privilege me to raise children and grandchildren who are wise and understanding, who love HASHEM and fear God, people of truth, holy offspring, attached to HASHEM, who illuminate the world with Torah and good deeds and with every labor in the service of the Creator. Please, hear my supplication at this time, in the merit of Sarah, Rebecca, Rachel, and Leah, our mothers, and cause our light to illuminate that it not be extinguished forever, and let Your countenance shine so that we are saved. Amen.

הסדר
THE SEDER

סימני הסדר
The Order of the Seder

KADDESH	**Sanctify** the day with the recitation of Kiddush.	קדש
URECHATZ	**Wash** the hands before eating Karpas.	ורחץ
KARPAS	Eat a **vegetable** dipped in salt water.	כרפס
YACHATZ	**Break** the middle matzah. Put away larger half for Afikoman.	יחץ
MAGGID	**Narrate** the story of the Exodus from Egypt.	מגיד
RACHTZAH	**Wash** the hands prior to the meal.	רחצה
MOTZI	Recite the blessing, **Who brings forth**, over matzah as a food.	מוציא
MATZAH	Recite the blessing over **Matzah.**	מצה
MAROR	Recite the blessing for the eating of the **bitter herbs.**	מרור
KORECH	Eat the **sandwich** of matzah and bitter herbs.	כורך
SHULCHAN ORECH	The **table prepared** with the festive meal.	שלחן עורך
TZAFUN	Eat the afikoman which had been **hidden** all during the Seder.	צפון
BARECH	Recite Bircas Hamazon, the **blessings** after the meal.	ברך
HALLEL	Recite the **Hallel** Psalms of praise.	הלל
NIRTZAH	Pray that God **accept** our observance and speedily send the Messiah.	נרצה

THE ORDER OF THE PESACH SEDER

Yesod V'Shoresh Ha'Avodah writes that great and wondrous secrets are hidden in the titles of the fifteen stages of the Pesach Seder. One should therefore announce the name of each stage before he begins it. Before Kiddush, one should announce "Kaddesh!", before Urchatz, he should announce, "Urchatz!", and so on, throughout the entire Seder.

Before each stage of the Seder, one should recite the Kabbalistic declaration of intent and the verse beginning, "Let the pleasantness of the Lord, our God, be upon us." Most important, one should have in mind that he is bringing HASHEM satisfaction, and he should perform every aspect of the Seder with great joy, since HASHEM desires the sincerity of our hearts.

The custom to recite the verse, "Let the pleasantness of the Lord, our God, be upon us," is a worthy practice, which finds its source in Zohar (Parashas Yisro). It was the custom of pious people in earlier generations to prepare themselves before any mitzvah by reciting the name of the mitzvah followed by the verse, "Let the pleasantness ..."

קַדֵּשׁ וּרְחַץ —
Kaddesh, Urechatz

Throughout the year, Urechatz — cleansing ourselves from our sins — must precede Kaddesh, sanctifying ourselves with mitzvos, as the verse states, "Turn from evil and do good" (Tehillim 34:15). On Pesach, however, Hashem sanctifies us even before we have cleansed ourselves of sin.

Shir HaShirim Rabbah (5:2) says that Hashem tell the Jewish people, "If you open the doors of repentance as wide as pinhole, I will open them for you as wide as the doors to the Sanctuary."

Kedushas Levi writes that on Pesach we do not need to open the doors to repentance. Hashem "passes over" the doorways; He takes the initiative and inspires us to repent.

These holy days are the only time that Kaddesh (sanctification) can precede Urechatz (cleansing ourselves of sin).

In describing the Exodus from Egypt, Hashem says, "I have borne you on the wings of eagles and brought you to Me" (Shemos 19:4).

Rashi explains that most birds carry their young in their claws, below their bodies. Eagles take pity on their young and carry them

אַתְקִינוּ סְעוּדָתָא דְּמַלְכָּא דָא הִיא סְעוּדָתָא
דְּקוּדְשָׁא בְּרִיךְ הוּא וּשְׁכִינְתֵּיהּ:

רִבּוֹנוֹ שֶׁל עוֹלָם אַתָּה יוֹדֵעַ כִּי בָשָׂר אֲנַחְנוּ וְלֹא
בִינַת אָדָם לָנוּ וְאֵין אִתָּנוּ יוֹדֵעַ
עַד מָה. לָכֵן יְהִי רָצוֹן מִלְּפָנֶיךָ יהוה אֱלֹהֵינוּ וֵאלֹהֵי
אֲבוֹתֵינוּ שֶׁיַּעֲלֶה וְיָבֹא וְיֵרָאֶה וְיֵרָצֶה לְנַחַת רוּחַ
לְפָנֶיךָ, כָּל הַמִּצְוֹת הַנַּעֲשִׂים בַּלַּיְלָה הַזֹּאת עַל
יָדֵינוּ, לְתַקֵּן כָּל אֲשֶׁר פָּגַמְנוּ בָּעוֹלָמוֹת הָעֶלְיוֹנִים
[עַל יְדֵי חֲטָאֵינוּ וַעֲוֹנוֹתֵינוּ וּפְשָׁעֵנוּ] וּלְתַקֵּן כָּל
הַנִּצוֹצוֹת שֶׁנָּפְלוּ תּוֹךְ הַקְּלִיפּוֹת, וְלִגְרוֹם שֶׁפַע
וּבְרָכָה רַבָּה בְּכָל הָעוֹלָמוֹת, וְאַל יְעַכֵּב שׁוּם חֵטְא
וְעָוֹן וְהִרְהוּר רַע אֶת מַעֲשֵׂה הַמִּצְוֹת הָאֵלֶּה.

וִיהִי רָצוֹן מִלְּפָנֶיךָ יהוה אֱלֹהֵינוּ וֵאלֹהֵי אֲבוֹתֵינוּ
שֶׁתְּצָרֵף מַחְשְׁבוֹתֵינוּ זֹאת הַפְּשׁוּטָה, עִם כַּוָּנַת בָּנֶיךָ
יְדִידֶיךָ הַיּוֹדְעִים וּמְכֻוָּנִים כָּל שְׁמוֹתֶיךָ הַקְּדוֹשִׁים
וְהַנּוֹרָאִים, וְכָל כַּוָּנוֹת וְזִוּוּגֵי מִדּוֹת הָעֶלְיוֹנִים
הַנַּעֲשִׂים עַל יְדֵי מִצְוַת הָאֵלֶּה.

וִיהִי נֹעַם יהוה אֱלֹהֵינוּ עָלֵינוּ וּמַעֲשֵׂה יָדֵינוּ כּוֹנְנָה
עָלֵינוּ וּמַעֲשֵׂה יָדֵינוּ כּוֹנְנֵהוּ:

---

on their wings, so that if an archer shoots an arrow into the air, it
would harm the adult eagle, not the child.

The eagle wants to provide protection for its eaglet, notes Rav
Shamshon Raphael Hirsch, but it does not have arms with which to
place it onto its wings. How do eaglets get onto their parents' wings?

Prepare the feast of the King. This is the Feast of the Holy One, Blessed is He, and His *Shechinah.*

Master of the universe, You well know that we are mere mortal flesh, and have not the wisdom of great men, and we have no depth of understanding. Therefore, may it be Your will, HASHEM our God and God of our forefathers, that they may ascend and arrive and be seen and be favored as a *nachas ruach* before You, all the mitzvos that we perform on this night — to correct all that we have damaged in the Higher Worlds (through our accidental sins, deliberate sins, and rebellious sins); and to rectify all the sparks that have fallen into the *klippos*; and to bring *shefa* and abundant blessing in all the worlds. May no sin, iniquity, or evil thought of ours hinder these mitzvos.

May it be Your will, HASHEM our God and God of our forefathers, to unite these simple intentions of ours, with the deep intentions of Your beloved children who recognize and contemplate all Your holy and awesome Names; and have *kavanah* for all the unifications of supernal attributes that are enacted through these mitzvos.

May the pleasantness of HASHEM, our God, be upon us, and may He establish our handiwork for us; our handiwork may He establish.

They must invest effort into climbing onto the wings, and only then can they rely on their parents' protection.

Hashem wants to protect us, but we must take the necessary steps to climb onto our Father's "wings."

קַדֵּשׁ

Kiddush should be recited and the Seder begun as soon
after synagogue services as possible — however, not before nightfall.

The first cup of wine is poured. Each participant's cup
should be poured by someone else to symbolize
the majesty of the evening, as though each participant had a servant.

Some have the custom to recite the following
declaration of intent before Kiddush:

הֲרֵינִי מוּכָן וּמְזוּמָּן לְקַדֵּשׁ עַל הַיַּיִן, וּלְקַיֵּם מִצְוַת כּוֹס רִאשׁוֹן מֵאַרְבַּע
כּוֹסוֹת. לְשֵׁם יִחוּד קֻדְשָׁא בְּרִיךְ הוּא וּשְׁכִינְתֵּיהּ, עַל יְדֵי הַהוּא
טָמִיר וְנֶעְלָם, בְּשֵׁם כָּל יִשְׂרָאֵל. וִיהִי נֹעַם אֲדֹנָי אֱלֹהֵינוּ עָלֵינוּ, וּמַעֲשֵׂה
יָדֵינוּ כּוֹנְנָה עָלֵינוּ, וּמַעֲשֵׂה יָדֵינוּ כּוֹנְנֵהוּ.

[The cup is taken in both hands, and then held in the right hand. It must
be held one handbreadth (*tefach*) above the table while reciting Kiddush.
Before Kiddush, one should have in mind to fulfill the mitzvah of Kiddush
and the first of the four cups. The first cup corresponds to the expression
"וְהוֹצֵאתִי" — I shall take you out," the first of the four expressions
of redemption (*Minchas Asher*).]

On Friday night begin here:

[וַיְהִי עֶרֶב וַיְהִי בֹקֶר]

יוֹם הַשִּׁשִּׁי. וַיְכֻלּוּ הַשָּׁמַיִם וְהָאָרֶץ וְכָל צְבָאָם. וַיְכַל
אֱלֹהִים בַּיּוֹם הַשְּׁבִיעִי מְלַאכְתּוֹ אֲשֶׁר
עָשָׂה, וַיִּשְׁבֹּת בַּיּוֹם הַשְּׁבִיעִי מִכָּל מְלַאכְתּוֹ אֲשֶׁר עָשָׂה.
וַיְבָרֶךְ אֱלֹהִים אֶת יוֹם הַשְּׁבִיעִי וַיְקַדֵּשׁ אֹתוֹ, כִּי בוֹ
שָׁבַת מִכָּל מְלַאכְתּוֹ אֲשֶׁר בָּרָא אֱלֹהִים לַעֲשׂוֹת.¹

On all nights other than Friday, begin here;
on Friday night include all passages in parentheses.

סַבְרִי מָרָנָן וְרַבָּנָן וְרַבּוֹתַי:

בָּרוּךְ אַתָּה יהוה אֱלֹהֵינוּ מֶלֶךְ הָעוֹלָם, בּוֹרֵא פְּרִי
הַגָּפֶן:

בָּרוּךְ אַתָּה יהוה אֱלֹהֵינוּ מֶלֶךְ הָעוֹלָם, אֲשֶׁר
בָּחַר בָּנוּ מִכָּל עָם, וְרוֹמְמָנוּ מִכָּל לָשׁוֹן,
וְקִדְּשָׁנוּ בְּמִצְוֹתָיו. וַתִּתֶּן לָנוּ יהוה אֱלֹהֵינוּ בְּאַהֲבָה

KADDESH

Kiddush should be recited and the Seder begun as soon
after synagogue services as possible — however, not before nightfall.
The first cup of wine is poured. Each participant's cup
should be poured by someone else to symbolize
the majesty of the evening, as though each participant had a servant.

Some have the custom to recite the following
declaration of intent before Kiddush:

Behold, I am prepared and ready to recite the Kiddush over wine,
and to fulfill the mitzvah of the first of the Four Cups. For the sake of
unification of the Holy One, Blessed is He, and His Presence, through
Him Who is hidden and inscrutable — [I pray] in the name of all Israel.
May the pleasantness of HASHEM, our God, be upon us, and may He
establish our handiwork for us; our handiwork may He establish.

[The cup is taken in both hands, and then held in the right hand. It must
be held one handbreadth (*tefach*) above the table while reciting Kiddush.
Before Kiddush, one should have in mind to fulfill the mitzvah of Kiddush
and the first of the four cups. The first cup corresponds to the expression
"וְהוֹצֵאתִי" — I shall take you out," the first of the four expressions
of redemption (*Minchas Asher*).]

On Friday night begin here:
(And there was evening and there was morning)

The sixth day. Thus the heaven and the earth were
finished, and all their array. On the seventh day God
completed His work which He had done, and He abstained
on the seventh day from all His work which He had done.
God blessed the seventh day and hallowed it, because on it
He abstained from all His work which God created to
make.[1]

On all nights other than Friday, begin here;
on Friday night include all passages in parentheses.

By your leave, my masters and teachers:

Blessed are You, HASHEM, our God, King of the
universe, Who creates the fruit of the vine.

Blessed are You, HASHEM, our God, King of the universe, Who has chosen us from all nations, exalted
us above all tongues, and sanctified us with His commandments. And You, HASHEM, our God, have lovingly

---

(1) *Bereishis* 1:31-2:3.

[שַׁבָּתוֹת לִמְנוּחָה וּ]מוֹעֲדִים לְשִׂמְחָה, חַגִּים וּזְמַנִּים לְשָׂשׂוֹן, אֶת [יוֹם הַשַּׁבָּת הַזֶּה וְאֶת] יוֹם חַג הַמַּצּוֹת הַזֶּה, זְמַן חֵרוּתֵנוּ [בְּאַהֲבָה] מִקְרָא קֹדֶשׁ, זֵכֶר לִיצִיאַת מִצְרָיִם, כִּי בָנוּ בָחַרְתָּ וְאוֹתָנוּ קִדַּשְׁתָּ מִכָּל הָעַמִּים, [וְשַׁבָּת] וּמוֹעֲדֵי קָדְשֶׁךָ [בְּאַהֲבָה וּבְרָצוֹן] בְּשִׂמְחָה וּבְשָׂשׂוֹן הִנְחַלְתָּנוּ. בָּרוּךְ אַתָּה יהוה, מְקַדֵּשׁ [הַשַּׁבָּת וְ]יִשְׂרָאֵל וְהַזְּמַנִּים.

On Saturday night, add the following two paragraphs:

בָּרוּךְ אַתָּה יהוה אֱלֹהֵינוּ מֶלֶךְ הָעוֹלָם, בּוֹרֵא מְאוֹרֵי הָאֵשׁ.

בָּרוּךְ אַתָּה יהוה אֱלֹהֵינוּ מֶלֶךְ הָעוֹלָם, הַמַּבְדִּיל בֵּין קֹדֶשׁ לְחוֹל, בֵּין אוֹר לְחֹשֶׁךְ, בֵּין יִשְׂרָאֵל לָעַמִּים, בֵּין יוֹם הַשְּׁבִיעִי לְשֵׁשֶׁת יְמֵי הַמַּעֲשֶׂה. בֵּין קְדֻשַּׁת שַׁבָּת לִקְדֻשַּׁת יוֹם טוֹב הִבְדַּלְתָּ, וְאֶת יוֹם הַשְּׁבִיעִי מִשֵּׁשֶׁת יְמֵי הַמַּעֲשֶׂה קִדַּשְׁתָּ, הִבְדַּלְתָּ וְקִדַּשְׁתָּ אֶת עַמְּךָ יִשְׂרָאֵל בִּקְדֻשָּׁתֶךָ. בָּרוּךְ אַתָּה יהוה, הַמַּבְדִּיל בֵּין קֹדֶשׁ לְקֹדֶשׁ.

On all nights conclude here:

בָּרוּךְ אַתָּה יהוה אֱלֹהֵינוּ מֶלֶךְ הָעוֹלָם, שֶׁהֶחֱיָנוּ וְקִיְּמָנוּ וְהִגִּיעָנוּ לַזְּמַן הַזֶּה.

The wine should be drunk without delay while reclining on the left side.
It is preferable to drink the entire cup, but at the very least,
most of the cup should be drained. No blessing is recited after this cup.

תְּחִלָּה לְמִקְרָאֵי קֹדֶשׁ זֵכֶר לִיצִיאַת מִצְרָיִם

The first of all that is called holy, a remembrance of Exodus[1]

In *Haggadas Divrei Chaim*, R' Chaim of Sanz cites from his mentor, R' Naftali of Ropshitz, that the first and foremost call that inspires a person to grow in holiness is the remembrance of Exodus.

While in Egypt, Bnei Yisrael had reached such a terrible low that the angel appointed over the sea complained that it was unfair to

---

1. These words actually appear in the Kiddush we recite Friday night. Its relevance to the Haggadah is obvious.

given us (Sabbaths for rest,) holidays for rejoicing, feasts and seasons for joy, (this Sabbath and) this Feast of Matzos, the season of our freedom (in love,) a holy convocation in commemoration of the Exodus from Egypt. For You have chosen and sanctified us above all peoples, (and the Sabbath) and Your holy festivals (in love and favor), in gladness and joy have You granted us as a heritage. Blessed are You, HASHEM, Who sanctifies (the Sabbath,) Israel, and the festive seasons.

On Saturday night, add the following two paragraphs:

Blessed are You, HASHEM, our God, King of the universe, Who creates the illumination of the fire.

Blessed are You, HASHEM, our God, King of the universe, Who distinguishes between sacred and secular, between light and darkness, between Israel and the nations, between the seventh day and the six days of activity. You have distinguished between the holiness of the Sabbath and the holiness of a Festival, and have sanctified the seventh day above the six days of activity. You distinguished and sanctified Your nation, Israel, with Your holiness. Blessed are You, HASHEM, Who distinguishes between holiness and holiness.

On all nights conclude here:

Blessed are You, HASHEM, our God, King of the universe, Who has kept us alive, sustained us, and brought us to this season.

The wine should be drunk without delay while reclining on the left side.
It is preferable to drink the entire cup, but at the very least,
most of the cup should be drained. No blessing is recited after this cup.

---

drown the Egyptians and save the Jews. "They both worship idols," the angel protested. "Why do you save the Jews but destroy the Egyptians?" (*Zohar* II:170b).

Even by the basic standards of respectable behavior, Bnei Yisrael had fallen to a terrible low. The Talmud tells us that they "ate like chickens pecking around in garbage heaps, until Moshe Rabbeinu came and arranged for them a fixed schedule for meals" (*Yoma* 75b).

Yet in one swift moment they were elevated, and merited to witness a revelation of the Divine Presence at the splitting of the

וּרְחַץ

The head of the household — according to many opinions,
all participants in the Seder — washes his hands as if to eat bread
[pouring water from a cup, twice on the right hand and twice on the left],
but without reciting a blessing.

כַּרְפַּס

Some have the custom to recite the following
declaration of intent before Karpas.

לְשֵׁם יִחוּד קֻדְשָׁא בְּרִיךְ הוּא וּשְׁכִינְתֵּיהּ, עַל יְדֵי הַהוּא טָמִיר וְנֶעְלָם,
בְּשֵׁם כָּל יִשְׂרָאֵל. וִיהִי נֹעַם אֲדֹנָי אֱלֹהֵינוּ עָלֵינוּ, וּמַעֲשֵׂה יָדֵינוּ
כּוֹנְנָה עָלֵינוּ, וּמַעֲשֵׂה יָדֵינוּ כּוֹנְנֵהוּ.

All participants take a vegetable other than maror and dip it into salt water.
A piece smaller in volume than half an egg should be used.

The following blessing is recited [with the intention that i
t also applies to the maror which will be eaten during the meal]
before the vegetable is eaten.
[It is customary to eat Karpas while leaning to the left (*Minchas Asher*).]

בָּרוּךְ אַתָּה יהוה אֱלֹהֵינוּ מֶלֶךְ הָעוֹלָם, בּוֹרֵא פְּרִי
הָאֲדָמָה.

No blessing is made after Karpas.

יַחַץ

The head of the household breaks the middle matzah in two.
He puts the smaller part back between the two whole matzos,
and wraps up the larger part for later use as the afikoman.
Some briefly place the afikoman portion on their shoulders,
in accordance with the Biblical verse recounting that Israel left
Egypt carrying their matzos on their shoulders,
and say, בְּחִפָּזוֹן יָצָאנוּ מִמִּצְרָיִם,"In haste we went out of Egypt."

Yam Suf, the likes of which even Yechezkel the Prophet had never
seen (*Mechilta, Parashas Beshalach*). We can draw great encouragement by reflecting on this thought and realizing that "[Hashem]

URECHATZ

The head of the household — according to many opinions,
all participants in the Seder — washes his hands as if to eat bread
[pouring water from a cup, twice on the right hand and twice on the left],
but without reciting a blessing.

KARPAS

Some have the custom to recite the following
declaration of intent before Karpas.

For the sake of unification of the Holy One, Blessed is He, and His
Presence, through Him Who is hidden and inscrutable [I pray] in the
name of all Israel. May the pleasantness of HASHEM, our God, be upon
us, and may He establish our handiwork for us; our handiwork may He
establish.

All participants take a vegetable other than maror and dip it into salt water.
A piece smaller in volume than half an egg should be used.

The following blessing is recited [with the intention that
it also applies to the maror which will be eaten during the meal]
before the vegetable is eaten.

[It is customary to eat Karpas while leaning to the left (*Minchas Asher*).]

Blessed are You, HASHEM, our God, King of the
universe, Who creates the fruits of the earth.

No blessing is made after Karpas.

YACHATZ

The head of the household breaks the middle matzah in two.
He puts the smaller part back between the two whole matzos,
and wraps up the larger part for later use as the afikoman.
Some briefly place the afikoman portion on their shoulders,
in accordance with the Biblical verse recounting that Israel left
Egypt carrying their matzos on their shoulders,
and say, בְּבְהִלוּ יָצָאנוּ מִמִּצְרָיִם,"*In haste we went out of Egypt.*"

raises the needy from the dust, from the trash heaps He lifts the
destitute" (*Tehillim* 113:7). Hashem allows us to rise from the deep-
est pit to the highest peak.

מַגִּיד

The Haggadah — from "This is the bread of affliction" until "Who has redeemed Israel" — is recited. One should have in mind that he is fulfilling the Torah obligation to relate the story of the Exodus on Pesach night. It is proper for the head of the household to explain the stories of the miracles of the Exodus to his family in a language they understand.

The Haggadah should be recited with awe and trepidation.
One should not lean during its recitation.

While reciting the Haggadah, the matzos should be uncovered, in fulfillment of the Sages' interpretation of לֶחֶם עֹנִי (literally, *bread of poverty,* i.e., matzah): לֶחֶם שֶׁעוֹנִים עָלָיו דְּבָרִים הַרְבֵּה, *bread over which many matters are discussed.* When the second cup is raised, the matzos are covered again.

(Similarly, whenever the cup is raised, the matzos are covered.)

Some have the custom to recite a passage from Zohar Parashas Bo (below):

Some recite the following before *Maggid:*

הִנְנִי מוּכָן וּמְזוּמָן לְקַיֵּם הַמִּצְוָה לְסַפֵּר בִּיצִיאַת מִצְרָיִם. לְשֵׁם יִחוּד קֻדְשָׁא בְּרִיךְ הוּא וּשְׁכִינְתֵּיהּ, עַל יְדֵי הַהוּא טָמִיר וְנֶעְלָם, בְּשֵׁם כָּל יִשְׂרָאֵל. וִיהִי נֹעַם אֲדֹנָי אֱלֹהֵינוּ עָלֵינוּ, וּמַעֲשֵׂה יָדֵינוּ כּוֹנְנָה עָלֵינוּ, וּמַעֲשֵׂה יָדֵינוּ כּוֹנְנֵהוּ:

The broken matzah is lifted for all to see as the head of the household begins with the following brief explanation of the proceedings.

[The plate holding the matzos is lifted.]
(It is not necessary to remove the other foods.)

זהר פרשת בא

פְּקוּדָא בָּתַר דָּא לְסַפֵּר בְּשִׁבְחָא דִּיצִיאַת מִצְרָיִם דְּאִיהוּ חִיּוּבָא עַל בַּר נַשׁ לְאִשְׁתָּעֵי בְּהַאי שִׁבְחָא לְעָלְמִין, הָכִי אוּקִימְנָא, כָּל בַּר נַשׁ דְּאִשְׁתָּעֵי בִּיצִיאַת מִצְרָיִם וּבְהַהוּא סִפּוּר חָדֵי בְּחֶדְוָה, זַמִּין אִיהוּ לְמֶחֱדֵי בִּשְׁכִינְתָּא לְעָלְמָא דְּאָתֵי דְּהוּא חֶדוּ מִכֹּלָּא, דְּהַאי אִיהוּ בַּר נַשׁ דְּחָדֵי בְּמָרֵיהּ, וְקוּדְשָׁא בְּרִיךְ הוּא חָדֵי בְּהַהוּא סִפּוּר בֵּיהּ שַׁעְתָּא כָּנֵישׁ קוּדְשָׁא בְּרִיךְ הוּא לְכָל פַּמַלְיָא דִּילֵיהּ וַאֲמַר לוֹן, זִילוּ וְשִׁמְעוּ סִפּוּרָא דְּשִׁבְחָא דִּילִי דְּקָא מִשְׁתָּעֵי בָּנַי וְחַדָּאן בְּפוּרְקָנִי, כְּדֵין כֻּלְּהוּ מִתְכַּנְּשִׁין וְאַתְיָין וּמִתְחַבְּרִין בַּהֲדַיְיהוּ דְּיִשְׂרָאֵל, וְשָׁמְעוּ סִפּוּרָא דְּשִׁבְחָא דְּקָא חַדָּאן בְּחֶדְוָה דְּפוּרְקָנָא דְּמָרֵיהוֹן, כְּדֵין אַתְיָין וְאוֹדָן לֵיהּ לְקוּדְשָׁא בְּרִיךְ הוּא עַל כָּל אִינּוּן נִסִּין וּגְבוּרָן, וְאוֹדָאן לֵיהּ עַל עַמָּא קַדִּישָׁא דְּאִית לֵיהּ בְּאַרְעָא דְּחַדָּאן בְּחֶדְוָה דְּפוּרְקָנָא דְּמָרֵיהוֹן. כְּדֵין

MAGGID

The Haggadah — from "This is the bread of affliction" until "Who has redeemed Israel" — is recited. One should have in mind that he is fulfilling the Torah obligation to relate the story of the Exodus on Pesach night. It is proper for the head of the household to explain the stories of the miracles of the Exodus to his family in a language they understand.

The Haggadah should be recited with awe and trepidation.
One should not lean during its recitation.

While reciting the Haggadah, the matzos should be uncovered, in fulfillment of the Sages' interpretation of לֶחֶם עֹנִי (literally, *bread of poverty*, i.e., matzah): לֶחֶם שֶׁעוֹנִים עָלָיו דְּבָרִים הַרְבֵּה, *bread over which many matters are discussed*. When the second cup is raised, the matzos are covered again.

(Similarly, whenever the cup is raised, the matzos are covered.)

Some have the custom to recite a passage from Zohar Parashas Bo (below):

Some recite the following before Maggid:

Behold, I am prepared and ready to fulfill the mitzvah of telling of the Exodus from Egypt. For the sake of the unification of the Holy One, Blessed is He, and His presence, through Him Who is hidden and inscrutable — [I pray] in the name of all Israel. May the pleasantness of HASHEM, our God, be upon us, and may He establish our handiwork for us; our handiwork may He establish.

The broken matzah is lifted for all to see as the head of the household begins with the following brief explanation of the proceedings.

[The plate holding the matzos is lifted.]
(It is not necessary to remove the other foods.)

אִתּוֹסַף לֵיהּ חֵילָא וּגְבוּרְתָּא לְעֵלָּא, וְיִשְׂרָאֵל בְּהַהוּא סְפוּרָא יָהֲבֵי
חֵילָא לְמָרֵיהוֹן כְּמַלְכָּא דְּאִתּוֹסַף חֵילָא וּגְבוּרְתָּא כַּד מְשַׁבְּחִין
גְּבוּרְתֵּהּ וְאוֹדָן לֵיהּ וְכֻלְּהוּ דָּחֲלִין מִקַּמֵּיהּ וְאִסְתַּלַּק יְקָרֵהּ עַל כֻּלְּהוּ,
וּבְגִין כַּךְ אִית לְשַׁבָּחָא וּלְאִשְׁתָּעֵי בְּסִפּוּר דָּא כְּמָה דְּאִתְּמָר, כְּגַוְונָא
דָא חוֹבָא אִיהוּ עַל בַּר נָשׁ לְאִשְׁתָּעֵי תָּדִיר קַמֵּי קוּדְשָׁא בְּרִיךְ הוּא
וּלְפַרְסוּמֵי נִיסָא בְּכָל אִינּוּן נִסִּין דְּעָבַד. וְאִי תֵּימָא אַמַּאי אִיהוּ חוֹבְתָּא,
וְהָא קוּדְשָׁא בְּרִיךְ הוּא יָדַע כֹּלָּא כָּל מָה דַּהֲוָה וְיֶהֱוֵי לְבָתַר דְּנָא,
אַמַּאי פַּרְסוּמָא דָא קַמֵּיהּ עַל מַה דְּאִיהוּ עָבַד וְאִיהוּ יָדַע, אֶלָּא וַדַּאי
אִצְטְרִיךְ בַּר נָשׁ לְפַרְסוּמֵי נִיסָא וּלְאִשְׁתָּעֵי קַמֵּהּ בְּכָל מָה דְּאִיהוּ עָבַד,
בְּגִין דְּאִינּוּן מִלִּין סָלְקִין וְכָל פָּמַלְיָא דִּלְעֵילָא מִתְכַּנְשִׁין וַחֲמָאן לוֹן
וְאוֹדָאן כֻּלְּהוּ לְקוּדְשָׁא בְּרִיךְ הוּא וְאִסְתַּלַּק יְקָרֵהּ עֲלַיְיהוּ עֵילָּא וְתַתָּא,
בָּרוּךְ יהוה לְעוֹלָם אָמֵן וְאָמֵן:

The following passage is recited in a loud voice (*Minchas Asher*).]
This passage is not mentioned anywhere in the Gemara or Midrash.
Shibolei HaLeket writes that it was instituted in Eretz Yisrael,
but Ra'avya (528) writes that it was instituted in Babylon.

[כ]הָא לַחְמָא עַנְיָא דִי אֲכָלוּ אַבְהָתָנָא בְּאַרְעָא
דְמִצְרָיִם. כָּל דִּכְפִין יֵיתֵי וְיֵכוֹל, כָּל דִּצְרִיךְ
יֵיתֵי וְיִפְסַח. הָשַׁתָּא הָכָא, לְשָׁנָה הַבָּאָה בְּאַרְעָא
דְיִשְׂרָאֵל. הָשַׁתָּא עַבְדֵי, לְשָׁנָה הַבָּאָה בְּנֵי חוֹרִין.

The plate is set down and moved to the end of the table. Some have the
custom not to remove the plate, but simply to cover the matzos. The
second cup is poured, and the youngest present asks the Four Questions.

משנה, פסחים קטז, א

מַה נִּשְׁתַּנָּה הַלַּיְלָה הַזֶּה מִכָּל הַלֵּילוֹת?

הָא לַחְמָא עַנְיָא
This is the bread of affliction
Shibolei Haleket (218) cites two explanations as to why this passage is recited in Aramaic and not in *Lashon HaKodesh* like the rest
of the Haggadah.

1) The angels of destruction do not understand Aramaic. By
   reciting this passage in Aramaic, we avoid arousing their
   jealousy and having them try to spoil the Seder. *Shibolei
   Haleket* rejects this explanation, because the Seder night is a
   time of Divine protection — *Leil Shimurim* — when Hashem protects us from the destructive angels, just as He
   protected our forefathers on the night of Exodus when He
   unleashed the angels of destruction in Egypt.

2) Rabbeinu Binyamin's explanation — which *Shibolei Haleket*
   prefers — is that the passage was originally composed in
   Aramaic so the uneducated masses would understand it.
   (Aramaic was the commonly spoken language among Jewish
   communities in Babylon, and even in Eretz Yisrael for certain
   periods.)

This answer is also perplexing. Why is *Ha Lachma Anya* the only
passage that had to be recited in Aramaic, while the rest of the
Haggadah remained in *Lashon HaKodesh*? It would seem that there
are more important parts of the Haggadah for the unlearned to
understand, such as the crucial passages explaining the reasons

The following passage is recited in a loud voice (*Minchas Asher*).]

This passage is not mentioned anywhere in the Gemara or Midrash.
Shibolei HaLeket writes that it was instituted in Eretz Yisrael,
but Ra'avya (528) writes that it was instituted in Babylon.

This is the bread of affliction that our fathers ate in the land of Egypt. Whoever is hungry — let him come and eat! Whoever is needy — let him come and celebrate Pesach! Now, we are here; next year may we be in the Land of Israel! Now, we are slaves; next year may we be free men!

The plate is set down and moved to the end of the table. Some have the custom not to remove the plate, but simply to cover the matzos. The second cup is poured, and the youngest present asks the Four Questions.

Mishnah, Pesachim 116a

Why is this night different from all other nights?

---

why we eat *Korban Pesach*, matzah, and maror.

We have many reasons to believe that this passage was not part of the original text of the Haggadah at all. First of all, even in modern times it seems quite odd to begin inviting guests once the family is already seated around the Seder table. Furthermore, in the times of the Beis Hamikdash, a person had to decide which *Korban Pesach* he wanted to partake from *before* it was slaughtered. Once the *korban* was slaughtered, no guests could join the Seder, so an invitation at this point would have been empty and meaningless.

It seems probable, then, that the original custom was to declare, "Whoever is hungry — let him come and eat," early in the day, *before* the *Korban Pesach* was slaughtered, while potential guests were still milling about in the marketplaces searching for a host for the Seder. It was only logical to make the declaration in Aramaic, because that was the common language of the time.

To commemorate this noble practice, this declaration was later incorporated into the text of the Haggadah. Memories of Eretz Yisrael probably evoked strong emotions in the hearts of those in Babylon who chose to insert this passage into the text of the Haggadah, and those emotions led them to conclude, "Next year may we be in the Land of Israel."

מַה נִּשְׁתַּנָּה הַלַּיְלָה הַזֶּה — Why is this night different

On the Seder night, the children ask for an explanation of four unusual practices that arouse their curiosity. There are many other

שֶׁבְּכָל הַלֵּילוֹת אָנוּ אוֹכְלִין חָמֵץ וּמַצָּה, הַלַּיְלָה הַזֶּה כֻּלּוֹ מַצָּה.

שֶׁבְּכָל הַלֵּילוֹת אָנוּ אוֹכְלִין שְׁאָר יְרָקוֹת, הַלַּיְלָה הַזֶּה מָרוֹר.

שֶׁבְּכָל הַלֵּילוֹת אֵין אָנוּ מַטְבִּילִין אֲפִילוּ פַּעַם אֶחָת, הַלַּיְלָה הַזֶּה שְׁתֵּי פְעָמִים.

שֶׁבְּכָל הַלֵּילוֹת אָנוּ אוֹכְלִין בֵּין יוֹשְׁבִין וּבֵין מְסֻבִּין, הַלַּיְלָה הַזֶּה כֻּלָּנוּ מְסֻבִּין.

---

unusual practices performed on this night. Why were these four questions chosen above all others and incorporated into the Haggadah?

All four questions are based on one fundamental question: What are we trying to commemorate on Pesach — servitude or freedom; slavery or redemption?

On the one hand, we eat while reclining, like kings and noblemen. On the other hand, we eat maror, as a reminder of the bitter suffering we endured in Egypt. We eat matzah to commemorate the bread of affliction that our forefathers ate in Egypt, but it also reminds us of the Exodus, when we left Egypt so swiftly that we did not even have time to allow the bread to rise. We dip maror in charoses, which symbolize both extremes: it is reminiscent of the Jewish blood that was spilled in Egypt and of the cement we were forced to mix. Clearly, charoses is a sign of servitude. At the same time, however, the luxury of dipping food into a tasty condiment is one that is usually limited to freemen.

The severe contradictions between these symbols confuse our children, and prompt them to ask the Four Questions.

How do we respond? We tell our children, "We were slaves to Pharaoh in Egypt, and Hashem our God brought us out."

Our objective during the Seder is indeed twofold. We are obligated to recall the suffering we once endured — in order to reach a more meaningful appreciation of the freedom Hashem has granted us when He redeemed us. In the words of the prophet, "For though I fell, I will rise! Though I sit in darkness, Hashem is my light" (Michah 7:8).

1. On all other nights we may eat chametz and matzah, but on this night — only matzah.

2. On all other nights we eat many vegetables, but on this night — we eat maror.

3. On all other nights we do not dip even once, but on this night — twice.

4. On all other nights we eat either sitting or reclining, but on this night — we all recline.

⋅⟶▬◉◖▬⟵⋅

Vilna Gaon explains that the word לַיְלָה — night — is feminine, and the word יוֹם — day — is masculine (which is why the plural of יוֹם is יָמִים, and the plural of לַיְלָה is לֵילוֹת). Why is this so?

Men are obligated to perform many mitzvos from which women are exempt. Similarly, many mitzvos can be performed only by day, and very few can be performed only at night. Day is considered masculine because of the abundance of mitzvos in which only men are obligated and that must be performed by day. Night is considered feminine because night is a time of relatively few mitzvos, just as women are exempt from many mitzvos.

In a deeper sense, מַה נִּשְׁתַּנָּה הַלַּיְלָה הַזֶּה מִכָּל הַלֵּילוֹת — *Why is this night different from all other nights?* — can mean, "Why do we have so many mitzvos that can only be performed on this night — such as eating matzah, maror, and recounting the story of the Exodus — to the extent that it seems accurate to deem it הַלַּיְלָה הַזֶּה, in masculine form (the feminine form would be הַלַּיְלָה הַזֹּאת).

The Vilna Gaon adds that the answer is implicit in the question. The word מַה has the same *gematria* (numerical value) as the word אָדָם, man. Indeed, the night of Pesach is a masculine night, for it has the characteristics of day.

Many ask why the Vilna Gaon considers לַיְלָה feminine, considering the numerous instances in which it appears with the masculine term זֶה.

The Gaon — with his legendary, encyclopedic knowledge of all areas of the Torah — certainly did not overlook the associations between לַיְלָה and זֶה. Rather, he considered the choice of לֵילוֹת for the plural form to be a sign that there is some feminine connotation to the word לַיְלָה, and he therefore explained why it appears with the masculine term זֶה in this question.

The Seder plate is returned to its place, the matzos are uncovered, and the Haggadah is recited in unison. The Haggadah should be translated, if necessary, and the story of the Exodus should be amplified upon.

משנה, פסחים קטז, א

עֲבָדִים הָיִינוּ לְפַרְעֹה בְּמִצְרַיִם, וַיּוֹצִיאֵנוּ יהוה אֱלֹהֵינוּ מִשָּׁם בְּיָד חֲזָקָה וּבִזְרוֹעַ נְטוּיָה. וְאִלּוּ לֹא הוֹצִיא הַקָּדוֹשׁ בָּרוּךְ הוּא אֶת אֲבוֹתֵינוּ מִמִּצְרַיִם, הֲרֵי אָנוּ וּבָנֵינוּ וּבְנֵי בָנֵינוּ מְשֻׁעְבָּדִים הָיִינוּ לְפַרְעֹה בְּמִצְרַיִם. וַאֲפִילוּ כֻּלָּנוּ חֲכָמִים, כֻּלָּנוּ נְבוֹנִים, כֻּלָּנוּ זְקֵנִים, כֻּלָּנוּ יוֹדְעִים אֶת הַתּוֹרָה, מִצְוָה עָלֵינוּ לְסַפֵּר בִּיצִיאַת מִצְרַיִם.

עֲבָדִים הָיִינוּ לְפַרְעֹה בְּמִצְרַיִם
We were slaves to Pharaoh in Egypt

"To He Who perceives what is hidden on the Day of Judgment; to He Who acquires His servants with judgment" (prayer service for Rosh Hashanah and Yom Kippur).

The Talmud (Kiddushin 11a) implies that if a person purchases a slave and then finds hidden blemishes that prevent him from working or discovers that he engages in armed robbery and might be put to death by the king, he may renege on the purchase, since he was unaware of this information.

On Rosh Hashanah and Yom Kippur, we are overcome with fear that Hashem may decide that our numerous blemishes and sins render us unworthy of serving Him, and invoke this halachah as grounds for absolving Himself of his acquisition of us and abandoning us.

The Talmud states, however, that visible wounds are not considered grounds for nullifying the sale, since the buyer was certainly aware of them and he still considered the purchase worthwhile.

Thus we declare, "Hashem perceives all that is hidden." He knew all our faults, and he still chose us as His servants, so the acquisition remains valid forever.

⋆⇨◉⇦⋆

"For Bnei Yisrael are servants to Me, they are My servants, whom I have taken out of the land of Egypt" (Vayikra 25:55).

This verse seems to contain an unnecessary redundancy. Why does it repeat that we are Hashem's servants?

הגדה של פסח [106]

The Seder plate is returned to its place, the matzos are uncovered, and the Haggadah is recited in unison. The Haggadah should be translated, if necessary, and the story of the Exodus should be amplified upon.

Mishnah, Pesachim 116a

We were slaves to Pharaoh in Egypt, and Hashem our God brought us out from there with a mighty hand and an outstretched arm. Had not the Holy One, Blessed is He, taken our fathers out from Egypt, then we, our children, and our children's children would have remained subservient to Pharaoh in Egypt. Even if we were all men of wisdom, understanding, experience, and knowledge of the Torah — it would still be an obligation upon us to tell about the Exodus from Egypt.

When Hashem came to offer us the Torah, He held Mount Sinai above our heads and threatened to bury us there if we would not accept the Torah. We might claim, then, that we are not truly Hashem's servants, since according to Torah law a Jew cannot be enslaved against his will. Since our servitude to Hashem was forced upon us, it is not legally binding (see *Shabbos* 88a).

The rejoinder to that question appears in this verse in the Torah.

It is true that a Jew who is free cannot be forced into slavery against his will, but a servant may be sold from one master to another even against his will (*Gittin* 13a). Hashem acquired us from the land of Egypt, where we were slaves to Pharaoh, so our status as His servants is valid according to the Torah.

In this verse, Hashem declares that we are His servants — and rightfully so — because he took us as slaves from the land of Egypt.

וַאֲפִילוּ כֻּלָּנוּ חֲכָמִים, כֻּלָּנוּ נְבוֹנִים, וכו׳, מִצְוָה עָלֵינוּ לְסַפֵּר בִּיצִיאַת מִצְרַיִם

Even if we were all men of wisdom ... it would still be an obligation upon us to tell about the Exodus from Egypt.

Many commentaries discuss the difference between the obligation to remember the Exodus every night and day (which we fulfill by reciting the third paragraph of *Shema*), and the obligation to recount the story of the Exodus on the night of Pesach.

We can suggest that during the rest of the year we are required to mention Exodus to affirm that we *know* that the Exodus occurred. On the night of Pesach, however, we must *feel* as if we left Egypt.

וְכָל הַמַּרְבֶּה לְסַפֵּר בִּיצִיאַת מִצְרָיִם, הֲרֵי זֶה מְשֻׁבָּח.

כְּעֵין זֶה מוּזְכָּר בְּתוֹסֶפְתָּא פְּסָחִים י, יב.

מַעֲשֶׂה בְּרַבִּי אֱלִיעֶזֶר וְרַבִּי יְהוֹשֻׁעַ וְרַבִּי אֶלְעָזָר בֶּן עֲזַרְיָה וְרַבִּי עֲקִיבָא וְרַבִּי טַרְפוֹן שֶׁהָיוּ מְסֻבִּין בִּבְנֵי בְרַק, וְהָיוּ מְסַפְּרִים בִּיצִיאַת מִצְרָיִם כָּל אוֹתוֹ הַלַּיְלָה.

We must rejoice as a slave would upon being redeemed from slavery, and praise and thank Hashem for His overwhelming kindness in liberating us from Egypt. In fact, *Rambam* (*Sefer Hamitzvos*: Positive Commandment 157) rules that thanking Hashem for redeeming us from Egypt is part of the obligation to recount the Exodus on the night of Pesach.

This is why the Haggadah stresses the requirement for all Jews — even learned, wise people — to tell the story of the Exodus. There is no purpose in requiring the learned and wise to recount the minutiae of the Exodus if the entire objective of the Seder is to remind us that the Exodus occurred. Since the true goal of the Seder is to stimulate a deep feeling of joy and gratitude toward Hashem for redeeming us, each Jew — wise or simple, learned or ignorant — must tell the story of the Exodus in a manner that will touch him, and bring him to appreciate Hashem's kindness.

וַאֲפִילוּ כֻּלָּנוּ חֲכָמִים כֻּלָּנוּ נְבוֹנִים
Even if we were all men of wisdom

The Talmud (*Shabbos* 11a) tells us that a person who engrosses himself entirely in Torah study, like R' Shimon bar Yochai and his peers, is exempt from prayer.

Talmud Yerushalmi (*Berachos* 8a) adds that they are exempt even from reciting *Shema*. "Since both are forms of study," explains the *Yerushalmi*, "we need not pause from one study to engage in another" (see *Minchas Asher*, Talmud Torah 10).

We might presume, then, that the same exemption applies to the mitzvah of recounting the Exodus on the Seder night. Studying the details of the Exodus is a form of Torah study, so perhaps a person like R' Shimon bar Yochai would not be required to take a break from his studies to fulfill this mitzvah.

The more one tells about the discussion of the Exodus, the more he is praiseworthy.

A passage similar to the following is found in Tosefta, Pesachim 10:8.

It happened that Rabbi Eliezer, Rabbi Yehoshua, Rabbi Elazar ben Azaryah, Rabbi Akiva, and Rabbi Tarfon were gathered (at the Seder) in Bnei Brak. They discussed the Exodus from Egypt all that night

---

The Haggadah makes a point of teaching us that even a person who devotes his entire life to Torah study is obligated to pause from his studies and tell the story of the Exodus on the night of Pesach. This is because apart from the element of Torah study involved in telling the story of the Exodus, there is also an element of thanksgiving to Hashem for rescuing us from Egypt — and that element cannot be overlooked no matter how diligently a person studies Torah.

מַעֲשֶׂה בְּרַבִּי אֱלִיעֶזֶר וכו'
וְהָיוּ מְסַפְּרִים בִּיצִיאַת מִצְרַיִם כָּל אוֹתוֹ הַלַּיְלָה

It happened that R' Eliezer... discussed the Exodus from Egypt all that night.

Tosefta (*Pesachim* 10:8) cites a similar story in which Sages studied the *laws* of Pesach through the night. The Brisker Rav cites this *Tosefta* as proof that studying the laws of Pesach is a fulfillment of the obligation to recount the story of the Exodus.

Simple logic dictates that this is only true if a person spends some time telling the story of the Exodus, for *Rambam* (*Hilchos Chametz U'Matzah* Ch. 7) states that we are required to recall the wondrous miracles that Hashem performed for us when He redeemed us from Egypt on the night of Pesach. The Brisker Rav's proof from *Tosefta* teaches us that once we have already told the story of the Exodus, discussing the laws of Pesach is considered a fulfillment of the precept, "The more one tells of the Exodus, the more he is praise-worthy."[1]

We must wonder, then, why the Sages relied on a secondary form

---

1. Similarly, *Raavad* and *Rash* of Shantz write (*Sifra*, Parashas Bechukosai) that studying the laws of *Megillah* is a fulfillment of the obligation to remember the story of Amalek. Studying the laws of *Megillah* obviously cannot serve as our *only* fulfillment of remembering the story of Amalek, but as an additional fulfillment of the obligation once we have already fulfilled it in the basic sense.

עַד שֶׁבָּאוּ תַּלְמִידֵיהֶם וְאָמְרוּ לָהֶם: רַבּוֹתֵינוּ הִגִּיעַ זְמַן קְרִיאַת שְׁמַע שֶׁל שַׁחֲרִית.

of fulfilling the mitzvah rather than fulfilling the mitzvah in its conventional manner, by recounting the details of the Exodus all night.

Perhaps we can answer that the Sages chose to study the laws of Pesach as a compromise between two Torah giants, R' Elazar ben Azariah and R' Akiva, both of whom were present at that Seder.

The Talmud (*Pesachim* 120b) states that R' Elazar ben Azariah holds that we must finish eating the *Korban Pesach* by midnight, and R' Akiva maintains that we can eat it until the morning.

We might suggest that as midnight struck, R' Elazar ben Azariah rose and headed toward the *Beis Midrash*, because he probably held that the obligation to tell the story of the Exodus ends when we are no longer allowed to eat the *Korban Pesach*. If we are no longer obligated to discuss the story of the Exodus, then the time should be spent studying Torah. R' Akiva held that the mitzvah continues until the morning, and wanted to keep discussing the Exodus until daybreak. Rather than disband and have each go his separate way, they decided to compromise. They studied the laws of Pesach, thereby satisfying both opinions.

One might object that unlike the story from the Mishnah that we recite in the Haggadah, the *Tosefta*'s story does not state that R' Akiva and R' Elazar ben Azariah took part in the Seder. In fact, only Rabban Gamliel is mentioned by name, and the other participants are referred to anonymously as "the Sages." How do we know that R' Akiva and R' Elazar were there?

Although there is no concrete proof that they were present, it does seem likely that the Sages who joined Rabban Gamliel were none other than R' Yehoshua, R' Akiva, and R' Elazar ben Azariah, who are mentioned frequently in stories regarding Rabban Gamliel (aside from the Mishnah cited here; see *Makkos* 24a and *Succah* 41b).

עַד שֶׁבָּאוּ תַּלְמִידֵיהֶם וְאָמְרוּ לָהֶם: רַבּוֹתֵינוּ הִגִּיעַ זְמַן קְרִיאַת שְׁמַע שֶׁל שַׁחֲרִית
Until their students came and said to them: "Our teachers, the time has come for the reading of the morning *Shema*."

Pirkei D'Rabbi Eliezer (2) relates, "R' Eliezer sat and taught Torah until their students came and said to them: "Our teachers, the time has come for the reading of the morning *Shema*."

---

and his face shone with the radiance of the sun; rays of light would emanate from his face — similar to those of Moshe Rabbeinu — such that no one present could distinguish between day and night."

Therefore, the students who were seated together with R' Eliezer at the Seder could not see the sunrise, and they had to rely on the students who were outside to inform them that it was time to recite *Shema*.

⊷⊜⊶

R' Levi Yitzchak of Berditchev was well known as the "advocate" of the Jewish people. He would always see the Jewish people in a positive light and pray to Hashem on their behalf.

On his way home from shul on the Seder night, R' Levi Yitzchak would hide outside the homes of simple Jews to hear how they would conduct their Seder.

Once, he paused by the home of a Jew who was totally unlearned, and heard him reading the Haggadah with great passion. When reciting the passage, "Concerning four sons does the Torah speak: A wise one, a wicked one, a simple one, and one who is unable to ask," he drew out the word *echad* (one) each time, saying, "echaaaaad." He explained to his family that this was how was father taught him to say *echad* when reciting *Shema* (as taught in *Shulchan Aruch*, O.C. 61:6), and he extrapolated that the same applies to the word *echad* in the Haggadah.

When R' Levi Yitzchak heard this, he lifted his hands to the Heavens and said, "Master of the universe! Who is like Your nation Israel? The entire purpose of the Seder is to come to the realization that Hashem is One, and to accept His Sovereignty upon ourselves. The greatest *Tannaim* spent the entire night telling stories of the Exodus until they finally achieved this goal, and only then did their students determine that it was time to recite *Shema*. This simple Jew just began his Seder, and he already drew out the word *echad* as he does when saying *Shema*!"

R' Levi Yitzchak jokingly added that this simpleton's idea appears in the Haggadah. The word שַׁחֲרִית in the passage, "The time has come to recite the *Shema* of *Shacharis*," is an acronym for the four sons: שֶׁאֵינוֹ יוֹדֵעַ לִשְׁאוֹל תָּם, רָשָׁע, חָכָם.

אָמַר רַבִּי אֶלְעָזָר בֶּן עֲזַרְיָה, הֲרֵי אֲנִי כְּבֶן שִׁבְעִים
שָׁנָה, וְלֹא זָכִיתִי שֶׁתֵּאָמֵר יְצִיאַת מִצְרַיִם
בַּלֵּילוֹת, עַד שֶׁדְּרָשָׁהּ בֶּן זוֹמָא, שֶׁנֶּאֱמַר, לְמַעַן תִּזְכֹּר

הֲרֵי אֲנִי כְּבֶן שִׁבְעִים שָׁנָה
I am like a seventy-year-old man

The Talmud (*Berachos* 28a) tells us that when R' Elazar ben Azariah was offered the position of Rosh Yeshivah, he was only eighteen years old. A miracle occurred, and eighteen streaks of white hair appeared in his beard, giving him the semblance of a seventy-year old sage worthy of serving as a Rosh Yeshivah. Thus R' Elazar said, "I am *like* a man of seventy years," although he was not actually seventy.

What is the connection between this observation, and the dispute of whether the Exodus must be remembered each night?

R' Elazar exact words were וְלֹא זָכִיתִי שֶׁתֵּאָמֵר יְצִיאַת מִצְרַיִם בַּלֵּילוֹת. R' Ovadiah of Bartenura interprets the word זָכִיתִי in this context to mean "victorious."

R' Elazar stated that although his peers had seen the miracle Hashem performed, turning his beard white so that he would command respect as Rosh Yeshivah, he still was not victorious in his struggle to convince them to accept his opinion. (A similar explanation is offered by *Shibolei Haleket, Seder Haggadah* 218 quoting R' Ephraim Kalai, *Abudraham*, and *Yaaros Devash* 2:18).

Rambam (*Peirush HaMishnayos, Berachos* 1:5) writes that R' Elazar ben Azariah aged prematurely because he toiled so intensely in Torah study that by the age of eighteen he appeared to be seventy years old.

Rambam interprets the word זָכִיתִי to mean "merit," and explains that R' Elazar was surprised that despite his efforts to toil in Torah study and associate himself with men of great wisdom, he still did not *merit* to find a source in the Torah for the obligation to mention the Exodus at night, until Ben Zoma finally revealed it to him. (See *Tosafos Yom Tov*.)

In *Divrei Shaul*, R' Yosef Shaul Nathanson offers a similar insight based on the *Talmud Yerushalmi's* teaching (*Berachos* 2:8) that R' Bon was able to achieve a level of scholarliness in 28 years that others did not achieve in 100 years. *Yefei Toar* explains that the human mind is limited, but R' Bon surpassed those limits. Similarly, R' Elazar had attained the level of wisdom of a seventy-year-old man

Rabbi Elazar ben Azaryah said: I am like a seventy-year-old man, but I could not succeed that the Exodus from Egypt be mentioned every night, until Ben Zoma expounded it: "In order that you may remember

---

at the age of eighteen, yet he was still unable to find a source for mentioning the Exodus at night until Ben Zoma revealed it to him.

וְלֹא זָכִיתִי . . . עַד שֶׁדְּרָשָׁהּ בֶּן זוֹמָא
But I could not succeed ... until Ben Zoma expounded

Malbim writes that the Sages did not wish to follow R' Elazar ben Azariah's opinion because he was only eighteen years old. This is surprising, because Ben Zoma — whose opinion was accepted — was not much older than R' Elazar ben Azariah. Both were contemporaries of R' Akiva and were apparently born in the same generation (see *Chagigah* 14b; *Tosafos, Yevamos* 86a). Why did the Sages accept Ben Zoma's proof if they had an issue with accepting the opinion of the younger Sages?[1]

Ben Zoma is quoted in *Pirkei Avos* (4:1) as teaching, "Who is wise? He who learns from all people."

Because the Sages accepted Ben Zoma's teaching in *Pirkei Avos*, they were able to accept his opinion regarding the mention of the Exodus at night.

שֶׁתֵּאָמֵר יְצִיאַת מִצְרַיִם בַּלֵּילוֹת
That the Exodus from Egypt be mentioned every night

The wording of R' Elazar's statement, שֶׁתֵּאָמֵר יְצִיאַת מִצְרַיִם בַּלֵּילוֹת, *that the Exodus from Egypt be mentioned every night,* implies that the Exodus must be mentioned verbally every night; contemplating the Exodus in our hearts is insufficient. This is the view held by *Rashash* (*Berachos* 12b) and *Shaagas Aryeh* (13), who cite various proofs to this effect.

Besamim Rosh (173) maintains that the mitzvah of telling the story of the Exodus at the Seder must be performed verbally,[2] but the

---

1. It is interesting to note that R' Elazar ben Azariah was not necessarily so young when he argued with the Sages about remembering the Exodus at night. *Seder Hadoros* contends that while he was eighteen when he became Rosh Yeshivah, this dispute actually occurred much later when he was at least seventy.

2. As per the verse וְהִגַּדְתָּ לְבִנְךָ בַּיּוֹם הַהוּא, *And you shall tell your son on that day* (Pesach) (*Shemos* 13:8).

אֶת יוֹם צֵאתְךָ מֵאֶרֶץ מִצְרַיִם כֹּל יְמֵי חַיֶּיךָ.[1] יְמֵי חַיֶּיךָ הַיָּמִים, כֹּל יְמֵי חַיֶּיךָ הַלֵּילוֹת. וַחֲכָמִים אוֹמְרִים, יְמֵי חַיֶּיךָ הָעוֹלָם הַזֶּה, כֹּל יְמֵי חַיֶּיךָ לְהָבִיא לִימוֹת הַמָּשִׁיחַ.

בָּרוּךְ הַמָּקוֹם, בָּרוּךְ הוּא. בָּרוּךְ שֶׁנָּתַן תּוֹרָה

---

obligation to remember the Exodus all year round can be fulfilled by means of contemplation. *Pri Megadim* (Introduction to *Hilchos Kerias Shema*, 4) takes the same approach, and uses it to explain why *Rambam* seems to limit the Torah commandment to remember the Exodus to Pesach night if the same mitzvah exists all year round. Since Pesach is the only time of the year that we are obligated to recount the Exodus verbally, it is the only time that it is considered a Torah-level positive commandment.[1]

בָּרוּךְ הַמָּקוֹם, בָּרוּךְ הוּא. בָּרוּךְ שֶׁנָּתַן תּוֹרָה לְעַמּוֹ יִשְׂרָאֵל, בָּרוּךְ הוּא
Blessed is the Omnipresent, Blessed is He.[2] Blessed is the One Who has given the Torah to His people Israel; Blessed is He.

In *Rambam* and *Abarbanel's* versions of the Haggadah, the words בָּרוּךְ הוּא, *Blessed is He*, are omitted from this passage. It seems that these words are indeed redundant; they do not seem to add any meaning to the passage.

It is possible that the Haggadah was originally recited in a responsive format. The person leading the Seder would declare, "Blessed is the Omnipresent," and the attendees would respond, "Blessed is He," similar to the way we respond to the mention of Hashem's Name in a blessing, בָּרוּךְ הוּא וּבָרוּךְ שְׁמוֹ, *Blessed is He, and Blessed is His Name.*

However, the phrase *Blessed is He* appears in two places where it does not seem to be a response. The text of *Baruch She'amar* (daily morning prayers) reads: "Blessed is He Who spoke and the world came into being, *Blessed is He.*" In addition, the Mishnah (*Middos* 5:4) tells us that the Sanhedrin would investigate the lineage of the Kohanim to ascertain if they were fit to serve in the Beis Hamikdash. When a Kohen was found fit to serve, they would celebrate with a festive meal,

---

1. See *Teshuvos Chasam Sofer*, *Orach Chaim* 15.

2. *Eitz Yosef* (in *Siddur Otzar Hatefillos*) explains that we say, "Blessed is He," not "Blessed are You," because we refer to the hidden and unfathomable Essence of Hashem, which we cannot refer to as "You."

the day you left Egypt all the days of your life."[1] The phrase "the days of your life" would have indicated only the days; the addition of the word "all" includes the nights as well. But the Sages declare that "the days of your life" would mean only the present world; the addition of "all" includes the era of the Messiah.

Blessed is the Omnipresent; Blessed is He. Blessed is the One Who has given the Torah

_____

(1) *Devarim* 16:3.

_____

at which they would declare, "Blessed is the Omnipresent — *Blessed is He* — that no blemish was found in Aharon's lineage" (*Middos* 5:4).

In both of these instances, "Blessed is He" must be part of the prayer, not a response, because these prayers are not necessarily recited in the presence of a congregation who could respond. It stands to reason that in our version of the Haggadah too, this phrase is not a response, but part of the text.

In his commentary to the Mishnah regarding the Kohanim found fit to serve, *Tosafos Yom Tov* explains that people might think that the phrase, "*Baruch HaMakom*" — literally, "blessed is the place" — refers to the place where they were located, i.e., the Beis Hamikdash. In truth, *HaMakom* is a reference to Hashem, Whose Presence is in no way limited by space. The phrase "Blessed is *He*" was added to clarify that the blessing is not directed toward the Beis Hamikdash, but to Hashem.

Since the same mistake can occur whenever we refer to Hashem as "*HaMakom*," it is reasonable that "Blessed is He" would be added in all such instances — including this passage in the Haggadah.

The question remains, however, why we say "Blessed is He" in *Baruch She'amar*, in which we do not refer to Hashem as *HaMakom*. Perhaps the reason for its addition is because the words that follow *Baruch She'amar* are *vehayah haolam* (the world came to be), which is remarkably similar to *Baruch HaMakom*. Here too, then, we must stress that the blessing is directed towards Hashem, not towards the world.[1]

בָּרוּךְ הַמָּקוֹם — Blessed is the Omnipresent

Two explanations are offered for the perplexing reference toward Hashem as *HaMakom*, the Omnipresent.

_____

1. In commenting on *Baruch She'amar*, *Siddur Avodas Yisrael* cites from *Sefer Hayuchsin* that when they would install a new *Reish Galusa* (Head of the Diaspora)

לְעַמּוֹ יִשְׂרָאֵל, בָּרוּךְ הוּא. כְּנֶגֶד אַרְבָּעָה בָנִים
דִּבְּרָה תוֹרָה — אֶחָד חָכָם, וְאֶחָד רָשָׁע, וְאֶחָד
תָּם, וְאֶחָד שֶׁאֵינוֹ יוֹדֵעַ לִשְׁאוֹל.

מכילתא שמות יג, יד

חָכָם מָה הוּא אוֹמֵר? מָה הָעֵדֹת וְהַחֻקִּים
וְהַמִּשְׁפָּטִים אֲשֶׁר צִוָּה יהוה אֱלֹהֵינוּ
אֶתְכֶם?[1] וְאַף אַתָּה אֱמָר לוֹ כְּהִלְכוֹת הַפֶּסַח,
אֵין מַפְטִירִין אַחַר הַפֶּסַח אֲפִיקוֹמָן.

The Midrash (*Bereishis Rabbah*, 68:9) explains that the world exists within the Place — i.e., Hashem; He does not exist within the world. Hashem encompasses the entire world, for the world cannot possibly encompass Him.

In a similar vein, *Midrash Tanchuma* (*Parashas Ki Sisa*) notes that Hashem told Moshe Rabbeinu, "Behold, there is a place *near* Me; you may stand on the rock" (*Shemos* 33:21), not, "Behold, I am in such and such place," because Hashem is the Place in which everything exists, so it is impossible for Him to be located in a spot that is within Him.

In *Moreh Nevuchim* (1:8), *Rambam* explains that *HaMakom* is a reference to Hashem's utterly exalted standing, far above all that He created.[1]

---

in Babylon, the congregation would sing *Baruch She'amar* responsively. The *chazzan* would recite each segment beginning with *Baruch*, and the young men would respond, "*Baruch Hu!*"

A contemporary scholar concluded that practice was actually the traditional manner in which *Baruch She'amar* was recited on a daily basis, and the reason why we only find the words *Baruch Hu* once in our version of *Baruch She'amar* is because the *chazzan* would recite it once, after *vehayah haolam*, to signal to the congregation to follow suit.

This conclusion is mistaken; *Baruch Hu* is an integral part of *Baruch She'amar*, not a response recited by the congregation. It was recited responsively in order to glorify and honor the *Reish Gelusa* upon his installment, not because it was the traditional manner in which it was recited. We find the expression "He Who spoke and the world came into being, Blessed is He," as a self-contained phrase in *Bereishis Rabbah* (6:2), where it could not possibly be due to a responsive form of recitation.

1. We find the root word of *HaMakom* used in the Talmud in the context of, "*Adayin machlokes bimekomo omedes* — the argument still **stands**." *Rambam* understands the word *HaMakom* in this context; it refers to Hashem's unique position, or, in other words, His standing.

to His people Israel; Blessed is He. Concerning four sons does the Torah speak — a wise one, a wicked one, a simple one, and one who is unable to ask.

Mechilta, Shemos 13:14

The wise son — what does he say? "What are the testimonies, decrees, and ordinances which HASHEM, our God, has commanded you?"[1] Therefore explain to him the laws of the Pesach offering: that one may not eat dessert after the final taste of the Pesach offering.

---

(1) *Devarim* 6:20.

חָכָם מָה הוּא אוֹמֵר?

The wise son — what does he say?

How is the wise son's wisdom apparent from his question?

The wise son's question is actually a profound one. He analyzed all of the mitzvos of the Torah and observed that they are divided into three categories:

1) *Eidos* (testimonies): These are mitzvos that commemorate important events. Shabbos, for instance, is a commemoration of Creation. Pesach, Shavuos, and Succos commemorate and affirm our faith in the Exodus, and the mitzvos we fulfill during the Seder commemorate various aspects of the exile in Egypt and the subsequent Redemption.

2) *Chukim* (decrees): Included in the category are most of the *mitzvos bein adam l'Makom* (mitzvos between man and God), such as *kashrus* and *sha'atnez*. These are decrees of the King, which are often incomprehensible, but may not be challenged, for they show our faithful subservience to Hashem.

3) *Mishpatim* (ordinances): This category includes the laws that govern interpersonal relationships (*mitzvos bein adam l'chaveiro*). For the most part, these mitzvos seem just and wise even to our limited intellects, for we realize that the world cannot function without justice.

The wise son tries to understand why the mitzvos fall under these three categories.

What do we answer? "We are forbidden to eat after the afikoman." Why? Because we want to preserve the taste of the afikoman as long as possible.

The same is true of all mitzvos. Mitzvos are supposed to perfect

רָשָׁע מַה הוּא אוֹמֵר? מָה הָעֲבֹדָה הַזֹּאת לָכֶם?[1] לָכֶם וְלֹא לוֹ, וּלְפִי שֶׁהוֹצִיא אֶת עַצְמוֹ מִן הַכְּלָל, כָּפַר בְּעִקָּר – וְאַף אַתָּה הַקְהֵה אֶת שִׁנָּיו

---

us, draw us close to God, and leave an indelible imprint of holiness on the soul. The imprint of holiness left by a mitzvah inspires us to perform more and more mitzvos, as our Sages tell us, "A mitzvah draws after it another mitzvah" (*Pirkei Avos* 4:2).

For a mitzvah to produce the desired effect on the soul, we must prepare ourselves to receive its holiness. *Ramban* (*Vayikra* 18:4) writes that the positive effect that a mitzvah will have on us is directly proportional to the amount of preparation we invest into performing it.

The first precept of the philosophy of Chassidus is that mitzvos require preparation; the second is to distance ourselves from evil by refraining from sin and theft. Only after fulfilling these two steps can we truly draw close to Hashem through the mitzvos.

The three categories of mitzvos represent these three foundations of our service of Hashem. The *eidos* prepare our souls, uplifting them and make them worthy of drawing close to Hashem and His service. The *mishpatim* distance us from sin, theft, and dishonesty. The *chukim* are the ultimate goal that we strive for, for they require us to display sincere subservience to Hashem's Will.

רָשָׁע מַה הוּא אוֹמֵר?
The wicked son — what does he say?

The dialogues with the wise and simple sons are introduced with the words, "And it shall be when your son will *ask* you" (*Shemos* 13:14; *Devarim* 6:20). They ask sincere questions, and truly desire a response.

The dialogue with the wicked son is introduced with the words, "And it shall be when your children *say* to you" (*Shemos* 12:26). The wicked son does not ask a question. He makes a statement in the form of a rhetorical question, launched as a derogatory attack against the mitzvos he sees performed at the Seder. He does not want to hear an answer to his question. He would prefer that his question remain unanswered, as a lasting mockery to the service he so despises (*Meshech Chochmah, Shemos* 13:14).

We can add that the sincere questions of the wise and simple sons deserve a direct response, as the Torah states, "You shall say to him" (*Shemos* 13:14), and, "You shall say to your child" (*Devarim* 6:21).

The wicked son — what does he say? "Of what purpose is this work to you?"[1] He says, "To you," thereby excluding himself. By excluding himself from the community of believers, he denies the basic principle of Judaism. Therefore, blunt his teeth

(1) *Shemos* 12:26.

The response to the wicked son's rhetorical attack is not directed toward anyone in particular: "You shall say, 'It is a Pesach offering to Hashem'" (*Shemos* 12:27). We have no reason to carry on any sort of dialogue with the wicked son. Rather, we provide an answer for the others gathered at the Seder so that they are aware of the reasons for the mitzvos and are not influenced by his snide remarks.

The fact that we are addressing the others gathered and not the wicked son is explicit in *Talmud Yerushalmi's* (*Pesachim* 10:4) version of the dialogue with the wicked son: "What does the wicked son say? 'What is this *service* to you? Why do you impose such difficulties and inconveniences upon us each year?'"

Since he has removed himself from the community, you should answer, "It is because of this that Hashem did so for *me* when I left Egypt." He did it for *me*, not for *that man*. Had *that man* been in Egypt, he would not have been worthy of redemption.

Since the wicked son has no interest in understanding the depth and beauty of the mitzvos and only wishes to complain about the difficulty and inconvenience Pesach imposes upon him, we do not bother to address him directly. We refer to the wicked son as "that man," and respond to his remarks only to prevent the others gathered at the table from being affected by his evil ways.

מָה הָעֲבֹדָה הַזֹּאת לָכֶם?
Of what purpose is this work to you?

The wicked son complains of the difficulties of Seder night, as we quoted above from the *Talmud Yerushalmi*: "Why do you impose upon me the difficulties and the inconveniences of the Seder each year?"

In other words, the wicked son wonders why it is necessary to perform so many mitzvos. Is it not enough to be a good Jew at heart? Is it not enough to love Hashem and honor Him, without performing all of the "burdensome service"? "We are Hashem's children," he claims, "not His servants!"

In each generation, some group or another adopts this line of

וְאָמַר לוֹ, בַּעֲבוּר זֶה עָשָׂה יהוה לִי בְּצֵאתִי
מִמִּצְרָיִם.¹ לִי וְלֹא לוֹ, אִלּוּ הָיָה שָׁם לֹא הָיָה
נִגְאָל.

reasoning as an excuse to divest themselves of the yoke of serving Hashem. The response to their claim is that we are not only sons of Hashem, we are also His servants. Hashem only redeemed us from Egypt so that we would serve Him, and we must do so with every fiber of our being.

This idea is implicit in our response to the wicked son's statement. We tell the others gathered at the Seder that the wicked son would not have been redeemed from slavery in Egypt. Why? Because the Redemption was contingent on our willingness to serve Hashem, as the Torah states, "For Bnei Yisrael are servants to Me, they are My servants, whom I have taken out of the land of Egypt" (*Vayikra* 25:55). Those who were unwilling to serve Hashem did not have the basic merit necessary to be redeemed.

בַּעֲבוּר זֶה עָשָׂה ה׳ לִי בְּצֵאתִי מִמִּצְרָיִם
It is because of this that Hashem did so for me when I went out of Egypt.

R' Saadiah Gaon, in his commentary on the Torah, seems to reverse the order of two words in his explanation of this verse. He writes that the mitzvos that we perform at the Seder commemorate the miracles of Exodus, with each mitzvah commemorating a portion of the slavery and redemption, as we specify later in the Haggadah. This explanation would be accurate if the words of the verse would be: זֶה בַּעֲבוּר עָשָׂה ה׳ לִי בְּצֵאתִי מִמִּצְרָיִם, *This [service] is because Hashem did [miracles] for me when I went out of Egypt.*

The Brisker Rav offers an explanation that follows the true order of the words in the Torah. We do not perform the mitzvos because we were taken out of from Egypt; we were take out of Egypt so that we would fulfill the mitzvos of matzah and maror: בַּעֲבוּר זֶה עָשָׂה ה׳ לִי בְּצֵאתִי מִמִּצְרָיִם, *It is because of this [service] that Hashem did so for me when I went out of Egypt.*

We can also offer a simpler interpretation of the verse based on *Rashi*'s comment on the words בַּעֲבוּר זֶה: "So that I will keep [Hashem's] commandments."

Hashem redeemed us from Egypt so that we will become His loyal servants and perform all of his commandments (not only the ones performed on Pesach). In the words of *Chazal* (*Shemos Rabbah*

and tell him: "It is because of this that HASHEM did so for me when I went out of Egypt."[1] "For me," but not for him — had he been there, he would not have been redeemed.

---

(1) *Shemos* 13:8.

29:3), [Hashem said,] "I removed you from Egypt on condition that you accept My Sovereignty upon yourselves."

⋆⟞⟝⊙⟝⋆

This verse appears three times in the Haggadah. When responding to the wicked son, we say, "It is because of this that Hashem did so *for me*" — for me, but not for him. We say this verse when opening a discussion with the son who does not know how to ask. And we derive from this verse that the mitzvah of relating the story of the Exodus applies on the Seder night when matzah and maror lie before us: "It is because of *this*" — i.e., the matzah and maror.

The repetition of this verse indicates that it carries a message fundamental to the mitzvah of relating the story of the Exodus.

The mitzvah of relating the story of the Exodus is meant to inspire us to accept the yoke of Heaven upon ourselves, as the verse states (*Vayikra* 25:55): "For Bnei Yisrael are servants to Me, they are My servants, whom I have taken out of the land of Egypt." *Chazal* expound this verse to mean, "For this purpose I took you out of Egypt — so that you would be My servants."

Of all the verses in the Torah that mention the Exodus, the Men of the Great Assembly chose the verse, "I am Hashem, your God, Who has removed you from the land of Egypt **to be a God to you**" (*Bamidbar* 15:41), as the verse with which we fulfill the mitzvah of remembering the Exodus every morning and evening.

The *Rishonim* are divided over the meaning of the verse, "It is because of this that Hashem did so for me when I left Egypt." In explaining the verse, *Ramban* and *R' Saadiah Gaon* invert the first two words, from בַּעֲבוּר זֶה, to זֶה בַּעֲבוּר: "This (the matzah and maror that we eat) is because Hashem did so for me when I left Egypt." *Rashi*, however, rejects this explanation and writes, according to the simple interpretation of the verse, "It is because of this — in order that I fulfill His commandments." In other words, the purpose of the Exodus was that we should accept the yoke of Heaven upon ourselves and fulfill Hashem's commandments.

Only one of the four sons, the wise son, grasps this fundamental idea and goes on to ask which commandments we are meant to

תָּם מָה הוּא אוֹמֵר? מַה זֹּאת? וְאָמַרְתָּ אֵלָיו, בְּחֹזֶק
יָד הוֹצִיאָנוּ יהוה מִמִּצְרַיִם מִבֵּית עֲבָדִים.[1]

וְשֶׁאֵינוֹ יוֹדֵעַ לִשְׁאוֹל, אַתְּ פְּתַח לוֹ. שֶׁנֶּאֱמַר,
וְהִגַּדְתָּ לְבִנְךָ בַּיּוֹם הַהוּא לֵאמֹר,
בַּעֲבוּר זֶה עָשָׂה יהוה לִי בְּצֵאתִי מִמִּצְרָיִם.[2]

מכילתא בא יז

יָכוֹל מֵרֹאשׁ חֹדֶשׁ, תַּלְמוּד לוֹמַר בַּיּוֹם הַהוּא. אִי
בַּיּוֹם הַהוּא, יָכוֹל מִבְּעוֹד יוֹם, תַּלְמוּד לוֹמַר
בַּעֲבוּר זֶה. בַּעֲבוּר זֶה לֹא אָמַרְתִּי אֶלָּא בְּשָׁעָה שֶׁיֵּשׁ
מַצָּה וּמָרוֹר מֻנָּחִים לְפָנֶיךָ.

פסחים קטז, א

מִתְּחִלָּה, עוֹבְדֵי עֲבוֹדָה זָרָה הָיוּ אֲבוֹתֵינוּ,
וְעַכְשָׁו קֵרְבָנוּ הַמָּקוֹם לַעֲבוֹדָתוֹ.
שֶׁנֶּאֱמַר, וַיֹּאמֶר יְהוֹשֻׁעַ אֶל כָּל הָעָם, כֹּה אָמַר
יהוה אֱלֹהֵי יִשְׂרָאֵל, בְּעֵבֶר הַנָּהָר יָשְׁבוּ אֲבוֹתֵיכֶם
מֵעוֹלָם, תֶּרַח אֲבִי אַבְרָהָם וַאֲבִי נָחוֹר, וַיַּעַבְדוּ
אֱלֹהִים אֲחֵרִים. וָאֶקַּח אֶת אֲבִיכֶם אֶת אַבְרָהָם
מֵעֵבֶר הַנָּהָר, וָאוֹלֵךְ אוֹתוֹ בְּכָל אֶרֶץ כְּנַעַן,
וָאַרְבֶּה אֶת זַרְעוֹ, וָאֶתֶּן לוֹ אֶת יִצְחָק. וָאֶתֵּן
לְיִצְחָק אֶת יַעֲקֹב וְאֶת עֵשָׂו, וָאֶתֵּן לְעֵשָׂו אֶת

---

perform: "What are the testimonies, decrees, and ordinances which
Hashem, our God, has commanded you?"

The evil son, on the other hand, is not interested in hearing or
knowing. We answer him, "It is because of this that Hashem did so
for me when I went out of Egypt" — the purpose of leaving Egypt
was to fulfill Hashem's commandments — "had he been there, he
would not have been redeemed," since he does not wish to fulfill
those commandments.

The simple son — what does he say? "What is this?" Tell him: "With a strong hand did HASHEM take us out of Egypt, from the house of bondage."[1]

And as for the son who is unable to ask, you must initiate the subject for him, as it is stated: "You shall tell your son on that day: It is because of this that HASHEM did so for me when I went out of Egypt."[2]

Cf. Mechilta, Parashas Bo 17

One might think that the obligation to discuss the Exodus commences with the first day of the month of Nissan, but the Torah says: "You shall tell your son on that day." But the expression "on that day" could be understood to mean only during the daytime; therefore the Torah adds: "It is because of this that HASHEM did so for me when I went out of Egypt." The pronoun "this" implies something tangible, thus, "You shall tell your son" applies only at the time when matzah and maror lie before you — at the Seder.

Pesachim 116a

Originally our ancestors were idol worshipers, but now the Omnipresent has brought us near to His service, as it is written: "Yehoshua said to all the people: So says HASHEM, God of Israel: Your fathers always lived beyond the Euphrates River, Terach the father of Avraham and Nachor, and they served other gods. Then I took your father Avraham from beyond the river and I led him through all the land of Canaan. I multiplied his offspring and gave him Yitzchak. To Yitzchak I gave Yaakov and Eisav, to Eisav I gave

(1) *Shemos* 13:14. (2) Ibid. 13:8.

The son who does not know how to ask sits at the Seder as well, not understanding what is told to him. Nevertheless, we tell him that "It is because of this." Even if he does not understand the profound significance of the Exodus, we must still teach him to perform the commandments, for that was the entire purpose of the Exodus.

הַר שֵׂעִיר לָרֶשֶׁת אוֹתוֹ, וְיַעֲקֹב וּבָנָיו יָרְדוּ מִצְרָיִם.[1]

בָּרוּךְ שׁוֹמֵר הַבְטָחָתוֹ לְיִשְׂרָאֵל, בָּרוּךְ הוּא. שֶׁהַקָּדוֹשׁ בָּרוּךְ הוּא חִשַּׁב אֶת הַקֵּץ, לַעֲשׂוֹת כְּמָה שֶׁאָמַר לְאַבְרָהָם אָבִינוּ בִּבְרִית בֵּין

שֶׁהַקָּדוֹשׁ בָּרוּךְ הוּא חִשַּׁב אֶת הַקֵּץ
**For the Holy One, Blessed is He,
calculated the end of the bondage**

We find much discussion in *Chazal* and the *Rishonim* regarding the discrepancy between the *Bris Bein Habesarim* (Covenant between the Parts[1]), when Hashem informed Avraham that his descendants would be enslaved for 400 years, and the actual exile, which lasted only 210 years. Three basic explanations are offered:

1) Hashem had mercy on the Jews in merit of our forefathers and redeemed them before the designated time.

2) The grueling slave labor they performed in those 210 years was equivalent to 400 years of ordinary labor.

3) *Arizal* explains that the verse וְלֹא יָכְלוּ לְהִתְמַהְמֵהַּ, *for they could not delay* (Shemos 12:39), means that Hashem saw that the Jews in Egypt were mired in the 49th level of impurity, and were on the verge of slipping into the 50th level, from which they could never emerge. Hashem redeemed them immediately because if they would have remained in Egypt any longer, they would have been stuck there forever, and He would have had to renege on the promise of redemption made to the Patriarchs years earlier.

We find allusions to these three reasons in the opening verses of *Parashas Va'eira*, when Hashem assured Moshe that the Redemption was imminent:

"God spoke to Moshe, and said to him, 'I am Hashem. I appeared to Avraham, to Yitzchak, and to Yaakov [an allusion to the merit of the forefathers] ... Moreover, I established My covenant with them to give them the Land of Canaan [an allusion to His promise to redeem their children] ... Moreover, I have heard the groan of Bnei Yisrael whom Egypt enslaves [an allusion to the intensity of the labor]" (*Shemos* 6:2-5).

--◦◦◦--

---

1. See *Bereishis* 15:7-21.

Mount Seir to inherit, but Yaakov and his children went down to Egypt."[1]

Blessed is He Who keeps His pledge to Israel; Blessed is He! For the Holy One, Blessed is He, calculated the end of the bondage in order to do as He said to our father Avraham at the Covenant between

---

(1) *Yehoshua* 24:2-4.

There is a small discrepancy between two verses in the Torah's description of the events leading up to the Redemption.

In one verse Hashem tells Moshe, "So shall you say to Bnei Yisrael, 'Hashem, the God of your forefathers, the God of Avraham, the God of Yitzchak, and the God of Yaakov, has dispatched me to you. This is My Name forever, and this is My remembrance from generation to generation'" (*Shemos* 3:15).

Just one verse later Hashem says, "Go and gather the elders of Israel and say to them, 'Hashem, the God of your forefathers, has appeared to me, the God of Avraham, Yitzchak, and Yaakov, saying: I have surely remembered you, and what is done to you in Egypt'" (ibid. 3:16).

In the first verse Hashem presents Himself as the God of each of the forefathers separately: "The God of Avraham, the God of Yitzchak, and the God of Yaakov." In the second verse, He presents Himself as the God of all three together: "The God of Avraham, Yitzchak, and Yaakov." What is the reason for the discrepancy between these two verses?

The Talmud (*Bava Metzia* 85a) tells us that Eliyahu HaNavi would come to Rebbi's[1] study hall each day. One Rosh Chodesh Eliyahu came late. When Rebbi asked him why he came late, he explained that first he had to rouse Avraham Avinu, wash his hands, wait for him to pray, and then send him back to rest, then he had to do the same for Yitzchak, and then for Yaakov.

Rebbi asked why Eliyahu did not have them pray together. Eliyahu explained that if the forefathers prayed together, their prayers would be so powerful that they might bring Mashiach before the designated time for the ultimate Redemption.

We can use this passage from the Talmud to reconcile these two verses.

The first verse refers to the ultimate Redemption: "This is My

---

1. The name *Rebbi* in the *Mishnah* and *Talmud* refers to R' Yehudah HaNassi, the codifier of Mishnah.

Name forever, and this is My remembrance *from generation to generation.*" Hashem presented Himself as the God of each of the forefathers individually in the context of the ultimate Redemption to hint to Moshe that if they were ever allowed to pray together they might bring Mashiach too soon.

The second verse refers to the Redemption from Egypt: "I have remembered you, and what has been done to you in Egypt."

Hashem told Moshe that although the forefathers were never allowed to gather to hasten the ultimate Redemption, they had already prayed to hasten the Exodus; thus he could gather the elders and inform them that the Redemption was indeed imminent.

[אֶהְיֶה שְׁלָחַנִי אֲלֵיכֶם — I Shall Be sent me to you]

When Hashem first revealed Himself to Moshe Rabbeinu in the burning bush and instructed him to tell Bnei Yisrael that they would soon be redeemed, Moshe asked Him, "Behold, when I come to Bnei Yisrael and say to them, 'The God of your forefathers has sent me to you,' and they say to me, 'What is His Name?' — what shall I say to them (*Shemos* 3:13)?"

Hashem answered, "So shall you say to Bnei Yisrael, "א-ה-י-ה, *I Shall Be* has sent me to you" (ibid. 3:14).

Rashbam explains that the Name א-ה-י-ה is a variation of י-ה-ו-ה which means *He Shall Be.* We refer to Hashem in the third person form, and He refers to Himself in the first person.

The Name י-ה-ו-ה represents Hashem's Attribute of Mercy. The same is true of א-ה-י-ה. This Name is the key to our redemption. The Name א-ה-י-ה was first revealed during the Exodus, yet it will be fully revealed only when the final Redemption arrives. Hashem told Moshe Rabbeinu to inform Bnei Yisrael, "א-ה-י-ה sent me to you," assuring them that despite the terrible darkness of their slavery, they must not despair. They would not be forced to carry the burden of slavery forever. The Redemption was soon to occur — "א-ה-י-ה sent me to you."

This same message is a beacon of hope for us in our present Exile. It has given us strength to persevere through these thousands of years of hardship and affliction, as we wander from one county to another, subject to the mockery and abuse of the nations that surround us. We stand proud in our faith in Hashem, and our

the Parts, as it is stated: "He said to Avram: Know with certainty that your offspring will be aliens in a land not their own, they will serve them, and they will oppress

---

assurance that He will be with us throughout all our hardships. We raise our eyes to Hashem with hope and faith that He will soon redeem us, and we pray to him three times each day that the Divine Presence should soon return to Zion with mercy.

We recognize that exile is a decree from Heaven, and that the righteous are not meant to experience tranquility in this world. Nevertheless, we know that there will be an end to our travails. Hashem is with us, as He was with our forefathers in Egypt. "*I Shall Be as I Shall Be*," as *Rashi* explains: "I will be with them in future exiles, as I was with them in Egypt."

The Jewish people find strength in this knowledge, and in the recognition that this world is like a fleeting dream. It is only an entrance room leading into the palace that awaits us in the World to Come. Therefore, the suffering of exile in this world should not make us sink into despondency.

→〓◎〓←

Before Yaakov Avinu died, he instructed his children, "Assemble yourselves and I will tell you what will befall you in the End of Days" (*Bereishis* 49:1). *Rashi* explains that he wished to reveal the קֵץ, end (i.e., the date of the final Redemption), to the tribes, but the Divine Presence departed from him, and he was unable to reveal it.

R' Shimshon of Ostropoli explains that Yaakov knew that the exile of his children in Egypt was a punishment for their sale of Yosef,[1] which caused a blemish in Hashem's Name א-ה-י-ה. Only nine brothers were involved in the sale, since Reuven and Binyamin were not present at the time of the sale. Yaakov reasoned that since the product of nine (tribes) multiplied by the *gematria* (numerical value) of א-ה-י-ה (21) is 189, his descendants would be forced to endure 189 years of exile, and they would be redeemed in the 190th year — which is the *gematria* of קֵץ. When *Rashi* says that Yaakov wished to reveal the קֵץ, he means that Yaakov wanted to tell the tribes that they would be redeemed in the 190th year.

Yaakov failed to realize, however, that the nine tribes present decided to impose a *cheirem* (ban of excommunication) on anyone who would reveal the story of the sale of Yosef, and in order to do so

---

1. As discussed in the Midrash and the writings of the *Arizal*. See *Ohr Hachaim, Parashas Vayechi.*

אֹתָם, אַרְבַּע מֵאוֹת שָׁנָה. וְגַם אֶת הַגּוֹי אֲשֶׁר יַעֲבֹדוּ דָן אָנֹכִי, וְאַחֲרֵי כֵן יֵצְאוּ בִּרְכֻשׁ גָּדוֹל.[1]

The matzos are covered and the cups lifted as the following paragraph
is proclaimed joyously. Upon its conclusion, the cups are
put down and the matzos are uncovered.

וְהִיא שֶׁעָמְדָה לַאֲבוֹתֵינוּ וְלָנוּ, שֶׁלֹּא אֶחָד בִּלְבָד עָמַד עָלֵינוּ לְכַלּוֹתֵנוּ. אֶלָּא שֶׁבְּכָל דּוֹר וָדוֹר עוֹמְדִים עָלֵינוּ לְכַלּוֹתֵנוּ, וְהַקָּדוֹשׁ בָּרוּךְ הוּא מַצִּילֵנוּ מִיָּדָם.

---

they needed a quorum of ten. They decided to include the Divine Presence to round out the quorum. Hashem told Yaakov that the exile would actually last 210 years, and Yaakov did not understand why, because "the Divine Presence departed from him" — i.e., he did not realize that the Jews would have to remain in exile for an additional 21 years to atone for including the Divine Presence in their plot.

When Hashem appeared to Moshe in the burning bush as the 210th year drew near, Moshe made a similar mathematical miscalculation. Moshe knew that there were ten participants in Yosef's sale, but he thought that they had caused a blemish in the Name י-ה-ו-ה, not א-ה-י-ה, and they would therefore have to remain in exile for 260 years (10 participants, multiplied by 26, the *gematria* of י-ה-ו-ה).

When Moshe turned to investigate the amazing sight of the burning bush, the Torah states, "וַיַּרְא ה' כִּי סָר לִרְאוֹת, *Hashem saw that he [Moshe] turned aside to see*" (*Shemos* 3:4).

Simply understood, this verse means that Hashem saw that Moshe took the time to investigate this wondrous sight. On a deeper level, however, it means that Hashem saw that Moshe was under the mistaken impression that the exile would last for an amount of years equivalent to the word סָר. Hashem informed Moshe that he was wrong — the exile was determined based on the Name א-ה-י-ה, not י-ה-ו-ה, and the Redemption that Moshe thought was 50 years away was actually imminent.

וְאַחֲרֵי כֵן יֵצְאוּ בִּרְכֻשׁ גָּדוֹל
Afterward they shall leave with great possessions.

On the eve of the Exodus from Egypt, Hashem tells Moshe, "*Please* speak in the ears of the people: Let each man request of

them four hundred years; but also upon the nation which they shall serve will I execute judgment, and afterward they shall leave with great possessions."[1]

The matzos are covered and the cups lifted as the following paragraph is proclaimed joyously. Upon its conclusion, the cups are put down and the matzos are uncovered.

It is this that has stood by our fathers and us. For not only one has risen against us to annihilate us, but in every generation they rise against us to annihilate us. But the Holy One, Blessed is He, rescues us from their hand.

---

(1) *Bereishis* 15:13-14.

---

his fellow and each woman from her fellow silver vessels and gold vessels" (*Shemos* 11:2).

Rashi explains that Hashem did not want Avraham Avinu to complain that He had fulfilled the prophecy of "They [the Jews] will serve them [the Egyptians] and they will oppress them — four hundred years," but not the accompanying pledge, "Afterward they shall leave with great wealth" (*Bereishis* 15:14-15).

Rashi's explanation is perplexing.

Chazal (*Bamidbar Rabbah* 13:20) tell us that the treasures removed from the bodies of the Egyptians who had drowned in the Yam Suf were far more valuable than those taken from Egypt. Why was it necessary to request valuables of the Egyptians if the promise, "Afterward they shall leave with great wealth," would be fulfilled at the Yam Suf?

Moreover, *Rashi* implies that Hashem only wanted Bnei Yisrael to request valuables from the Egyptians to prevent Avraham Avinu from complaining that His promise had not been fulfilled. Hashem certainly would not renege on a promise, even if Avraham Avinu would not complain!

It would seem that one question answers the other. Bnei Yisrael did not need the riches they took from Egypt; they would end up receiving all of Egypt's valuables at the Yam Suf either way. Yet Hashem did not want Avraham to see his children leaving Egypt empty-handed and think — even for a moment — that Hashem had not fulfilled His promise. Hashem instructed Bnei Yisrael to take riches from Egypt to avoid causing His beloved servant Avraham to be disappointed, even if that disappointment would not last long.

צֵא וּלְמַד מַה בִּקֵּשׁ לָבָן הָאֲרַמִּי לַעֲשׂוֹת לְיַעֲקֹב אָבִינוּ, שֶׁפַּרְעֹה לֹא גָזַר אֶלָּא עַל הַזְּכָרִים, וְלָבָן בִּקֵּשׁ לַעֲקוֹר אֶת הַכֹּל. שֶׁנֶּאֱמַר:

צֵא וּלְמַד מַה בִּקֵּשׁ לָבָן הָאֲרַמִּי
Go and learn what Lavan the Aramean attempted

Why do we mention Lavan in the Haggadah, which focuses primarily on the Exodus?

This passage expands on a statement made in the previous one: "In every generation they rise against us to annihilate us."

We mention Lavan here to indicate that throughout our history, two forms of destruction threaten our existence: physical annihilation and spiritual destruction.

Pharaoh subjected us to both threats. He decreed that all male children be drowned, thus threatening our physical existence, and he also wanted to prevent us from serving Hashem. This is why we conclude *Maggid* with a blessing, in which we thank Hashem "for our redemption and for the liberation of our souls."

Lavan tried to uproot us, not by trying to annihilate us in a physical sense, but by attempting to influence Yaakov and his children to become idolaters.

We find these two threats reappearing time and again throughout our history. Haman tried to eradicate the Jewish nation in a physical sense. The Greeks tried to put an end to our spiritual existence by preventing us from learning Torah and fulfilling Hashem's mitzvos.

When Yaakov's sons asked him to send Binyamin to Egypt with them, Yaakov cried, "I am the one whom you bereaved! Yosef is gone, Shimon is gone, and now you would take away Binyamin? עָלַי הָיוּ כֻלָּנָה, *Upon me has it all fallen!"* (Bereishis 42:36).

The Vilna Gaon[1] notes that years earlier, when Yaakov was afraid to pose as Eisav to claim his father's blessings lest his father curse him instead of blessing him, Rivkah assured him, עָלַי קִלְלָתְךָ בְּנִי, *Your curse be upon me, my son"* (Bereishis 27:13).

The word עָלַי is and acronym for Eisav, Lavan, and Yosef (עֵשָׂו, לָבָן, יוֹסֵף). Rivkah foresaw that there was an unavoidable Heavenly decree that Yaakov would have to deal with three difficulties in life — those of Eisav, Lavan, and Yosef.

When the tribes wanted to take Binyamin to Egypt, Yaakov ex-

---

1. See also *Teshuvos Zayis Ra'anan*, end of vol. 2.

Go and learn what Lavan the Aramean attempted to do to our father Yaakov! For Pharaoh decreed only against the males, and Lavan attempted to uproot everything, as it is said:

---

claimed, "עָלַי הָיוּ כֻלָּנָה!" I have already suffered through the difficulties of Eisav, Lavan, and Yosef. I don't have to face the trial of being bereft of Binyamin. (Yaakov did not realize that this was not a trial, but a salvation from the loss of Yosef.)

Ramban (Introduction to *Shemos*) writes that the events in the lives of our forefathers are symbolic; they foretell the future of the Jewish people.

Yaakov had to face the tests of Eisav, Lavan, and Yosef, and so must we. Eisav wanted to murder Yaakov, and we have faced similar threats from various nations in the course of history. Lavan tried to sever our connection to the Torah and mitzvos, and several nations have tried to follow his lead.

The trial of Yosef is even worse than those of Eisav and Lavan. Yosef was sold as a result of strife and baseless hatred between brothers. The conflicts that tear our nation apart are more destructive than the harshest decrees that others can impose upon us.

We witness manifestations of these three trials in our own times, as well. First came Hitler and the Nazis *ym"s*. Like Pharaoh and Eisav, they sought to obliterate our nation. When they were defeated, Stalin and the Bolsheviks followed in the footsteps of Lavan and the Greeks by trying to prevent us from studying Torah and observing mitzvos.

Thanks to Hashem's infinite mercy, we have survived both of these trials. The Jewish nation lives on and prevails, battered but enduring.

We are now in the midst of facing the most difficult challenge of all, a trial similar to the trial of Yosef. The baseless hatred that caused the destruction of the Beis Hamikdash and brought untold suffering upon us continues to plague us. Hashem does not save us from the battle against inner conflict, for it is our task to defeat it. When we succeed in uprooting this terrible trait from our nation and leave no trace of it behind, we will be able to come together in love and unity, and then our enemies will have no power over us.

.⊹⇒◎⇐⊹.

When and how did Lavan attempt to destroy our nation?

אֲרַמִּי אֹבֵד אָבִי, וַיֵּרֶד מִצְרַיְמָה וַיָּגָר שָׁם בִּמְתֵי מְעָט, וַיְהִי שָׁם לְגוֹי, גָּדוֹל עָצוּם וָרָב.[1] וַיֵּרֶד מִצְרַיְמָה – אָנוּס עַל פִּי הַדִּבּוּר.

Tzror Hamor (*Parashas Vayeitzei*) writes that Lavan wanted to use words to destroy Yaakov, by placing some sort of spell upon him. Hashem stopped Lavan in his tracks, telling him, "Beware, lest you speak with Yaakov" (*Bereishis* 31:25).

Sefer Hayashar (ibid.) states that Lavan sent messengers to Eisav, asking him to kill Yaakov.

Others explain that Lavan tried to destroy our nation by attempting to poison Avraham's servant Eliezer when he came to find a bride for Yitzchak. How would Eliezer's death destroy our nation?

The Talmud (*Nazir* 11b-12a) tells us that if a person appoints an agent to choose a woman and betroth her on his behalf and the agent dies while away, the sender cannot marry any woman in the world, because the agent may have betrothed her relative to him. Had Lavan been successful in killing Eliezer, Yitzchak could never have married, and Yaakov would never have been born.

The simplest explanation is that Lavan tried to destroy the Jewish people by trying to persuade Yaakov to stay in his home — "Your daughters are my daughters and your sons are my sons" (*Bereishis* 31:43). It is only when we are apart from Lavan and the rest of the world that we can exist: "It is a nation that will dwell in solitude and not be reckoned among the nations" (*Bamidbar* 23:9).

אֲרַמִּי אֹבֵד אָבִי
An Aramean tried to destroy my father

We can deduce from the Mishnah (*Pesachim* 116a) that we cannot simply read the passage cited from the Torah (*Devarim* 26:5-8), beginning with, "An Aramean tried to destroy my forefather." We have to spend time expounding these verses to extract all the information about the exile in Egypt that cannot be discerned through a superficial reading of the verse.

Thus we find that the author of the Haggadah emphasizes the symbolism hidden in each word of these verses, showing their connection to the terrible suffering we endured in Egypt, and the great miracles we experienced during the Redemption.

The need to delve into this passage is also apparent from the *Rambam* (*Hilchos Chametz U'Matzah* 7:4): "One must expound on

"An Aramean tried to destroy my father, and he descended to Egypt and sojourned there, with few people; and there he became a nation — great, mighty, and numerous."[1]

And he descended to Egypt — compelled by Divine decree.

_____
(1) *Devarim* 26:5.

---

the passage, 'An Aramean tried to destroy my forefather'; one who discusses this passage at length is praiseworthy."

וַיְהִי שָׁם לְגוֹי, גָּדוֹל עָצוּם וָרָב

There he became a nation — great, mighty, and numerous.

The Torah tells us that the Jewish midwives, Shifrah and Puah, defied Pharaoh's direct order and helped the Jewish women deliver their babies. What was their reward? The Torah states, "God benefited the midwives, and the people increased and became very strong" (*Shemos* 1:20).

Why was the proliferation of the Jewish people considered a reward for the midwives?

Ohr Hachaim explains that a person is rewarded not only for the performance of a good deed, but also for indirect consequences of that deed.

The midwives were rewarded not only for the children they delivered, but for all the descendants of those children as well. The Torah emphasizes the exponential growth of the Jewish people to teach us that the reward of the midwives increased accordingly.

In a similar vein, my *rebbi*, the Klausenberger Rebbe *zt"l*, quoted the Chafetz Chaim as saying that the *rebbi* who taught Torah to Leon Trotsky as a child will have to account for the millions of Jewish souls that were torn away from their heritage by the Communist Party that Trotsky helped found. Had Trotsky's *rebbi* applied himself towards the young "Leibele's" education, he would never have dropped to the spiritual nadir that he did.

The Talmud (*Sotah* 11a; *Sanhedrin* 100b) tells us that Hashem rewards on a scale five hundred times greater than the scale by which he punishes. If Trotsky's *rebbi* was responsible for the suffering that came as a result of his laxity, then the midwives were certainly deserving of reward for all of the generations of Jews that came into the world because of them.

וַיָּגָר שָׁם – מְלַמֵּד שֶׁלֹּא יָרַד יַעֲקֹב אָבִינוּ לְהִשְׁתַּקֵּעַ בְּמִצְרַיִם, אֶלָּא לָגוּר שָׁם. שֶׁנֶּאֱמַר, וַיֹּאמְרוּ אֶל פַּרְעֹה, לָגוּר בָּאָרֶץ בָּאנוּ, כִּי אֵין מִרְעֶה לַצֹּאן אֲשֶׁר לַעֲבָדֶיךָ, כִּי כָבֵד הָרָעָב בְּאֶרֶץ כְּנַעַן, וְעַתָּה יֵשְׁבוּ נָא עֲבָדֶיךָ בְּאֶרֶץ גֹּשֶׁן.[1]

בִּמְתֵי מְעָט – כְּמָה שֶׁנֶּאֱמַר, בְּשִׁבְעִים נֶפֶשׁ יָרְדוּ אֲבֹתֶיךָ מִצְרָיְמָה, וְעַתָּה שָׂמְךָ יהוה אֱלֹהֶיךָ כְּכוֹכְבֵי הַשָּׁמַיִם לָרֹב.[2]

וַיְהִי שָׁם לְגוֹי – מְלַמֵּד שֶׁהָיוּ יִשְׂרָאֵל מְצֻיָּנִים שָׁם.

גָּדוֹל עָצוּם – כְּמָה שֶׁנֶּאֱמַר, וּבְנֵי יִשְׂרָאֵל פָּרוּ וַיִּשְׁרְצוּ וַיִּרְבּוּ וַיַּעַצְמוּ בִּמְאֹד מְאֹד, וַתִּמָּלֵא הָאָרֶץ אֹתָם.[3]

וָרָב – כְּמָה שֶׁנֶּאֱמַר, רְבָבָה כְּצֶמַח הַשָּׂדֶה נְתַתִּיךְ, וַתִּרְבִּי וַתִּגְדְּלִי וַתָּבֹאִי בַּעֲדִי עֲדָיִים, שָׁדַיִם נָכֹנוּ וּשְׂעָרֵךְ צִמֵּחַ, וְאַתְּ עֵרֹם וְעֶרְיָה: וָאֶעֱבֹר עָלַיִךְ וָאֶרְאֵךְ מִתְבּוֹסֶסֶת בְּדָמָיִךְ, וָאֹמַר לָךְ, בְּדָמַיִךְ חֲיִי, וָאֹמַר לָךְ, בְּדָמַיִךְ חֲיִי.[4]

בְּדָמַיִךְ חֲיִי
Through your blood shall you live

Chazal (Yalkut Shimoni, Parashas Bo, 195) cite this verse as proof that we were redeemed from Egypt in the merit of the two kinds of blood.

Rashi (Shemos 12:6) explains that when the time had come for Hashem to fulfill His promise to Avraham Avinu and redeem Bnei Yisrael from Egypt, we had no merit by which to be redeemed. Hashem commanded us to perform the mitzvos of *Korban Pesach* and *Bris Milah* to provide us with merits by which to be redeemed.

Upon closer inspection we find that there are actually four kinds

He sojourned there — this teaches that our father Yaakov did not descend to Egypt to settle, but only to sojourn temporarily, as it says: "They (the sons of Yaakov) said to Pharaoh: We have come to sojourn in this land because there is no pasture for the flocks of your servants, because the famine is severe in the Land of Canaan. And now, please let your servants dwell in the land of Goshen."[1]

With few people — as it is written: "With seventy persons, your forefathers descended to Egypt, and now HASHEM, your God, has made you as numerous as the stars of heaven."[2]

There he became a nation — this teaches that the Israelites were distinctive there.

Great, mighty — as it says: "And Bnei Yisrael were fruitful, increased greatly, multiplied, and became very, very mighty; and the land was filled with them."[3]

Numerous — as it says: "I made you as numerous as the plants of the field; you grew and developed, and became charming, beautiful of figure; your hair grown long; but you were naked and bare. And I passed over you and saw you downtrodden in your blood and I said to you: Through your blood shall you live! And I said to you: Through your blood shall you live!"[4]

---

(1) *Bereishis* 47:4. (2) *Devarim* 10:22.
(3) *Shemos* 1:7. (4) *Yechezkel* 16:7,6.

---

of blood mentioned in this verse. The word דָּמַיִךְ is a plural form of the word, meaning "your bloods," and it appears twice in the verse: "By your blood(s) you shall live; by your blood(s) you shall live."

When we look at this verse in context, it appears that the blood of the *Korban Pesach* and the *Bris Milah* are both referred to in the second half of the verse, and the first half refers to a different form of blood entirely — it refers to the Jewish blood that has been spilled throughout our history.

The verses that lead up to this verse express the hardship that the Jewish people endure. We are compared to a baby who is born with

וַיָּרֵעוּ אֹתָנוּ הַמִּצְרִים, וַיְעַנּוּנוּ, וַיִּתְּנוּ עָלֵינוּ עֲבֹדָה קָשָׁה.[1]

וַיָּרֵעוּ אֹתָנוּ הַמִּצְרִים – כְּמָה שֶׁנֶּאֱמַר, הָבָה נִתְחַכְּמָה לוֹ, פֶּן יִרְבֶּה, וְהָיָה כִּי תִקְרֶאנָה מִלְחָמָה, וְנוֹסַף גַּם הוּא עַל שֹׂנְאֵינוּ, וְנִלְחַם בָּנוּ, וְעָלָה מִן הָאָרֶץ.[2]

וַיְעַנּוּנוּ – כְּמָה שֶׁנֶּאֱמַר, וַיָּשִׂימוּ עָלָיו שָׂרֵי מִסִּים, לְמַעַן עַנֹּתוֹ בְּסִבְלֹתָם, וַיִּבֶן עָרֵי מִסְכְּנוֹת לְפַרְעֹה, אֶת פִּתֹם וְאֶת רַעַמְסֵס.[3]

---

no one to tend to its basic needs: "On the day you were born your umbilical cord was not cut, nor were you washed with water to smooth [your skin], nor were you salted, nor were you swaddled. No one pitied you to do any one of these things for you, to show you compassion; you were cast out upon the open field because of the loathsomeness of your being, on the day you were born. Then I passed before you and saw you wallowing in your blood, and I said to you, 'In your blood you shall live'; I said to you, 'In your blood you shall live'" (Yechezkel 16: 4-6).

The expression, "By your blood you shall live," is repeated to include the two forms of blood by which the Jewish people are known. The first is the blood of our hardship and affliction. The second is the blood of our noble mission in this world, the blood of the korbanos and Bris Milah.

It is the unfathomable will of the Creator that His beloved children must endure persecution, harsh decrees, and exile. Our destiny in this world is one of bloodshed, which at times cannot be escaped by any means. During the Holocaust, the pious and righteous were slaughtered together with heretics who had no affiliation with their Jewish heritage. No person can escape the destiny that was chosen for his nation by the Creator and Conductor of the world.

Aside from the suffering that the Jewish people endure, we are distinguished by another characteristic: our sense of purpose in the world, our fine character traits, and our loyal adherence to Torah and mitzvos, symbolized by the blood of the Korban Pesach and Bris Milah.

When Bnei Yisrael built the Mishkan in the desert, they made a

‘‘The Egyptians did evil to us and afflicted us; and imposed hard labor upon us.’’[1]

The Egyptians did evil to us — as it says: ‘‘Let us deal with them wisely lest they multiply and, if we happen to be at war, they may join our enemies and fight against us and then leave the country.’’[2]

And they afflicted us — as it says: ‘‘They set tax-collectors over them in order to oppress them with their burdens; and they built Pisom and Raamses as treasure cities for Pharaoh.’’[3]

---

(1) *Devarim* 26:6. (2) *Shemos* 1:10. (3) Ibid. 1:11.

---

central support beam, called the *bariach hatichon*, which went through the *kerashim* (upright beams) on all three sides, joining and supporting them. The commentaries debate what the *bariach hatichon* was made out of. *Da'as Zekeinim* (*Shemos* 25:5) states that it was made out of the staff with which Yaakov Avinu crossed the Jordan River when he fled from his brother Eisav. *Targum Yonasan* (*Shemos* 26:28) suggests that it was made from the tree planted by Avraham Avinu to provide shade for his guests as they rested and enjoyed his hospitality.

Yaakov's staff represents the destiny of Bnei Yisrael. His children must endure affliction in their exile, just as he was forced into exile, penniless and persecuted, owning nothing but the staff that he held. Avraham's tree represents the purpose and unique mission of Bnei Yisrael. It represents Avraham Avinu's trademark of kindness and hospitality, through which he sanctified Hashem's Name in the world.

וַיָּשִׂימוּ עָלָיו שָׂרֵי מִסִּים
They set tax-collectors over them

Every country collects taxes from its citizens, and Jewish citizens are obligated to pay the taxes of their respective countries faithfully, in keeping with the principle of *Dina demalchusa dina* (the laws of the land are binding under Torah law; see *Nedarim* 28a et al.). What right did we have, then, to complain about the taxes levied upon us by the Egyptians?

Taxes that are collected by a government in order to finance projects for the benefit of its people are just and fair taxes, and the Torah obligates us to pay them. But Pharaoh and the wicked Egyptians did not subject the Jewish people to taxes because they

וַיִּתְּנוּ עָלֵינוּ עֲבֹדָה קָשָׁה - כְּמָה שֶׁנֶּאֱמַר,
וַיַּעֲבִדוּ מִצְרַיִם אֶת בְּנֵי יִשְׂרָאֵל בְּפָרֶךְ.¹

וַנִּצְעַק אֶל יהוה אֱלֹהֵי אֲבֹתֵינוּ, וַיִּשְׁמַע יהוה
אֶת קֹלֵנוּ, וַיַּרְא אֶת עָנְיֵנוּ, וְאֶת
עֲמָלֵנוּ, וְאֶת לַחֲצֵנוּ.²

---

needed our money. They did so only to afflict us, as we see in this
verse. Such taxes are unjustified.

וַיַּעֲבִדוּ מִצְרַיִם אֶת בְּנֵי יִשְׂרָאֵל בְּפָרֶךְ
The Egyptians subjugated Bnei Yisrael with hard labor.

Moshe Rabbeinu was instructed to console Bnei Yisrael with two
assurances of their imminent salvation: (1) "So shall you say to Bnei
Yisrael, 'Hashem, the God of your forefathers, the God of Avraham,
the God of Yitzchak, and the God of Yaakov, has dispatched me to
you. This is My Name forever, and this is My remembrance from
generation to generation'" (*Shemos* 3:15), and (2) "Go and gather the
elders of Israel and say to them... I have surely remembered you
and what is done to you in Egypt" (Ibid. 3:16).

These two assurances appear to have been directed at two different segments of Jewish society. To the simple Jews, Moshe spoke
words of encouragement, to prevent them from despairing of ever
being freed from their grueling labor. Moshe told them in Hashem's
Name, "This is My Name forever, and this is My remembrance from
generation to generation." In doing so, Moshe used the Name
ה-י-ה-א, *I Shall Be*, the meaning of which is, "I will be with you in
this exile, as I will be with you in future exiles."

To the elders and spiritually uplifted members of Bnei Yisrael,
Moshe felt no need to mention the ultimate Redemption. They had a
tradition from their ancestors that Hashem would redeem us from the
final exile in the End of Days, and they had full faith that He would do
so. Moshe only needed to encourage them concerning their present
exile, assuring them that the Exodus was imminent. To them he said,
"I have remembered you and what has been done to you in Egypt."

אֶת עָנְיֵנוּ, וְאֶת עֲמָלֵנוּ, וְאֶת לַחֲצֵנוּ
Our affliction, our travail, and our oppression.

This verse refers to three different forms of hardship Bnei Yisrael

They imposed hard labor upon us — as it says: "The Egyptians subjugated Bnei Yisrael with hard labor."[1]

"We cried out to HASHEM, the God of our fathers; and HASHEM heard our voice and saw our affliction, our travail, and our oppression."[2]

---

(1) *Shemos* 1:13. (2) *Devarim* 26:7.

---

suffered from in Egypt: עָנְיֵנוּ, *our affliction*; עֲמָלֵנוּ, *our travail*, and לַחֲצֵנוּ, *our oppression*.

A slave generally suffers from three distinct hardships: he is afflicted by the loss of personal freedom and the stigma of being a slave; he is required to engage in backbreaking physical labor; and he is usually subject to degrading treatment from his master.

Bnei Yisrael in Egypt suffered all these forms of hardship. We were redeemed when Hashem saw our affliction, our difficult labors, and the humiliation of our oppression.

וַנִּצְעַק אֶל ה'
We cried out to Hashem

When Bnei Yisrael stood at the Yam Suf, with the raging sea before them and their Egyptian pursuers approaching from behind, they cried out to Hashem for help. "Why do you cry out to Me?" Hashem asked Moshe. "Speak to Bnei Yisrael, and let them journey forth!" (*Shemos* 14:15). With Nachshon ben Aminadav in the lead, the entire nation marched into the Yam Suf, and the sea split before them.

Mechilta (*Beshalach* 3) comments on this verse:

> Hashem told Moshe, "My children are in distress and you stand before Me in lengthy prayer? Why do you cry to Me?"
>
> R' Eliezer derives from here that there are times for lengthy prayers and times for hurried prayers. Moshe Rabbeinu's prayer for his sister Miriam's recovery was "Please, God, heal her now (*Bamidbar* 12:13)." Those circumstances called for a hurried prayer. When Bnei Yisrael sinned with the Golden Calf, Moshe Rabbeinu prayed for their forgiveness for forty days and nights. Those circumstances called for lengthy prayers."

Similarly, *Sifri* (*Parashas Beha'alosecha*) states, "R' Eliezer's students asked him how long a person's prayers should be. He answered that one should not pray for more time than Moshe Rabbeinu, who prayed for forty days and forty nights; and one

וַנִּצְעַק אֶל יהוה אֱלֹהֵי אֲבֹתֵינוּ – כְּמָה
שֶׁנֶּאֱמַר, וַיְהִי בַיָּמִים הָרַבִּים הָהֵם וַיָּמָת מֶלֶךְ
מִצְרַיִם, וַיֵּאָנְחוּ בְנֵי יִשְׂרָאֵל מִן הָעֲבֹדָה, וַיִּזְעָקוּ,
וַתַּעַל שַׁוְעָתָם אֶל הָאֱלֹהִים מִן הָעֲבֹדָה.[1]

---

should not pray a shorter prayer than Moshe Rabbeinu did when he
prayed, 'Please, God, heal her.' "

A similar discussion is also found in the Talmud (*Berachos* 34a).

Our Sages teach us that there are times for lengthy prayers, and
times for hurried prayers, but they do not tell us when to engage in
each form of prayer. How did Moshe Rabbeinu decide when each
type of prayer was appropriate?

My *rebbi*, the Klausenberger Rebbe *zt"l*, would often quote R'
Pinchas of Koritz as saying that when a person finds himself in grave
danger, he cannot rely only on prayer; he must also have *bitachon*
that Hashem will make things turn out right. When Bnei Yisrael were
stuck between the sea and the Egyptians, Hashem admonished
Moshe Rabbeinu for praying, because the correct response in such
a situation was to demonstrate faith in Hashem: "Speak to Bnei
Yisrael, and let them journey forth!"

We learn from here that *bitachon* has the power to complement
prayer.

The power of prayer lies in its ability to open the gates of Divine
blessing, and draw through them an abundance of Heavenly mercy
and lovingkindness. *Rashba* (*Teshuvos* 5:51) explains that the word
berachah (blessing) comes from the same root as *bereichah* — a
reservoir. Just as a reservoir contains vast quantities of water, Hashem's *berachos* are an endless reservoir of mercy and lovingkindness, and our prayers and blessings are the pipelines via which we
can draw those *berachos*.

The same *berachos* can be drawn through *bitachon*.

Based on this concept, we can understand why Moshe Rabbeinu
did not need to pray at length for Miriam. The righteous Miriam
certainly had *bitachon* in Hashem's ability to heal her, and that
bitachon complemented Moshe's brief prayer. When Moshe prayed
that Hashem forgive Bnei Yisrael for the sin of the Golden Calf, he
could not rely on *bitachon* complementing his prayer, because Bnei
Yisrael's actions had demonstrated that their *bitachon* in Hashem
was far from perfect. Moshe had to rely entirely on his prayer, and
therefore needed to pray at length.

We cried out to HASHEM, the God of our fathers —
as it says: "It happened in the course of those many
days that the king of Egypt died; and Bnei Yisrael
groaned because of the servitude and cried; their cry
because of the servitude rose up to God."[1]

(1) *Shemos* 2:23.

When Hashem told Moshe Rabbeinu not to cry out to Him in
prayer, but to instruct Bnei Yisrael to march into the sea, they were
given a choice. If they would have complete faith in Hashem and
march fearlessly into the sea in keeping with His command, then the
power of their *bitachon* would create a miraculous salvation on their
behalf even with a minimal amount of prayer.

Alternatively, we can suggest that Bnei Yisrael were in fact unworthy of salvation, because they had demonstrated a lack of
bitachon by complaining, "Were there no graves in Egypt that you
took us to die in the Wilderness?" (*Shemos* 14:11). To merit salvation, they had to repent for their lack of *bitachon* by demonstrating
an equal level of *bitachon*. Hashem instructed Moshe not to cry out
to Him in prayer, but to lead Bnei Yisrael into the depths of the sea.
By following Hashem's orders, they displayed a level of *bitachon*
that atoned for their earlier lack thereof, and made them worthy of a
miraculous salvation.

וַיָּמָת מֶלֶךְ מִצְרַיִם, וַיֵּאָנְחוּ בְנֵי יִשְׂרָאֵל מִן הָעֲבֹדָה, וַיִּזְעָקוּ,
**The king of Egypt died; and Bnei Yisrael
groaned because of the servitude and cried**

Why did Bnei Yisrael wait until after Pharaoh died to cry out, and
how did his death intensify the difficulty of their servitude?

R' Itzele of Volozhin explains that as long as the first Pharaoh
lived, Bnei Yisrael anxiously awaited his death, hoping that it would
cause their situation to improve. They assumed that their sorrowful
state was the result of Pharaoh's terrible wickedness, and that when
he would die, a more merciful king would take his place. When
Pharaoh died and their condition did not improve in the least, they
realized that they had no hope but to daven for Hashem's mercy. It
was then that they began to cry out to Hashem.

My master and teacher, the Klausenberger Rebbe *zt"l*, would
often tell the story of a poor woman who came before the *Divrei
Chaim* of Sanz in tears. She told him that her son was sick, and asked
for his blessing that the child should have a complete recovery. The

וַיִּשְׁמַע יהוה אֶת קֹלֵנוּ – כְּמָה שֶׁנֶּאֱמַר, וַיִּשְׁמַע
אֱלֹהִים אֶת נַאֲקָתָם, וַיִּזְכֹּר אֱלֹהִים אֶת בְּרִיתוֹ אֶת
אַבְרָהָם, אֶת יִצְחָק, וְאֶת יַעֲקֹב.¹

Divrei Chaim told her that if she would give him one thousand *reinish* coins, he would assure her son's recovery. The woman pleaded with him to pray for her son without the requested payment, but the Rebbe was adamant; he would not pray unless she paid. In desperation and anguish, she cried out, "If the Rebbe won't help me, then Hashem will!"

The *Divrei Chaim*'s face lit up. "Finally!" the Rebbe exclaimed. "That is what I was waiting to hear. Now I can assure you that your son will merit a complete and speedy recovery." And recover he did.

As long as a person places his trust in human beings, he locks the gates of Heavenly mercy.

When the king of Egypt died, Bnei Yisrael finally understood that their situation was not determined by one king or another. They realized that they had nowhere else to turn but to their Father in Heaven. It was then that they cried out to Hashem and were saved.

⊷═◉═⊷

Rashi explains that Pharaoh was stricken with *tzaraas*,¹ and he would slaughter Jewish infants to bathe in their blood. If so, why does the verse state that they groaned because of their work? It should say that they groaned from the loss of their children!

Apparently, the loss of their children affected their attitude toward their work.

As long as a person has children and sees *nachas* from them, he can withstand tremendous difficulty. Jewish parents throughout the generations have adopted King David's stance: "Give Your judgments to the king, and Your righteousness to the king's son" (*Tehillim* 72:1). *Rashi* explains that David prayed that suffering should befall him alone, so that his son Shlomo would have a peaceful life. This feeling has become ingrained in our nation. Let us suffer, and let our children enjoy peace.

When the evil Pharaoh subjected Jewish children to his ruthless

---

1. The popular translation of *tzaraas* is 'leprosy.' R' Hirsch proves that this translation is incorrect, because *tzaraas* is not a physical disease, but a spiritual disease with physical manifestations.

And HASHEM heard our voice — as it says: "God heard their groaning, and God recalled His covenant with Avraham, with Yitzchak, and with Yaakov."[1]

_____

(1) *Shemos* 2:24.

_____

decree of mass murder, their parents could no longer bear their own affliction and difficult conditions. Broken in body and spirit, they cried out to Hashem for salvation.

וַיִּשְׁמַע ה' אֶת קֹלֵנוּ

And Hashem heard our voice

Interestingly, the verse states that, "Hashem heard קֹלֵנוּ, *our voice*." It does not say that He heard our prayers or our supplications, but that He heard our voice, implying a wordless call, similar to the call of the shofar.

The Midrash (*Devarim Rabbah* 2:1) tells us that Moshe Rabbeinu said to Hashem, "Master of the universe, when You see Your children in distress, and there is no one to pray for mercy on their behalf, answer them immediately."

Hashem answered, "Moshe, by your life I swear that whenever they call out to Me, I will answer them, as the verse states: 'Hashem our God is close to us whenever we call out to Him'" (*Devarim* 4:7).

This Midrash is perplexing. Moshe Rabbeinu requested Hashem's mercy for the times that there would be no one to cry out! How does Hashem's assurance that He would answer whenever we call out to Him fulfill Moshe's request?

Moshe's request is also somewhat paradoxical. Moshe asked that Hashem should *answer* when there would be no one to pray. If no one asks, whom should Hashem answer? Moshe should have requested that Hashem *save* them even if there is no one to beg for salvation.

The answers to these questions lie in the distinction between בַּקָשָׁה, request, and קְרִיאָה, crying out. When someone requests something, he articulates a specific request, which is on a higher level than someone who simply cries out for help.

The Talmud (*Bava Basra* 116a) teaches us that if a member of one's household becomes ill, he should ask a Torah scholar to pray for mercy on his behalf.

Nimukei Yosef specifies that one should ask the head of a yeshivah to pray for sick people, as was customary in France during the era of the *Rishonim*. We see that a person must be a Torah scholar in order to request Hashem's mercy properly. Calling out to Hashem,

וַיַּרְא אֶת עָנְיֵנוּ – זוֹ פְּרִישׁוּת דֶּרֶךְ אֶרֶץ,
כְּמָה שֶׁנֶּאֱמַר, וַיַּרְא אֱלֹהִים אֶת בְּנֵי יִשְׂרָאֵל, וַיֵּדַע
אֱלֹהִים.[1]

וְאֶת עֲמָלֵנוּ – אֵלּוּ הַבָּנִים, כְּמָה שֶׁנֶּאֱמַר,
כָּל הַבֵּן הַיִּלּוֹד הַיְאֹרָה תַּשְׁלִיכֻהוּ, וְכָל הַבַּת
תְּחַיּוּן.[2]

וְאֶת לַחֲצֵנוּ – זוֹ הַדְּחַק, כְּמָה שֶׁנֶּאֱמַר, וְגַם
רָאִיתִי אֶת הַלַּחַץ אֲשֶׁר מִצְרַיִם לֹחֲצִים אֹתָם.[3]

on the other hand, does not require any level of scholarliness. Even a simple person can call out to Hashem.

Moshe Rabbeinu prayed that in the times when there would be no Torah scholars to properly beseech Hashem to have mercy on the Jewish people, He should still hear the simple calls of the unlearned, and have mercy on His nation. And indeed, Hashem responded that He would listen to us whenever we cry out to Him.

This is also the meaning of the verse quoted here in the Haggadah. At the time, Bnei Yisrael were not on a high enough level to beseech Hashem articulately, but He heard our voice, our simple call for mercy.

כָּל הַבֵּן הַיִּלּוֹד הַיְאֹרָה תַּשְׁלִיכֻהוּ
Every son that is born you shall cast into the river

"The midwives feared God and they did not do as the king of Egypt spoke to them, and they caused the boys to live" (*Shemos* 1:17).

This verse implies that the midwives' fear of God prevented them from killing the baby boys in Egypt. Murdering innocent babies is an act of unspeakable cruelty. Only a person who is corrupt to the very depths of his or her soul could perpetrate so heinous a crime. Can we really consider it a given that a person who does not fear God will commit infanticide?

When Pharaoh instructed the midwives to kill the Jewish babies, the midwives knew that defying his order would be punishable by death. Nevertheless, they were willing to risk their own lives to save the baby boys. Such an act of self-sacrifice — risking one's own life to save another person's — can only come from true fear of God.

And He saw our affliction — that is the disruption of family life, as it says: "God saw Bnei Yisrael and God knew."[1]

Our travail — refers to the children, as it says: "Every son that is born you shall cast into the river, but every daughter you shall let live."[2]

Our oppression — refers to the pressure expressed in the words: "I have also seen how the Egyptians are oppressing them."[3]

---

(1) *Shemos* 2:25. (2) Ibid. 1:22. (3) Ibid. 3:9

A person may be a kindhearted and noble soul who would never dream of killing a baby, but who knows what choice he would make if he had to choose between his own life and that of an innocent baby? The only time we can be sure that a person will pass this test is if the person possesses true fear of God.

כָּל הַבֵּן הַיִּלּוֹד הַיְאֹרָה תַּשְׁלִיכֻהוּ, וְכָל הַבַּת תְּחַיּוּן

**Every son that is born you shall cast into the river,
but every daughter you shall let live.**

There seems to be a redundancy in this verse. If only the male children were thrown into the Nile, obviously the girls were saved. Why is it necessary to tell us that the girls were spared?

The cruel Pharaoh did not spare the girls because he had mercy on them. Rather, he spared them for his own evil motives. The Egyptians were known for their licentiousness, and they wanted to take the Jewish girls as wives (*Shemos Rabbah* 1:18). The Torah indicates that the girls were not *excluded* from Pharaoh's evil decree, but that he *spared* them with ulterior motives.

וְאֶת לַחֲצֵנוּ – זוֹ הַדְּחַק

Our oppression — refers to the pressure

Rabbeinu Bechaye (*Shemos* 3:9) quotes Rabbeinu Chananel's teaching that although the Jewish population exploded way beyond the seventy souls that descended to Egypt with Yaakov Avinu, the Egyptians did not allow them to settle outside Goshen. The "pressure" described in this verse refers to the terrible overcrowding caused by the presence of hundreds of thousands of people in an area — or more aptly, a ghetto — that was once inhabited by seventy people.

וַיּוֹצִאֵנוּ יהוה מִמִּצְרַיִם בְּיָד חֲזָקָה, וּבִזְרֹעַ
נְטוּיָה, וּבְמֹרָא גָּדֹל, וּבְאֹתוֹת
וּבְמֹפְתִים.[1]

וַיּוֹצִאֵנוּ יהוה מִמִּצְרַיִם – לֹא עַל יְדֵי מַלְאָךְ,
וְלֹא עַל יְדֵי שָׂרָף, וְלֹא עַל יְדֵי שָׁלִיחַ, אֶלָּא הַקָּדוֹשׁ
בָּרוּךְ הוּא בִּכְבוֹדוֹ וּבְעַצְמוֹ. שֶׁנֶּאֱמַר, וְעָבַרְתִּי
בְאֶרֶץ מִצְרַיִם בַּלַּיְלָה הַזֶּה, וְהִכֵּיתִי כָל בְּכוֹר
בְּאֶרֶץ מִצְרַיִם מֵאָדָם וְעַד בְּהֵמָה, וּבְכָל אֱלֹהֵי
מִצְרַיִם אֶעֱשֶׂה שְׁפָטִים, אֲנִי יהוה.[2]

וְעָבַרְתִּי בְאֶרֶץ מִצְרַיִם בַּלַּיְלָה הַזֶּה – אֲנִי וְלֹא
מַלְאָךְ. וְהִכֵּיתִי כָל בְּכוֹר בְּאֶרֶץ מִצְרַיִם – אֲנִי וְלֹא
שָׂרָף. וּבְכָל אֱלֹהֵי מִצְרַיִם אֶעֱשֶׂה שְׁפָטִים – אֲנִי וְלֹא
הַשָּׁלִיחַ. אֲנִי יהוה – אֲנִי הוּא, וְלֹא אַחֵר.

בְּיָד חֲזָקָה – זוֹ הַדֶּבֶר, כְּמָה שֶׁנֶּאֱמַר, הִנֵּה יַד
יהוה הוֹיָה בְּמִקְנְךָ אֲשֶׁר בַּשָּׂדֶה, בַּסּוּסִים בַּחֲמֹרִים
בַּגְּמַלִּים בַּבָּקָר וּבַצֹּאן, דֶּבֶר כָּבֵד מְאֹד.[3]

בְּיָד חֲזָקָה – זוֹ הַדֶּבֶר

With a mighty hand — refers to the pestilence

The Torah states that Hashem took us out of Egypt with a mighty
hand and an outstretched arm. On a simple level, this seems to refer
either to the entire process of the Exodus, through which Hashem
showed His Omnipotence. It could also refer to the harshest plague
— which we would assume to be the final plague, the death of the
firstborn. Why does the author of the Haggadah consider the plague
of pestilence a sign of Hashem's mighty hand more than all the
other plagues?

Torah Temimah explains that each of the plagues was called a
"finger of Hashem." Since pestilence was the fifth plague, it was the
"fifth finger," so to speak, representing the completion of Hashem's
hand, with which He struck Egypt.

"**H**ASHEM took us out of Egypt with a mighty hand and with an outstretched arm, with great awe, with signs and with wonders."[1]

HASHEM **took us out of Egypt** — not through an angel, not through a seraph, not through a messenger, but the Holy One, Blessed is He, in His glory, Himself, as it says: "I will pass through the land of Egypt on that night; I will slay all the firstborn in the land of Egypt from man to beast; and upon all the gods of Egypt will I execute judgments; I, HASHEM."[2]

"I will pass through the land of Egypt on that night" — I and no angel; "I will slay all the firstborn in the land of Egypt" — I and no seraph; "And upon all the gods of Egypt will I execute judgments" — I and no messenger; "I, HASHEM" — it is I and no other.

With a mighty hand — refers to the pestilence, as it says: "Behold, the hand of HASHEM shall strike your cattle which are in the field, the horses, the donkeys, the camels, the herds, and the flocks — a very severe pestilence."[3]

---

(1) *Devarim* 26:8. (2) *Shemos* 12:12. (3) Ibid. 9:3.

However, the verse refers to this plague as the *mighty* hand of Hashem, which implies that some unique aspect of His might was exhibited through the plague of pestilence.

Perhaps the pestilence mentioned here does not refer to the fifth of the ten plagues, but to a different plague that accompanied each of the plagues. The Midrash (*Shemos Rabbah* 10:2) tells us that each plague that befell Egypt was accompanied by pestilence, which was indeed a manifestation of Hashem's mighty hand.

In his commentary to the Haggadah, *Ritva* gives an explanation that follows the simple meaning of the words. He writes that the death of the firstborn was the culminatino of the plague of pestilence; pestilence affected animals, and death of the firstborn affected humans. Thus, concludes the *Ritva*, the pestilence is referred to as the "hand of Hashem" (*Shemos* 9:3), whereas the plague of the firstborn is called, "The *mighty* hand" (*Sifri* on *Devarim* 34:12).

וּבִזְרֹעַ נְטוּיָה – זוֹ הַחֶרֶב, כְּמָה שֶׁנֶּאֱמַר, וְחַרְבּוֹ שְׁלוּפָה בְּיָדוֹ, נְטוּיָה עַל יְרוּשָׁלָיִם.[1]

וּבְמֹרָא גָּדֹל – זוֹ גִּלּוּי שְׁכִינָה, כְּמָה שֶׁנֶּאֱמַר, אוֹ הֲנִסָּה אֱלֹהִים לָבוֹא לָקַחַת לוֹ גוֹי מִקֶּרֶב גּוֹי, בְּמַסֹּת, בְּאֹתֹת, וּבְמוֹפְתִים, וּבְמִלְחָמָה, וּבְיָד חֲזָקָה, וּבִזְרוֹעַ נְטוּיָה, וּבְמוֹרָאִים גְּדֹלִים, כְּכֹל אֲשֶׁר עָשָׂה לָכֶם יהוה אֱלֹהֵיכֶם בְּמִצְרַיִם לְעֵינֶיךָ.[2]

וּבְאֹתוֹת – זֶה הַמַּטֶּה, כְּמָה שֶׁנֶּאֱמַר, וְאֶת הַמַּטֶּה הַזֶּה תִּקַּח בְּיָדֶךָ, אֲשֶׁר תַּעֲשֶׂה בּוֹ אֶת הָאֹתֹת.[3]

וּבִזְרֹעַ נְטוּיָה – זוֹ הַחֶרֶב
With an outstretched arm — refers to the sword

The commentaries wonder what the author of the Haggadah's source was for this "sword," which we do not find mentioned in any of the plagues.

Some commentaries answer, citing *Tosafos* (*Shabbos* 87b, s.v. *V'oso*), that the Egyptian firstborns demanded that Pharaoh release Bnei Yisrael, for fear that Hashem would strike them with the final plague. When he refused, a civil war erupted, in which many Egyptian firstborns slew their parents with swords, as described in the verse, "To He Who struck the Egyptians with their firstborn, for His kindness is eternal" (*Tehillim* 136:10). The sword in the Haggadah refers to those used by the Egyptian firstborns.

Shibolei HaLeket (218) cites this explanation, and adds that the sword refers to Hashem's Name, which was called, "The sword of Moshe," because Moshe Rabbeinu used it to bring the plagues upon the Egyptians.

I believe I remember seeing another explanation in the writings of R' Avraham, son of the *Rambam*. He writes that all the suffering and misfortune that exist in the world can be grouped into two categories, symbolized by pestilence and the sword. Pestilence represents all forms of *internal* sickness and disease, and the sword represents tragedies that befall a person as a result of external circumstances. Thus we find in the rebuke in *Sefer Vayikra* (26:25), "I will bring *upon* you a sword of vengeance … and I will send

With an outstretched arm — refers to the sword, as it says: "His drawn sword in His hand, outstretched over Jerusalem."[1]

With great awe — alludes to the revelation of the *Shechinah*, as it says: "Has God ever attempted to take unto Himself a nation from the midst of another nation by trials, miraculous signs, and wonders, by war and with a mighty hand and outstretched arm and by awesome revelations, as all that HASHEM your God did for you in Egypt, before your eyes?"[2]

With signs — refers to the miracles performed with the staff as it says: "Take this staff in your hand, that you may perform the miraculous signs with it."[3]

---

(1) *I Divrei Hayamim* 21:16. (2) *Devarim* 4:34. (3) *Shemos* 4:17.

---

pestilence *within* you."

Similarly, when we pray in *Hashkiveinu* (recited after the evening *Shema*) that Hashem should protect us from pestilence and sword, pestilence represents all forms of death that are sent directly from Heaven, and the sword represents forms of death inflicted by people.

The ten plagues that struck Egypt included both forms of punishment. Some plagues caused sickness and disease; others brought about death and destruction. Therefore, the Haggadah mentions both pestilence and sword.

Alternatively, we can explain that Hashem's sword and outstretched arm refer to the ultimate Redemption. As we know, the Exodus was a model after which all subsequent redemptions were patterned. The hand of Hashem, which was outstretched to rescue us from Egypt, is still outstretched to strike and exact retribution from our enemies when Hashem determines that the time has come to redeem us from our exile and gather us back to our homeland, may it be speedily in our days.

וּבְאֹתוֹת – זֶה הַמַּטֶּה

With signs — refers to the miracles performed with the staff

When Hashem instructed Moshe to confront Pharaoh and warn him of the impending plagues, He said: "Go to Pharaoh in the morning — behold! he goes out to the water — and you shall stand opposite him at the River's bank, and the staff that was turned into a snake you shall take in your hand" (*Shemos* 7:15). Moshe

וּבְמֹפְתִים – זֶה הַדָּם, כְּמָה שֶׁנֶּאֱמַר, וְנָתַתִּי
מוֹפְתִים בַּשָּׁמַיִם וּבָאָרֶץ:[1]

As each of the words דָּם, *blood*, אֵשׁ, *fire*, and עָשָׁן, *smoke*, is said, a bit of wine is removed from the cup. [It is customary to remove the wine using the forefinger — which in Hebrew is called *etzba* — corresponding to the verse, "It is a finger (*etzba*) of God." One should not use his little finger to remove wine. According to some opinions he should toss the wine from the cup using his index finger. Others hold that he should not use his finger at all, but should instead pour the wine directly out of the cup. If one is easily disgusted by touching his food, he should follow the last opinion] (*Rema 473:7; Mishnah Berurah 74, Shaar HaTzion 81*), (*Minchas Asher*).

[1]. דָּם וָאֵשׁ וְתִמְרוֹת עָשָׁן.

דָּבָר אַחֵר – בְּיָד חֲזָקָה, שְׁתַּיִם. וּבִזְרֹעַ נְטוּיָה,
שְׁתַּיִם. וּבְמוֹרָא גָּדֹל, שְׁתַּיִם.
וּבְאֹתוֹת, שְׁתַּיִם. וּבְמֹפְתִים, שְׁתַּיִם.

אֵלּוּ עֶשֶׂר מַכּוֹת שֶׁהֵבִיא הַקָּדוֹשׁ בָּרוּךְ הוּא עַל
הַמִּצְרִים בְּמִצְרַיִם, וְאֵלּוּ הֵן:

---

confronted Pharaoh and said in Hashem's Name: "Through this shall you know that I am Hashem; behold, with the staff that is in my hand I shall strike the waters that are in the River, and they shall change to blood" (ibid. v. 17).

Why did Hashem emphasize that Moshe should take the staff that had turned into a snake? What implications did this have on the plague of blood? Furthermore, why did Moshe tell Pharaoh that he would strike the river with the stick that was in his hand in order to turn it into blood? Why did he have to tell Pharaoh how he would turn the water into blood?

We can answer these questions based on a concept discussed in *Pardes Yosef* (*Shemos* 7:35).

When Aharon's staff turned into a snake and swallowed the snakes that Pharaoh's sorcerers had produced, Pharaoh was unimpressed. True, sorcery cannot transform a lifeless stick into a living snake that can swallow staffs, but Pharaoh suspected that Moshe's staff had originally been a snake and Moshe used sorcery to disguise it as a staff. It is no wonder that a snake can swallow other snakes.

It was known, however, that sorcery is rendered powerless by

With wonders — alludes to the blood, as it says: "I will set wonders in the heavens and on the earth."[1]

As each of the words דָּם, *blood*, אֵשׁ, *fire*, and עָשָׁן, *smoke*, is said, a bit of wine is removed from the cup. [It is customary to remove the wine using the forefinger — which in Hebrew is called *etzba* — corresponding to the verse, "It is a finger (*etzba*) of God." One should not use his little finger to remove wine. According to some opinions he should toss the wine from the cup using his index finger. Others hold that he should not use his finger at all, but should instead pour the wine directly out of the cup. If one is easily disgusted by touching his food, he should follow the last opinion] (*Rema* 473:7; *Mishnah Berurah* 74, *Shaar HaTzion* 81), (*Minchas Asher*).

"Blood, fire, and columns of smoke."[1]

Another explanation of the preceding verse: [Each phrase represents two plagues,] hence: mighty hand — two; outstretched arm — two; great awe — two; signs — two; wonders — two.

These are the ten plagues which the Holy One, Blessed is He, brought upon the Egyptians in Egypt, namely:

---

(1) *Yoel* 3:3.

---

contact with water (see *Sanhedrin* 67b). When Moshe struck the water with his staff and it remained a staff, it proved to Pharaoh that it was truly a piece of wood, and its transformation into a snake that ate the snakes that his sorcerers had created was truly miraculous.

Hashem commanded Moshe to take the staff that had been transformed into a snake, and Moshe made it clear to Pharaoh that this was the very same staff that now touched the water, to prove that the events he was witnessing were miracles, not sorcery.

עֲשֶׂרֶת הַמַּכּוֹת — The Ten Plagues

The plagues served two functions: They served to punish the Egypt for their terrible cruelty, to shatter their feeling of power, and humble them; and they caused a firm, unwavering faith in Hashem to take root in the hearts of the Jewish people. Both of these functions are referred to in the verse, "So that you may relate in the ears of your son and your son's son that I made a mockery of Egypt [i.e., I punished the Egyptians and humbled them] and My signs that I placed among them [I placed signs of My Sovereignty into the hearts of Bnei Yisrael]" (*Shemos* 10:2).

With the mention of each of the ten plagues, one should remove a small amount of wine from his cup using his finger (or pour it out of the cup).

As each of the plagues is mentioned, a bit of wine is removed from the cup (with the finger, or by pouring).

The same is done by each word of Rabbi Yehudah's mnemonic.

דָּם. צְפַרְדֵּעַ. כִּנִּים. עָרוֹב. דֶּבֶר. שְׁחִין. בָּרָד. אַרְבֶּה. חֹשֶׁךְ. מַכַּת בְּכוֹרוֹת.

דָּם — Blood

"Take your staff and stretch out your hand over the waters of Egypt; over their rivers, over their canals, over their reservoirs, and all over their gatherings of water, and they shall become blood; there shall be blood throughout the land of Egypt" (Shemos 7:19).

"The sorcerers of Egypt did the same by means of their incantations; so Pharaoh's heart was strong and he did not heed them" (Ibid. 7:22).

There seems to be a redundancy in the first verse cited here. Why does it say, "And they shall become blood ... there shall be blood?"

Furthermore, if all the water in Egypt had already been turned into blood, where did the Egyptian sorcerers obtain water to transform into blood with their incantations?

The Midrash (Shemos Rabbah 9:10) tells us that when the Egyptians purchased water from Bnei Yisrael, the water did not turn into blood. The hapless Egyptians were forced to pay whatever price Bnei Yisrael asked. Thus Bnei Yisrael became extremely wealthy during the plague of blood.

It appears, then, that the Egyptian sorcerers bought water from Bnei Yisrael, and used their sorcery to transform that water into blood. It is quite possible, however, that the water was not transformed to blood as a result of their sorcery. Rather, as soon as they attempted to use sorcery to discredit Moshe's miraculous plague, they revealed their evil intent. The merit of having purchased the water from Bnei Yisrael then failed to protect their water, and the water was immediately transformed to blood as a result of the original miracle.

The Torah states, "And they shall become blood," referring to all the water in Egypt, and then adds, "And there shall be blood," referring to water supposedly turned into blood through Egyptian sorcery, which in reality was also a result of the plague.

We can also explain the redundancy based on Rashi's statement that the words, "There shall be blood throughout the land of Egypt," refer to the water in the Egyptians' bathhouses and in the bathtubs in their homes.

With the mention of each of the ten plagues, one should remove a small amount of wine from his cup using his finger (or pour it out of the cup).

As each of the plagues is mentioned, a bit of wine is removed from the cup (with the finger, or by pouring).

The same is done by each word of Rabbi Yehudah's mnemonic.

1. Blood 2. Frogs 3. Lice 4. Wild Beasts 5. Pestilence 6. Boils 7. Hail 8. Locusts 9. Darkness 10. Plague of the Firstborn.

According to *Rashi*, the first half of the verse refers to the water in the lakes and rivers; the second half refers to the water gathered in the homes of the Egyptians.

⚜

"Behold, with the staff that is in my hand I shall strike the waters that are in the River, and they shall change to blood" (*Shemos* 7:17).

Baal HaTurim comments that there was so much blood in the water that the water was discolored by the redness of the blood. This is a very puzzling comment, since it seems from the verses that all the water in Egypt had turned into blood and there was no water left to be discolored.

Perhaps *Baal HaTurim* understood that all the water that was in Egypt when Moshe's staff smote the river turned into blood, but the water that was outside of Egypt then and only flowed into the rivers of Egypt afterward remained water. Hashem performed another miracle and prevented the blood in the Egyptian rivers from being washed away by the fresh water flowing in. The blood remained in its place, and the fresh water streamed over it and was discolored by the blood.

We can use this approach to explain the seeming redundancy we noted earlier. "And they shall become blood" refers to the water that was in Egypt at the time that the plague began, all of which became actual blood. "There shall be blood throughout the land of Egypt" refers to the water that streamed into Egypt afterward. This water did not become blood, but was tainted by the blood that was there already.

צְפַרְדֵּעַ — Frogs

Chazal note (*Shemos Rabbah* 10:4; *Sanhedrin* 67b) that the words, "The *frog* ascended (from the Nile)" (*Shemos* 8:2), imply that only one frog emerged from the Nile at first.

Some explain that it was indeed only one frog at first, but the Egyptians struck it out of anger, and swarms of frogs began to pour out of it. Others explain that at first one frog emerged, but when it began to croak on shore, swarms of frogs followed.

It seems that an additional miracle occurred, and aside from the frog that emerged from the river and produced others with it, millions of other frogs formed spontaneously from the earth of Egypt, with no apparent means of reproduction. This miracle is alluded to in the verse, "Their land swarmed with frogs, *in the chambers* of their kings" (*Tehillim* 105:30).

Why was this additional miracle necessary?

When the Egyptians heard of the impending plague of frogs, they undoubtedly attempted to barricade their homes to prevent the frogs from entering. We can be certain that the kings and noblemen used all means at their disposal to fortify the walls and floors of their homes. But Hashem circumvented their preventative measures by causing the frogs to propagate spontaneously inside their chambers.

--=◉=--

The Talmud (*Sanhedrin* 67b) records a dispute between *Tannaim* regarding the exact process of the plague of frogs.

R' Akiva said that only one frog emerged from the Nile at first, but as the Egyptians struck it, swarms of frogs began to pour out of it.

"Akiva!" retorted R' Elazar ben Azariah, "What business do you have interpreting teachings of *aggadah*? Contain your words and return to the subjects of *Negaim* and *Ohalos*.

"Rather," continued R' Elazar ben Azariah, "one frog emerged from the Nile, and then croaked to the other frogs to come."

There are many disputes in the Talmud, in the realms of both halachah and *aggadah*. Granted, R' Elazar had the right to disagree with R' Akiva — as he did in other instances — but why did he contest R' Akiva's right to offer his opinion in matters of *aggadah*?

The Talmud (*Pesachim* 53b) states: "From where did Chananyah, Mishael, and Azariah learn to offer their lives in sanctification of Hashem's Name?[1] They learned from the frogs [that leaped into the ovens of the Egyptians to sanctify Hashem's Name]."

Tosafos (ibid., s.v. *Mah*) asks why they had to derive this lesson from the frogs in Egypt; we all know that we are required to sacrifice our lives rather than succumb to coercion to commit idolatry in public.

Rabbeinu Tam answers that the statue of Nebuchadnezzar was

---

1. Chananyah, Mishael, and Azariah were given the choice of either bowing to a statue of Nebuchadnezzar or being cast into a fiery furnace, and they chose the latter. Hashem performed a miracle and the flames did not burn them. See *Daniel* 3 for the full story.

not originally constructed with the intention to be served as an idol; it was constructed to honor Nebuchadnezzar. According to halachah, they were permitted to bow to the statue, but they learned from the frogs to sacrifice their lives even though they were not required to do so.

The lesson they learned from the frogs is only true if we assume that the frogs in Egypt were normal, natural frogs that chose to sacrifice their lives to sanctify Hashem's Name. According to R' Akiva, however, these were not natural frogs. They were created miraculously, leaping from the body of the first frog that emerged from the Nile. It is no wonder that such frogs would sacrifice their lives by leaping into the Egyptians' ovens, because they were created only for that purpose.

R' Elazar was sharply opposed to R' Akiva's opinion, because if R' Akiva was correct, then Chananyah, Mishael, and Azariah erred in sacrificing their lives when they were not required to.

Furthermore, R' Akiva himself followed their example and sacrificed his life despite not being required to do so (*Berachos* 61b, see *Maharsha*). The Romans passed an edict that anyone caught learning Torah would be executed. R' Akiva gathered his students and taught Torah publicly, in open defiance of the Roman decree.

Had R' Akiva concurred with R' Elazar's opinion, he could have drawn proof from the frogs that he, too, was permitted to sacrifice his life to sanctify Hashem's Name. According to his own opinion, however, the frogs in Egypt were supernatural, so he had no basis for the assumption that a person born under normal circumstances may risk his life to sanctify Hashem's Name.

R' Elazar ben Azariah was prompted to respond to R' Akiva's explanation of the plague of frogs so sharply because according to R' Akiva's explanation, one would not have the right to die in honor of Hashem's Name.

עָרוֹב — Wild Beasts

Moshe Rabbeinu's warning of the impending plague of wild beasts reads as follows: "Behold, I shall incite against you (הִנְנִי מַשְׁלִיחַ בְּךְ), your servants, your people, and your houses, (the swarm of) wild beasts" (*Shemos* 8:17).

This is the only plague in which Hashem threatens to *incite* against the Egyptians. Hashem *brought* locusts upon the Egyptians (*Shemos* 10:4); He *struck* them with frogs (ibid. 8:2). Why is the expression "I shall incite" appropriate for the plague of wild beasts?

The Mishnah (*Taanis* 19a) tells us that when danger threatens a community, they must fast and blow horns to stir everyone to repent. The Talmud (*Taanis* 22a) notes that not all sightings of wild beasts constitute a danger that requires the inhabitants to fast. The sighting of animals only warrants sounding of the shofar if it is clear that they were incited, and are therefore liable to attack.

The Torah emphasizes that the wild beasts that invaded Egypt were incited, and therefore represented a clear and present danger to the Egyptians.

"The houses of the Egyptians will be filled with (the swarm of) wild beasts, and even the ground upon which they are" (*Shemos* 8:17).

Simply understood, this verse warned Pharaoh that the wild beasts would not only fill the homes of the Egyptians, they would fill the entire land of Egypt. If this is the true interpretation, however, then the verse should have been written in a slightly different order: "The houses of the Egyptians, and even the ground upon which they are, will be filled with (the swarm of) wild beasts."

Animals only thrive in their natural habitats. Animals used to desert conditions could not survive in a jungle; animals that are used to living in a jungle could not survive in a desert. Pharaoh thought he did not have to fear the onslaught of wild beasts, because many wild beasts could not survive the desert climate of Egypt, and would quickly perish.

Hashem had taken this into account, however. Egypt was filled with beasts, *and the land upon which they are* — i.e., the land upon which the beasts dwelled was brought with them into Egypt, providing each animal with a suitable environment.

This approach also explains the verse, "The land was being ruined by (the swarm of) wild breasts" (ibid. 8:20). The very *land* of Egypt was ruined by the sudden adjustments to allow for desert, plains, and forest climates to exist simultaneously, providing suitable environments for various ferocious animals to inhabit Egypt and wreak havoc on its citizens.

The Mishnah (*Kilayim* 8:5) mentions beasts called *adnei hasadeh*, which have human features and are extremely dangerous to those who come near them. *Adnei hasadeh* are connected to the ground with an apparatus similar to an umbilical cord, and can only live if that cord remains attached to the ground.

The Vilna Gaon writes that *adnei hasadeh* were among the beasts

Rabbi Yehudah abbreviated them
by their Hebrew initials:
D'TZACH, ADASH, B'ACHAV.

that attacked Egypt. Thus the Torah tells us, "The houses of the Egyptians will be filled with (the swarm of) wild beasts, *and even the ground upon which they are,* because if the land had not come along with them, they could not have survived.[1]

בָּרָד — Hail

"As I leave the city, I will stretch my hands to Hashem" (*Shemos* 9:29).

Rashi explains that Moshe could not daven while he stood in the city, since it was filled with idolatry. Why does the Torah wait until the plague of hail to inform us that Moshe would not pray in Egypt? Surely the same was true when he prayed to halt all the previous plagues. If Moshe saw no need to tell Pharaoh how or where he intended to pray to halt those plagues, why did he decide to do so with this plague?

The Talmud (*Avodah Zarah* 52b) tells us that if an idolater nullifies his deity, not only does the idol itself lose its status as a false deity, but all the paraphernalia used to serve it also lose that status.

Under the barrage of the plague of hail, Pharaoh finally declared, "This time I have sinned; Hashem is the Righteous One, and I and my people are the wicked ones" (*Shemos* 9:27). One might have thought that with this statement Pharaoh nullified all the idols in Egypt, by recognizing that Hashem is the One and Only God of Creation. If that were so, Moshe could now pray in Egypt, since all the idols there had been nullified.

But Moshe told Pharaoh that he knew that his confession was insincere: "I know that you are not yet afraid of Hashem" (ibid. 9:30).

The Torah emphasizes that despite Pharaoh's declaration, Moshe still had to leave Egypt to pray.

רַבִּי יְהוּדָה הָיָה נוֹתֵן בָּהֶם סִמָּנִים: דְּצַ"ךְ עַדַ"שׁ בְּאַחַ"ב
Rabbi Yehudah abbreviated them by their Hebrew initials

Many have asked what R' Yehudah meant to add by devising acronyms for the plagues. Why did he prefer to call the plagues by the first letters of their names, rather than by their full names?

---

1. After writing this explanation, I saw it cited by *Panim Yafos* in the name of his grandfather. He also cites further proof from *Bechoros* 8.

The cups are refilled. The wine that was removed is not used.

מכילתא דרבי ישמעאל בשלח פרשה ו.

רַבִּי יוֹסֵי הַגְּלִילִי אוֹמֵר: מִנַּיִן אַתָּה אוֹמֵר שֶׁלָּקוּ
הַמִּצְרִים בְּמִצְרַיִם עֶשֶׂר מַכּוֹת וְעַל
הַיָּם לָקוּ חֲמִשִּׁים מַכּוֹת? בְּמִצְרַיִם מָה הוּא אוֹמֵר,
וַיֹּאמְרוּ הַחַרְטֻמִּם אֶל פַּרְעֹה, אֶצְבַּע אֱלֹהִים הוּא.[1]

(1) *Shemos* 8:15.

The Talmud[1] tells us that we should never let a word that represents negativity or hardship leave our lips, since a person's words
may inadvertently be fulfilled.[2] R' Yehudah therefore felt that it was
better not to mention the plagues by name.

Those who argue with R' Yehudah had no aversion to mentioning
the plagues by name because recounting the Exodus is a mitzvah,
and "He who obeys the commandments will know no evil" (*Koheles*
8:5). Furthermore, it is possible that the plagues are not classified as
hardships, since they harmed only the Egyptians and caused Hashem's Name to be sanctified.

We can suggest another explanation as to why R' Yehudah abbre-
viated the names of the plagues based on an insight from the
Raviyah (*Pesachim* 2:424).

When we look at R' Yehudah's abbreviation, we find that the third
plagues of the three groups were lice, boils, and darkness. These
three plagues always struck simultaneously, one as the primary plague and the others as peripheral plagues. The primary plague always
struck hardest. When lice was the primary plague, the Egyptians
suffered from boils and darkness as secondary ills; when the plague
of boils was primary, lice and darkness served as secondary plagues,
and when darkness struck, the Egyptians were also infested with lice
and stricken with boils. This is alluded to in the Hebrew words for
these three plagues, which can be arranged in a table as follows:

כ ש ח

נ ח ש

ם נ כ

The names of the plagues can be read as an acrostic, starting from
any letter of the first word. R' Yehudah alluded to this insight by

---

1. *Moed Katan* 18a; see also *Midrash Tanchuma, Korach* 6.
2. For instance, it is customary not to mention terrible diseases by name, but to hint
to them.

The cups are refilled. The wine that was removed is not used.

Mechilta D'Rabbi Yishmael, Parashas Beshalach 6a

Rabbi Yose the Galilean said: How does one derive that the Egyptians were struck with ten plagues in Egypt, but with fifty plagues at the Sea? — Concerning the plagues in Egypt the Torah states: The magicians said to Pharaoh, "It is the finger of God."[1]

---

developing an abbreviation that placed these plagues third in each series.

שֶׁלָּקוּ הַמִּצְרִים בְּמִצְרַיִם עֶשֶׂר מַכּוֹת —
The Egyptians were struck with ten plagues in Egypt

The ten plagues that struck Egypt correspond to the ten utterances with which the world was created, which is why the Mishnah in *Pirkei Avos* (5:1) lists these two sets of ten together.[1]

The two sets of ten actually achieved opposite results.

Before Creation, the Divine Presence was entirely revealed. With each utterance, the physical world took on greater form, and the Divine Presence became more concealed. During the Exodus, the opposite occurred. The Divine Presence was concealed during the exile in Egypt, and it was revealed a bit more with each plague, until Hashem's Sovereignty over Creation was completely revealed.

We find another parallel between Creation and the Exodus in a Midrash (*Shemos Rabbah* 19:8): "Just as at first there were seven days of Creation, and just as Shabbos occurs once every seven days, so too shall these seven days (of Pesach) occur each year." The Exodus corresponds to Creation, just as the ten plagues correspond to the ten utterances.

When we study the ten plagues and the ten utterances, we find that the parallel between them is actually in reverse order.

The first of the utterances was בְּרֵאשִׁית בָּרָא, *In the beginning of God's creating*; the last of the plagues struck רֵאשִׁית אוֹנִים, *the first fruit* (*Tehillim* 78:51), of the Egyptians. The second utterance was יְהִי אוֹר, *Let there be light*; the second-to-last plague cast the Egyptians into total darkness, but וּלְכָל בְּנֵי יִשְׂרָאֵל הָיָה אוֹר בְּמוֹשְׁבֹתָם, for all the Bnei Yisrael there was light in their dwellings (*Shemos* 10:23).

The same parallel holds true for the other eight utterances and plagues.

---

1. See *Rashi* to *Avos*, *Ruach Chaim* by Rav Chaim of Volozhin, and *Derech Chaim* from the Maharal.

וְעַל הַיָּם מָה הוּא אוֹמֵר, וַיַּרְא יִשְׂרָאֵל אֶת הַיָּד הַגְּדֹלָה אֲשֶׁר עָשָׂה יהוה בְּמִצְרַיִם, וַיִּירְאוּ הָעָם אֶת יהוה, וַיַּאֲמִינוּ בַּיהוה וּבְמֹשֶׁה עַבְדּוֹ.[1] כַּמָּה לָקוּ בְאֶצְבַּע? עֶשֶׂר מַכּוֹת. אֱמוֹר מֵעַתָּה, בְּמִצְרַיִם לָקוּ עֶשֶׂר מַכּוֹת, וְעַל הַיָּם לָקוּ חֲמִשִּׁים מַכּוֹת.

שם

רַבִּי אֱלִיעֶזֶר אוֹמֵר. מִנַּיִן שֶׁכָּל מַכָּה וּמַכָּה שֶׁהֵבִיא הַקָּדוֹשׁ בָּרוּךְ הוּא עַל הַמִּצְרִים בְּמִצְרַיִם הָיְתָה שֶׁל אַרְבַּע מַכּוֹת? שֶׁנֶּאֱמַר, יְשַׁלַּח בָּם חֲרוֹן אַפּוֹ – עֶבְרָה, וָזַעַם, וְצָרָה, מִשְׁלַחַת מַלְאֲכֵי רָעִים.[2] עֶבְרָה, אַחַת. וָזַעַם, שְׁתַּיִם. וְצָרָה, שָׁלֹשׁ. מִשְׁלַחַת מַלְאֲכֵי רָעִים, אַרְבַּע. אֱמוֹר מֵעַתָּה, בְּמִצְרַיִם לָקוּ אַרְבָּעִים מַכּוֹת, וְעַל הַיָּם לָקוּ מָאתַיִם מַכּוֹת.

שם

רַבִּי עֲקִיבָא אוֹמֵר. מִנַּיִן שֶׁכָּל מַכָּה וּמַכָּה שֶׁהֵבִיא הַקָּדוֹשׁ בָּרוּךְ הוּא עַל הַמִּצְרִים בְּמִצְרַיִם הָיְתָה שֶׁל חָמֵשׁ מַכּוֹת? שֶׁנֶּאֱמַר, יְשַׁלַּח בָּם חֲרוֹן אַפּוֹ, עֶבְרָה, וָזַעַם, וְצָרָה, מִשְׁלַחַת מַלְאֲכֵי רָעִים. חֲרוֹן אַפּוֹ, אַחַת. עֶבְרָה, שְׁתַּיִם. וָזַעַם, שָׁלֹשׁ. וְצָרָה, אַרְבַּע. מִשְׁלַחַת מַלְאֲכֵי רָעִים, חָמֵשׁ. אֱמוֹר מֵעַתָּה,

---

וַיַּרְא יִשְׂרָאֵל אֶת הַיָּד הַגְּדֹלָה
Israel saw the great "hand"

Hashem's "hand" is usually used to hide His interaction with Creation, as *Ohr Hachaim* (*Shemos* 24:11) notes in his explanation of the verses, "When My glory passes by, I will place you in the cleft of the rock, and *I shall cover you with My hand* until I pass. I will then remove My hand, and you will see My back, but My face may

However, of those at the Sea, the Torah relates: "Israel saw the great 'hand' which HASHEM laid upon the Egyptians, the people feared HASHEM, and they believed in HASHEM and in His servant Moses."[1] How many plagues did they receive with the finger? Ten! Then conclude that if they suffered ten plagues in Egypt [where they were struck with a finger], they must have been made to suffer fifty plagues at the Sea [where they were struck with a whole hand].

Ibid.

Rabbi Eliezer said: How does one derive that every plague that the Holy One, Blessed is He, inflicted upon the Egyptians in Egypt was equal to four plagues? — for it is written: "He sent upon them His fierce anger: wrath, fury, and trouble, a band of emissaries of evil."[2] [Since each plague in Egypt consisted of] (1) wrath, (2) fury, (3) trouble, and (4) a band of emissaries of evil, therefore conclude that in Egypt they were struck by forty plagues and at the Sea by two hundred!

Ibid.

Rabbi Akiva said: How does one derive that each plague that the Holy One, Blessed is He, inflicted upon the Egyptians in Egypt was equal to five plagues? — for it is written: "He sent upon them His fierce anger, wrath, fury, trouble, and a band of emissaries of evil." [Since each plague in Egypt consisted of] (1) fierce anger, (2) wrath, (3) fury, (4) trouble, and (5) a band of emissaries of evil, therefore conclude that

(1) *Shemos* 14:31. (2) *Tehillim* 78:49.

not be seen" (*Shemos* 33:22-23), and "Against the nobles of Bnei Yisrael, Hashem did not send His hand" (ibid. 24:11).[1]

One of the wonders of Exodus was that Hashem's "hand" was used to *reveal* His might and His Sovereignty over Creation through the miracles that He performed in Egypt.

1. I.e., Hashem did not conceal His Glory from the nobles as He usually does.

בְּמִצְרַיִם לָקוּ חֲמִשִּׁים מַכּוֹת, וְעַל הַיָּם לָקוּ חֲמִשִּׁים וּמָאתַיִם מַכּוֹת.

Abarbanel, in his commentary Zevach Pesach, writes
that the following — until the section "Rabban Gamliel would say"
— is a continuation of R' Akiva's statement.

כַּמָּה מַעֲלוֹת טוֹבוֹת לַמָּקוֹם עָלֵינוּ.

אִלּוּ הוֹצִיאָנוּ מִמִּצְרַיִם,

וְלֹא עָשָׂה בָהֶם שְׁפָטִים,   דַּיֵּנוּ.

אִלּוּ עָשָׂה בָהֶם שְׁפָטִים,

וְלֹא עָשָׂה בֵאלֹהֵיהֶם,   דַּיֵּנוּ.

אִלּוּ עָשָׂה בֵאלֹהֵיהֶם,

וְלֹא הָרַג אֶת בְּכוֹרֵיהֶם,   דַּיֵּנוּ.

אִלּוּ הָרַג אֶת בְּכוֹרֵיהֶם,

וְלֹא נָתַן לָנוּ אֶת מָמוֹנָם,   דַּיֵּנוּ.

אִלּוּ נָתַן לָנוּ אֶת מָמוֹנָם,

וְלֹא קָרַע לָנוּ אֶת הַיָּם,   דַּיֵּנוּ.

אִלּוּ קָרַע לָנוּ אֶת הַיָּם,

וְלֹא הֶעֱבִירָנוּ בְתוֹכוֹ בֶּחָרָבָה,   דַּיֵּנוּ.

אִלּוּ קָרַע לָנוּ אֶת הַיָּם
Had He split the Sea for us

וַיָּשָׁב הַיָּם לִפְנוֹת בֹּקֶר לְאֵיתָנוֹ, *Toward morning, the water went back to its power* (Shemos 14:27).

Chazal[1] note that the word לְאֵיתָנוֹ, *to its power,* is comprised of the same letters as לִתְנָאוֹ, *to its original stipulation,* and explain that when Hashem created the world, He stipulated that the sea would split for Bnei Yisrael. After Bnei Yisrael had passed through, the sea returned to its "original stipulation."

---

1. This idea appears in many Midrashim, but the question and explanation here are based on the text of the Midrash as it is cited in many *sefarim*, and also fits with the version found in *Yalkut Shimoni, Shemos* 236. It does not explain the version that appears in Shemos Rabbah 21:6.

in Egypt they were struck by fifty plagues and at the Sea by two hundred and fifty!

Abarbanel, in his commentary Zevach Pesach, writes that the following — until the section "Rabban Gamliel would say" — is a continuation of R' Akiva's statement.

The Omnipresent has bestowed so many favors upon us!

Had He brought us out of Egypt,
    but not executed judgments against the
    Egyptians,   it would have sufficed us.
Had He executed judgments against them,
    but not upon their gods, it would have sufficed us.
Had He executed judgments against their gods,
    but not slain their firstborn,
                        it would have sufficed us.
Had He slain their firstborn,
    but not given us their wealth,
                        it would have sufficed us.
Had He given us their wealth,
    but not split the Sea for us,
                        it would have sufficed us.
Had He split the Sea for us,
    but not led us through it on dry land,
                        it would have sufficed us.

The Midrash implies that there were two stipulations: the original stipulation that caused the sea to flow in its natural form, and a second stipulation requiring it to split for Bnei Yisrael. Logic would dictate, however, that only the stipulation requiring the sea to split was necessary, and that no stipulation was necessary in order for it to return to its natural state.

We can explain the "original stipulation" based on a principle described at length by *Akeidas Yitzchak* (*Parashas Noach*).

When Hashem created the world, He designed it so that all the forces of Creation would be subservient to the will of mankind. The Talmud (*Kiddushin* 81b) tells us that world was created to serve man, just as man was created to serve his Creator. Before Adam sinned, even angels served him, filtering wine and roasting meat for him

אִלּוּ הֶעֱבִירָנוּ בְתוֹכוֹ בֶּחָרָבָה,
וְלֹא שִׁקַּע צָרֵינוּ בְּתוֹכוֹ, דַּיֵּנוּ.

(Sanhedrin 59b). The fruits that grew from the earth were perfect, and everything in Creation was ready to serve him.

But Adam sinned, and the curse of "thorns and thistles will sprout for you" was imposed upon him. From then on, whenever man fails to obey his Creator, the world is no longer subject to his will. Nevertheless, man remains the focal point of Creation until this very day. Only humans can bring the world to perfection through the observance of Torah and mitzvos. All of Creation remains subservient to us as long as we strive to fulfill our purpose and bring it to perfection.

Akeidas Yitzchak teaches us that the "original stipulation" was that all of Creation should be subservient to humans, as long as they attempt to fulfill the spiritual end for which they were placed into this world.

Similarly, *Ramban* (*Vayikra* 26:6) writes, "When Bnei Yisrael fulfill the mitzvos, Eretz Yisrael is as perfect as the world was before Adam's sin. Beasts and vermin will not kill people, as the Talmud (*Berachos* 33a) states, 'A viper does not kill — sin kills.' Wild beasts only became dangerous as a result of Adam's sin. When Eretz Yisrael attains perfection, wild beasts will cease to be dangerous, and they will return to their original, peaceful nature, as they were when they were first created."

The *original* stipulation was that Creation is subservient to humans when they observe Torah and mitzvos. A second stipulation was necessary in order for the sea to split for Bnei Yisrael, since they were not worthy of the sea's cooperation at the time.

When Bnei Yisrael finished passing through the Yam Suf, the sea returned to its original stipulation — in which those who sin are subject to the natural order of creation — and drowned the Egyptian pursuers.

בִּקְשׁוּ מַלְאֲכֵי הַשָּׁרֵת לוֹמַר שִׁירָה אָמַר לָהֶם הַקָּבָּ"ה
מַעֲשֵׂה יָדַי טוֹבְעִים בַּיָּם וְאַתֶּם אוֹמְרִים שִׁירָה

The angels requested permission to sing (praises). Said Hashem,
"My creatures are drowning in the sea, and you wish to sing?"

If there was something wrong with singing praise while the Egyptians drowned, why were Bnei Yisrael permitted to sing *Az Yashir*, the Song at Sea, in which they praised Hashem specifically for drowning the Egyptians?

Unlike the angels, Bnei Yisrael never asked for permission to sing. Had they requested permission, they might have been denied. But

> Had He led us through it on dry land,
>
> but not drowned our oppressors in it,
>
> it would have sufficed us.

---

they did not stop and think about it; the songs and praises welled up in their hearts spontaneously until they burst forth on their own.

שִׁירַת הַיָּם — The Song at Sea

The opening words to the Song at Sea are אָז יָשִׁיר, *Then* they sang. The Midrash (*Shemos Rabbah* 23:4) explains that from the day that Hashem created the world, no one sang *shirah* to Him, until Bnei Yisrael sang the Song at Sea.

We find, however, that Adam sang, *"Mizmor Shir L'Yom HaShabbos — A Song for the Shabbos Day,"* after he was forgiven for his sin. How could the Midrash state that no one sang *shirah* before Bnei Yisrael at the Yam Suf?

There are several distinctions between the song of Adam and the song of Bnei Yisrael. Adam sang over his personal forgiveness and his salvation; Bnei Yisrael sang the praises of Hashem. Furthermore, Adam only praised Hashem for His Attribute of Mercy, which had spared him from death and forgiven him for his sin; Bnei Yisrael went a step further and praised Hashem for the mercy that He blends into His Attribute of Justice. "Who is like You among the powers (בָּאֵלִם), Hashem," they sang. (*Chazal* (*Gittin* 56b) expound the word בָּאֵלִם to read בָּאִלְּמִים, *the mute ones*. Hashem is able to watch His Name being disgraced and remain silent because even His Attribute of Justice is diluted with mercy.)

Another Midrash (*Shemos Rabbah* 23:3) tells us that Moshe Rabbeinu said to Hashem, "I know that I sinned before You with the word אָז when I said, וּמֵאָז בָּאתִי אֶל פַּרְעֹה לְדַבֵּר בִּשְׁמֶךָ הֵרַע לָעָם הַזֶּה וְהַצֵּל לֹא הִצַּלְתָּ אֶת עַמֶּךָ, *From the time that I came to Pharaoh to speak in Your name he did evil to this people, but You did not rescue Your people'* (*Shemos* 5:23). Now that you drowned Pharaoh, I will sing *shirah* with אָז."

At the Yam Suf, Bnei Yisrael saw that all the difficulties they had endured in Egypt were precursors to their redemption.[1] They then understood that Hashem's Attribute of Justice is also filled with mercy, so they sang *shirah* over the Attribute of Justice as well.

---

1. Some explain that the extra work that Pharaoh placed on the Jewish people hastened the Redemption, which — as we noted in our commentary to the passage "The Holy One, Blessed is He, calculated the end of the bondage [page 124] — had to be hastened in order to prevent us from falling to the 50th level of impurity and being mired in Egypt forever.

אִלּוּ שִׁקַּע צָרֵינוּ בְּתוֹכוֹ,

וְלֹא סִפֵּק צָרְכֵּנוּ בַּמִּדְבָּר אַרְבָּעִים שָׁנָה,   דַּיֵּנוּ.

אִלּוּ סִפֵּק צָרְכֵּנוּ בַּמִּדְבָּר אַרְבָּעִים שָׁנָה,

וְלֹא הֶאֱכִילָנוּ אֶת הַמָּן,   דַּיֵּנוּ.

אִלּוּ הֶאֱכִילָנוּ אֶת הַמָּן,

וְלֹא נָתַן לָנוּ אֶת הַשַּׁבָּת,   דַּיֵּנוּ.

אִלּוּ נָתַן לָנוּ אֶת הַשַּׁבָּת,

וְלֹא קֵרְבָנוּ לִפְנֵי הַר סִינַי,   דַּיֵּנוּ.

אִלּוּ קֵרְבָנוּ לִפְנֵי הַר סִינַי,

וְלֹא נָתַן לָנוּ אֶת הַתּוֹרָה,   דַּיֵּנוּ.

אִלּוּ נָתַן לָנוּ אֶת הַתּוֹרָה,

וְלֹא הִכְנִיסָנוּ לְאֶרֶץ יִשְׂרָאֵל,   דַּיֵּנוּ.

אִלּוּ הִכְנִיסָנוּ לְאֶרֶץ יִשְׂרָאֵל,

וְלֹא בָנָה לָנוּ אֶת בֵּית הַבְּחִירָה,   דַּיֵּנוּ.

עַל אַחַת כַּמָּה, וְכַמָּה טוֹבָה כְפוּלָה וּמְכֻפֶּלֶת לַמָּקוֹם עָלֵינוּ. שֶׁהוֹצִיאָנוּ מִמִּצְרַיִם, וְעָשָׂה בָהֶם שְׁפָטִים, וְעָשָׂה בֵאלֹהֵיהֶם, וְהָרַג אֶת בְּכוֹרֵיהֶם, וְנָתַן לָנוּ אֶת מָמוֹנָם, וְקָרַע לָנוּ אֶת הַיָּם, וְהֶעֱבִירָנוּ בְתוֹכוֹ בֶּחָרָבָה, וְשִׁקַּע צָרֵינוּ בְּתוֹכוֹ, וְסִפֵּק צָרְכֵּנוּ בַּמִּדְבָּר אַרְבָּעִים שָׁנָה, וְהֶאֱכִילָנוּ אֶת הַמָּן, וְנָתַן לָנוּ אֶת הַשַּׁבָּת, וְקֵרְבָנוּ לִפְנֵי הַר סִינַי, וְנָתַן לָנוּ אֶת הַתּוֹרָה, וְהִכְנִיסָנוּ לְאֶרֶץ יִשְׂרָאֵל, וּבָנָה לָנוּ אֶת בֵּית הַבְּחִירָה, לְכַפֵּר עַל כָּל עֲוֹנוֹתֵינוּ.

וּבָנָה לָנוּ אֶת בֵּית הַבְּחִירָה
And built for us the Beis Hamikdash

The Talmud (*Pesachim* 88a) states:

Had He drowned our oppressors in it,
  but not provided for our needs in the desert
    for forty years,   it would have sufficed us.
Had He provided for our needs in the desert
  for forty years, but not fed us the Manna,
                  it would have sufficed us.
Had He fed us the Manna,
  but not given us the Sabbath,
                  it would have sufficed us.
Had He given us the Sabbath,
  but not brought us before Mount Sinai,
                  it would have sufficed us.
Had He brought us before Mount Sinai,
  but not given us the Torah,
                  it would have sufficed us.
Had He given us the Torah,
  but not brought us into the Land of Israel,
                  it would have sufficed us.
Had He brought us into the Land of Israel,
  but not built the Beis Hamikdash for us,
                  it would have sufficed us.

Thus, how much more so should we be grateful to the Omnipresent for all the numerous favors He showered upon us: He brought us out of Egypt; executed judgments against the Egyptians; acted against their gods; slew their firstborn; gave us their wealth; split the Sea for us; led us through it on dry land; drowned our oppressors in it; provided for our needs in the desert for forty years; fed us the manna; gave us the Sabbath; brought us close to Mount Sinai; gave us the Torah; brought us to the Land of Israel; and built for us the Beis Hamikdash, to atone for all our sins.

What is the meaning of the verse, "Let us go up to the Mountain of Hashem, to the House of the God of Yaakov" (Yeshayah 2:3)?

[The Beis Hamikdash is called the *house* of the God of *Yaakov*,] not like Avraham who called it a mountain in the verse, "On the

רַבָּן גַּמְלִיאֵל הָיָה אוֹמֵר. כָּל שֶׁלֹּא אָמַר שְׁלשָׁה דְבָרִים אֵלּוּ בַּפֶּסַח, לֹא יָצָא יְדֵי חוֹבָתוֹ, וְאֵלּוּ הֵן, פֶּסַח. מַצָּה. וּמָרוֹר.

---

mountain Hashem will be seen" (*Bereishis* 22:14); not like Yitzchak who called it a field in the verse, "Yitzchak went out to supplicate in the field" (ibid. 24:63); but like Yaakov who called it a house in the verse, "And he named the place the House of God" (ibid. 28:19).

Yaakov's name for the Beis Hamikdash was chosen over the names of Avraham and Yitzchak not to disparage our holy forefathers — it is impossible for us to understand the deep intentions of Avraham and Yitzchak — but to provide us with an important lesson in education.

Many people wish to influence the world and to perfect it. Some build their proverbial "Beis Hamikdash" on the mountaintops and call out to others to join them in their service of Hashem. This was the way of Avraham Avinu, who called the Beis Hamikdash a mountain. Avraham Avinu was not entirely successful, however — Yishmael was born from him.

Others build their "Beis Hamikdash" by going out into the fields, markets and other public places to search for Hashem's lost children, and draw them back into His service. This was the method of service chosen by Yitzchak Avinu, who called the Beis Hamikdash a field. Yitzchak did not meet with complete success, either — Eisav was born from him.

Yaakov called the Beis Hamikdash a house. He realized that the most stable and powerful influence a person can have on the world is to direct his efforts toward his own home. Yaakov built his home as a protective fortress to shield his children from the negative influences of the world. His home was not a mountain, exposed to the winds and other elements. It was not a field, free for all to enter. It was a fortified home. Therefore, he merited that all of his children grew to become great tzaddikim.

We find the Beis Hamikdash referred to as *Har HaBayis*, the Mountain of the House (*Yirmiyah* 26:18; *Michah* 3:12). This teaches us that the Jewish home can be both a protective fortress for our children, and also a mountaintop from which Torah is disseminated throughout the world. By protecting our homes from negative

Pesachim 116a

R abban Gamliel used to say: Whoever has not explained the following three things on Pesach has
not fulfilled his duty, namely:

Pesach — the Pesach Offering;
Matzah — the Unleavened Bread;
Maror — the Bitter Herbs.

---

influences, we can turn them into lighthouses that will spread the
rays of the Torah and Hashem throughout the world.

כָּל שֶׁלֹּא אָמַר שְׁלֹשָׁה דְּבָרִים אֵלּוּ
Whoever has not explained the following three things

The Talmud (*Bava Metzia* 115b, *Sanhedrin* 21b) records a dispute
between R' Yehudah and R' Shimon over whether we assume that
we know the reasons for the mitzvos of the Torah. In practice, we
follow the ruling of R' Yehudah, and we do not ascribe reasons for
mitzvos. If so, how could Rabban Gamliel say that whoever does not
explain the reasons for *Korban Pesach*, matzah, and maror does not
fulfill the mitzvah of relating the story of the Exodus?

Bach (*Orach Chaim* 8) writes that when a person performs a
mitzvah for which the Torah gives a reason, he is obligated to have
that reason in mind at the time of the mitzvah. For instance, when
performing the mitzvah of succah, a person must have in mind the
Clouds of Glory, as the Torah states, "So that your generations will
know that I caused Bnei Yisrael to dwell in booths" (*Vayikra* 23:43).
Similarly, with regard to the mitzvah of *tzitzis*, the Torah states, "So
that you may remember and perform all My commandments" (*Bamidbar* 15:40), and with regard to *tefillin*, the Torah states, "So that
Hashem's Torah may be in your mouth" (*Shemos* 13:9). According to
Bach, we need to have these ideas in mind when fulfilling the
mitzvos of *tzitzis* and *tefillin*.

Bach's opinion does not answer our question, but actually inten-
sifies it. If the Torah offers reasons for the mitzvos of *Korban Pesach*,
matzah, and maror, why didn't *Bach* enumerate these in his list of
mitzvos for which one must have in mind the Torah's reason?

Out of these three mitzvos, the reason for *Korban Pesach* is
alluded to in the Torah: "You shall say, 'It is a Pesach offering to
Hashem, *Who passed over the houses of Bnei Yisrael in Egypt*'"
(*Shemos* 12:27). The Torah does not give a reason for the mitzvos of
matzah and maror, however. Regarding matzah, the Torah simply

According to some opinions, if one neglects to mention these three things he does not fulfill his obligation in the ideal way (*Ran, Pesachim* 116; *Darkei Moshe* 473:19). Others hold that he does not fulfill his obligation at all (*Pri Megadim* 473, *Eishel Avraham* 1. This seems to be the opinion of *Tosafos*).

One must explain these three things to his family
in a language they can understand.

One should not hold meat in his hand when discussing the symbolism of the *Korban Pesach*, so that it should not appear as though he is sanctifying this meat as an offering (*Mishnah Berurah* 463:72). Some hold that he should nevertheless show it to the rest of the family (*Bach*).

פסחים קטז, ב

פֶּסַח שֶׁהָיוּ אֲבוֹתֵינוּ אוֹכְלִים בִּזְמַן שֶׁבֵּית הַמִּקְדָּשׁ הָיָה קַיָּם, עַל שׁוּם מָה? עַל שׁוּם שֶׁפָּסַח הַקָּדוֹשׁ בָּרוּךְ הוּא עַל בָּתֵּי אֲבוֹתֵינוּ בְּמִצְרָיִם. שֶׁנֶּאֱמַר, וַאֲמַרְתֶּם, זֶבַח פֶּסַח הוּא לַיהוה, אֲשֶׁר פָּסַח עַל בָּתֵּי בְנֵי יִשְׂרָאֵל בְּמִצְרַיִם בְּנָגְפּוֹ אֶת מִצְרַיִם, וְאֶת בָּתֵּינוּ הִצִּיל, וַיִּקֹּד הָעָם וַיִּשְׁתַּחֲווּ.¹

tells us that the dough that the Jews took with them as they left Egypt did not have time to rise, but it does not tell us that we eat matzah for that reason. And the Torah tells us that the Egyptians embittered the lives of the Jews, but not that we eat maror to commemorate the embitterment of our lives. If so, these mitzvos cannot belong to the category of mitzvos for which the Torah gives a reason, and we therefore cannot say that Rabban Gamliel's statement is in accordance with *Bach*'s opinion.[1]

Apparently, reasons that the Torah gives explicitly — such as the reasons for the mitzvos of succah, *tzitzis*, and *tefillin* — differ from non-explicit reasons, such as those given for matzah and maror. This distinction would explain why *Bach* does not list matzah and maror along with succah, *tzitzis*, and *tefillin*. But it still does not explain why *Korban Pesach* — which does have an explicit reason in the Torah — is not included in *Bach*'s list.

---

1. *Haggadah Divrei Shaul* and *Bikkurei Yaakov* (625) do use *Bach*'s opinion to explain Rabban Gamliel's statement. They write that if one does not tell the reasons for *Korban Pesach*, matzah, and maror, he does not fulfill his obligation to eat those foods. In my opinion, however, the fact that *Bach* does not enumerate these mitzvos is proof that this halachah only applies to succah, *tzitzis*, and *tefillin*, for if these are the reasons for these mitzvos, why do we not have to have the reasons in mind when performing these mitzvos?

According to some opinions, if one neglects to mention these three things he does not fulfill his obligation in the ideal way (*Ran, Pesachim* 116; *Darkei Moshe* 473:19). Others hold that he does not fulfill his obligation at all (*Pri Megadim* 473, *Eishel Avraham* 1. This seems to be the opinion of *Tosafos*).

One must explain these three things to his family
in a language they can understand.

One should not hold meat in his hand when discussing the symbolism of the *Korban Pesach*, so that it should not appear as though he is sanctifying this meat as an offering (*Mishnah Berurah* 463:72). Some hold that he should nevertheless show it to the rest of the family (*Bach*).

Pesachim 116b

Pesach — Why did our fathers eat a Pesach offering during the period when the Beis Hamikdash still stood? Because the Holy One, Blessed is He, passed over the houses of our fathers in Egypt, as it is written: "You shall say: 'It is a Pesach offering for HASHEM, Who passed over the houses of Bnei Yisrael in Egypt when He struck the Egyptians and spared our houses'; and the people bowed down and prostrated themselves."[1]

---

(1) *Shemos* 12:27.

To understand the difference between the mitzvos listed by *Bach* and the mitzvos of *Korban Pesach*, matzah, and maror, we have to distinguish between *reason* and *purpose*. *Bach*'s opinion is that the Torah requires us to have in mind the *purpose* of the mitzvah while performing it. He therefore enumerates the mitzvos whose purpose is explained by the Torah: "*So that* your generations will know," "*So that* you may remember," "*So that* Hashem's Torah may be in your mouth." In these instances, the Torah is telling us that the purpose of the mitzvah is to bring a person to a certain realization or achievement. According to *Bach*, that realization or achievement is the very purpose of the mitzvah, and is therefore an integral aspect of its performance.

When the Torah gives a *reason* for a mitzvah, however, that reason does not become the purpose of the mitzvah. One therefore does not have to consciously recall that reason at the time when he performs the mitzvah.

The Torah does not explain the purpose of *Korban Pesach*, matzah, and maror, and that is why *Bach* did not include these mitzvos along with succah, *tzitzis*, and *tefillin*. If so, what did Rabban Gamliel mean when he taught that fulfillment of the mitzvos of *Korban Pesach*,

The broken half of the middle matzah is lifted and displayed
while the following paragraph is recited.

פסחים קטז, ב

מַצָּה זוֹ שֶׁאָנוּ אוֹכְלִים, עַל שׁוּם מָה? עַל שׁוּם
שֶׁלֹּא הִסְפִּיק בְּצֵקָם שֶׁל אֲבוֹתֵינוּ לְהַחֲמִיץ,
עַד שֶׁנִּגְלָה עֲלֵיהֶם מֶלֶךְ מַלְכֵי הַמְּלָכִים הַקָּדוֹשׁ
בָּרוּךְ הוּא וּגְאָלָם. שֶׁנֶּאֱמַר, וַיֹּאפוּ אֶת הַבָּצֵק אֲשֶׁר
הוֹצִיאוּ מִמִּצְרַיִם עֻגֹת מַצּוֹת כִּי לֹא חָמֵץ, כִּי גֹרְשׁוּ
מִמִּצְרַיִם, וְלֹא יָכְלוּ לְהִתְמַהְמֵהַּ, וְגַם צֵדָה לֹא עָשׂוּ
לָהֶם.[1]

The maror is lifted and displayed
while the following paragraph is recited.

שם

מָרוֹר זֶה שֶׁאָנוּ אוֹכְלִים, עַל שׁוּם מָה? עַל שׁוּם

---

matzah, and maror is contingent upon explaining their reasons?

Furthermore, the Talmud (ibid.) teaches that one who swallows maror without chewing it does not fulfill his obligation to eat maror. *Rashbam* explains that Hashem specifically wanted us to taste the bitterness of the maror and recall how the Egyptians embittered our lives. This halachah seems to support the premise that the reason for eating maror is an integral part of the performance of the mitzvah.

The *Rishonim* take two approaches in explaining Rabban Gamliel's statement. *Tosafos* says that Rabban Gamliel's statement is based on the verse, "You shall say, 'It is a Pesach offering for Hashem.'" The words "You shall **say**" teach that the *Korban Pesach* must be accompanied by discussion of the mitzvah, and of the related mitzvos — matzah and maror — as well.

Shibolei Haleket (218) writes that Rabban Gamliel's statement is based on the verse, "**It is because of this** that Hashem did so for me when I left Egypt." *Chazal* derive from this verse that the mitzvah of relating the story of the Exodus is at the time when matzah and maror lie before us. This indicates that discussion of the mitzvos of matzah and maror is fundamental to the mitzvah of relating the story of the Exodus.

Both of these approaches suggest that because we are commanded

The broken half of the middle matzah is lifted and displayed
while the following paragraph is recited.

Pesachim 116b

Matzah — Why do we eat this unleavened bread? Because the dough of our fathers did not have time to become leavened before the King of kings, the Holy One, Blessed is He, revealed Himself to them and redeemed them, as it is written: "They baked the dough which they had brought out of Egypt into unleavened bread, for it had not fermented, because they were driven out of Egypt and could not delay, nor had they prepared any provisions for themselves."[1]

The maror is lifted and displayed
while the following paragraph is recited.

Ibid.

Maror — Why do we eat this bitter herb? Because

_____
(1) *Shemos* 12:39.

---

to explain the reasons for the mitzvos of matzah and maror, it became necessary for the Sages to expound and give reasons for these mitzvos.[1] Otherwise, we would not know how to explain them. If so, the mitzvah of relating the story of the Exodus and explaining the mitzvos of matzah and maror is included in the Sages' obligation to explain the reasons for the mitzvos with their Divine Inspiration and profound understanding.

מָרוֹר זֶה שֶׁאָנוּ אוֹכְלִים, עַל שׁוּם מָה
Why do we eat this bitter herb?

The first vegetable listed in the Mishnah (*Pesachim* 39a) as a bitter herb that may be used for maror is *chazeres*. The Talmud explains that *chazeres* is *chasah* (romaine lettuce). The symbolism of *chasah* is that Hashem was חָס, *had mercy*, on us and redeemed us from Egypt.

We can understand this passage from the Talmud on a deeper level. The word מָרוֹר has the same *gematria* (numeric value) as the word מָוֶת, *death*. The word חָס has the same *gematria* as חַיִּים *life*. Maror has the power to exchange strict justice for mercy, by removing a death sentence and inscribing us for life. Thus the Talmud is

_____
1. נִמְסַר הַדָּבָר לַחֲכָמִים, "This matter was given over to the Sages." See *Minchas Asher*, *Devarim* 27 for further discussion of this idea.

שֶׁמֵּרְרוּ הַמִּצְרִים אֶת חַיֵּי אֲבוֹתֵינוּ בְּמִצְרַיִם.
שֶׁנֶּאֱמַר, וַיְמָרְרוּ אֶת חַיֵּיהֶם, בַּעֲבֹדָה קָשָׁה,
בְּחֹמֶר וּבִלְבֵנִים, וּבְכָל עֲבֹדָה בַּשָּׂדֶה, אֵת כָּל
עֲבֹדָתָם אֲשֶׁר עָבְדוּ בָהֶם בְּפָרֶךְ.[1]

---

teaching us that Hashem is חָס *has mercy* on us when we eat the *chasah*.

Yismach Yisrael notes that the *mispar kattan*[1] of מַצָּה is equal to the *gematria* of the word חַי. We noted above that מָרוֹר has the same *gematria* as מָוֶת, *death*. When matzah and maror are eaten together — as we do in *Korech* in accordance with Hillel's custom — it is a hint that even those who are at the gates of death can merit long, blessed years of life by fulfilling the mitzvos of Pesach night.

Along the same lines, *Chasam Sofer* notes in his Haggadah that מַצָּה is an acronym for מִכָּל צָרָה הִצִּילָנוּ, *[Hashem] rescued us from all distress*, and *Zohar* (*Parashas Tetzaveh*, 183b) states that in the merit of the matzah we eat on Pesach, we are vindicated in our judgment on Rosh Hashanah.

עַל שׁוּם שֶׁמֵּרְרוּ הַמִּצְרִים אֶת חַיֵּי אֲבוֹתֵינוּ בְּמִצְרַיִם
Because the Egyptians embittered
the lives of our fathers in Egypt

We are supposed to conduct ourselves like free men on Pesach night. Why do we eat maror, a symbol of our servitude?

We eat maror to instill a firm awareness in our hearts that even when misfortune seems to strike it is also for the best, because all that Hashem does is for the best.

The Torah states, "You are children to Hashem, your God — you shall not cut yourselves and you shall not make a bald spot between your eyes for a dead person" (*Devarim* 14:1).

Ibn Ezra comments that Hashem loves us more than any father could ever love his son. We should therefore not mourn excessively over the sorrows that befall us, because all that happens to us is in our own best interests. We might not always understand Hashem's

---

1. *Mispar kattan* (lit. a small number) is a form of *gematria* in which a number that equals a multiple of 10 is assigned the value of its first digit. In *mispar kattan*, מ equals 4 instead of 40; צ equals 9 instead of 90; and ה remains 5 for a total of 18, which is the full *gematria* of the word חַי.

the Egyptians embittered the lives of our fathers
in Egypt, as it says: "They embittered their lives
with hard labor, with mortar and bricks, and with all
manner of labor in the field: Whatever service they
made them perform was with hard labor."[1]

---

(1) *Shemos* 1:14.

---

designs, but we should trust in Him just as a child trusts his father
even if he does not understand his decisions.

This was R' Akiva's approach to life. No matter what happened, he
would say, "All that the Merciful One does is for the best" (*Berachos*
60b). R' Akiva laughed even as he was being led to his execution for
teaching Torah (*Yerushalmi Berachos* 9:5; *Sotah* 5:5), and his positive
outlook extended to various other situations (see *Sanhedrin* 101a;
Makkos 24a). [**There should be a link here to the mussar essay in which
he records R' Akiva's positive reactions.**]

I heard from my *rebbi*, the Klausenberger Rebbe *zt"l*, that this is
why we cover our eyes when we accept Hashem's Sovereignty
upon ourselves in *Shema* (as discussed in *Berachos* 13a). In *Shema*
we declare, אֶחָד ה' אֱלֹקֵינוּ ה': The Name ה' (י-ה-ו-ה) represents
Hashem's Attribute of Mercy, and אֱלֹקֵינוּ the Attribute of Justice,
but in *Shema* we declare that both Names are one, since the Attribute of Justice is also a manifestation of Hashem's mercy. Hashem's
justice often appears to be so harsh that we must cover our eyes to
hide the outward appearance, and declare ה' אֱלֹקֵינוּ ה' אֶחָד,
expressing our firm belief that everything He does is for our best.

Kol Aryeh (Introduction, *Ma'amar Pesach Tov* 7) offers a beautiful
explanation of the verses in which Hashem tells Yaakov Avinu, "Do
not fear to descend to Egypt ... Yosef will place his hands over your
eyes" (*Bereishis* 46:3,4).

Yaakov considered his descent to Egypt a terrible misfortune, but
Hashem reassured him that in the end he would see that it was
actually for the best, like Yosef's descent into slavery. Yosef's descent also seemed like a terrible misfortune at first, but in the end it
became apparent that the entire story had been a manifestation of
Hashem's hidden kindness: Yosef became the viceroy to Pharaoh,
and was able to support Yaakov's family during the years of famine.

When Hashem told Yaakov that Yosef would place his hands over
his eyes, He was referring to the practice of covering our eyes when
we recite *Shema*. He reminded Yaakov that we must ignore outward
appearances, and trust that Hashem's Attribute of Justice is actually
part of His Attribute of Mercy.

בְּכָל דּוֹר וָדוֹר חַיָּב אָדָם לִרְאוֹת אֶת עַצְמוֹ כְּאִלוּ הוּא יָצָא מִמִּצְרַיִם. שֶׁנֶּאֱמַר, וְהִגַּדְתָּ לְבִנְךָ בַּיּוֹם הַהוּא לֵאמֹר, בַּעֲבוּר זֶה עָשָׂה יהוה לִי, בְּצֵאתִי מִמִּצְרָיִם.¹ לֹא אֶת אֲבוֹתֵינוּ בִּלְבָד גָּאַל הַקָּדוֹשׁ בָּרוּךְ הוּא, אֶלָּא אַף אֹתָנוּ גָּאַל עִמָּהֶם. שֶׁנֶּאֱמַר, וְאוֹתָנוּ הוֹצִיא מִשָּׁם, לְמַעַן הָבִיא אֹתָנוּ לָתֶת לָנוּ אֶת הָאָרֶץ אֲשֶׁר נִשְׁבַּע לַאֲבוֹתֵינוּ.²

This is why *Zohar* describes the incident of Yosef's sale to Egypt as "the secret of *Kerias Shema*."

Similarly, *Kol Aryeh* cites *Chasam Sofer's* explanation of the verse, "You will see My back, but My face you may not see" (*Shemos* 33:23): We cannot always see the face of Hashem and His kindness when tragedy descends upon us. Many years later, however, we can often see His kindness in retrospect — "from the back" — and realize that all was for the best.

As we noted earlier, the Talmud (*Pesachim* 39a) explains that *chasah* alludes to Hashem having mercy (*chas*) on us. *Chasam Sofer* (*Teshuvos*, O.C. 132) points out that תַּמְכָא, another herb that can be used as maror, is an acronym for תָּמִיד מְסַפְּרִים כְּבוֹד אֵל, *Constantly relating the honor of Hashem.*

Chasam Sofer adds that his *rebbi*, R' Nosson Adler, invested much effort into identifying the vegetable known as *karpas*, because *Maharil* said that the word כַּרְפַּס is comprised of the letters ס' פרך, which means that 600,000 people endured crushing harshness from the Egyptians.¹ He found that the vegetable commonly used is called אַפְיָא in most European languages, which can be an acronym for אַ-ל פּוֹעֵל יְשׁוּעוֹת אָתָּה, *For You effect salvations, O God.*

It would seem that *Chasam Sofer* and R' Nosson Adler were not simply trying to find acronyms for the items we use at the Seder. They were teaching us that the purpose of the maror is to remind us to constantly declare the Glory of God; even during the most bitter and painful episodes of our lives, we should realize that Hashem is

---

1. The ס', which has a *gematria* of 60, stands for the 60 ten-thousands who were enslaved under crushingly harsh conditions in Egypt.

In every generation, it is one's duty to view himself as if he personally had gone out of Egypt, as it is written: "You shall tell your son on that day: It is because of this that HASHEM did for 'me' when I went out of Egypt."[1] It was not only our fathers whom the Holy One, Blessed is He, redeemed from slavery; we, too, were redeemed with them, as it is written: "He brought 'us' out from there so that He might take us to the land which He had promised to our fathers."[2]

---

(1) *Shemos* 13:8. (2) *Devarim* 6:23.

---

truly looking to benefit us, and that He can prepare the remedy from the very ailment from which we are suffering.

בְּכָל דּוֹר וָדוֹר חַיָּב אָדָם לִרְאוֹת אֶת עַצְמוֹ כְּאִלּוּ הוּא יָצָא מִמִּצְרָיִם
In every generation, it is one's duty to view himself as if he personally had left Egypt

In the version of the Haggadah commonly recited, we say that it is our duty לִרְאוֹת, *to view* ourselves as if we left Egypt. The version *Rambam* cites in his halachic work, *Mishnah Torah* (*Hilchos Chametz U'Matzah* 7:6) contains a slight variation — instead of לִרְאוֹת, *to view*, it says לְהַרְאוֹת, *to demonstrate*. In his commentary to the Mishnah, however, he cites the commonly accepted wording of לִרְאוֹת, *to view*.

It would seem that this subtle difference in wording highlights two distinct aspects of the Seder night. Viewing ourselves as if we left Egypt requires us to internalize the appreciation we have toward Hashem for the miracles He performed for us. Demonstrating that it is as though we ourselves left Egypt requires us to publicize Hashem's miracles (*pirsumei nisa*). These two obligations are expressed in a verse in *Tehillim* (107:8): "Let them give thanks to Hashem for His kindness and [tell] His wonders to the children of man." The first part of the verse bids us to appreciate Hashem's miracles; the second half bids us to publicize those miracles.

In the introduction to *Sefer Hamitzvos, Rambam* writes: "We were commanded to read the *Megillah* in its appropriate time in order to relate the praises of Hashem and recall the miraculous salvations He

The matzos are covered and the cup is lifted and held until after the blessing אֲשֶׁר גְּאָלָנוּ, *Who redeemed us* (p. 184), so that this song of praise is recited over a cup of wine. According to some customs, however, the cup is put down after the following paragraph, in which case the matzos should once more be uncovered. If this custom is followed, the matzos are to be covered and the cup raised again upon reaching the blessing אֲשֶׁר גְּאָלָנוּ, *Who redeemed us* (p. 184).

פסחים קטז, ב

לְפִיכָךְ אֲנַחְנוּ חַיָּבִים לְהוֹדוֹת, לְהַלֵּל, לְשַׁבֵּחַ, לְפָאֵר, לְרוֹמֵם, לְהַדֵּר, לְבָרֵךְ, לְעַלֵּה, וּלְקַלֵּס, לְמִי שֶׁעָשָׂה לַאֲבוֹתֵינוּ וְלָנוּ אֶת כָּל הַנִּסִּים

performed for our forefathers when He drew close to answer their prayers. We are thereby inspired to bless and praise Him, and tell the generations that come after us that the Torah's assurances are all true — 'Hashem our God is close to us whenever we call out to Him" (*Devarim* 4:7).

Rambam teaches that a proper expression of gratitude contains two aspects: personal appreciation for the miracles that Hashem has performed for us, and the publicizing of those miracles.

לְפִיכָךְ אֲנַחְנוּ חַיָּבִים. . . לְמִי שֶׁעָשָׂה לַאֲבוֹתֵינוּ וְלָנוּ אֶת כָּל הַנִּסִּים הָאֵלּוּ
Therefore it is our duty to thank, praise, pay tribute,
glorify, exalt, honor, bless, extol, and acclaim Him
Who performed all these miracles for our fathers and for us.

It is interesting to note that we mention our forefathers before ourselves in this passage — "Who performed all these miracles for our fathers and for us" — but in the blessing that concludes *Maggid*, we reverse the order: "Who redeemed us and redeemed our ancestors from Egypt."[1]

Haggadas Maaseh Nissim (by the author of *Nesivos Hamishpat*) explains that when we thank Hashem for His miracles, we thank Him first for the miracles our forefathers experienced. This is because the miracles performed for our forefathers were much greater than those that we experience in our exile, in which the Divine Presence conceals Itself as much as possible.

When we thank Hashem for redeeming us from Egypt, on the

---

1. This only applies to our version of the text, which apparently follows that of R' Amram Gaon. This discrepancy does not exist in *Rambam's* version of the text (*Hilchos Chametz U'Matzah* 8:5), which places us before our forefathers in both instances.

The matzos are covered and the cup is lifted and held until after the blessing אֲשֶׁר גְּאָלָנוּ, *Who redeemed us* (p. 184), so that this song of praise is recited over a cup of wine. According to some customs, however, the cup is put down after the following paragraph, in which case the matzos should once more be uncovered. If this custom is followed, the matzos are to be covered and the cup raised again upon reaching the blessing אֲשֶׁר גְּאָלָנוּ, *Who has redeemed us* (p. 184).

Pesachim 116b

Therefore it is our duty to thank, praise, pay tribute, glorify, exalt, honor, bless, extol, and acclaim Him Who performed all these miracles for our fathers and

---

other hand, we thank Him first for our own redemption. Our fore-fathers suffered through many years of slavery and oppression before they were redeemed, but we did not have to suffer from Pharaoh's cruel decrees.

לְפִיכָךְ אֲנַחְנוּ חַיָּבִים לְהוֹדוֹת, לְהַלֵּל
Therefore it is our duty to thank, praise,

The words לְהוֹדוֹת לְהַלֵּל also appear in the prayer of *Al Hanissim* recited on Chanukah. Interestingly, some versions of *Al Hanissim* place them in the reverse order: וְקָבְעוּ שְׁמוֹנַת יָמִים אֵלּוּ, בְּהַלֵּל וּלְהוֹדָיָה.

What is the difference between *hallel* and *hoda'ah*, and why do some reverse the order on Chanukah?

As we discussed above,[1] a person who experiences Hashem's miraculous salvation has a twofold obligation: to appreciate Hashem's kindness and thank Him for it; to publicize the miracle (*pirsumei nisa*), in order to sanctify and exalt Hashem's Name in the world.

Hoda'ah is a person's private expression of thanks to Hashem, as we find in the first half of the verse cited above: יוֹדוּ לַה' חַסְדּוֹ, *Let them give thanks to Hashem for His kindness*. *Hallel* means to praise Hashem publicly for the miracles one experiences; this is alluded to in the second half of the verse: "and [tell] His wonders to the children of man."

On Pesach we are obligated to view ourselves as if we personally left Egypt. We are overcome with personal feelings of gratitude, and therefore we place *hoda'ah* before *hallel*. On Chanukah and Purim, however, there is no mitzvah to view ourselves as if we had personally been saved from the Greeks or from Haman. Our primary focus then is on *pirsumei nisa* — publicizing the miracles that

---

1. In our comment on the passage, "In every generation" (p. 176).

הָאֵלּוּ, הוֹצִיאָנוּ מֵעַבְדוּת לְחֵרוּת, מִיָּגוֹן לְשִׂמְחָה, וּמֵאֵבֶל לְיוֹם טוֹב, וּמֵאֲפֵלָה לְאוֹר גָּדוֹל, וּמִשִּׁעְבּוּד לִגְאֻלָּה, וְנֹאמַר לְפָנָיו שִׁירָה חֲדָשָׁה, הַלְלוּיָהּ.

[The matzos are now uncovered, and Hallel is begun.
It should be recited with joyous song.
The recitation of the following two chapters of Hallel follows
Beis Hillel's ruling (*Pesachim* 116b), (*Minchas Asher*).]

הַלְלוּיָהּ הַלְלוּ עַבְדֵי יהוה, הַלְלוּ אֶת שֵׁם יהוה. יְהִי שֵׁם יהוה מְבֹרָךְ, מֵעַתָּה וְעַד עוֹלָם. מִמִּזְרַח שֶׁמֶשׁ עַד מְבוֹאוֹ, מְהֻלָּל שֵׁם יהוה. רָם

Hashem performed for our forefathers. Therefore, *hallel* comes before *hoda'ah*.

⋯⟐⋯

The Vilna Gaon writes in his commentary to the Haggadah that there are nine expressions of thanksgiving in the beginning of this section, corresponding to the first nine plagues. The conclusion of this section, "And we shall sing before Him a new song, Halleluyah. — Halleluyah, give praise, O servants of Hashem," corresponds to the final plague, the plague of the firstborn.

Hallel can only be recited upon a complete redemption. The Talmud explains that we do not say Hallel on Purim because the Jews remained subservient to Achashveirosh even after Haman's downfall (*Megillah* 14a). For this same reason, we could not say Hallel until after the plague of the firstborn, when Bnei Yisrael were allowed to leave Egypt, and the yoke of Egyptian slavery was removed from us entirely.

⋯⟐⋯

Thanking Hashem for His salvation is part of the mitzvah of recounting the Exodus on Pesach night, as *Rambam* writes (*Sefer Hamitzvos*, Positive Commandment 157):

> We are commanded to tell the story of the Exodus on the fifteenth of Nissan, at the beginning of the night, each person according to his level of rhetorical skill. One should speak at length to dramatize the miracles Hashem performed for us — he should discuss the terrible iniquities that the Egyptians

for us, Who brought us forth from slavery to freedom, from grief to joy, from mourning to festivity, from darkness to great light, and from servitude to redemption. And we shall sing before Him a new song, Halleluyah!

[The matzos are now uncovered, and Hallel is begun.
It should be recited with joyous song.
The recitation of the following two chapters of Hallel follows
Beis Hillel's ruling (*Pesachim* 116b), (*Minchas Asher*).]

Halleluyah, give praise, O servants of HASHEM, praise the Name of HASHEM. Blessed is the Name of HASHEM from now and forever. From the rising of the sun to its setting, HASHEM's Name is praised. High

---

perpetrated against us, and how Hashem exacted retribution from them, and praise Him for all the kindness He has dealt us. In the words of the Haggadah, "The more one tells about the Exodus, the more he is praiseworthy."

הוֹצִיאָנוּ מֵעַבְדוּת לְחֵרוּת
Who brought us from slavery to freedom

"Therefore, say to Bnei Yisrael: 'I am Hashem, and I shall take you out from under the burdens of Egypt; I shall rescue you from their service; I shall redeem you with an outstretched arm and with great judgments. I shall take you to Me for a people" (*Shemos* 6:6-7).

Slavery is inherently difficult, but there are different levels of slavery. Some slaves suffer under the hands of cruel and tyrannical masters who beat them mercilessly, and are subject to incessant physical and verbal abuse. Others are lucky enough to have merciful masters who do not beat them, but they still suffer from the difficult workload imposed upon them. The most fortunate slaves are those that are only required to perform light household tasks. But even such slaves are subject to the will of their masters, and suffer from the lack of freedom intrinsic to servitude.

Pharaoh was a terribly evil master, and he subjected the Jews to death, torture, and grueling labor. Hashem rescued us from all the difficult circumstances that we endured. He *took us out* from the burden of their cruel abuse. He *rescued us* from the difficult labors

עַל כָּל גּוֹיִם יהוה, עַל הַשָּׁמַיִם כְּבוֹדוֹ. מִי כַּיהוה
אֱלֹהֵינוּ, הַמַּגְבִּיהִי לָשָׁבֶת. הַמַּשְׁפִּילִי לִרְאוֹת,
בַּשָּׁמַיִם וּבָאָרֶץ. מְקִימִי מֵעָפָר דָּל, מֵאַשְׁפֹּת יָרִים
אֶבְיוֹן. לְהוֹשִׁיבִי עִם נְדִיבִים, עִם נְדִיבֵי עַמּוֹ. מוֹשִׁיבִי
עֲקֶרֶת הַבַּיִת, אֵם הַבָּנִים שְׂמֵחָה, הַלְלוּיָהּ.[1]

---

they imposed upon us. He *redeemed us* from the degradation of
slavery. Above all, however, was the great kindness He showed us
by *taking us* to Himself and making us His people.

מִי כַה' אֱלֹהֵינוּ, הַמַּגְבִּיהִי לָשָׁבֶת.
הַמַּשְׁפִּילִי לִרְאוֹת, בַּשָּׁמַיִם וּבָאָרֶץ
Who is like Hashem, our God, Who is enthroned on high,
yet deigns to look upon Heaven and earth?

Many ancient cultures believed that Hashem created the world,
but they erred in their assumption that once He finished Creation,
He ascended to the highest Heavens and ceased to interact with
Creation. Those cultures denied the idea of Divine Providence,
and did not believe in any system of Heavenly reward and punishment.

This chapter in *Tehillim* addresses that false ideology. King David
writes, "High above all nations is Hashem, above the Heavens is His
glory" (113:4) — i.e., the nations believe that Hashem is so exalted
that He raises Himself above the Heavens (see *Ramban, Shemos*
13:16).

We know the truth. Hashem's true greatness lies in the fact that
despite His exaltedness, he lowers Himself to observe all that occurs
in Heaven and on earth — as the chapter continues, "Who is like
Hashem, our God, Who is enthroned on high, yet deigns to look
upon Heaven and earth?" Hashem's infinite Glory fills and surrounds all the worlds, both above and below. He pays specific
attention to all His creations, large and small.

מְקִימִי מֵעָפָר דָּל, מֵאַשְׁפֹּת יָרִים אֶבְיוֹן
He raises the destitute from the dust;
from the trash heaps He lifts the needy

It is from the darkest depths of exile that the light of redemption
will shine forth. The prophet said, "Do not rejoice over me, my

above all nations is HASHEM, above the Heavens is His glory. Who is like HASHEM, our God, Who is enthroned on high, yet deigns to look upon Heaven and earth? He raises the destitute from the dust; from the trash heaps He lifts the needy — to seat them with nobles, with nobles of His people. He transforms the barren wife into a glad mother of children. Halleluyah![1]

---

(1) *Tehillim* 113.

---

enemy, for though I fell, I will rise! Though I sit in the darkness, Hashem is a light unto me" (*Michah* 7:8). *Chazal* (*Midrash Tehillim,* 22) explain that one leads to the other — had we not fallen, we could not have risen; had we not sat in darkness, we could not have experienced Hashem's great light.

Rabbeinu Yonah (*Shaarei Teshuvah* 2:5) writes that a person who has firm faith in Hashem must realize in his most difficult moments that the darkness he is experiencing will enable him to achieve the greatest possible light. This is part of Hashem's unfathomable plan for Creation. When darkness seems to have completely engulfed the earth, and no ray of light is to be seen, "Then your light will burst out like the dawn and your healing will speedily sprout" (*Yeshayah* 58:8).

Hashem told Yaakov Avinu, "Your offspring shall be as the dust of the earth, and you shall spread out powerfully westward, eastward, northward, and southward" (*Bereishis* 28:14).

Sforno writes that when we — Yaakov's offspring — will become like the dust of the earth, reaching the lowest possible level of degradation, only then will we break forth beyond all boundaries and inherit Eretz Yisrael forever.

The ultimate Redemption will only come when we sink to the lowest possible level, as the Talmud states (*Sanhedrin* 98a), "If you see a generation in which a river of misfortune sweeps over the Jewish people, it is then that you should expect the coming of Mashiach."

From the trash heaps of poverty and suffering, Hashem will soon uplift the Jewish people to the greatest heights. May we merit seeing this prophecy fulfilled soon and in our days.

בְּצֵאת יִשְׂרָאֵל מִמִּצְרָיִם, בֵּית יַעֲקֹב מֵעַם לֹעֵז. הָיְתָה יְהוּדָה לְקָדְשׁוֹ, יִשְׂרָאֵל מַמְשְׁלוֹתָיו. הַיָּם רָאָה וַיָּנֹס, הַיַּרְדֵּן יִסֹּב לְאָחוֹר. הֶהָרִים רָקְדוּ כְאֵילִים, גְּבָעוֹת כִּבְנֵי צֹאן. מַה לְּךָ הַיָּם כִּי תָנוּס, הַיַּרְדֵּן תִּסֹּב לְאָחוֹר. הֶהָרִים תִּרְקְדוּ כְאֵילִים, גְּבָעוֹת כִּבְנֵי צֹאן. מִלִּפְנֵי אָדוֹן חוּלִי אָרֶץ, מִלִּפְנֵי אֱלוֹהַּ יַעֲקֹב. הַהֹפְכִי הַצּוּר אֲגַם מָיִם, חַלָּמִישׁ לְמַעְיְנוֹ מָיִם.[1]

Those who have the custom to put down the cup before Halleluyah, should lift it up again here until after the *berachah*. The matzos are covered, and the *berachah* is recited.

According to all customs the cup is lifted and the matzos covered during the recitation of this blessing.

בָּרוּךְ אַתָּה יהוה אֱלֹהֵינוּ מֶלֶךְ הָעוֹלָם, אֲשֶׁר גְּאָלָנוּ וְגָאַל אֶת אֲבוֹתֵינוּ מִמִּצְרָיִם, וְהִגִּיעָנוּ הַלַּיְלָה הַזֶּה לֶאֱכָל בּוֹ מַצָּה וּמָרוֹר.

קְרִיעַת יַם סוּף — The Splitting of the Yam Suf

When Bnei Yisrael left Egypt, "Hashem went before them by day in a pillar of cloud to lead them on the way" (*Shemos* 13:21). Immediately prior to the splitting of the Yam Suf, the pillar of cloud moved behind them: "The angel of Hashem who had been going in front of the camp of Israel moved and went behind them; and the pillar of cloud moved from before them and went behind them" (*Shemos* 14:19).

What is the significance of the pillar of cloud moving behind the Jews?

Zohar tells us that when the Jewish people perform Hashem's Will faithfully, He walks before us. When we disobey Him, He walks behind us (*Zohar, Parashas Shelach* IV, 166a). *Ateres Tzvi* cites from R' Moshe of P'shevorsk that when a master knows that his slave is faithful, he lets his slave walk behind him, because he is not worried that the slave will try to escape. When a master has a disloyal slave, however, then he makes the slave walk before him so that he can keep a sharp eye on his every movement.

When Israel went forth from Egypt, Jacob's household from a people of alien tongue, Judah became His sanctuary, Israel His dominion. The Sea
saw and fled; the Jordan turned backward. The
mountains skipped like rams, and the hills like young
lambs. What ails you, O Sea, that you flee? O Jordan,
that you turn backward? O mountains, that you skip
like rams? O hills, like young lambs? Before HASHEM's
presence — tremble, O earth, before the presence of
the God of Jacob, Who turns the rock into a pond of
water, the flint into a flowing fountain.[1]

Those who have the custom to put down the cup before Halleluyah,
should lift it up again here until after the *berachah*. The matzos are
covered, and the *berachah* is recited.
According to all customs the cup is lifted
and the matzos covered during the recitation of this blessing.

Blessed are You, HASHEM, our God, King of the
universe, Who redeemed us and redeemed our
ancestors from Egypt and enabled us to reach this
night that we may eat on it matzah and maror.

---

(1) *Tehillim* 114.

The same is true of the relationship between Hashem and the Jewish
people. When we are loyal to Him, He walks before us. When we are
disloyal, He walks behind us. When Hashem told the Jewish people,
"Behold! I am sending an angel before you, to guard you on the path"
(*Shemos* 23:20), He was warning them to remain faithful to Him so that
the angel should continue to go before them, and not be forced to
walk behind them. This is also the meaning of the verse, "Hashem,
your God, shall you follow" (*Devarim* 13:5) — we must prove ourselves to be loyal to Him so that that He can let us *follow* Him.

When Bnei Yisrael first left Egypt, they showed their faithfulness
and loyalty to Hashem's word: "Thus said Hashem, I recall for you
the kindness of your youth, the love of your nuptials, your following
Me into the Wilderness, into an unsown land" (*Yirmiyah* 2:2). When
they stood at the Yam Suf, however, they rebelled against Him by
complaining, "Were there no graves in Egypt that you took us to die
in the Wilderness?" (*Shemos* 14:11). These are not the words of a
loyal servant. Therefore, Hashem sent His emissary, the pillar of
cloud, to walk behind them.

(On Saturday night the phrase in parentheses
substitutes for the preceding phrase.)

כֵּן יהוה אֱלֹהֵינוּ וֵאלֹהֵי אֲבוֹתֵינוּ, יַגִּיעֵנוּ לְמוֹעֲדִים
וְלִרְגָלִים אֲחֵרִים הַבָּאִים לִקְרָאתֵנוּ לְשָׁלוֹם, שְׂמֵחִים
בְּבִנְיַן עִירֶךָ וְשָׂשִׂים בַּעֲבוֹדָתֶךָ, וְנֹאכַל שָׁם מִן
הַזְּבָחִים וּמִן הַפְּסָחִים [מִן הַפְּסָחִים וּמִן הַזְּבָחִים]
אֲשֶׁר יַגִּיעַ דָּמָם עַל קִיר מִזְבַּחֲךָ לְרָצוֹן. וְנוֹדֶה
לְךָ שִׁיר חָדָשׁ עַל גְּאֻלָתֵנוּ וְעַל פְּדוּת נַפְשֵׁנוּ.

יַגִּיעֵנוּ לְמוֹעֲדִים וְלִרְגָלִים אֲחֵרִים
Bring us also to future holidays and festivals

The three festivals — Pesach, Shavuos, and Succos — commemorate three different stages of the Exodus. They also represent three different stages in our service of Hashem: shunning evil, preparing ourselves for good, and ultimately performing good deeds.

Pesach commemorates our initial flight from Egypt, when the yoke of Egyptian bondage was removed from us. Egypt was the most perverse of nations. When Bnei Yisrael dwelt there, the Egyptians had a terrible influence on our souls; they corrupted and defiled us. When we were redeemed, their influence was also removed from us, and we began to purify ourselves from the corruption of Egypt. Therefore, Pesach represents the stage of a person's growth in which he abandons his evil ways.

Succos commemorates the Clouds of Glory with which Hashem shielded us when we traveled through the desert. The clouds purified us and prepared us to receive the Torah and enter Eretz Yisrael. Therefore, Succos represents the preparation of the soul to serve Hashem.

Shavuos was the final stage of the Exodus. The ultimate goal for which we left Egypt was to accept the Torah and commit ourselves to Hashem's service. Therefore, it represents the final stage of serving Hashem: the actual performance of good deeds.

We have to study the three festivals and follow the path of spiritual redemption that they provide for us. We have a tradition from the holy Baal Shem Tov that every Jew undergoes his own personal spiritual bondage — an "Egyptian Exile" of sorts — and his own Exodus. The Egyptian Exile represents the subjugation of the soul to the desires of the physical body that enslaves and oppresses it. A person undergoes his own Exodus when he frees his soul from

הגדה של פסח [186]

(On Saturday night the phrase in parentheses
substitutes for the preceding phrase.)

So, HASHEM, our God and God of our fathers, bring us also to future holidays and festivals in peace, gladdened in the rebuilding of Your city and joyful at Your service. There we shall eat of the offerings and Pesach sacrifices (of the Pesach sacrifices and offerings) whose blood will gain the sides of Your Altar for gracious acceptance. We shall then sing a new song of praise to You for our redemption and for the liberation of our souls.

---

the desires of the body, sanctifying and elevating it toward Hashem.

It is clear, then, that the three stages of the Exodus also represent three stages of each person's liberation from the clutches of his evil inclination. The liberation from the evil inclination is a constantly unfolding process that occurs in every generation, every day, and every moment of the day. The Baal Shem Tov taught that the verse, "Draw near to my soul, redeem it" (Tehillim 69:19), teaches us that when a person redeems his soul from the clutches of the evil inclination, he thereby hastens the ultimate Redemption of all of Bnei Yisrael (Toldos Yaakov Yosef, Parashas Shemini).

עַל גְּאֻלָּתֵנוּ וְעַל פְּדוּת נַפְשֵׁנוּ
For our redemption and for the liberation of our souls.

"And these are the names of Bnei Yisrael who were coming to Egypt; with Yaakov each man and his household came" (Shemos 1:1).

Baal HaTurim notes that the first and last letters of the words יִשְׂרָאֵל הַבָּאִים, Yisrael who were coming, can be rearranged to spell the word מִילָה. Similarly, the last letters of אֵת יַעֲקֹב אִישׁ, with Yaakov each man, can be rearranged to spell the word שַׁבָּת. This teaches us that Bnei Yisrael were redeemed from Egypt in the merit of Bris Milah and Shabbos.

To understand the special significance of these two mitzvos, we must first discuss an issue raised by many Rishonim. Hashem told Avraham Avinu that his descendants would be strangers in a foreign land for 400 years (Bereishis 15:13). However, the Egyptian Exile lasted only 210 years (see Rashi, ibid., who explains that the 400 years began with the birth of Yitzchak).

Chasam Sofer notes that Bnei Yisrael were indeed meant to be enslaved — מְשֻׁעְבָּד — for 400 years, and he offers a homiletic explanation as to why that decree was changed.

בָּרוּךְ אַתָּה יהוה, גָּאַל יִשְׂרָאֵל.

The word מְשֻׁעְבָּד is also used to mean that a borrower's possessions become collateral for a loan. If Reuven borrows money from Shimon, all properties and assets that Reuven owns at the time of the loan become מְשֻׁעְבָּד to the Shimon. If Reuven sells a property or an object and then defaults on the loan, the lender may seize that object or property from the buyer (if no other properties or assets are still in Reuven's possession).

The Talmud rules that there are three instances in which the lien on properties and assets is voided: (a) if the lien was on food that was chametz, and it belonged to a Jew on Pesach; (b) if the borrower consecrated[1] that object or property; (c) if the lien was on a slave owned by the borrower, and he freed the slave.

We were indeed supposed to be מְשֻׁעְבָּד to the Egyptians, says the *Chasam Sofer*, but we became sanctified to Hashem — as the verse states, "Israel is holy to Hashem, the first of His crop" (*Yirmiyah* 2:3) — so the שִׁעְבּוּד was nullified.

Of all the mitzvos, *Bris Milah* and Shabbos are especially capable of sanctifying a person. Shabbos is known as *Shabbos Kodesh*, and *Bris Milah* is known as *os* (sign of) *Bris Kodesh*. Together, these two mitzvos form the foundation for the holiness of the Jewish people. Shabbos sanctifies time, and *Bris Milah* sanctifies the person himself. As we cited above from the Baal Shem Tov, each person must free his own soul from the clutches of his evil inclination by observing Torah and mitzvos. By doing so, he hastens the ultimate Redemption of the Jewish people. Because Shabbos and *Bris Milah* sanctify a person, they have the ability to free a person from slavery to the evil inclination. Therefore, during the weeks of *Shovavim*, when the Torah portions of *Shemos* through *Mishpatim* are read, one must make special efforts to sanctify himself in these two areas.

גָּאַל יִשְׂרָאֵל — Who has redeemed Israel.

The *Talmud* (Berachos 4b) tells us that a person who prays *Shemoneh Esrei* immediately after reciting the blessing of גָּאַל יִשְׂרָאֵל, *Who has redeemed Israel*, is guaranteed a portion in the World to Come.

Rabbeinu Yonah (ibid., p. 2b of *Rif's* pages) suggests two reasons why a practice that seems so simple merits such a great reward.

One, Hashem redeemed us from Egypt in order that we may serve

---

1. A person consecrates an object or property by setting it aside for use in the Beis Hamikdash or to belong to *hekdesh*, the treasury of the Beis Hamikdash. The object or property then becomes sanctified, and may not be used for any other purpose.

Blessed are You, HASHEM, Who has redeemed Israel.

Him, as the verse states, "For Bnei Yisrael are servants to Me, they are My servants, whom I have taken out of the land of Egypt" (*Vayikra* 25:55). In גָּאַל יִשְׂרָאֵל we show our appreciation to Hashem for liberating us from Egypt, and immediately thereafter we begin serving Him through prayer. In this way, we show that we are indeed fulfilling the objective for which we were redeemed.

Two, after praising Hashem for the miraculous salvation He performed for our forefathers, we pray to Him to save us and provide for all of our needs. By doing so we show that we have *bitachon* (trust) in Hashem, and we believe that just as He protected our forefathers, so too will He protect us. In the merit of *bitachon*, one is rewarded with a portion in the World to Come.

We see from here an important principle of *emunah* and *bitachon*. The story of the Exodus is supposed to cause us to have *emunah* in Hashem's Providence. However, it is not enough to recognize Hashem's Providence intellectually or in theory. The intellectual recognition of Hashem's Providence must bring us to have *bitachon* in Hashem with all our heart, and feel confident with the knowledge that He protects us. *Bitachon* is the litmus test of the level of a person's *emunah*. A person can fool himself into thinking that he has sincere faith in Hashem, but when he is tested in a real-life situation, he will suddenly realize that he has no *bitachon* at all.

Chazon Ish (*Emunah U'Bitachon* 2:2) writes:
Emunah is like halachah, and *bitachon* is the hands-on application of that halachah. It is easy for a person to profess to have *bitachon* when he is not faced with any trial, but how difficult it is to have *bitachon* when it is truly necessary to trust in Hashem!

The real test of whether a person's words match the feeling in his heart — whether he has true *bitachon*, or he has simply trained his tongue to chirp, "*Bitachon! Bitachon!*" while his heart remains undecided — is when he is confronted with a situation that demands true *bitachon* to guide him, comfort him, and heal him. Does he turn to *bitachon* in such times, or does he cast his *bitachon* aside and begin to stray towards falsehood?

Emunah is a concept, and *bitachon* is the practical application of that concept. This is why we must pray immediately following גָּאַל יִשְׂרָאֵל. The words גָּאַל יִשְׂרָאֵל express our belief that Hashem redeemed us from Egypt and took us as His servants, and we follow this expression of belief by prayer, which the Talmud deems "the service of the heart" (*Taanis* 2a). We stand before Hashem, and like servants who have no possessions of their own and must rely on

The second cup corresponds to the expression of redemption,
וְהִצַּלְתִּי, *I shall rescue you.*
Some have the custom to recite the following declaration of intent.

הֲרֵינִי מוּכָן וּמְזוּמָּן לְקַיֵּם מִצְוַת כּוֹס שֵׁנִי מֵאַרְבַּע כּוֹסוֹת. לְשֵׁם יִחוּד
קֻדְשָׁא בְּרִיךְ הוּא וּשְׁכִינְתֵּיהּ, עַל יְדֵי הַהוּא טָמִיר וְנֶעְלָם, בְּשֵׁם
כָּל יִשְׂרָאֵל. וִיהִי נֹעַם אֲדֹנָי אֱלֹהֵינוּ עָלֵינוּ, וּמַעֲשֵׂה יָדֵינוּ כּוֹנְנָה עָלֵינוּ,
וּמַעֲשֵׂה יָדֵינוּ כּוֹנְנֵהוּ:

בָּרוּךְ אַתָּה יהוה אֱלֹהֵינוּ מֶלֶךְ הָעוֹלָם, בּוֹרֵא פְּרִי
הַגָּפֶן.

The wine should be drunk while leaning to the left side, in the manner of
free men. Preferably, one should drink the entire cup, but at least most of it.
If one drank without leaning to the side, he should drink another cup while
leaning. However, this is true only if he had in mind to drink more wine
during the meal. Otherwise, he should not drink an additional cup
(*Mishnah Berurah* 472:21, *Shaar HaTzion* 31).

רָחְצָה

Some recite the following declaration of intent before washing their
hands, so as not to interrupt between washing and reciting the blessing
on the matzah. Some authorities do not consider it an interruption. If one
does delay the recitation until after hand washing, it is best to contemplate
the words, not recite them.

הִנְנִי מוּכָן וּמְזוּמָּן לְקַיֵּם מִצְוַת אֲכִילַת מַצָּה. לְשֵׁם יִחוּד קֻדְשָׁא בְּרִיךְ
הוּא וּשְׁכִינְתֵּיהּ, עַל יְדֵי הַהוּא טָמִיר וְנֶעְלָם, בְּשֵׁם כָּל יִשְׂרָאֵל.
וִיהִי נֹעַם אֲדֹנָי אֱלֹהֵינוּ עָלֵינוּ, וּמַעֲשֵׂה יָדֵינוּ כּוֹנְנָה עָלֵינוּ, וּמַעֲשֵׂה יָדֵינוּ
כּוֹנְנֵהוּ:

---

their master for all their needs, we beg Hashem to provide for us.
We express our realization that without Him we have nothing.

Mentioning the Exodus immediately prior to praying also helps
instill in us a feeling of submissiveness toward Hashem that is
necessary for prayer.

אַרְבַּע כּוֹסוֹת — The Four Cups

Rashi and *Rashbam* (*Pesachim* 99b) write that the four cups of
wine correspond to the four expressions of redemption: I shall take
you out; I shall rescue you; I shall redeem you; and I shall take you
to Me (*Shemos* 6:6-7).

Between the first three cups of wine we are permitted to drink.

The second cup corresponds to the expression of redemption,
וְהִצַּלְתִּי, *I shall rescue you.*

Some have the custom to recite the following declaration of intent.

Behold, I am prepared and ready to fulfill the mitzvah of the second of the Four Cups. For the sake of the unification of the Holy One, Blessed is He, and His Presence, through Him Who is hidden and inscrutable — [I pray] in the name of all Israel. May the pleasantness of HASHEM, our God, be upon us, and may He establish our handiwork for us; our handiwork may He establish.

Blessed are You, HASHEM, our God, King of the universe, Who creates the fruit of the vine.

The wine should be drunk while leaning to the left side, in the manner of free men. Preferably, one should drink the entire cup, but at least most of it. If one drank without leaning to the side, he should drink another cup while leaning. However, this is true only if he had in mind to drink more wine during the meal. Otherwise, he should not drink an additional cup (*Mishnah Berurah* 472:21, *Shaar HaTzion* 31).

RACHTZAH

Some recite the following declaration of intent before washing their hands, so as not to interrupt between washing and reciting the blessing on the matzah. Some authorities do not consider it an interruption. If one does delay the recitation until after hand washing, it is best to contemplate the words, not recite them.

Behold, I am prepared and ready to fulfill the mitzvah of eating matzah. For the sake of the unification of the Holy One, Blessed is He, and His Presence, through Him Who is hidden and inscrutable — [I pray] in the name of all Israel. May the pleasantness of HASHEM, our God, be upon us, and may He establish our handiwork for us; our handiwork may He establish.

Between the third and fourth cups, however, we may not interrupt by eating or drinking. This comes to teach us an important lesson. Some people view the awaited redemption as no more than a national liberation, which will free us from the oppression we suffer from the nations of the world. They feel that first three expressions of redemption are sufficient; they want to be taken out, rescued, and redeemed, but they are willing to forgo the fourth aspect of redemption. They do not see the great importance of being taken to Hashem, of becoming His holy nation.

Chazal prohibited us from interrupting between the third and fourth cups to teach us that true redemption is that of the soul. We are only considered free when our souls are free to draw close to

The hands are washed for matzah and the following blessing is recited. If one is certain that from the time he washed his hands for *Urechatz* he has not touched anything impure, then he should make his hands impure (by scratching his head or the like) before washing hands again for *Rachtzah*, so that he may recite the blessing.
It is preferable to bring water and a basin
to the head of the household at the Seder table.

בָּרוּךְ אַתָּה יהוה אֱלֹהֵינוּ מֶלֶךְ הָעוֹלָם, אֲשֶׁר קִדְּשָׁנוּ בְּמִצְוֹתָיו, וְצִוָּנוּ עַל נְטִילַת יָדָיִם.

מוֹצִיא

The following two blessings are recited over matzah; the first is recited over matzah as food, and the second for the special mitzvah of eating matzah on the night of Pesach. [The latter blessing is to be made with the intention that it also apply to the *Korech* "sandwich" and the afikoman.]

The head of the household raises all the matzos on the Seder plate
(the broken one between the two whole ones)
and recites the following blessing:

בָּרוּךְ אַתָּה יהוה אֱלֹהֵינוּ מֶלֶךְ הָעוֹלָם, הַמּוֹצִיא לֶחֶם מִן הָאָרֶץ.

מַצָּה

The bottom matzah is put down and the following blessing is recited while the top (whole) matzah and the middle (broken) piece are still raised. One should have in mind that this blessing should also apply to the matzah eaten for *Korech* and afikoman.

בָּרוּךְ אַתָּה יהוה אֱלֹהֵינוּ מֶלֶךְ הָעוֹלָם, אֲשֶׁר קִדְּשָׁנוּ בְּמִצְוֹתָיו, וְצִוָּנוּ עַל אֲכִילַת מַצָּה.

Hashem, when we merit having the Beis Hamikdash and the Divine Presence in our midst.

Ramban (Introduction to *Shemos*) writes that the entire *Sefer Shemos* is a continuous story of redemption. It begins with the slavery of our forefathers and the miracles of the Exodus, and it concludes with the Divine Presence coming to rest among Bnei Yisrael in the Mishkan (Tabernacle). Only when the Divine Presence comes to rest among us — as it did among our forefathers — are we considered truly free from bondage.

The hands are washed for matzah and the following blessing is recited. If one is certain that from the time he washed his hands for *Urechatz* he has not touched anything impure, then he should make his hands impure (by scratching his head or the like) before washing hands again for *Rachtzah*, so that he may recite the blessing.

It is preferable to bring water and a basin to the head of the household at the Seder table.

Blessed are You, Hashem, our God, King of the universe, Who has sanctified us with His commandments, and has commanded us concerning the washing of the hands.

MOTZI

The following two blessings are recited over matzah; the first is recited over matzah as food, and the second for the special mitzvah of eating matzah on the night of Pesach. [The latter blessing is to be made with the intention that it also apply to the *Korech* "sandwich" and the afikoman.]

The head of the household raises all the matzos on the Seder plate (the broken one between the two whole ones) and recites the following blessing:

Blessed are You, Hashem, our God, King of the universe, Who brings forth bread from the earth.

MATZAH

The bottom matzah is put down and the following blessing is recited while the top (whole) matzah and the middle (broken) piece are still raised. One should have in mind that this blessing should also apply to the matzah eaten for *Korech* and afikoman.

Blessed are You, Hashem, our God, King of the universe, Who has sanctified us with His commandments, and has commanded us concerning the eating of the matzah.

מַצָּה — **Matzah**

Some have written that one must make a legal transfer of ownership (קִנְיָן) when giving pieces of matzah to his family and guests so that they can fulfill the mitzvah with matzah that belongs to them. *Sefas Emes* (*Succah* 35) mentions this idea, but writes that he has not seen people following this practice.

It seems to me that this practice is unnecessary. If a person gives

Each participant is required to eat an amount of matzah equal in volume to an egg. Ideally, each person should receive a half-egg volume from both the top and middle pieces. However, since it is usually impossible to provide a sufficient amount of matzah from the two matzos for all members of the household, each participant should receive a piece from each of the top two matzos, and other matzos should be available at the head of the table from which to complete the required amounts. The matzos are to be eaten while reclining on the left side and without delay; they need not be dipped in salt. They should be eaten with the intention to fulfill the Torah obligation of eating matzah.

מָרוֹר

The head of the household takes a *k'zayis* (half-egg volume) of maror, dips it into charoses, and gives each participant a like amount. The following blessing is recited with the intention that it also apply to the maror of the *Korech* "sandwich." The maror is eaten without reclining, and without delay.

Minchas Asher writes that some have the custom to dip only the tip of the maror in charoses. The maror should not be left to soak in the charoses, so that its bitter taste is not weakened. The charoses should be shaken off before the maror is eaten. Although one need not recline while eating maror, he may do so if he wishes.

Some recite the following before eating the maror:

הִנְנִי מוּכָן וּמְזֻמָּן לְקַיֵּם מִצְוַת אֲכִילַת מָרוֹר. לְשֵׁם יְחוּד קֻדְשָׁא בְּרִיךְ הוּא וּשְׁכִינְתֵּיהּ, עַל יְדֵי הַהוּא טָמִיר וְנֶעְלָם, בְּשֵׁם כָּל יִשְׂרָאֵל. וִיהִי נֹעַם אֲדֹנָי אֱלֹהֵינוּ עָלֵינוּ, וּמַעֲשֵׂה יָדֵינוּ כּוֹנְנָה עָלֵינוּ, וּמַעֲשֵׂה יָדֵינוּ כּוֹנְנֵהוּ:

בָּרוּךְ אַתָּה יהוה אֱלֹהֵינוּ מֶלֶךְ הָעוֹלָם, אֲשֶׁר קִדְּשָׁנוּ בְּמִצְוֹתָיו, וְצִוָּנוּ עַל אֲכִילַת מָרוֹר.

The maror must be chewed before it is swallowed (*Shulchan Aruch HaRav* 473:31). Preferably, an entire *k'zayis* of maror should be eaten at once. However, if it is eaten within *kdei achilas pras*, several minutes, one still fulfills his obligation (*Mishnah Berurah* 473:43). If one eats maror after midnight (*chatzos*), he should not recite a blessing (ibid. 477:6).

an item to his friend to use and expects him to return it, then we can say that no legal transfer of ownership has been made. For instance, a person who gives his lulav and esrog to his friend to use on the first day of Succos must make a proper transfer of ownership in order for the other person to fulfill his obligation.

Each participant is required to eat an amount of matzah equal in volume to an egg. Ideally, each person should receive a half-egg volume from both the top and middle pieces. However, since it is usually impossible to provide a sufficient amount of matzah from the two matzos for all members of the household, each participant should receive a piece from each of the top two matzos, and other matzos should be available at the head of the table from which to complete the required amounts. The matzos are to be eaten while reclining on the left side and without delay; they need not be dipped in salt. They should be eaten with the intention to fulfill the Torah obligation of eating matzah.

MAROR

The head of the household takes a *k'zayis* (half-egg volume) of maror, dips it into charoses, and gives each participant a like amount. The following blessing is recited with the intention that it also apply to the maror of the *Korech* "sandwich." The maror is eaten without reclining, and without delay.

Minchas Asher writes that some have the custom to dip only the tip of the maror in charoses. The maror should not be left to soak in the charoses, so that its bitter taste is not weakened. The charoses should be shaken off before the maror is eaten. Although one need not recline while eating maror, he may do so if he wishes.

Some recite the following before eating the maror:

Behold, I am prepared and ready to fulfill the mitzvah of eating maror. For the sake of unification of the Holy One, Blessed is He, and His Presence, through Him Who is hidden and inscrutable — [I pray] in the name of all Israel. May the pleasantness of HASHEM, our God, be upon us, and may He establish our handiwork for us; our handiwork may He establish.

Blessed are You, HASHEM, our God, King of the universe, Who has sanctified us with His commandments, and has commanded us concerning the eating of maror.

The maror must be chewed before it is swallowed (*Shulchan Aruch HaRav* 473:31). Preferably, an entire *k'zayis* of maror should be eaten at once. However, if it is eaten within *kdei achilas pras*, several minutes, one still fulfills his obligation (*Mishnah Berurah* 473:43). If one eats maror after midnight (*chatzos*), he should not recite a blessing (ibid. 477:6).

When one gives his friend an object that can only be used in a way that will consume it — such as matzah — he realizes that he will not get it back. The transfer of ownership in such cases is implicit, so a formal transfer of ownership is unnecessary.

כּוֹרֵךְ

The bottom (thus far unbroken) matzah is now taken. From it, with the addition of other matzos, each participant receives a half-egg volume of matzah with an equal-volume portion of maror (dipped into charoses, which is shaken off). According to some opinions the matzah and maror should be dipped together in charoses (*Shulchan Aruch*). According to other opinions it should not (*Rema*). Each person should therefore follow his own custom (*Magen Avraham*). The following paragraph is recited and the "sandwich" is eaten while reclining.

The following declaration is recited:

זֵכֶר לְמִקְדָּשׁ כְּהִלֵּל. כֵּן עָשָׂה הִלֵּל בִּזְמַן שֶׁבֵּית הַמִּקְדָּשׁ הָיָה קַיָּם. הָיָה כּוֹרֵךְ [פֶּסַח] מַצָּה וּמָרוֹר וְאוֹכֵל בְּיַחַד. לְקַיֵּם מַה שֶׁנֶּאֱמַר, עַל מַצּוֹת וּמְרֹרִים יֹאכְלֻהוּ.[1]

שֻׁלְחָן עוֹרֵךְ

The meal should be eaten in a combination of joy and solemnity, for the meal, too, is part of the Seder service. While it is desirable that *zemiros* and discussion of the laws and events of Pesach be part of the meal, extraneous conversation should be avoided. It should be remembered that the afikoman must be eaten while there is still some appetite for it. In fact, if one is so sated that he must literally force himself to eat it, he is not credited with the performance of the mitzvah of afikoman. Therefore, it is unwise to eat more than a moderate amount during the meal.

Minchas Asher writes that it is preferable to recline while eating the meal. It is customary to eat eggs during this meal.

It is proper to learn about the Korban Pesach at the meal, for studying a mitzvah is considered as if we actually performed it. The following description was composed by Yaavetz.

אֲכִילַת בָּשָׂר הַפֶּסַח בְּלֵיל חֲמִשָּׁה עָשָׂר שֶׁל חֹדֶשׁ הָאָבִיב מִצְוַת עֲשֵׂה מִן הַתּוֹרָה, שֶׁנֶּאֱמַר וְאָכְלוּ אֶת הַבָּשָׂר בַּלַּיְלָה הַזֶּה צְלִי אֵשׁ וּמַצּוֹת עַל מְרוֹרִים יֹאכְלֻהוּ. מִצְוָה מִן הַמֻּבְחָר לֶאֱכוֹל בְּשַׂר הַפֶּסַח עַל הַשּׂוֹבַע, לְפִיכָךְ אִם הִקְרִיב שַׁלְמֵי חֲגִיגָה בְּאַרְבָּעָה עָשָׂר אוֹכֵל מֵהֶן תְּחִלָּה. וְאַחַר כָּךְ אוֹכֵל בְּשַׂר הַפֶּסַח כְּדֵי לְשָׂבְעוֹ מִמֶּנּוּ. וְאִם לֹא אָכַל אֶלָּא כְּזַיִת יָצָא יְדֵי חוֹבָתוֹ, וּשְׁנֵיהֶן אֵין נֶאֱכָלִים אֶלָּא צְלִי אֵשׁ. וּצְרִיכִין בְּרָכָה לְכָל אֶחָד בִּפְנֵי עַצְמוֹ, עַל הַפֶּסַח אוֹמֵר אֲשֶׁר קִדְּשָׁנוּ

_____
(1) *Bamidbar* 9:11.

KORECH

The bottom (thus far unbroken) matzah is now taken. From it, with the addition of other matzos, each participant receives a half-egg volume of matzah with an equal-volume portion of maror (dipped into charoses, which is shaken off). According to some opinions the matzah and maror should be dipped together in charoses (*Shulchan Aruch*). According to other opinions it should not (*Rema*). Each person should therefore follow his own custom (*Magen Avraham*). The following paragraph is recited and the "sandwich" is eaten while reclining.

The following declaration is recited:

In remembrance of the Beis Hamikdash [we do] as Hillel [did]. So did Hillel do at the time that the Beis Hamikdash was still standing: He would combine (the Pesach offering,) matzah and maror in a sandwich and eat them together, to fulfill what it states: They shall eat it with matzos and bitter herbs.[1]

SHULCHAN ORECH

The meal should be eaten in a combination of joy and solemnity, for the meal, too, is part of the Seder service. While it is desirable that *zemiros* and discussion of the laws and events of Pesach be part of the meal, extraneous conversation should be avoided. It should be remembered that the afikoman must be eaten while there is still some appetite for it. In fact, if one is so sated that he must literally force himself to eat it, he is not credited with the performance of the mitzvah of afikoman. Therefore, it is unwise to eat more than a moderate amount during the meal.

Minchas Asher writes that it is preferable to recline while eating the meal. It is customary to eat eggs during this meal.

It is proper to learn about the Korban Pesach at the meal, for studying a mitzvah is considered as if we actually performed it. The following description was composed by Yaavetz.

It is a positive commandment from the Torah to eat from the *Korban Pesach* on the night of the fifteenth of Nissan, as the *pasuk* states, "You will eat the meat on this night, roasted over the fire. With matzos and maror you will eat it." It is a *mitzvah min hamuvchar* (ideal way of performing the mitzvah) to eat the *Korban Pesach* [to satisfaction/ after he has been satisfied with other foods]. Therefore, if one offered a *Shalmei Chagigah korban* on the fourteenth, he should eat it before he eats the *Korban Pesach*. Afterward he should eat the *Korban Pesach* to satisfaction. Even if one eats only a *k'zayis* of the *Korban Pesach*, he fulfills his obligation. Both *korbanos* should be eaten after having been roasted over a fire. Each one requires its own *berachah*. Before eating the *Korban Pesach*, one recites: "Blessed are You, HASHEM ... Who has sanctified us

בְּמִצְוֹתָיו וְצִוָּנוּ לֶאֱכוֹל הַפֶּסַח, וְעַל הַחֲגִיגָה לֶאֱכוֹל הַזֶּבַח. הַפֶּסַח טָעוּן הַלֵּל בַּאֲכִילָתוֹ. וְאָמַר רַב מְשׁוּם רַבִּי חִיָּיא כְּזַיְתָא פִּסְחָא וְהַלֵּלָא פָּקַע אִיגְּרָא. אֵין צוֹלִין אֶת הַפֶּסַח עַל גַּבֵּי כְּלִי אֶבֶן אוֹ כְּלִי מַתֶּכֶת, וְלֹא בְּשַׁפּוּד שֶׁל מַתֶּכֶת. כֵּיצַד צוֹלִין אוֹתוֹ, מְבִיאִין שַׁפּוּד שֶׁל רִמּוֹן, וְתוֹחֲבוֹ מִתּוֹךְ פִּיו עַד בֵּית נְקוּבָתוֹ, וְתוֹחֵב כְּרָעָיו וּבְנֵי מֵעָיו בְּשַׁפּוּד לְמַעֲלָה מִפִּיו שֶׁל טָלֶה. וְתוֹלֵהוּ לְתוֹךְ הַתַּנּוּר וְהָאֵשׁ לְמַטָּה. אֵין הַפֶּסַח נֶאֱכָל נָא וּמְבֻשָּׁל, וְאֵינוֹ נֶאֱכָל בִּשְׁתֵּי חֲבוּרוֹת. וְאֵין מוֹצִיאִין מֵחֲבוּרָה לַחֲבוּרָה. וְלֹא הָאוֹכֵל רַשַּׁאי לֶאֱכוֹל מִשְּׁנֵי פְסָחִים. שֶׁאֵין נִמְנִין עַל שְׁנֵי פְסָחִים כְּאַחַת. וְאֵינוֹ נֶאֱכָל אֶלָּא לִמְנוּיָו (בִּשְׁעַת הַשְּׁחִיטָה), יִשְׂרָאֵל מָהוּל טָהוֹר בֶּן בְּרִית, וּכְשֵׁם שֶׁמִּילַת בָּנָיו וַעֲבָדָיו מְעַכַּבְתּוֹ מִלִּשְׁחוֹט הַפֶּסַח, כָּךְ מְעַכַּבְתּוֹ מִלְּאָכְלוֹ בּוֹ. הַשּׁוֹבֵר עֶצֶם בַּפֶּסַח הַטָּהוֹר לוֹקֶה. וַאֲפִלּוּ שֶׁלֹּא בְלֵיל פֶּסַח. לְפִיכָךְ שׂוֹרְפִין עַצְמוֹת הַפֶּסַח בִּכְלַל הַנּוֹתָר מִבְּשָׂרוֹ, כְּדֵי שֶׁלֹּא יָבֹאוּ בָּהֶן לִידֵי תַקָּלָה. אֵין רַשַּׁאי לֶאֱכוֹל מִגְּדֵי הָרַךְ אֶלָּא מַה שֶּׁנֶּאֱכַל בְּשׁוֹר הַגָּדוֹל. הַפֶּסַח אֵינוֹ נֶאֱכָל אֶלָּא עַד חֲצוֹת הַלַּיְלָה הַזֶּה. בְּשַׂר חֲגִיגָה שֶׁעָלָה עִם הַפֶּסַח עַל הַשֻּׁלְחָן, וְכֵן כָּל הַתַּבְשִׁילִין הָעוֹלִין עִמּוֹ מִתְבַּעֲרִין עִמּוֹ. וְאֵינָן נֶאֱכָלִין אֶלָּא עַד חֲצוֹת כְּפֶסַח. חָלוּק פֶּסַח דּוֹרוֹת מִפֶּסַח מִצְרַיִם בִּשְׁלשָׁה דְבָרִים: שֶׁהוּא הָיָה מִקְחוֹ מִבֶּעָשׂוֹר, וְטָעוּן הַגָּעַת דָּם בַּאֲגוּדַּת אֵזוֹב עַל הַמַּשְׁקוֹף וּשְׁתֵּי הַמְּזוּזוֹת, וְשֶׁנֶּאֱכַל בְּחִפָּזוֹן. זֶהוּ מִצְוַת אֲכִילַת הַפֶּסַח. הָרַחֲמָן יְזַכֵּנוּ לְאָכְלוֹ בְּעִיר מִקְדָּשֵׁנוּ בִּמְהֵרָה בְיָמֵינוּ, וִיקֻיַּם בָּנוּ מִקְרָא שֶׁכָּתוּב "כִּי לֹא בְחִפָּזוֹן תֵּצֵאוּ וּבִמְנוּסָה לֹא תֵלֵכוּן כִּי הֹלֵךְ לִפְנֵיכֶם יהוה וּמְאַסִּפְכֶם אֱלֹהֵי יִשְׂרָאֵל." "כִּימֵי צֵאתְךָ מֵאֶרֶץ מִצְרַיִם אַרְאֶנּוּ נִפְלָאוֹת." "וּדְבַר אֱלֹהֵינוּ יָקוּם לְעוֹלָם." "יְמִינוֹ רוֹמֵמָה עָשָׂה נִרְאוֹת":

Yaavetz writes that it is proper to recite
the following passage from *Zohar* (*Parashas Bo*, 38a).

זוהר פרשת בא דף ל"ח ע"א

תָּנִינָן כְּתִיב הַיּוֹם אַתֶּם יוֹצְאִים. וּכְתִיב הוֹצִיאֲךָ יהוה אֱלֹהֶיךָ מִמִּצְרַיִם לָיְלָה. אֶלָּא תָּאנָא. עִיקָּרָא דְּפוּרְקָנָא דְיִשְׂרָאֵל לָא הֲוֵה אֶלָּא בַּלֵּילְיָא. דְּלֵילְיָא שָׁרָא קְטָרִין וְעָבֵד נוּקְמִין וְיוֹמָא אַפִּיק לוֹן בְּרֵישׁ גַּלֵּי. הֲדָא הוּא דִכְתִיב יָצְאוּ בְנֵי יִשְׂרָאֵל בְּיָד רָמָה לְעֵינֵי כָל מִצְרַיִם (נ"א וְעוֹד לַיְלָה שָׁרֵי קְטָרִין וְעָבֵד נוּקְמִין וְדִינִין. וְיוֹמָא גַּלֵּי וּפִרְסֵם נִסָּא וְנוּקְמָא דְאִתְעֲבִיד. הֲדָא הוּא דִכְתִיב יָצְאוּ בְנֵי יִשְׂרָאֵל בְּיָד רָמָה וְגו'). וּכְתִיב וּמִצְרַיִם מְקַבְּרִים אֵת אֲשֶׁר הִכָּה יהוה בָּהֶם כָּל בְּכוֹר דָּא הוּא פַּרְסוּמֵי נִיסָּא. אָתוּ ר' חִיָּיא וְר' יוֹסֵי אִשְׁתַּטָּחוּ קַמֵּיהּ וְנַשְׁקוּ יְדוֹי וכו'. אָמַר לוֹן עַד הַשְׁתָּא לָא סַיָּימְנָא מִלָּה דְשָׁאֶלְתָּא דִּלְכוֹן דְּהָא תָּנִינָן וַיהוה הִכָּה כָל בְּכוֹר. סָתַם כִּדְקָאָמְרָן וְכֻלָּא הֲוֵה כְּמָה דְּאִינוּן דְּמִיתוּ אִינּוּן קְטוּרֵי קְטָרִין דַּהֲווֹ מִשְׁתַּמְּשֵׁי בְּחַרְשַׁיְיהוּ בְּאִנּוּן

with His commandments, and commanded us to eat the *Korban Pesach*." Before eating the *Chagigah*, one recites: "... and commanded us to eat the slaughtered *korban*."

Hallel must be recited while eating the *Korban Pesach*. Rav said in the name of Rebbe Chiya, that they eat only a *k'zayis* of *Korban Pesach*, but their songs of Hallel burst through the attic.

The *Korban Pesach* must not be roasted over stoneware or metal vessels, or on a metal spit. How then is it roasted? A spit of pomegranate wood is brought, and thrust through the mouth of the *korban* to its backside. The legs and intestines are hung on the spit, above the mouth of the animal. The spit is then hung inside an oven, with a fire beneath it.

The *Korban Pesach* must not be eaten undercooked, or cooked in water. It may not be eaten in two different companies. It many not be taken out from one company to another. No one person may eat from two different *Pesachim*, since he may not join two different companies.

It may only be eaten by those who have joined into a company to eat it, (before it was slaughtered), and who are Jewish, circumcised, ritually pure, and a *ben bris*. Just as one may not slaughter a *Korban Pesach* unless his children and slaves are circumcised, so too he may not eat from it unless they are circumcised.

If a person breaks the bone of a ritually pure *Korban Pesach*, he is liable for lashes, even at times other than Pesach night. Therefore, the bones of the *Korban Pesach* are burned together with the leftover meat, in order that people not come to transgress this law.

Even though the *Korban Pesach* is a tender, young lamb, one may only eat from it those portions that are edible in a full-grown ox. The *Korban Pesach* may only be eaten before midnight.

The meat of the *Chagigah* that is served on the same table as the *Korban Pesach*, as well as the other dishes served with it, must all be destroyed together with it [on the following morning]. They may only be eaten before midnight, like the *Korban Pesach*.

In three ways, the *Korban Pesach* offered throughout the generations was different from the original *Korban Pesach* offered in Egypt. The *Korban Pesach* offered in Egypt had to be acquired on the tenth of the month. Its blood was applied to the doorposts using sprigs of hyssop, and it was eaten in haste.

This is the mitzvah of eating the *Korban Pesach*. May the Merciful One grant us the merit to eat from it in the Holy City soon and in our days. May He fulfill with us the *pasuk*, "You will not need to exit in haste, nor will you flee. For HASHEM walks before you, your Gatherer, the God of Israel." "As in the days when you left the land of Egypt, I will show you wonders." "The word of our God endures forever." "His uplifted hand performs wonders."

Yaavetz writes that it is proper to recite
the passage from *Zohar* (*Parashas Bo*, 38a).

צָפוּן

From the afikoman matzah (and from additional matzos to make up the required amount) a half-egg volume portion — according to some, a full egg's volume portion — is given to each participant. It should be eaten while reclining, without delay, uninterruptedly, and before midnight (chatzos), just as the *Korban Pesach* was eaten before midnight. Nothing may be eaten or drunk after the afikoman (with the exception of water and the like) except for the last two Seder cups of wine.

Some recite the following declaration of intent.

הִנְנִי מוּכָן וּמְזוּמָּן לְקַיֵּם מִצְוַת אֲכִילַת אֲפִיקוֹמָן. לְשֵׁם יְחוּד קֻדְשָׁא בְּרִיךְ הוּא וּשְׁכִינְתֵּיהּ, עַל יְדֵי הַהוּא טָמִיר וְנֶעְלָם, בְּשֵׁם כָּל יִשְׂרָאֵל. וִיהִי נֹעַם אֲדֹנָי אֱלֹהֵינוּ עָלֵינוּ, וּמַעֲשֵׂה יָדֵינוּ כּוֹנְנָה עָלֵינוּ, וּמַעֲשֵׂה יָדֵינוּ כּוֹנְנֵהוּ:

בָּרֵךְ

The third cup is poured. The hands are washed for *mayim acharonim*, and *Bircas HaMazon* (Grace After Meals) is recited.

Minchas Asher writes that it is a mitzvah to have three people present in order to make a *Zimun* (formal invitation). The head of the household should lead the *Zimun*. He should take the cup in his right hand, and hold it a *tefach* (handbreadth) above the table. He should recite *Bircas HaMazon* aloud, while everyone else recites it quietly. They should complete each of the blessings before him, so that they may answer "Amen" to his.

According to some customs, the Cup of Eliyahu is poured at this point.

שִׁיר הַמַּעֲלוֹת, בְּשׁוּב יהוה אֶת שִׁיבַת צִיּוֹן, הָיִינוּ כְּחֹלְמִים. אָז יִמָּלֵא שְׂחוֹק פִּינוּ וּלְשׁוֹנֵנוּ רִנָּה, אָז יֹאמְרוּ בַגּוֹיִם, הִגְדִּיל יהוה לַעֲשׂוֹת עִם אֵלֶּה. הִגְדִּיל יהוה לַעֲשׂוֹת עִמָּנוּ, הָיִינוּ שְׂמֵחִים.

כְּתָרִין. מִנְהוֹן מִשְׁתַּמְּשֵׁי בְּעֶלָּאֵי וּמִנְהוֹן בְּתַתָּאֵי. וְאַף עַל גַּב דְּכוּלְּהוּ תַּתָּאִין אִינּוּן. וְכָל אַרְעָא דְּמִצְרַיִם מַלְיָא חַרְשִׁין הֲוָה. וּכְתִיב כִּי אֵין בַּיִת אֲשֶׁר אֵין שָׁם מֵת. וְאִתְעֲבִיד דִּינָא בְּכוּלָּא בְּשַׁעֲתָּא דְּאִתְכְּנָשׁוּ כּוּלְּהוּ בְּבָתֵּיהוֹן וְלָא הֲווֹ מִתְפַּזְּרֵי בְּמַדְבְּרָא וּבְחַקְלָא. אֶלָּא כּוּלְּהוּ אִשְׁתַּכְּחוּ בְּבָתֵּיהוֹן וְעָבַד לֵילְיָא דִּינוֹי בְּכוּלָּא בְּהַהִיא שַׁעֲתָּא וְתָנָא הֲוָה נָהִיר לֵילְיָא כִּיוֹמָא דְּתִקּוּפָה דְּתַמּוּז. וְחָמָא כָּל עַמָּא דִּינוֹי דְּקוּדְשָׁא בְּרִיךְ הוּא הֲדָא הוּא דִכְתִיב וְלַיְלָה כַּיוֹם יָאִיר

TZAFUN

From the afikoman matzah (and from additional matzos to make up the required amount) a half-egg volume portion — according to some, a full egg's volume portion — is given to each participant. It should be eaten while reclining, without delay, uninterruptedly, and before midnight (*chatzos*), just as the *Korban Pesach* was eaten before midnight. Nothing may be eaten or drunk after the afikoman (with the exception of water and the like) except for the last two Seder cups of wine.

Some recite the following declaration of intent.

Behold, I am prepared and ready to fulfill the mitzvah of eating the afikoman. For the sake of the unification of the Holy One, Blessed is He, and his Presence, through Him Who is hidden and inscrutable — [I pray] in the name of all Israel. May the pleasantness of HASHEM, our God, be upon us, and may He establish our handiwork for us; our handiwork may He establish.

BARECH

The third cup is poured. The hands are washed for *mayim acharonim*, and *Bircas HaMazon* (Grace After Meals) is recited.

Minchas Asher writes that it is a mitzvah to have three people present in order to make a *Zimun* (formal invitation). The head of the household should lead the *Zimun*. He should take the cup in his right hand, and hold it a *tefach* (handbreadth) above the table. He should recite *Bircas HaMazon* aloud, while everyone else recites it quietly. They should complete each of the blessings before him, so that they may answer "Amen" to his.

According to some customs, the Cup of Eliyahu is poured at this point.

A song of Ascents. When HASHEM brings back the exiles to Zion, we will have been like dreamers. Then our mouth will be filled with laughter, and our tongue with glad song. Then will it be said among the nations: HASHEM has done great things for these, HASHEM has done great things for us, and we rejoiced.

כַּחֲשֵׁכָה כָּאוֹרָה. וּבְשַׁעֲתָא דְּנָפְקוּ אִשְׁתַּבְּחוּ כּוּלְּהוֹן מֵתִין בְּשׁוּקִין לְעֵינֵיהוֹן דְּכוֹלָא. בָּעְיַין לְאַקְבְּרָא לְהוּ וְלֹא אַשְׁכְּחוּ [אֲתַר נ"ל דכצ"ל. ר"ל מֵאין מָקוֹם לקבור] וְדָא אַקְשֵׁי לְהוּ מְכּוֹלָא. חֲמוּ לְיִשְׂרָאֵל נָפְקִין לְעֵינֵיהוֹן בְּחַד גִּיסָא. וְחָמוּ לְמֵיתֵיהוֹן בְּאִידָךְ גִּיסָא. וּבְכּוּלָּא הֲוָה פַּרְסוּמֵי נִיסָא. דְּלָא הֲוָה כְּהַאי מִיּוֹמָא דְּאִתְבְּרִי עָלְמָא וכו'. וְעַל דָּא מְחַבְּאָן יִשְׂרָאֵל. דִּכְתִיב זֶה יהוה קִוִּינוּ לוֹ נָגִילָה וְנִשְׂמְחָה בִּישׁוּעָתוֹ. מִשּׁוּם דְּהָכִי זַמִּין לְמֶעֱבַד לְהוּ. דִּכְתִיב כִּימֵי צֵאתְךָ מֵאֶרֶץ מִצְרַיִם אַרְאֶנּוּ נִפְלָאוֹת.

שׁוּבָה יהוה אֶת שְׁבִיתֵנוּ, כַּאֲפִיקִים בַּנֶּגֶב. הַזֹּרְעִים
בְּדִמְעָה בְּרִנָּה יִקְצֹרוּ. הָלוֹךְ יֵלֵךְ וּבָכֹה נֹשֵׂא מֶשֶׁךְ
הַזָּרַע, בֹּא יָבֹא בְרִנָּה, נֹשֵׂא אֲלֻמֹּתָיו.[1]

Some recite the following declaration of intent before *Bircas HaMazon*.

הִנְנִי מוּכָן וּמְזוּמָּן לְקַיֵּם מִצְוַת עֲשֵׂה שֶׁל בִּרְכַּת הַמָּזוֹן, כַּכָּתוּב,
וְאָכַלְתָּ וְשָׂבָעְתָּ וּבֵרַכְתָּ אֶת יהוה אֱלֹהֶיךָ עַל הָאָרֶץ הַטֹּבָה
אֲשֶׁר נָתַן לָךְ:

If three or more males, aged thirteen or older, participated in the meal, the
leader is required to formally invite the others to join him in the recitation
of Grace After Meals. Following is the *Zimun*, formal invitation.

The leader begins:

רַבּוֹתַי נְבָרֵךְ. (מִיר וֶועלִין בֶּענְטְשִׁין)

The group responds:

יְהִי שֵׁם יהוה מְבֹרָךְ מֵעַתָּה וְעַד עוֹלָם.[2]

The leader continues:

יְהִי שֵׁם יהוה מְבֹרָךְ מֵעַתָּה וְעַד עוֹלָם.[2]

If ten men join in the *Zimun*, the words (in parentheses) are included.

בִּרְשׁוּת מָרָנָן וְרַבָּנָן וְרַבּוֹתַי, נְבָרֵךְ [אֱלֹהֵינוּ] שֶׁאָכַלְנוּ מִשֶּׁלּוֹ.

The group responds:

בָּרוּךְ [אֱלֹהֵינוּ] שֶׁאָכַלְנוּ מִשֶּׁלּוֹ וּבְטוּבוֹ חָיִינוּ.

The leader continues:

בָּרוּךְ [אֱלֹהֵינוּ] שֶׁאָכַלְנוּ מִשֶּׁלּוֹ וּבְטוּבוֹ חָיִינוּ.

The following line is recited if ten men join in the *Zimun*.

בָּרוּךְ הוּא וּבָרוּךְ שְׁמוֹ.

בָּרוּךְ אַתָּה יהוה אֱלֹהֵינוּ מֶלֶךְ הָעוֹלָם, הַזָּן אֶת
הָעוֹלָם כֻּלּוֹ, בְּטוּבוֹ, בְּחֵן בְּחֶסֶד וּבְרַחֲמִים,
הוּא נֹתֵן לֶחֶם לְכָל בָּשָׂר, כִּי לְעוֹלָם חַסְדּוֹ[3] וּבְטוּבוֹ
הַגָּדוֹל, תָּמִיד לֹא חָסַר לָנוּ, וְאַל יֶחְסַר לָנוּ מָזוֹן
לְעוֹלָם וָעֶד. בַּעֲבוּר שְׁמוֹ הַגָּדוֹל, כִּי הוּא אֵל זָן
וּמְפַרְנֵס לַכֹּל, וּמֵטִיב לַכֹּל, וּמֵכִין מָזוֹן לְכָל בְּרִיּוֹתָיו
אֲשֶׁר בָּרָא. (כָּאָמוּר: פּוֹתֵחַ אֶת יָדֶךָ וּמַשְׂבִּיעַ לְכָל
חַי רָצוֹן.[4]) בָּרוּךְ אַתָּה יהוה, הַזָּן אֶת הַכֹּל.

---

(1) *Tehillim* 126. (2) Ibid. 113:2. (3) Ibid. 136:25. (4) Ibid. 145:16.

Restore our captives, HASHEM, like streams in the dry land. Those who sow in tears shall reap in joy. Though the farmer bears the measure of seed to the field in tears, he shall come home with joy, bearing his sheaves.[1]

Some recite the following declaration of intent before *Bircas HaMazon*.

Behold, I am prepared and ready to fulfill the mitzvah of Grace After Meals, as it is stated: "And you shall eat and you shall be satisfied and you shall bless HASHEM, your God, for the good land which He gave you."

If three or more males, aged thirteen or older, participated in the meal, the leader is required to formally invite the others to join him in the recitation of Grace After Meals. Following is the *Zimun*, formal invitation.

The leader begins:

Gentlemen, let us bless.

The group responds:

Blessed is the Name of HASHEM from this moment and forever![2]

The leader continues:

Blessed is the Name of HASHEM from this moment and forever![2]

If ten men join in the *Zimun*, אֱלֹהֵינוּ, *our God* (in parentheses), is included.

With the permission of the distinguished people present, let us bless [our God] for we have eaten from what is His.

The group responds:

Blessed is He [our God] of Whose we have eaten and through Whose goodness we live.

The leader continues:

Blessed is He [our God] of Whose we have eaten and through Whose goodness we live.

The following line is recited if ten men join in the *Zimun*.

Blessed is He and Blessed is His Name.

Blessed are You, HASHEM, our God, King of the universe, Who nourishes the entire world; in His goodness, with grace, with lovingkindness, and with mercy. He gives nourishment to all flesh, for His lovingkindness is eternal.[3] And through His great goodness, nourishment was never lacking to us, and may it never be lacking to us forever. For the sake of His Great Name, because He is God Who nourishes and sustains all, and benefits all, and He prepares food for all of His creatures that He has created. (As it is said: "You open Your hand, and satisfy the desire of every living thing."[4]) Blessed are You, HASHEM, Who nourishes all.

נוֹדֶה לְךָ יהוה אֱלֹהֵינוּ, עַל שֶׁהִנְחַלְתָּ לַאֲבוֹתֵינוּ אֶרֶץ חֶמְדָּה טוֹבָה וּרְחָבָה. וְעַל שֶׁהוֹצֵאתָנוּ יהוה אֱלֹהֵינוּ מֵאֶרֶץ מִצְרַיִם, וּפְדִיתָנוּ מִבֵּית עֲבָדִים, וְעַל בְּרִיתְךָ שֶׁחָתַמְתָּ בִּבְשָׂרֵנוּ, וְעַל תּוֹרָתְךָ שֶׁלִּמַּדְתָּנוּ, וְעַל חֻקֶּיךָ שֶׁהוֹדַעְתָּנוּ, וְעַל חַיִּים חֵן וָחֶסֶד שֶׁחוֹנַנְתָּנוּ, וְעַל אֲכִילַת מָזוֹן שָׁאַתָּה זָן וּמְפַרְנֵס אוֹתָנוּ תָּמִיד, בְּכָל יוֹם וּבְכָל עֵת וּבְכָל שָׁעָה.

וְעַל הַכֹּל יהוה אֱלֹהֵינוּ אֲנַחְנוּ מוֹדִים לָךְ, וּמְבָרְכִים אוֹתָךְ, יִתְבָּרַךְ שִׁמְךָ בְּפִי כָּל חַי תָּמִיד לְעוֹלָם וָעֶד. כַּכָּתוּב, וְאָכַלְתָּ וְשָׂבָעְתָּ, וּבֵרַכְתָּ אֶת יהוה אֱלֹהֶיךָ, עַל הָאָרֶץ הַטֹּבָה אֲשֶׁר נָתַן לָךְ.[1] בָּרוּךְ אַתָּה יהוה, עַל הָאָרֶץ וְעַל הַמָּזוֹן.

רַחֵם נָא יהוה אֱלֹהֵינוּ עַל יִשְׂרָאֵל עַמֶּךָ, וְעַל יְרוּשָׁלַיִם עִירֶךָ, וְעַל צִיּוֹן מִשְׁכַּן כְּבוֹדֶךָ, וְעַל מַלְכוּת בֵּית דָּוִד מְשִׁיחֶךָ, וְעַל הַבַּיִת הַגָּדוֹל וְהַקָּדוֹשׁ שֶׁנִּקְרָא שִׁמְךָ עָלָיו. אֱלֹהֵינוּ אָבִינוּ רְעֵנוּ זוּנֵנוּ פַּרְנְסֵנוּ וְכַלְכְּלֵנוּ וְהַרְוִיחֵנוּ, וְהַרְוַח לָנוּ יהוה אֱלֹהֵינוּ מְהֵרָה מִכָּל צָרוֹתֵינוּ. וְנָא אַל תַּצְרִיכֵנוּ יהוה אֱלֹהֵינוּ, לֹא לִידֵי מַתְּנַת בָּשָׂר וָדָם, וְלֹא לִידֵי הַלְוָאָתָם, כִּי אִם לְיָדְךָ הַמְּלֵאָה הַפְּתוּחָה הַקְּדוֹשָׁה וְהָרְחָבָה, שֶׁלֹּא נֵבוֹשׁ וְלֹא נִכָּלֵם לְעוֹלָם וָעֶד.

We thank You, HASHEM, our God, because You have given to our forefathers as a heritage a desirable, good, and spacious land; because You removed us, HASHEM, our God, from the land of Egypt and You redeemed us from the house of bondage; for Your covenant which You sealed in our flesh; for Your Torah that You taught us and for Your statutes that You made known to us; for life, grace, and loving-kindness which You granted us; and for the provision of food with which You nourish and sustain us constantly, in every day, in every season and in every hour.

For all, HASHEM, our God, we thank You and bless You. May Your Name be blessed by the mouth of all the living, continuously for all eternity. As it is written: "And you shall eat and you shall be satisfied, and you shall bless HASHEM, your God, for the good land which He gave you."[1] Blessed are You, HASHEM, for the land and for the food.

Have mercy we beg You, HASHEM, our God, on Your people Israel, on Your city Jerusalem, on Zion the resting place of Your Glory, on the monarchy of the house of David, Your anointed, and on the great and holy House upon which Your Name is called. Our God, our Father — tend us, nourish us, sustain us, support us, relieve us; HASHEM, our God, grant us speedy relief from all our troubles. Please, HASHEM, our God, make us not needful of the gifts of human hands nor of their loans, but only of Your Hand that is full, open, holy, and generous, that we not feel inner shame nor be humiliated for ever and ever.

---

(1) *Devarim* 8:10.

רְצֵה וְהַחֲלִיצֵנוּ יהוה אֱלֹהֵינוּ בְּמִצְוֹתֶיךָ, וּבְמִצְוַת יוֹם הַשְּׁבִיעִי הַשַּׁבָּת הַגָּדוֹל וְהַקָּדוֹשׁ הַזֶּה, כִּי יוֹם זֶה גָּדוֹל וְקָדוֹשׁ הוּא לְפָנֶיךָ, לִשְׁבָּת בּוֹ וְלָנוּחַ בּוֹ בְּאַהֲבָה כְּמִצְוַת רְצוֹנֶךָ, וּבִרְצוֹנְךָ הָנִיחַ לָנוּ יהוה אֱלֹהֵינוּ, שֶׁלֹּא תְהֵא צָרָה וְיָגוֹן וַאֲנָחָה בְּיוֹם מְנוּחָתֵנוּ, וְהַרְאֵנוּ יהוה אֱלֹהֵינוּ בְּנֶחָמַת צִיּוֹן עִירֶךָ, וּבְבִנְיַן יְרוּשָׁלַיִם עִיר קָדְשֶׁךָ, כִּי אַתָּה הוּא בַּעַל הַיְשׁוּעוֹת וּבַעַל הַנֶּחָמוֹת.

אֱלֹהֵינוּ וֵאלֹהֵי אֲבוֹתֵינוּ, יַעֲלֶה, וְיָבֹא, וְיַגִּיעַ, וְיֵרָאֶה, וְיֵרָצֶה, וְיִשָּׁמַע, וְיִפָּקֵד, וְיִזָּכֵר זִכְרוֹנֵנוּ וּפִקְדוֹנֵנוּ, וְזִכְרוֹן אֲבוֹתֵינוּ, וְזִכְרוֹן מָשִׁיחַ בֶּן דָּוִד עַבְדֶּךָ, וְזִכְרוֹן יְרוּשָׁלַיִם עִיר קָדְשֶׁךָ, וְזִכְרוֹן כָּל עַמְּךָ בֵּית יִשְׂרָאֵל לְפָנֶיךָ, לִפְלֵיטָה לְטוֹבָה לְחֵן וּלְחֶסֶד וּלְרַחֲמִים, לְחַיִּים (טוֹבִים) וּלְשָׁלוֹם בְּיוֹם חַג הַמַּצּוֹת הַזֶּה. זָכְרֵנוּ יהוה אֱלֹהֵינוּ בּוֹ לְטוֹבָה, וּפָקְדֵנוּ בּוֹ לִבְרָכָה, וְהוֹשִׁיעֵנוּ בוֹ לְחַיִּים טוֹבִים. וּבִדְבַר יְשׁוּעָה וְרַחֲמִים, חוּס וְחָנֵּנוּ וְרַחֵם עָלֵינוּ וְהוֹשִׁיעֵנוּ, כִּי אֵלֶיךָ עֵינֵינוּ, כִּי אֵל מֶלֶךְ חַנּוּן וְרַחוּם אָתָּה.[1]

וּבְנֵה יְרוּשָׁלַיִם עִיר הַקֹּדֶשׁ בִּמְהֵרָה בְיָמֵינוּ. בָּרוּךְ אַתָּה יהוה, בּוֹנֵה (בְרַחֲמָיו) יְרוּשָׁלָיִם. אָמֵן.

בָּרוּךְ אַתָּה יהוה אֱלֹהֵינוּ מֶלֶךְ הָעוֹלָם, הָאֵל אָבִינוּ מַלְכֵּנוּ אַדִּירֵנוּ בּוֹרְאֵנוּ גּוֹאֲלֵנוּ יוֹצְרֵנוּ קְדוֹשֵׁנוּ קְדוֹשׁ יַעֲקֹב, רוֹעֵנוּ רוֹעֵה יִשְׂרָאֵל, הַמֶּלֶךְ הַטּוֹב וְהַמֵּטִיב לַכֹּל, שֶׁבְּכָל יוֹם וָיוֹם הוּא הֵטִיב, הוּא מֵטִיב, הוּא יֵיטִיב לָנוּ. הוּא גְמָלָנוּ הוּא גוֹמְלֵנוּ הוּא יִגְמְלֵנוּ לָעַד, לְחֵן

---

(1) *Nechemiah* 9:31.

May it please You to strengthen us, HASHEM, our God, through Your commandments, and through the commandment of the seventh day, this great and holy Sabbath. For this day is great and holy before You to rest on it and be content on it in love, as ordained by Your will. May it be Your will, HASHEM, our God, that there be no distress, grief, or lament on this day of our contentment. And show us, HASHEM, our God, the consolation of Zion, Your city, and the rebuilding of Jerusalem, city of Your holiness, for You are the Master of salvations and Master of consolations.

Our God and God of our fathers, may there rise, come, reach, be noted, be favored, be heard, be considered, and be remembered before You — the remembrance and consideration of ourselves; the remembrance of our fathers; the remembrance of Mashiach, son of David, Your servant; the remembrance of Jerusalem, Your holy city; and the remembrance of Your entire people, the House of Israel — for deliverance, for well-being, for grace, for lovingkindness, and for mercy, for (good) life and for peace on this day of the Festival of Matzos. Remember us on it, HASHEM, our God, for goodness; consider us on it for blessing; and help us on it for good life. In the matter of salvation and mercy, have pity, show grace and be merciful upon us and help us, for our eyes are turned to You; for You are the Almighty, the gracious, and generous.[1]

Rebuild Jerusalem, the Holy City, soon in our days. Blessed are You, HASHEM, Who rebuilds Jerusalem (in His mercy). Amen.

Blessed are You, HASHEM, our God, King of the universe, the Almighty, our Father, our King, our Sovereign, our Creator, our Redeemer, our Maker, our Holy One, Holy One of Yaakov, our Shepherd, the Shepherd of Israel, the good and beneficent King. For every single day He did good, does good, and will do good to us. He was bountiful with us, is bountiful with us, and will forever be bountiful with us — with grace

וּלְחֶסֶד וּלְרַחֲמִים וּלְרֶוַח הַצָּלָה וְהַצְלָחָה, בְּרָכָה
וִישׁוּעָה נֶחָמָה פַּרְנָסָה וְכַלְכָּלָה וְרַחֲמִים וְחַיִּים
וְשָׁלוֹם וְכָל טוֹב, וּמִכָּל טוּב לְעוֹלָם אַל יְחַסְּרֵנוּ.

The Talmud (*Berachos* 46a) gives a rather lengthy text of the blessing that a
guest inserts here for the host. It is quoted with minor variations in
Shulchan Aruch (*Orach Chaim* 201) and many authorities are at a loss to
explain why the prescribed text has fallen into disuse in favor of the briefer
version commonly used. The text found in *Shulchan Aruch* is:

יְהִי רָצוֹן שֶׁלֹּא יֵבוֹשׁ בַּעַל הַבַּיִת בָּעוֹלָם הַזֶּה וְלֹא יִכָּלֵם
לְעוֹלָם הַבָּא, וְיִצְלַח מְאֹד בְּכָל נְכָסָיו, וְיִהְיוּ
נְכָסָיו וּנְכָסֵינוּ מוּצְלָחִים וּקְרוֹבִים לָעִיר, וְאַל יִשְׁלוֹט שָׂטָן
לֹא בְּמַעֲשֵׂה יָדָיו וְלֹא בְּמַעֲשֵׂה יָדֵינוּ, וְאַל יִזְדַּקֵּק לֹא לְפָנָיו וְלֹא
לְפָנֵינוּ שׁוּם דְּבַר הִרְהוּר חֵטְא וַעֲבֵירָה וְעָוֹן, מֵעַתָּה וְעַד עוֹלָם.

הָרַחֲמָן הוּא יִמְלוֹךְ עָלֵינוּ לְעוֹלָם וָעֶד. הָרַחֲמָן
הוּא יִתְבָּרַךְ בַּשָּׁמַיִם וּבָאָרֶץ. הָרַחֲמָן
הוּא יִשְׁתַּבַּח לְדוֹר דּוֹרִים, וְיִתְפָּאַר בָּנוּ לָעַד
וּלְנֵצַח נְצָחִים, וְיִתְהַדַּר בָּנוּ לָעַד וּלְעוֹלְמֵי
עוֹלָמִים. הָרַחֲמָן הוּא יְפַרְנְסֵנוּ בְּכָבוֹד. הָרַחֲמָן
הוּא יִשְׁבּוֹר עוֹל הַגּוֹיִם מֵעַל צַוָּארֵנוּ, וְהוּא יוֹלִיכֵנוּ
[מְהֵרָה] קוֹמְמִיּוּת לְאַרְצֵנוּ. הָרַחֲמָן הוּא יִשְׁלַח
לָנוּ בְּרָכָה מְרֻבָּה בַּבַּיִת הַזֶּה, וְעַל שֻׁלְחָן זֶה
שֶׁאָכַלְנוּ עָלָיו. הָרַחֲמָן הוּא יִשְׁלַח לָנוּ אֶת
אֵלִיָּהוּ הַנָּבִיא זָכוּר לַטּוֹב, וִיבַשֶּׂר לָנוּ [בִּמְהֵרָה]
בְּשׂוֹרוֹת טוֹבוֹת יְשׁוּעוֹת וְנֶחָמוֹת.

הָרַחֲמָן הוּא יְבָרֵךְ

Guests recite the following.
Children at their parents' table add words in parentheses.

אֶת (אָבִי מוֹרִי) בַּעַל הַבַּיִת הַזֶּה,
וְאֶת (אִמִּי מוֹרָתִי) בַּעֲלַת הַבַּיִת הַזֶּה,

and with lovingkindness and with mercy, with relief, salvation, success, blessing, help, consolation, sustenance, support, mercy, life, peace, and all good; and of all good things may He never deprive us.

The Talmud (*Berachos* 46a) gives a rather lengthy text of the blessing that a guest inserts here for the host. It is quoted with minor variations in *Shulchan Aruch* (*Orach Chaim* 201) and many authorities are at a loss to explain why the prescribed text has fallen into disuse in favor of the briefer version commonly used. The text found in *Shulchan Aruch* is:

May it be God's will that this host not be shamed in this world nor humiliated in the World to Come. May he be very successful in all his dealings. May his dealings and our dealings be successful and conveniently close at hand. May no evil impediment reign over his handiwork or over our handiwork and may no semblance of iniquitous thought or transgression or sin attach itself to him or to us from this time and forever.

The compassionate One! May He reign over us forever. The compassionate One! May He be blessed in heaven and on earth. The compassionate One! May He be praised throughout all generations, may He be glorified through us forever to the ultimate ends, and be honored through us to the inscrutable everlasting. The compassionate One! May He sustain us in honor. The compassionate One! May He break the yoke of the nations from our necks and speedily guide us erect to our Land. The compassionate One! May He send us abundant blessing to this house and upon this table at which we have eaten. The compassionate One! May He send us Eliyahu, the Prophet — may he be remembered for good — to proclaim [speedily] to us good tidings, salvations, and consolations.

The compassionate One! May He bless

Guests recite the following.
Children at their parents' table add words in parentheses.

(my father, my teacher) the master of this house, and (my mother, my teacher) lady of this house,

Those eating at their own table recite the following,
adding the appropriate parenthesized phrases:

אוֹתִי (וְאֶת אִשְׁתִּי/בַּעֲלִי, וְאֶת זַרְעִי)
וְאֶת כָּל אֲשֶׁר לִי.

All guests recite the following:

אוֹתָם וְאֶת בֵּיתָם וְאֶת זַרְעָם וְאֶת כָּל אֲשֶׁר לָהֶם.

All continue here:

אוֹתָנוּ וְאֶת כָּל אֲשֶׁר לָנוּ, כְּמוֹ שֶׁנִּתְבָּרְכוּ אֲבוֹתֵינוּ
אַבְרָהָם יִצְחָק וְיַעֲקֹב בַּכֹּל מִכֹּל כֹּל, כֵּן יְבָרֵךְ אוֹתָנוּ
כֻּלָּנוּ יַחַד בִּבְרָכָה שְׁלֵמָה, וְנֹאמַר, אָמֵן.

בַּמָּרוֹם יְלַמְּדוּ עֲלֵיהֶם וְעָלֵינוּ זְכוּת, שֶׁתְּהֵא
לְמִשְׁמֶרֶת שָׁלוֹם. וְנִשָּׂא בְרָכָה מֵאֵת
יהוה, וּצְדָקָה מֵאֱלֹהֵי יִשְׁעֵנוּ, וְנִמְצָא חֵן וְשֵׂכֶל
טוֹב בְּעֵינֵי אֱלֹהִים וְאָדָם.[1]

On Shabbos add the following sentence:

הָרַחֲמָן הוּא יַנְחִילֵנוּ יוֹם שֶׁכֻּלּוֹ שַׁבָּת (וּקְדֻשָׁה) וּמְנוּחָה
לְחַיֵּי הָעוֹלָמִים.

The words in brackets are added
on the two Seder nights in some communities.

הָרַחֲמָן הוּא יַנְחִילֵנוּ יוֹם שֶׁכֻּלּוֹ טוֹב. [לְיוֹם
שֶׁכֻּלּוֹ אָרוּךְ. יוֹם שֶׁצַּדִּיקִים יוֹשְׁבִין
וְעַטְרוֹתֵיהֶם בְּרָאשֵׁיהֶם וְנֶהֱנִים מִזִּיו הַשְּׁכִינָה
וִיהְיֶה חֶלְקֵנוּ עִמָּהֶם.]

הָרַחֲמָן הוּא יְזַכֵּנוּ לִימוֹת הַמָּשִׁיחַ וּלְחַיֵּי הָעוֹלָם
הַבָּא. מִגְדוֹל יְשׁוּעוֹת מַלְכּוֹ וְעֹשֶׂה חֶסֶד
לִמְשִׁיחוֹ לְדָוִד וּלְזַרְעוֹ עַד עוֹלָם.[2] עֹשֶׂה שָׁלוֹם
בִּמְרוֹמָיו, הוּא יַעֲשֶׂה שָׁלוֹם עָלֵינוּ וְעַל כָּל
יִשְׂרָאֵל. וְאִמְרוּ, אָמֵן.

me (my wife/husband and family)
and all that is mine,

them, their house, their family, and all that is theirs,

ours and all that is ours — just as our forefathers Avraham, Yitzchak, and Yaakov were blessed in everything, from everything, with everything. So may He bless all of us together, with a perfect blessing. And let us say: Amen!

On high, may merit be pleaded upon them and upon us, for a safeguard of peace. May we receive a blessing from HASHEM and just kindness from the God of our salvation, and find favor and good understanding in the eyes of God and man.[1]

On Shabbos add the following sentence:
The compassionate One! May He cause us to inherit the day which will be completely a Shabbos (and holiness) and rest day for eternal life.

The words in brackets are added
on the two Seder nights in some communities.

The compassionate One! May He cause us to inherit that day which is altogether good [that everlasting day, the day when the just will sit with crowns on their heads, enjoying the reflection of God's majesty — and may our portion be with them!].

The compassionate One! May He make us worthy of the days of Messiah and the life of the World to Come. He Who is a tower of salvations to His king and shows lovingkindness for His anointed, to David and his descendants forever.[2] He Who makes peace in His heavenly heights, may He make harmony for us and for all Israel. Say: Amen!

---

(1) Cf. *Mishlei* 3:4. (1) *II Shmuel* 22:51.

יְראוּ אֶת יהוה קְדֹשָׁיו, כִּי אֵין מַחְסוֹר לִירֵאָיו. כְּפִירִים רָשׁוּ וְרָעֵבוּ, וְדֹרְשֵׁי יהוה לֹא יַחְסְרוּ כָל טוֹב.[1] הוֹדוּ לַיהוה כִּי טוֹב, כִּי לְעוֹלָם חַסְדּוֹ.[2] פּוֹתֵחַ אֶת יָדֶךָ, וּמַשְׂבִּיעַ לְכָל חַי רָצוֹן.[3] בָּרוּךְ הַגֶּבֶר אֲשֶׁר יִבְטַח בַּיהוה, וְהָיָה יהוה מִבְטַחוֹ.[4] נַעַר הָיִיתִי גַּם זָקַנְתִּי, וְלֹא רָאִיתִי צַדִּיק נֶעֱזָב, וְזַרְעוֹ מְבַקֶּשׁ לָחֶם.[5] יהוה עֹז לְעַמּוֹ יִתֵּן, יהוה יְבָרֵךְ אֶת עַמּוֹ בַשָּׁלוֹם.[6]

Upon completion of *Bircas HaMazon* the blessing over wine is recited and the third cup is drunk while reclining on the left side. This cup corresponds to the third expression of redemption, וְגָאַלְתִּי, *I shall redeem you*. It is preferable to drink the entire cup, but at the very least, most of the cup should be drained.

Some have the custom to recite the following declaration of intent.

הִנְנִי מוּכָן וּמְזוּמָּן לְקַיֵּם מִצְוַת כּוֹס שְׁלִישִׁי שֶׁל אַרְבַּע כּוֹסוֹת. לְשֵׁם יִחוּד קֻדְשָׁא בְּרִיךְ הוּא וּשְׁכִינְתֵּיהּ, עַל יְדֵי הַהוּא טָמִיר וְנֶעְלָם, בְּשֵׁם כָּל יִשְׂרָאֵל. וִיהִי נֹעַם אֲדֹנָי אֱלֹהֵינוּ עָלֵינוּ, וּמַעֲשֵׂה יָדֵינוּ כּוֹנְנָה עָלֵינוּ, וּמַעֲשֵׂה יָדֵינוּ כּוֹנְנֵהוּ:

בָּרוּךְ אַתָּה יהוה אֱלֹהֵינוּ מֶלֶךְ הָעוֹלָם, בּוֹרֵא פְּרִי הַגָּפֶן.

The fourth cup is poured, and the door is opened in accordance with the verse, "It is a guarded night." In the merit of this expression of faith, Mashiach will come and pour his wrath on those who deny Hashem's existence (*Rema* 480:1).
According to most customs, the Cup of Eliyahu is poured at this point. This cup is a sign of our belief that just as Hashem redeemed us from Egypt, he will redeem us again and send Eliyahu to herald the final Redemption.

כּוֹס שֶׁל אֵלִיָּהוּ — Cup of Eliyahu

The Cup of Eliyahu corresponds to the fifth expression of redemption: "And I shall bring you to the land (Eretz Yisrael)" (*Shemos* 6:8). Why do we pour this cup but not drink it?

The fulfillment of the fifth aspect of redemption is contingent upon the verse that precedes it: "And you shall know that I am Hashem your God, Who takes you out from under the burdens of Egypt."

F ear HASHEM, His holy ones, for those who fear Him feel no deprivation. Young lions may feel want and hunger, but those who seek HASHEM will not lack any good.[1] Give thanks to God for He is good; His loving-kindness is eternal.[2] You open up Your hand and satisfy the desire of every living thing.[3] Blessed is the man who trusts in HASHEM, and HASHEM will be his trust.[4] I was a youth and also have aged, and I have not seen a righteous man forsaken, with his children begging for bread.[5] HASHEM will give might to His nation; HASHEM will bless His nation with peace.[6]

Upon completion of Bircas HaMazon the blessing over wine is recited and the third cup is drunk while reclining on the left side. This cup corresponds to the third expression of redemption, וְגָאַלְתִּי, I shall redeem you. It is preferable to drink the entire cup, but at the very least, most of the cup should be drained.

Some have the custom to recite the following declaration of intent.

B ehold, I am prepared and ready to fulfill the mitzvah of the third of the Four Cups. For the sake of the unification of the Holy One, Blessed is He, and His presence, through Him Who is hidden and inscrutable — [I pray] in the name of all Israel. May the pleasantness of HASHEM, our God, be upon us, and may He establish our handiwork for us; our handiwork may He establish.

B lessed are You, HASHEM, our God, King of the universe, Who creates the fruit of the vine.

The fourth cup is poured, and the door is opened in accordance with the verse, "It is a guarded night." In the merit of this expression of faith, Mashiach will come and pour his wrath on those who deny Hashem's existence (Rema 480:1).

According to most customs, the Cup of Eliyahu is poured at this point. This cup is a sign of our belief that just as Hashem redeemed us from Egypt, he will redeem us again and send Eliyahu to herald the final Redemption.

---

(1) *Tehillim* 34:10-11. (2) Ibid. 136:1. (3) Ibid. 145:16. (4) *Yirmiyahu* 17:7. (5) *Tehillim* 37:25. (6) Ibid. 29:11.

If we recognize Hashem's Sovereignty over us, then He promises, "I shall bring you to the land about which I raised My hand to give it to Avraham, Yitzchak, and Yaakov; and I shall give it to you as a heritage — I am Hashem."

If we fail to meet the condition of knowing that Hashem is God, we will not merit the fulfillment of the fifth stage of redemption. The

The following paragraph is recited.

שְׁפֹךְ חֲמָתְךָ אֶל הַגּוֹיִם אֲשֶׁר לֹא יְדָעוּךָ וְעַל מַמְלָכוֹת אֲשֶׁר בְּשִׁמְךָ לֹא קָרָאוּ. כִּי אָכַל אֶת יַעֲקֹב וְאֶת נָוֵהוּ הֵשַׁמּוּ.[1] שְׁפֹךְ עֲלֵיהֶם זַעְמֶךָ וַחֲרוֹן אַפְּךָ יַשִּׂיגֵם.[2] תִּרְדֹּף בְּאַף וְתַשְׁמִידֵם מִתַּחַת שְׁמֵי יהוה.[3]

הַלֵּל

The door is closed. Hallel is recited while seated,
in the manner of free men.

לֹא לָנוּ יהוה לֹא לָנוּ, כִּי לְשִׁמְךָ תֵּן כָּבוֹד, עַל חַסְדְּךָ עַל אֲמִתֶּךָ. לָמָּה יֹאמְרוּ הַגּוֹיִם, אַיֵּה נָא אֱלֹהֵיהֶם. וֵאלֹהֵינוּ בַשָּׁמַיִם, כֹּל אֲשֶׁר חָפֵץ עָשָׂה. עֲצַבֵּיהֶם כֶּסֶף וְזָהָב, מַעֲשֵׂה יְדֵי אָדָם. פֶּה לָהֶם וְלֹא יְדַבֵּרוּ, עֵינַיִם לָהֶם וְלֹא יִרְאוּ. אָזְנַיִם לָהֶם וְלֹא יִשְׁמָעוּ, אַף לָהֶם וְלֹא יְרִיחוּן. יְדֵיהֶם וְלֹא יְמִישׁוּן, רַגְלֵיהֶם וְלֹא יְהַלֵּכוּ, לֹא יֶהְגּוּ בִּגְרוֹנָם. כְּמוֹהֶם יִהְיוּ עֹשֵׂיהֶם, כֹּל אֲשֶׁר בֹּטֵחַ בָּהֶם.

fifth cup gets poured; whether we get to drink from it is dependent on us.

הַלֵּל — Hallel

We divide Hallel into two parts on Pesach. The first two chapters are recited before the meal, and the rest is recited after *Bircas HaMazon*. Why?

We might suggest that the first half of the Seder focuses on the Exodus from Egypt, and the second half focuses on the ultimate Redemption.

Before *Bircas HaMazon*, we tell the story of the Exodus in *Maggid*, we eat matzah and maror to commemorate various aspects of the exile and redemption, and we eat a festive meal to celebrate our redemption. The first two chapters of Hallel are recited during the

Pour Your wrath upon the nations that do not recognize You and upon the kingdoms that do not invoke Your Name. For they have devoured Yaakov and destroyed His habitation.[1] Pour Your anger upon them and let Your fiery wrath overtake them.[2] Pursue them with wrath and annihilate them from beneath the heavens of HASHEM.[3]

HALLEL

The door is closed. Hallel is recited while seated,
in the manner of free men.

Not for our sake, HASHEM, not for our sake, but for Your Name's sake give glory, for the sake of Your kindness and Your truth! Why should the nations say, "Where is their God?" Our God is in the heavens; whatever He pleases, He does! Their idols are silver and gold, the handiwork of man. They have a mouth, but cannot speak; they have eyes, but cannot see; they have ears, but cannot hear; they have a nose, but cannot smell; their hands — they cannot feel; their feet — they cannot walk; nor can they utter a sound with their throat. Those who make them should become like them, whoever trusts in them!

(1) *Tehillim* 79:6-7. (2) Ibid. 69:25. (3) *Eichah* 3:66.

first half of the Seder because they also focus on the Exodus. The first chapter (*Tehillim* 113), "Give praise, O servants of Hashem," corresponds to the verse, "For Bnei Yisrael are servants to Me, they are My servants, whom I have taken out of the land of Egypt" (*Vayikra* 25:55). The second chapter (*Tehillim* 114) obviously focuses on the Exodus; it begins with the words, "When Israel went forth from Egypt."

From *Bircas HaMazon*, our attention shifts to the long-awaited redemption from our current exile. We pray, "Pour Your wrath upon the nations," and then proceed to the second half of Hallel, which also relates to the ultimate Redemption, as evidenced by the references to the future: "Not for our sake, O Lord, not for our sake, but for Your Name's sake give glory"; "Hashem Who has remembered

יִשְׂרָאֵל בְּטַח בַּיהוה, עֶזְרָם וּמָגִנָּם הוּא. בֵּית אַהֲרֹן בִּטְחוּ בַיהוה, עֶזְרָם וּמָגִנָּם הוּא. יִרְאֵי יהוה בִּטְחוּ בַיהוה, עֶזְרָם וּמָגִנָּם הוּא.

יהוה זְכָרָנוּ יְבָרֵךְ, יְבָרֵךְ אֶת בֵּית יִשְׂרָאֵל, יְבָרֵךְ אֶת בֵּית אַהֲרֹן. יְבָרֵךְ יִרְאֵי יהוה, הַקְּטַנִּים עִם הַגְּדֹלִים. יֹסֵף יהוה עֲלֵיכֶם, עֲלֵיכֶם וְעַל בְּנֵיכֶם. בְּרוּכִים אַתֶּם לַיהוה, עֹשֵׂה שָׁמַיִם וָאָרֶץ. הַשָּׁמַיִם שָׁמַיִם לַיהוה, וְהָאָרֶץ נָתַן לִבְנֵי אָדָם. לֹא הַמֵּתִים יְהַלְלוּ יָהּ, וְלֹא כָּל יֹרְדֵי דוּמָה. וַאֲנַחְנוּ נְבָרֵךְ יָהּ, מֵעַתָּה וְעַד עוֹלָם, הַלְלוּיָהּ.[1]

אָהַבְתִּי, כִּי יִשְׁמַע יהוה אֶת קוֹלִי, תַּחֲנוּנָי. כִּי הִטָּה אָזְנוֹ לִי, וּבְיָמַי אֶקְרָא. אֲפָפוּנִי חֶבְלֵי מָוֶת, וּמְצָרֵי שְׁאוֹל מְצָאוּנִי, צָרָה וְיָגוֹן אֶמְצָא. וּבְשֵׁם יהוה אֶקְרָא, אָנָּה יהוה מַלְּטָה נַפְשִׁי. חַנּוּן יהוה וְצַדִּיק, וֵאלֹהֵינוּ מְרַחֵם. שֹׁמֵר פְּתָאִים יהוה,

---

us will bless — He will bless the House of Israel"; "I love Him, for Hashem hears my voice, my supplications," and so on.

We can attribute this distinction to *Yerushalmi* (*Megillah* 2:1), which explains the focus of the verses in Hallel as follows: "When Israel went forth from Egypt" refers to the past; "Not for our sake" refers to the present generations; "I have loved Hashem, for He hears the voice of my supplications" refers to the era of Mashiach; "Bind the festival offering with cords" refers to the days of Gog and Magog; "You are my God, and I shall thank You" refers to Days to Come.

יִרְאֵי ה' בִּטְחוּ בַה', עֶזְרָם וּמָגִנָּם הוּא
You who fear Hashem — trust in Hashem,
He is their help and their shield!

There are three opinions which group is referred to as "You who fear Hashem."

O Israel! Trust in HASHEM; He is their help and their shield! House of Aharon! Trust in HASHEM! He is their help and their shield! You who fear HASHEM — trust in HASHEM, He is their help and their shield!

HASHEM Who has remembered us will bless — He will bless the House of Israel; He will bless the House of Aharon; He will bless those who fear HASHEM, the small as well as the great. May HASHEM add upon you, upon you and your children! You are blessed of HASHEM, Maker of heaven and earth. As for the heaven — the heaven is HASHEM's, but the earth He has given to mankind. Neither the dead can praise God, nor any who descend into silence; but we will bless God henceforth and forever. Halleluyah![1]

I love Him, for HASHEM hears my voice, my supplications. For He has inclined His ear to me, all my days I will call upon Him. The pains of death surround me; the confines of the grave have found me; disease and heartache I have found. In the Name of HASHEM I call: "Please, HASHEM, save my soul." Gracious is HASHEM and righteous, our God is merciful. HASHEM protects the simple;

---

(1) *Tehillim* 115.

Ibn Ezra and *Metzudas David* explain that this appellation refers to righteous gentiles, who also fear Hashem, and are therefore helped and shielded by His benevolence.

Rashi explains that it refers to converts. If so, it is interesting to note that the converts receive their own classification as "You who fear Hashem," and are not included in the first group, "Israel trusts in Hashem," even though they are regular members of the Jewish people.

Radak explains that "You who fear Hashem" are individuals in *Klal Yisrael* whose greatness surpasses that of the members of the House of Aharon: "wise men, who seclude themselves in the House of Hashem to study and pursue wisdom so that they can reach a deep recognition of Hashem, for they know that they can rely on no one but Him."

דַלּוֹתִי וְלִי יְהוֹשִׁיעַ. שׁוּבִי נַפְשִׁי לִמְנוּחָיְכִי, כִּי יהוה גָּמַל עָלָיְכִי. כִּי חִלַּצְתָּ נַפְשִׁי מִמָּוֶת, אֶת עֵינִי מִן דִּמְעָה, אֶת רַגְלִי מִדֶּחִי. אֶתְהַלֵּךְ לִפְנֵי יהוה, בְּאַרְצוֹת הַחַיִּים. הֶאֱמַנְתִּי כִּי אֲדַבֵּר, אֲנִי עָנִיתִי מְאֹד. אֲנִי אָמַרְתִּי בְחָפְזִי, כָּל הָאָדָם כֹּזֵב.

מָה אָשִׁיב לַיהוה, כָּל תַּגְמוּלוֹהִי עָלָי. כּוֹס יְשׁוּעוֹת אֶשָּׂא, וּבְשֵׁם יהוה אֶקְרָא. נְדָרַי לַיהוה אֲשַׁלֵּם, נֶגְדָה נָּא לְכָל עַמּוֹ. יָקָר בְּעֵינֵי יהוה,

---

כּוֹס יְשׁוּעוֹת אֶשָּׂא, וּבְשֵׁם ה' אֶקְרָא
I will raise the cup of salvations and call in the Name of Hashem

The imagery of the cup is used to represent the four expressions of redemption. It is also used to represent four kinds of misfortune (see *Yerushalmi Pesachim* 68b). Sometimes we are forced to drink from the cup of misfortunes, and sometimes we are allowed to drink from the cup of salvations. King David said, "I will raise the cup of salvations, and call in the Name of Hashem." He also said, "The pains of death surround me … disaster and heartache I have found. In the Name of Hashem I call."

King David called to Hashem in prayer both in times of joy and times of suffering. He turned to Hashem in recognition of the hidden kindness that sustained him even in his most difficult moments — as *Chazal* teach us, one must bless Hashem for his difficulties, just as he would bless Hashem for his good fortune (*Berachos* 54a).

◆══◎══◆

Two almost identical verses appear in *Tehillim*, with very slight variations:

מִי יִתֵּן מִצִּיּוֹן יְשׁוּעוֹת יִשְׂרָאֵל בְּשׁוּב אֱלֹהִים שְׁבוּת עַמּוֹ יָגֵל יַעֲקֹב יִשְׂמַח יִשְׂרָאֵל, *O, that out of Zion would come Yisrael's salvations! When God (Elokim) restores the captivity of his people, Yaakov will exult, Yisrael will be glad"* (53:7). In this verse, the word "salvations" is plural, and Hashem's Name *Elokim* is used, indicating that the salvation will come about through the Attribute of Justice.

מִי יִתֵּן מִצִּיּוֹן יְשׁוּעַת יִשְׂרָאֵל בְּשׁוּב י-ה-ו-ה שְׁבוּת עַמּוֹ יָגֵל יַעֲקֹב יִשְׂמַח יִשְׂרָאֵל, *O, that out of Zion would come Yisrael's salvation! When*

I was brought low but He saved me. Return to your rest, my soul, for HASHEM has been kind to you. You delivered my soul from death, my eyes from tears, and my feet from stumbling. I shall walk before HASHEM in the lands of the living. I kept faith although I say: "I suffer exceedingly." I said in my haste: "All mankind is deceitful."

How can I repay HASHEM for all His kindness to me? I will raise the cup of salvations and call in the Name of HASHEM. My vows to HASHEM I pay in the presence of His entire people. Precious in the eyes of HASHEM

Hashem restores the captivity of his people, Yaakov will exult Yisrael will be glad" (14:7). In this verse, "salvation" appears in singular form, and the Tetragrammaton, י-ה-ו-ה, is used, which means that the salvation will emanate from the Attribute of Mercy.

Chida (Chomas Anach, Tehillim 116) cites R' Yosef Piamanta's explanation of these variations. When Hashem's salvation comes about through the Attribute of Mercy, it is considered only one salvation. When it comes about through the Attribute of Justice, it is considered a double salvation.

Chida uses this idea to explain the plural form in the verse, "I will raise the cup of salvations." Since the word כּוֹס, cup, has the same gematria (numerical value) as Elokim, the verse refers to Hashem's salvations in the plural form.

As we have explained previously, Hashem's greatest mercy emanates from the most trying, difficult times in our lives.

In a similar vein, the Vilna Gaon notes that the phrase, "He sustains the living with kindness," is found in the second blessing of Shemoneh Esrei — which is known as Gevuros (Hashem's Might) — since Hashem's greatest kindness emanates from His Might.

This concept is also expressed in the verse, "With might, His right hand saves" (Tehillim 20:7). Hashem's "right hand" represents His Mercy, and His "left hand," His Justice. King David teaches us that Hashem's might also emanates from His right hand, the hand of mercy.

Appropriately, when we raise the cup of salvations — which emanate from the Attribute of Justice — we go on to "call in the Name of Hashem י-ה-ו-ה," — because we realize that this is an expression of the highest form of Hashem's mercy.

הַמָּוְתָה לַחֲסִידָיו. אָנָּה יהוה כִּי אֲנִי עַבְדֶּךָ, אֲנִי
עַבְדְּךָ, בֶּן אֲמָתֶךָ, פִּתַּחְתָּ לְמוֹסֵרָי. לְךָ אֶזְבַּח זֶבַח
תּוֹדָה, וּבְשֵׁם יהוה אֶקְרָא. נְדָרַי לַיהוה אֲשַׁלֵּם, נֶגְדָה
נָא לְכָל עַמּוֹ. בְּחַצְרוֹת בֵּית יהוה, בְּתוֹכֵכִי יְרוּשָׁלַיִם
הַלְלוּיָהּ.[1]

הַלְלוּ אֶת יהוה, כָּל גּוֹיִם, שַׁבְּחוּהוּ כָּל הָאֻמִּים.
כִּי גָבַר עָלֵינוּ חַסְדּוֹ, וֶאֱמֶת יהוה לְעוֹלָם,
הַלְלוּיָהּ.[2]

אָנָּה ה' כִּי אֲנִי עַבְדֶּךָ

Please, Hashem for I am Your servant

The Lev Simchah of Gur recounted in the name of his father, the Imrei Emes, that one Succos, the Sefas Emes said that while praying, אָנָּה ה', Please, Hashem, during Hallel, one can achieve great spiritual accomplishments.

The next day, a debate erupted between the Chassidim: Was the Sefas Emes referring to the verse אָנָּא ה' הוֹשִׁיעָה נָּא, Please, Hashem, save now, or to the verse אָנָּא ה' הַצְלִיחָה נָא, Please, Hashem, bring success now?

During Hallel, some shouted the verse, "Please, Hashem, save now," with intense concentration, while others fervently recited, "Please, Hashem, grant success now."

The Imrei Emes said that he understood that both groups were wrong. The Sefas Emes was referring to the verse, אָנָּה ה' כִּי אֲנִי עַבְדֶּךָ, Please, Hashem, for I am Your servant.

This story conveys a profound idea. The highest level that a Jew can attain is to be able to serve Hashem with joy. Moshe Rabbeinu reached the pinnacle of human achievement — Hashem conferred the title "My servant" upon him — because he accepted upon himself to serve Hashem with joy.

When a person accepts Hashem's Sovereignty with joy, he merits the "crown of royalty" with which Bnei Yisrael were crowned at Mount Sinai. The Talmud (*Shabbos* 88) tells us that when Bnei Yisrael were offered the Torah and they proclaimed, "We will do and we will listen," six hundred thousand angels descended and crowned them with two crowns each; one for "We will do," and one for "We will listen." By accepting Hashem's Torah without waiting to

is the death of His devout ones. Please, HASHEM — for I am Your servant, I am Your servant, son of Your handmaid — You have released my bonds. To You I sacrifice thanksgiving offerings, and the Name of HASHEM I will call. My vows to HASHEM I will pay in the presence of His entire people; in the courtyards of the House of HASHEM, in your midst, O Jerusalem, Halleluyah![1]

Praise HASHEM, all you nations; praise Him all you peoples! For His kindness to us was overwhelming, and the truth of HASHEM is eternal, Halleluyah![2]

---

(1) *Tehillim* 116. (2) Ibid. 117.

---

hear what His decrees entailed, they showed their great love and enthusiasm to enter into His service, and therefore merited the great reward of being crowned by the angels.

Similarly, we pray (Shabbos morning *Shemoneh Esrei*), "Moshe will rejoice in the gift of his portion: that You called him a faithful servant. A crown of splendor You placed on his head, when he stood before You on Mount Sinai." Because Moshe rejoiced when he was called a servant of Hashem, he merited the crown of splendor at Mount Sinai.

Succos is a time to rejoice. *Rambam* (*Hilchos Lulav* 8:12) writes: "Although there is a mitzvah to rejoice on all festivals, the holiday of Succos was celebrated in the Beis Hamikdash with *simchah yeseirah* (exceptional joy)."

Rambam uses the expression *simchah yeseirah* again in reference to the mitzvah of reciting Hallel: "On Rosh Hashanah and Yom Kippur, Hallel is not recited, since these are days of repentance, awe, and fear; and not days of *simchah yeseirah*" (*Hilchos Chanukah* 3:6). If so, the Hallel recited on Succos is certainly a unique expression of *simchah yeseirah*. We can understand, then, that if we use the zenith of joy of the entire year to exclaim, "Please, Hashem, for I am Your servant," that we can attain some of the highest spiritual levels possible.[1]

---

1. It is noteworthy that the word אָנָּה in the verse אָנָּה ה' כִּי אֲנִי עַבְדֶּךָ is written with a 'ה, whereas the words at the end of Hallel are אָנָּא, with an 'א. אָנָּה is an expression of appreciation; אָנָּא is a request. Thus, the true translation of the verse אָנָּה ה' כִּי אֲנִי עַבְדֶּךָ is, "I thank Hashem for the kindness He bestowed upon me in that I am Your servant" (*Radak*).

Some have the custom that the head of the household says, "Give thanks to HASHEM," and those present respond, as long as at least three people are present (i.e., two people to respond to the head of the household).

כִּי לְעוֹלָם חַסְדּוֹ.	**הוֹדוּ** לַיהוה כִּי טוֹב,
כִּי לְעוֹלָם חַסְדּוֹ.	יֹאמַר נָא יִשְׂרָאֵל,
כִּי לְעוֹלָם חַסְדּוֹ.	יֹאמְרוּ נָא בֵית אַהֲרֹן,
כִּי לְעוֹלָם חַסְדּוֹ.	יֹאמְרוּ נָא יִרְאֵי יהוה,

מִן הַמֵּצַר קָרָאתִי יָּהּ, עָנָנִי בַמֶּרְחָב יָהּ. יהוה לִי לֹא אִירָא, מַה יַּעֲשֶׂה לִי אָדָם. יהוה לִי בְּעֹזְרָי, וַאֲנִי אֶרְאֶה בְשֹׂנְאָי. טוֹב לַחֲסוֹת בַּיהוה, מִבְּטֹחַ בָּאָדָם. טוֹב לַחֲסוֹת בַּיהוה, מִבְּטֹחַ בִּנְדִיבִים. כָּל גּוֹיִם סְבָבוּנִי, בְּשֵׁם יהוה כִּי אֲמִילַם. סַבּוּנִי גַם סְבָבוּנִי, בְּשֵׁם יהוה כִּי אֲמִילַם. סַבּוּנִי כִדְבֹרִים דֹּעֲכוּ כְּאֵשׁ קוֹצִים, בְּשֵׁם יהוה כִּי אֲמִילַם. דָּחֹה דְחִיתַנִי לִנְפֹּל, וַיהוה עֲזָרָנִי. עָזִּי וְזִמְרָת יָהּ, וַיְהִי לִי לִישׁוּעָה. קוֹל רִנָּה וִישׁוּעָה, בְּאָהֳלֵי צַדִּיקִים, יְמִין יהוה עֹשָׂה חָיִל. יְמִין יהוה רוֹמֵמָה, יְמִין יהוה עֹשָׂה חָיִל. לֹא אָמוּת כִּי אֶחְיֶה, וַאֲסַפֵּר מַעֲשֵׂי יָהּ. יַסֹּר יִסְּרַנִּי יָּהּ, וְלַמָּוֶת לֹא נְתָנָנִי. פִּתְחוּ לִי שַׁעֲרֵי צֶדֶק, אָבֹא בָם אוֹדֶה יָהּ. זֶה הַשַּׁעַר לַיהוה, צַדִּיקִים יָבֹאוּ בוֹ. אוֹדְךָ כִּי עֲנִיתָנִי, וַתְּהִי לִי לִישׁוּעָה.

אוֹדְךָ כִּי עֲנִיתָנִי
I thank You for You answered me
Most of the classic commentators interpret the word עֲנִיתָנִי in this verse to mean, "You have answered me." They understood that עֲנִיתָנִי stems from the word עוֹנֶה, which means answer. According to this interpretation, King David thanked Hashem for answering all his prayers.

Give thanks to HASHEM for He is good;
His kindness endures forever!
Let Yisrael say: His kindness endures forever!
Let the House of Aaron say:
His kindness endures forever!
Let those who fear HASHEM say:
His kindness endures forever!

From the straits did I call to God; God answered me with expansiveness. HASHEM is with me; I have no fear; how can man affect me? HASHEM is for me through my helpers; therefore I can face my foes. It is better to take refuge in HASHEM than to rely on man. It is better to take refuge in HASHEM than to rely on princes. All the nations encompass me; but in the Name of HASHEM I cut them down! They encompass me; they swarm around me; but in the Name of HASHEM I cut them down! They swarm around me like bees, but they are extinguished as a fire does thorns; in the Name of HASHEM I cut them down! You pushed me hard that I might fall, but HASHEM assisted me. My strength and song is God; He became my salvation. The sound of rejoicing and salvation is in the tents of the righteous: "The right hand of HASHEM does valiantly! The right hand of HASHEM is raised triumphantly! The right hand of HASHEM does valiantly!" I shall not die! I shall live and relate the deeds of God. God chastened me exceedingly but He did not let me die. Open for me the gates of righteousness, I will enter them and thank God. This is the gate of HASHEM; the righteous shall enter through it. I thank You for You answered me and became my salvation!

אוֹדְךָ כִּי עֲנִיתָנִי, וַתְּהִי לִי לִישׁוּעָה. אֶבֶן מָאֲסוּ
הַבּוֹנִים, הָיְתָה לְרֹאשׁ פִּנָּה. אֶבֶן מָאֲסוּ הַבּוֹנִים,
הָיְתָה לְרֹאשׁ פִּנָּה. מֵאֵת יהוה הָיְתָה זֹּאת, הִיא
נִפְלָאת בְּעֵינֵינוּ. מֵאֵת יהוה הָיְתָה זֹּאת, הִיא
נִפְלָאת בְּעֵינֵינוּ. זֶה הַיּוֹם עָשָׂה יהוה, נָגִילָה
וְנִשְׂמְחָה בוֹ. זֶה הַיּוֹם עָשָׂה יהוה, נָגִילָה וְנִשְׂמְחָה
בוֹ.

אָנָּא יהוה הוֹשִׁיעָה נָּא.

אָנָּא יהוה הוֹשִׁיעָה נָּא.

אָנָּא יהוה הַצְלִיחָה נָּא.

אָנָּא יהוה הַצְלִיחָה נָּא.

בָּרוּךְ הַבָּא בְּשֵׁם יהוה, בֵּרַכְנוּכֶם מִבֵּית יהוה.
בָּרוּךְ הַבָּא בְּשֵׁם יהוה, בֵּרַכְנוּכֶם מִבֵּית
יהוה. אֵל יהוה וַיָּאֶר לָנוּ, אִסְרוּ חַג בַּעֲבֹתִים, עַד
קַרְנוֹת הַמִּזְבֵּחַ. אֵל יהוה וַיָּאֶר לָנוּ, אִסְרוּ חַג
בַּעֲבֹתִים, עַד קַרְנוֹת הַמִּזְבֵּחַ. אֵלִי אַתָּה וְאוֹדֶךָּ,
אֱלֹהַי אֲרוֹמְמֶךָּ. אֵלִי אַתָּה וְאוֹדֶךָּ, אֱלֹהַי אֲרוֹמְמֶךָּ.
הוֹדוּ לַיהוה כִּי טוֹב, כִּי לְעוֹלָם חַסְדּוֹ. הוֹדוּ לַיהוה כִּי
טוֹב, כִּי לְעוֹלָם חַסְדּוֹ.[1]

Chida (Haggadah shel Pesach Peh Echad) understands the word to
mean, "You have caused me to suffer," from the root word עִנּוּי,
suffering. According to this interpretation, King David thanked
Hashem for the suffering he endured.

Rabbeinu Yonah writes in *Shaarei Teshuvah* (2:4) that although we
must pray to Hashem to protect us from misfortune, we must nevertheless rejoice when misfortune strikes. We must realize that we will
benefit from our suffering as much as we would from a profitable
business venture.

I thank You for You answered me and became my salvation! The stone which the builders despised has become the cornerstone! The stone which the builders despised has become the cornerstone! This has emanated from HASHEM; it is wondrous in our eyes! This has emanated from HASHEM; it is wondrous in our eyes! This is the day HASHEM has made; we will rejoice and be glad in Him! This is the day HASHEM has made; we will rejoice and be glad in Him!

Please, HASHEM, save now!
  Please, HASHEM, save now!
Please, HASHEM, grant success now!
Please, HASHEM, grant success now!

Blessed be he who comes in the Name of HASHEM; we bless you from the House of HASHEM. Blessed be he who comes in the Name of HASHEM; we bless you from the House of HASHEM. HASHEM is God and He illuminated for us; bind the festival offering with cords to the corners of the Altar. HASHEM is God and He illuminated for us; bind the festival offering with cords to the corners of the Altar. You are my God and I shall thank You; my God and I shall exalt You. You are my God, and I shall thank You; my God and I shall exalt You. Give thanks to HASHEM, for He is good; His kindness endures forever! Give thanks to HASHEM, for He is good; His kindness endures forever![1]

---

(1) *Tehillim* 118.

Similarly, when R' Eliezer HaGadol was ill, R' Akiva visited him and said, "Suffering is beloved," for it can cause a person's merits to outweigh his misdeeds (*Sanhedrin* 101a).

According to the rules of Hebrew grammar, the first interpretation seems more correct, since עֲנִיתָנִי is spelled with a *pasach*, similar to the word for "answer," not with a *chirik*, like the word for "suffering."

Nusach Ashkenaz recites the following passage here.
Nusach Sefard recites it later, after Yishtabach.
According to the Vilna Gaon, this passage is not recited at all.

יְהַלְלוּךְ יהוה אֱלֹהֵינוּ כָּל מַעֲשֶׂיךָ, וַחֲסִידֶיךָ צַדִּיקִים עוֹשֵׂי רְצוֹנֶךָ, וְכָל עַמְּךָ בֵּית יִשְׂרָאֵל בְּרִנָּה יוֹדוּ וִיבָרְכוּ וִישַׁבְּחוּ וִיפָאֲרוּ וִירוֹמְמוּ וְיַעֲרִיצוּ וְיַקְדִּישׁוּ וְיַמְלִיכוּ אֶת שִׁמְךָ מַלְכֵּנוּ, כִּי לְךָ טוֹב לְהוֹדוֹת וּלְשִׁמְךָ נָאֶה לְזַמֵּר, כִּי מֵעוֹלָם וְעַד עוֹלָם אַתָּה אֵל.

על פי פסחים קיח, א

הוֹדוּ לַיהוה כִּי טוֹב   כִּי לְעוֹלָם חַסְדּוֹ.
הוֹדוּ לֵאלֹהֵי הָאֱלֹהִים   כִּי לְעוֹלָם חַסְדּוֹ.
הוֹדוּ לַאֲדֹנֵי הָאֲדֹנִים   כִּי לְעוֹלָם חַסְדּוֹ.
לְעֹשֵׂה נִפְלָאוֹת גְּדֹלוֹת לְבַדּוֹ   כִּי לְעוֹלָם חַסְדּוֹ.
לְעֹשֵׂה הַשָּׁמַיִם בִּתְבוּנָה   כִּי לְעוֹלָם חַסְדּוֹ.
לְרֹקַע הָאָרֶץ עַל הַמָּיִם   כִּי לְעוֹלָם חַסְדּוֹ.
לְעֹשֵׂה אוֹרִים גְּדֹלִים   כִּי לְעוֹלָם חַסְדּוֹ.
אֶת הַשֶּׁמֶשׁ לְמֶמְשֶׁלֶת בַּיּוֹם   כִּי לְעוֹלָם חַסְדּוֹ.
אֶת הַיָּרֵחַ וְכוֹכָבִים לְמֶמְשְׁלוֹת בַּלַּיְלָה
  כִּי לְעוֹלָם חַסְדּוֹ.
לְמַכֵּה מִצְרַיִם בִּבְכוֹרֵיהֶם   כִּי לְעוֹלָם חַסְדּוֹ.
וַיּוֹצֵא יִשְׂרָאֵל מִתּוֹכָם   כִּי לְעוֹלָם חַסְדּוֹ.
בְּיָד חֲזָקָה וּבִזְרוֹעַ נְטוּיָה   כִּי לְעוֹלָם חַסְדּוֹ.
לְגֹזֵר יַם סוּף לִגְזָרִים   כִּי לְעוֹלָם חַסְדּוֹ.

Nusach Ashkenaz recites the following passage here.
Nusach Sefard recites it later, after *Yishtabach*.
According to the Vilna Gaon, this passage is not recited at all.

They shall praise You, HASHEM our God, all Your works, along with Your pious followers, the righteous, who do Your will, and Your entire people, the House of Israel, with joy will thank, bless, praise, glorify, exalt, revere, sanctify, and coronate Your Name, our King! For to You it is fitting to give thanks, and unto Your Name it is proper to sing praises, for from eternity to eternity You are God.

Our recitation of Psalm 136 is based on Pesachim 118a

Give thanks to HASHEM, for He is good;
His kindness endures forever!
Give thanks to the God of gods;
His kindness endures forever!
Give thanks to the Master of masters;
His kindness endures forever!
To Him Who alone does great wonders;
His kindness endures forever!
To Him Who makes the heaven with understanding;
His kindness endures forever!
To Him Who stretched out the earth over the waters;
His kindness endures forever!
To Him Who makes great luminaries;
His kindness endures forever!
The sun for the reign of the day;
His kindness endures forever!
The moon and the stars for the reign of the night;
His kindness endures forever!
To Him Who struck the Egyptians
through their firstborn;
His kindness endures forever!
And took Israel out from their midst;
His kindness endures forever!
With strong hand and outstretched arm;
His kindness endures forever!
To Him Who divided the Sea of Reeds into parts;
His kindness endures forever!

כִּי לְעוֹלָם חַסְדּוֹ.	וְהֶעֱבִיר יִשְׂרָאֵל בְּתוֹכוֹ
כִּי לְעוֹלָם חַסְדּוֹ.	וְנִעֵר פַּרְעֹה וְחֵילוֹ בְיַם סוּף
כִּי לְעוֹלָם חַסְדּוֹ.	לְמוֹלִיךְ עַמּוֹ בַּמִּדְבָּר
כִּי לְעוֹלָם חַסְדּוֹ.	לְמַכֵּה מְלָכִים גְּדֹלִים
כִּי לְעוֹלָם חַסְדּוֹ.	וַיַּהֲרֹג מְלָכִים אַדִּירִים
כִּי לְעוֹלָם חַסְדּוֹ.	לְסִיחוֹן מֶלֶךְ הָאֱמֹרִי
כִּי לְעוֹלָם חַסְדּוֹ.	וּלְעוֹג מֶלֶךְ הַבָּשָׁן
כִּי לְעוֹלָם חַסְדּוֹ.	וְנָתַן אַרְצָם לְנַחֲלָה
כִּי לְעוֹלָם חַסְדּוֹ.	נַחֲלָה לְיִשְׂרָאֵל עַבְדּוֹ
כִּי לְעוֹלָם חַסְדּוֹ.	שֶׁבְּשִׁפְלֵנוּ זָכַר לָנוּ
כִּי לְעוֹלָם חַסְדּוֹ.	וַיִּפְרְקֵנוּ מִצָּרֵינוּ
כִּי לְעוֹלָם חַסְדּוֹ.	נֹתֵן לֶחֶם לְכָל בָּשָׂר
כִּי לְעוֹלָם חַסְדּוֹ.[1]	הוֹדוּ לְאֵל הַשָּׁמָיִם

על פי פסחים קיח, א

נִשְׁמַת כָּל חַי תְּבָרֵךְ אֶת שִׁמְךָ יהוה אֱלֹהֵינוּ וְרוּחַ כָּל בָּשָׂר תְּפָאֵר וּתְרוֹמֵם זִכְרְךָ מַלְכֵּנוּ תָּמִיד. מִן הָעוֹלָם וְעַד הָעוֹלָם אַתָּה אֵל. וּמִבַּלְעָדֶיךָ

נִשְׁמַת כָּל חַי
The soul of every living thing

It is customary to recite *Nishmas Kol Chai* on Shabbos morning, since on Shabbos we are granted a *neshamah yeseirah* — an additional soul (*Chida, Haggadah shel Pesach Safah Achas*). Although some *Rishonim* hold that we do not receive a *neshamah yeseirah* on Yom Tov (see *Pesachim* 102b, *Tosafos* s.v. *Rav amar*), on the Seder night we experience such an incomparable elevation of the soul that it has become a universally accepted practice to recite *Nishmas* on this night.

❖

The aspect of the soul known as *neshamah* is loftier than the aspect known as *ru'ach* (see *Reishis Chochmah, Shaar HaAhavah* Ch.

And caused Israel to pass through it;
His kindness endures forever!
And threw Pharaoh and his army into the Sea of Reeds;
His kindness endures forever!
To Him Who led His people through the Wilderness;
His kindness endures forever!
To Him Who smote great kings;
His kindness endures forever!
And slew mighty kings;
His kindness endures forever!
Sichon, king of the Emorites;
His kindness endures forever!
And Og, king of Bashan;
His kindness endures forever!
And gave their land as an inheritance;
His kindness endures forever!
An inheritance to Israel His servant;
His kindness endures forever!
Who remembered us in our lowliness;
His kindness endures forever!
And released us from our foes;
His kindness endures forever!
He gives food to all living creatures;
His kindness endures forever!
Give thanks to God of heaven;
His kindness endures forever![1]

Our recitation of the following selection is based on Pesachim 118a

The soul of every living thing shall bless Your Name, HASHEM, our God; the spirit of all flesh shall always glorify and exalt Your remembrance, our King. From eternity to eternity You are God, and except for You

(1) *Tehillim* 136.

---

11). We can therefore explain that the first words of this prayer — "The soul (*neshamah*) of every *living thing* shall bless Your Name" — refers to righteous individuals, for a Midrash tells us that the righteous are considered alive even after their passing, while the

אֵין לָנוּ מֶלֶךְ גּוֹאֵל וּמוֹשִׁיעַ, פּוֹדֶה וּמַצִּיל וּמְפַרְנֵס
וְעוֹנֶה וּמְרַחֵם בְּכָל עֵת צָרָה וְצוּקָה, אֵין לָנוּ
מֶלֶךְ עוֹזֵר וְסוֹמֵךְ אֶלָּא אָתָּה. אֱלֹהֵי הָרִאשׁוֹנִים
וְהָאַחֲרוֹנִים. אֱלוֹהַּ כָּל בְּרִיּוֹת. אֲדוֹן כָּל תּוֹלָדוֹת,
הַמְהֻלָּל בְּרֹב הַתִּשְׁבָּחוֹת הַמְנַהֵג עוֹלָמוֹ
בְּחֶסֶד וּבְרִיּוֹתָיו בְּרַחֲמִים. וַיהוה עֵר. הִנֵּה
לֹא יָנוּם וְלֹא יִישָׁן. הַמְּעוֹרֵר יְשֵׁנִים וְהַמֵּקִיץ
נִרְדָּמִים. וְהַמֵּשִׂיחַ אִלְּמִים וְהַמַּתִּיר אֲסוּרִים
וְהַסּוֹמֵךְ נוֹפְלִים וְהַזּוֹקֵף כְּפוּפִים, וְהַמְפַעֲנֵחַ

---

wicked are considered like dead even while they live (*Midrash Tanchuma, Parashas Vezos HaBerachah*). They merit blessing Hashem's Name, since they can recognize His greatness.

The next words read: "The spirit (*ru'ach*) of all flesh shall always glorify and exalt Your remembrance." This refers to the wicked who are not considered truly alive. They are mere flesh, and exhibit only the faculty of *ru'ach*. Even they will merit to exalt Hashem's remembrance.

מְחַיֶּה מֵתִים, וְרוֹפֵא חוֹלִים
Who revives the dead and heals the sick[1]

Chida (*Haggadah shel Pesach Simchas HaRegel*) explains these words based on the passage in the Talmud (*Sanhedrin* 91b) that states that when the dead return to life, each one will return with the physical blemishes he had when he died. This will make it easier for us to recognize one another. Afterward, Hashem will heal all our blemishes. Therefore, we say first that Hashem revives the dead, and then that He heals the sick.

The same explanation can be applied to the second blessing of *Shemoneh Esrei*, in which we say, "He revives the dead with abundant mercy," and then, "He supports the fallen and heals the sick." We go on to say that Hashem is the "King Who causes death and restores life and makes salvation sprout." After He revives the dead, He will make salvation sprout by healing all their ills.

---

1. These words appear in the *Nusach Sefard* version of *Nishmas*.

we have no king, redeemer or helper. O Rescuer, and Redeemer, Sustainer, Responder, and Merciful One in every time of trouble and distress. We have no king, helper, or supporter but You — God of the first and of the last, God of all creatures, Master of all generations, Who is extolled through a multitude of praises, Who guides His world with kindness and His creatures with mercy. HASHEM is awake, behold, He neither slumbers nor sleeps; He rouses the sleepers and awakens the slumberers; He makes the mute speak and releases the bound; He supports the fallen and raises erect the bowed down and uncovers

---

וְהַמֵּשִׂיחַ אִלְּמִים . . . וְהַמְפַעֲנֵחַ נֶעְלָמִים

He makes the mute speak ... and uncovers the hidden[1]

Chida (ibid.) explains this based on *Sefer HaYashar*, who writes that when Potiphar's wife accused Yosef of attempting to seduce her, Potiphar was overcome with wrath and decided to kill Yosef. Hashem performed a miracle, and an infant in its crib began to speak, and revealed that it was actually Potiphar's wife who attempted to seduce Yosef. Potiphar and his household saw the great miracle and realized the truth. They spared Yosef's life, but in order to protect their own honor, they condemned him to imprisonment.

A similar incident occurred in Jerusalem during the days of Rabbeinu Klonimus. A group of Arabs killed an Arab child and threw him into the courtyard of a shul. They planned on creating a blood libel and use it to justify a massacre of the Jewish community.

Rabbeinu Klonimus prayed for mercy, and a miracle occurred. The dead Arab child began to speak and he told how the Arabs themselves had killed him and thrown him into the courtyard. The authorities heard about the miracle, and the Jews were saved. Rabbeinu Klonimus thus became known as "Rabbeinu Klonimus, *Baal HaNess* (the Master of the Miracle)."

These stories are examples of how Hashem "makes the mute speak ... and (thereby) uncovers the hidden."[1]

---

1. R' Galanti, a student of R' Moshe Cordovero (*RaMaK*), writes that the entire section from "אֱלֹהֵי הָרִאשׁוֹנִים וְהָאַחֲרוֹנִים — God of the first and of the last," until "אֲנַחְנוּ מוֹדִים — we give thanks," is actually an addition to the original text of *Nishmas*. This addition, which includes the words, "He makes the mute speak ... and uncovers the hidden," was inserted after the murdered Arab child miraculously spoke and the Jewish community of Yerushalayim was saved.

נֶעְלָמִים, וּלְךָ לְבַדְּךָ אֲנַחְנוּ מוֹדִים. וְאִלּוּ פִינוּ מָלֵא
שִׁירָה כַּיָּם, וּלְשׁוֹנֵנוּ רִנָּה כַּהֲמוֹן גַּלָּיו, וְשִׂפְתוֹתֵינוּ
שֶׁבַח כְּמֶרְחֲבֵי רָקִיעַ, וְעֵינֵינוּ מְאִירוֹת כַּשֶּׁמֶשׁ
וְכַיָּרֵחַ וְיָדֵינוּ פְרוּשׂוֹת כְּנִשְׁרֵי שָׁמַיִם, וְרַגְלֵינוּ
קַלּוֹת כָּאַיָּלוֹת, אֵין אֲנַחְנוּ מַסְפִּיקִים לְהוֹדוֹת לְךָ
יְהוָה אֱלֹהֵינוּ וֵאלֹהֵי אֲבוֹתֵינוּ וּלְבָרֵךְ אֶת שִׁמְךָ
מַלְכֵּנוּ עַל אַחַת מֵאֶלֶף אֶלֶף אַלְפֵי אֲלָפִים וְרִבֵּי
רְבָבוֹת פְּעָמִים הַטּוֹבוֹת נִסִּים וְנִפְלָאוֹת שֶׁעָשִׂיתָ עִם
אֲבוֹתֵינוּ וְעִמָּנוּ. מִלְּפָנִים מִמִּצְרַיִם גְּאַלְתָּנוּ יְהוָה
אֱלֹהֵינוּ, וּמִבֵּית עֲבָדִים פְּדִיתָנוּ, בְּרָעָב זַנְתָּנוּ,
וּבְשָׂבָע כִּלְכַּלְתָּנוּ, מֵחֶרֶב הִצַּלְתָּנוּ, וּמִדֶּבֶר
מִלַּטְתָּנוּ, וּמֵחֳלָיִם רָעִים וְרַבִּים וְנֶאֱמָנִים דִּלִּיתָנוּ.
עַד הֵנָּה עֲזָרוּנוּ רַחֲמֶיךָ, וְלֹא עֲזָבוּנוּ חֲסָדֶיךָ יְהוָה
אֱלֹהֵינוּ. וְאַל תִּטְּשֵׁנוּ יְהוָה אֱלֹהֵינוּ לָנֶצַח.
עַל כֵּן אֵבָרִים שֶׁפִּלַּגְתָּ בָּנוּ, וְרוּחַ וּנְשָׁמָה שֶׁנָּפַחְתָּ

בְּרָעָב זַנְתָּנוּ וּבְשָׂבָע כִּלְכַּלְתָּנוּ
In famine You nourished us and in plenty You supported us.

The Talmud tells us that when a person performs a mitzvah, an
angel is created that will walk before him in the World to Come.
When he sins, an angel is created that clings to him and walks
behind him on the Day of Judgment (*Avodah Zarah* 5a).

Maharsha notes that the angel created by mitzvos walks before a
person, while the angel created by his sins walks behind him. He explains that when a person is invited to a wedding or other joyous event,
the messenger need only show the way, and the guest is happy to
follow after him. When a person is summoned to jail, execution, or any
difficult judgment, the court officers walk behind him to ensure that he
does not escape. So too, the angels created by mitzvos walk before a
person, to guide him to his reward. The angels created by sins walk
behind him, to ensure that he does not attempt to escape judgment.

Based on this, *Yeshuos Yaakov* explains the prayer, "Remove the

the hidden. To You alone we give thanks.

Were our mouth as full of song as the sea, and our tongue as full of jubilation as its multitude of waves, and our lips as full of praise as the breadth of the heavens, and our eyes as brilliant as the sun and the moon, and our hands as outspread in prayer as eagles of the sky and our feet as swift as deer — we still could not sufficiently thank You, HASHEM our God and God of our fathers, and bless Your Name our King for even one of the thousands upon thousands, and myriads upon myriads of favors, miracles and wonders, that You performed for our ancestors and for us. At first You redeemed us from Egypt, HASHEM our God, and liberated us from the house of bondage. In famine You nourished us and in plenty You supported us. From the sword You saved us; from the plague You let us escape; and You spared us from severe, numerous and enduring diseases. Until now Your mercy has helped us and Your kindness has not forsaken us, HASHEM, our God; do not abandon us, HASHEM our God, forever.

Therefore, the organs that You have set within us, and the spirit and soul which You breathed

---

Satan from before us and from behind us." The Satan, the Evil Inclination, and the Angel of Death are all one and the same. He incites us to sin, then ascends to the Heavens to prosecute, and eventually returns to claim our souls as punishment for our sins (see *Bava Basra* 16a). We tell Hashem that we have no desire to follow the Evil Inclination, and we have no interest in "either its honey or its sting." Let him not lead us into the festivities of sin, and let him not follow us to our punishment.

When Bnei Yisrael traveled into the barren desert on Hashem's command, they did not wait to be driven from behind, as could be expected in such a frightful journey. They willingly and joyously followed after Him, with complete *bitachon* that He would cater to all their needs, as the verse says, "Your following Me into the

בְּאַפֵּינוּ, וְלָשׁוֹן אֲשֶׁר שַׂמְתָּ בְּפֵינוּ, הֵן הֵם יוֹדוּ וִיבָרְכוּ
וִישַׁבְּחוּ וִיפָאֲרוּ וִישׁוֹרְרוּ וִירוֹמְמוּ וְיַעֲרִיצוּ וְיַקְדִּישׁוּ
וְיַמְלִיכוּ אֶת שִׁמְךָ מַלְכֵּנוּ תָּמִיד. כִּי כָל פֶּה לְךָ יוֹדֶה,
וְכָל לָשׁוֹן לְךָ תִשָּׁבַע, וְכָל עַיִן לְךָ תְצַפֶּה, וְכָל בֶּרֶךְ
לְךָ תִכְרַע, וְכָל קוֹמָה לְפָנֶיךָ תִשְׁתַּחֲוֶה, וְכָל הַלְּבָבוֹת
יִירָאוּךָ, וְכָל קֶרֶב וּכְלָיוֹת יְזַמְּרוּ לִשְׁמֶךָ, כַּדָּבָר
שֶׁכָּתוּב: כָּל עַצְמֹתַי תֹּאמַרְנָה יהוה מִי כָמוֹךָ,[1]
מַצִּיל עָנִי מֵחָזָק מִמֶּנּוּ, וְעָנִי וְאֶבְיוֹן מִגֹּזְלוֹ. שַׁוְעַת
עֲנִיִּים אַתָּה תִשְׁמַע צַעֲקַת הַדַּל תַּקְשִׁיב וְתוֹשִׁיעַ. מִי
יִדְמֶה לָּךְ, וּמִי יִשְׁוֶה לָּךְ, וּמִי יַעֲרָךְ לָךְ. הָאֵל הַגָּדוֹל
הַגִּבּוֹר וְהַנּוֹרָא, אֵל עֶלְיוֹן קֹנֵה שָׁמַיִם וָאָרֶץ. נְהַלֶּלְךָ
וּנְשַׁבֵּחֲךָ וּנְפָאֶרְךָ וּנְבָרֵךְ אֶת שֵׁם קָדְשֶׁךָ, כָּאָמוּר:
לְדָוִד, בָּרְכִי נַפְשִׁי אֶת יהוה, וְכָל קְרָבַי אֶת שֵׁם קָדְשׁוֹ:

הָאֵל בְּתַעֲצֻמוֹת עֻזֶּךָ, הַגָּדוֹל בִּכְבוֹד שְׁמֶךָ, הַגִּבּוֹר
לָנֶצַח וְהַנּוֹרָא בְּנוֹרְאוֹתֶיךָ, הַמֶּלֶךְ הַיּוֹשֵׁב
עַל כִּסֵּא רָם וְנִשָּׂא:

שׁוֹכֵן עַד מָרוֹם וְקָדוֹשׁ שְׁמוֹ. וְכָתוּב: רַנְּנוּ צַדִּיקִים
בַּיהוה, לַיְשָׁרִים נָאוָה תְהִלָּה: בְּפִי יְשָׁרִים
תִּתְרוֹמָם. וּבְשִׂפְתֵי צַדִּיקִים תִּתְבָּרַךְ. וּבִלְשׁוֹן
חֲסִידִים תִּתְקַדָּשׁ. וּבְקֶרֶב קְדוֹשִׁים תִּתְהַלָּל:

Wilderness, into an unsown land" (*Yirmiyah* 2:2).

It is interesting to note that Bnei Yisrael brought with them the treasures of Egypt — gold, silver, and elegant clothes — but they did not prepare food or drink for themselves. A person traveling through the desert has no need for gold and silver, nor does he need elegant clothes. But he does need food and drink to ensure his survival.

Bnei Yisrael had no concern for their survival. They had complete trust in Hashem to provide for them. They did not take the treasures

into our nostrils, and the tongue which You have placed in our mouth — they shall thank and bless, praise and glorify, sing about, exalt, be devoted to, sanctify and do homage to Your Name, our King continuously. For every mouth shall offer thanks to You; every tongue shall vow allegiance to You; every eye shall look toward You; every knee shall bend to You; all who stand erect shall bow before You; all hearts shall fear You; and all men's innermost feelings and thoughts shall sing praises to Your Name, as it is written: "All my bones declare: 'HASHEM, who is like You?'[1] You save the poor man from one stronger than him, the poor and needy from one who would rob him." The outcry of the poor You hear, the screams of the destitute You listen to, and You save. Who may be likened to You? Who is equal to You? Who can be compared to You? O great, mighty, and awesome God, supreme God, Creator of heaven and earth. We shall praise, acclaim, and glorify You and bless Your holy Name, as it is said: "A psalm of David: Bless HASHEM, O my soul, and let my whole inner being bless His holy Name!"[2]

O God, in the omnipotence of Your strength, great in the honor of Your Name, powerful forever and awesome through Your awesome deeds, O King enthroned upon a high and lofty throne!

He Who abides forever, exalted and holy is His Name. And it is written: "Rejoice in HASHEM, you righteous; for the upright, His praise is pleasant."[3] By the mouth of the upright You shall be exalted; by the lips of the righteous You shall be blessed; by the tongue of the pious You shall be sanctified; and amid the holy You shall be praised.

---

(1) *Tehillim* 35:10. (2) Ibid. 103:1. (3) Ibid. 33:1.

---

of Egypt to fill their own desires, but simply to obey Moshe Rabbeinu, who instructed them to do so.

וּבְמַקְהֵלוֹת רִבְבוֹת עַמְּךָ בֵּית יִשְׂרָאֵל, בְּרִנָּה יִתְפָּאַר שִׁמְךָ מַלְכֵּנוּ בְּכָל דּוֹר וָדוֹר.

שֶׁכֵּן חוֹבַת כָּל הַיְצוּרִים, לְפָנֶיךָ יהוה אֱלֹהֵינוּ וֵאלֹהֵי אֲבוֹתֵינוּ, לְהוֹדוֹת לְהַלֵּל לְשַׁבֵּחַ לְפָאֵר לְרוֹמֵם לְהַדֵּר וּלְנַצֵּחַ לְבָרֵךְ לְעַלֵּה וּלְקַלֵּס, עַל כָּל דִּבְרֵי שִׁירוֹת וְתִשְׁבָּחוֹת דָּוִד בֶּן יִשַׁי עַבְדְּךָ מְשִׁיחֶךָ.

[וּבְכֵן] יִשְׁתַּבַּח שִׁמְךָ לָעַד, מַלְכֵּנוּ, הָאֵל הַמֶּלֶךְ הַגָּדוֹל וְהַקָּדוֹשׁ, בַּשָּׁמַיִם וּבָאָרֶץ. כִּי לְךָ נָאֶה, יהוה אֱלֹהֵינוּ וֵאלֹהֵי אֲבוֹתֵינוּ, שִׁיר וּשְׁבָחָה, הַלֵּל וְזִמְרָה, עֹז וּמֶמְשָׁלָה, נֶצַח גְּדֻלָּה וּגְבוּרָה, תְּהִלָּה וְתִפְאֶרֶת, קְדֻשָּׁה וּמַלְכוּת, בְּרָכוֹת וְהוֹדָאוֹת לְשִׁמְךָ הַגָּדוֹל וְהַקָּדוֹשׁ, [וּמֵעוֹלָם וְעַד עוֹלָם אַתָּה אֵל] (מֵעַתָּה וְעַד עוֹלָם).

Those who recited יְהַלְלוּךָ earlier conclude the blessing here
and continue with drinking the fourth cup.
Others continue יְהַלְלוּךָ below with its concluding blessing.

בָּרוּךְ אַתָּה יהוה, אֵל מֶלֶךְ גָּדוֹל בַּתִּשְׁבָּחוֹת, אֵל הַהוֹדָאוֹת, אֲדוֹן הַנִּפְלָאוֹת, הַבּוֹחֵר בְּשִׁירֵי זִמְרָה, מֶלֶךְ, אֵל, חֵי הָעוֹלָמִים.

Those who did not recite יְהַלְלוּךָ earlier continue יְהַלְלוּךָ
with its concluding blessing.

יְהַלְלוּךָ יהוה אֱלֹהֵינוּ כָּל מַעֲשֶׂיךָ, וַחֲסִידֶיךָ צַדִּיקִים עוֹשֵׂי רְצוֹנֶךָ, וְכָל עַמְּךָ בֵּית יִשְׂרָאֵל בְּרִנָּה יוֹדוּ וִיבָרְכוּ וִישַׁבְּחוּ וִיפָאֲרוּ וִישׁוֹרְרוּ וִירוֹמְמוּ וְיַעֲרִיצוּ וְיַקְדִּישׁוּ וְיַמְלִיכוּ אֶת שִׁמְךָ מַלְכֵּנוּ תָּמִיד, כִּי לְךָ טוֹב לְהוֹדוֹת וּלְשִׁמְךָ נָאֶה לְזַמֵּר, כִּי מֵעוֹלָם וְעַד עוֹלָם אַתָּה אֵל. בָּרוּךְ אַתָּה יהוה מֶלֶךְ מְהֻלָּל בַּתִּשְׁבָּחוֹת:

And in the assemblies of the myriads of Your people, the House of Israel, with jubilation shall Your Name, our King, be glorified in every generation. For such is the duty of all creatures — before You, HASHEM, our God and God of our fathers, to thank, praise, laud, glorify, exalt, adore, render triumphant, bless, raise high, and sing praises — even beyond all expressions of the songs and praises of David the son of Yishai, Your servant, Your anointed.

[And] thus may Your Name be praised forever, our King, the God, and King Who is great and holy in heaven and on earth; for to You, HASHEM, our God and the God of our fathers, it is fitting to render song and praise, hallel and hymns, power and dominion, victory, greatness and might, praise and glory, holiness and sovereignty, blessings and thanksgivings to Your Great and Holy Name; [from this World to the World to Come You are God] (from this time and forever).

Those who recited "They shall praise You" earlier conclude the blessing here and continue with drinking the fourth cup. Others continue "They shall praise You" below with its concluding blessing.

Blessed are You, HASHEM, God, King, great in praises, God of thanksgivings, Master of wonders, Who favors songs of praise — King, God, Life-giver of the world.

Those who did not recite "They shall praise You" earlier continue "They shall praise You" with its concluding blessing.

They shall praise You, HASHEM our God, all Your works, along with Your pious followers, the righteous, who do Your will, and Your entire people, the House of Israel, with joy will thank, bless, praise, glorify, sing about, exalt, revere, sanctify, and coronate Your Name, our King, continuously! For to You it is fitting to give thanks, and unto Your Name it is proper to sing praises, for from eternity to eternity You are God. Blessed are You, HASHEM, the King, Who is lauded with praises.

The fourth cup corresponds to the fourth expression of redemption,
וְלָקַחְתִּי, *I shall take you to Me for a people.*
Another blessing is recited over this cup of wine
(since Hallel interrupts between the third and fourth cups).

Some recite the following declaration of intent.

הִנְנִי מוּכָן וּמְזוּמָּן לְקַיֵּם מִצְוַת כּוֹס רְבִיעִי שֶׁל אַרְבַּע כּוֹסוֹת. לְשֵׁם יִחוּד קֻדְשָׁא בְּרִיךְ הוּא וּשְׁכִינְתֵּיהּ, עַל יְדֵי הַהוּא טָמִיר וְנֶעְלָם, בְּשֵׁם כָּל יִשְׂרָאֵל. וִיהִי נֹעַם אֲדֹנָי אֱלֹהֵינוּ עָלֵינוּ, וּמַעֲשֵׂה יָדֵינוּ כּוֹנְנָה עָלֵינוּ, וּמַעֲשֵׂה יָדֵינוּ כּוֹנְנֵהוּ:

The blessing over wine is recited and the fourth cup is drunk while reclining to the left side. It is preferable that the entire cup be drunk. *Minchas Asher* writes that a *revi'is* must be drunk in order to recite the concluding blessing.

בָּרוּךְ אַתָּה יהוה אֱלֹהֵינוּ מֶלֶךְ הָעוֹלָם בּוֹרֵא פְּרִי הַגָּפֶן:

After drinking the fourth cup, the concluding blessing is recited.
On the Sabbath, include the passage in parentheses.

בָּרוּךְ אַתָּה יהוה אֱלֹהֵינוּ מֶלֶךְ הָעוֹלָם, עַל הַגֶּפֶן וְעַל פְּרִי הַגֶּפֶן, וְעַל תְּנוּבַת הַשָּׂדֶה, וְעַל אֶרֶץ חֶמְדָּה טוֹבָה וּרְחָבָה, שֶׁרָצִיתָ וְהִנְחַלְתָּ לַאֲבוֹתֵינוּ, לֶאֱכוֹל מִפִּרְיָהּ וְלִשְׂבּוֹעַ מִטּוּבָהּ. רַחֶם נָא יהוה אֱלֹהֵינוּ עַל יִשְׂרָאֵל עַמֶּךְ, וְעַל יְרוּשָׁלַיִם עִירֶךְ, וְעַל צִיּוֹן מִשְׁכַּן כְּבוֹדֶךְ, וְעַל מִזְבְּחֶךְ וְעַל הֵיכָלֶךְ. וּבְנֵה יְרוּשָׁלַיִם עִיר הַקֹּדֶשׁ בִּמְהֵרָה בְיָמֵינוּ, וְהַעֲלֵנוּ לְתוֹכָהּ, וְשַׂמְּחֵנוּ בְּבִנְיָנָהּ, וְנֹאכַל מִפִּרְיָהּ, וְנִשְׂבַּע מִטּוּבָהּ, וּנְבָרֶכְךָ עָלֶיהָ בִּקְדֻשָּׁה וּבְטָהֳרָה. [וּרְצֵה וְהַחֲלִיצֵנוּ בְּיוֹם הַשַּׁבָּת הַזֶּה] וְשַׂמְּחֵנוּ בְּיוֹם חַג הַמַּצּוֹת הַזֶּה. כִּי אַתָּה יהוה טוֹב וּמֵטִיב לַכֹּל, וְנוֹדֶה לְּךָ עַל הָאָרֶץ וְעַל פְּרִי הַגָּפֶן: בָּרוּךְ אַתָּה יהוה, עַל הָאָרֶץ וְעַל פְּרִי הַגָּפֶן (גַּפְנָהּ—on wine from Eretz Yisrael).

The fourth cup corresponds to the fourth expression of redemption,
וְלָקַחְתִּי, *I shall take you to Me for a people.*
Another blessing is recited over this cup of wine
(since Hallel interrupts between the third and fourth cups).

Some recite the following declaration of intent.

Behold, I am prepared and ready to fulfill the mitzvah of the fourth of the Four Cups. For the sake of the unification of the Holy One, Blessed is He, and His Presence, through Him Who is hidden and inscrutable — [I pray] in the name of all Israel. May the pleasantness of HASHEM, our God, be upon us, and may He establish our handiwork for us; our handiwork may He establish.

The blessing over wine is recited and the fourth cup is drunk while reclining to the left side. It is preferable that the entire cup be drunk. *Minchas Asher* writes that a *revi'is* must be drunk in order to recite the concluding blessing.

Blessed are You, HASHEM, our God, King of the universe, Who creates the fruit of the vine.

After drinking the fourth cup, the concluding blessing is recited.
On the Sabbath, include the passage in parentheses.

Blessed are You, HASHEM, our God, King of the universe, for the vine and the fruit of the vine, and for the produce of the field. For the desirable, good, and spacious land that You were pleased to give our forefathers as a heritage, to eat of its fruit and to be satisfied with its goodness. Have mercy, we beg You, HASHEM, our God, on Israel Your people; on Jerusalem, Your city; on Zion, resting place of Your glory; on Your Altar, and on Your Beis Hamikdash. Rebuild Jerusalem the city of holiness, speedily in our days. Bring us up into it and gladden us in its rebuilding, and let us eat from its fruit and be satisfied with its goodness and bless You upon it in holiness and purity. (Favor us and strengthen us on this Sabbath day) and grant us happiness on this Festival of Matzos; for You, HASHEM, are good and do good to all, and we thank You for the land and for the fruit of the vine. Blessed are You, HASHEM, for the land and for the fruit of the vine. (on wine from Eretz Yisrael substitute — its vine).

נִרְצָה

If the Seder has been conducted according to this order, may it be accepted favorably before Hashem.

The following prayer is part of the Yotzros (additions to Shemoneh Esrei) for Shabbos HaGadol. It was composed by R' Yosef Tov Ileim, who lived in the generation before Rashi. (Some say that he is the author of Halachos Gedolos.)

חֲסַל סִדּוּר פֶּסַח כְּהִלְכָתוֹ. כְּכָל מִשְׁפָּטוֹ וְחֻקָּתוֹ. כַּאֲשֶׁר זָכִינוּ לְסַדֵּר אוֹתוֹ. כֵּן נִזְכֶּה לַעֲשׂוֹתוֹ: זָךְ שׁוֹכֵן מְעוֹנָה. קוֹמֵם קְהַל עֲדַת מִי מָנָה. בְּקָרוֹב נַהֵל נִטְעֵי כַנָּה. פְּדוּיִם לְצִיּוֹן בְּרִנָּה:

Recite three times:

לְשָׁנָה הַבָּאָה בִּירוּשָׁלָיִם:

Outside Eretz Yisrael, the following is recited only on the first night. Some say that the refrain, "It came to pass at midnight," should not be recited at the conclusion of the *piyut*. Some suggest that it should not even be recited at the conclusion of every stanza, but only once at the beginning of the *piyut (Siddur HaYaavetz).*

This piyut is arranged according to the order of the Aleph-Beis. It is taken from the Yotzros for Shabbos HaGadol. It was written by R' Yannai, whom the Geonim referred to as a "sage of earlier times" (see R' Saadiah Gaon's introduction to his work Ha'Igron; see also Shibolei HaLeket 28).

On the second night continue on page 244.

וּבְכֵן וַיְהִי בַּחֲצִי הַלָּיְלָה:

בַּלָּיְלָה.	אָז רוֹב נִסִּים הִפְלֵאתָ
הַלָּיְלָה.	בְּרֹאשׁ אַשְׁמוֹרֶת זֶה
לָיְלָה.	גֵּר צֶדֶק נִצַּחְתּוֹ כְּנֶחֱלַק לוֹ
	וַיְהִי בַּחֲצִי הַלָּיְלָה.
הַלָּיְלָה.	דַּנְתָּ מֶלֶךְ גְּרָר בַּחֲלוֹם
לָיְלָה.	הִפְחַדְתָּ אֲרַמִּי בְּאֶמֶשׁ

NIRTZAH

The following prayer is part of the Yotzros (additions to Shemoneh Esrei) for Shabbos HaGadol. It was composed by R' Yosef Tov Ileim, who lived in the generation before Rashi. (Some say that he is the author of Halachos Gedolos.)

The Seder is now concluded in accordance with its laws, with all its ordinances and statutes. Just as we were privileged to arrange it, so may we merit to perform it. O Pure One, Who dwells on high, raise up the countless congregation, soon — guide the offshoots of Your plants, redeemed to Zion with glad song.

Recite three times:

NEXT YEAR IN JERUSALEM

Outside Eretz Yisrael, the following is recited only on the first night. Some say that the refrain, "It came to pass at midnight," should not be recited at the conclusion of the *piyut*. Some suggest that it should not even be recited at the conclusion of every stanza, but only once at the beginning of the *piyut* (*Siddur HaYaavetz*).

This piyut is arranged according to the order of the Aleph-Beis. It is taken from the Yotzros for Shabbos HaGadol. It was written by R' Yannai, whom the Geonim referred to as a "sage of earlier times" (see R' Saadiah Gaon's introduction to his work Ha'Igron; see also Shibolei HaLeket 28).

On the second night continue on page 244.

It came to pass at midnight.

You have, of old, performed many wonders by
    night.
At the head of the watches of this   night.
To the righteous convert (Avraham),
    You gave triumph by dividing for him the   night.
        It came to pass at midnight.
You judged the king of Gerar (Avimelech),
    in a dream by   night.
You frightened the Aramean (Lavan),
    in the dark of   night.

וַיָּשַׂר יִשְׂרָאֵל לְמַלְאָךְ וַיּוּכַל לוֹ   לַיְלָה.
וַיְהִי בַּחֲצִי הַלַּיְלָה.

זֶרַע בְּכוֹרֵי פַתְרוֹס מָחַצְתָּ בַּחֲצִי   הַלַּיְלָה.
חֵילָם לֹא מָצְאוּ בְּקוּמָם   בַּלַּיְלָה.
טִיסַת נְגִיד חֲרוֹשֶׁת סִלִּיתָ בְּכוֹכְבֵי   לַיְלָה.
וַיְהִי בַּחֲצִי הַלַּיְלָה.

יָעַץ מְחָרֵף לְנוֹפֵף אִוּוּי הוֹבַשְׁתָּ פְגָרָיו   בַּלַּיְלָה.
כָּרַע בֵּל וּמַצָּבוֹ בְּאִישׁוֹן   לַיְלָה.
לְאִישׁ חֲמוּדוֹת נִגְלָה רָז חֲזוֹת   לַיְלָה.
וַיְהִי בַּחֲצִי הַלַּיְלָה.

מִשְׁתַּכֵּר בִּכְלֵי קֹדֶשׁ נֶהֱרַג בּוֹ   בַּלַּיְלָה.
נוֹשַׁע מִבּוֹר אֲרָיוֹת פּוֹתֵר בִּעֲתוּתֵי   לַיְלָה.
שִׂנְאָה נָטַר אֲגָגִי וְכָתַב סְפָרִים   בַּלַּיְלָה.
וַיְהִי בַּחֲצִי הַלַּיְלָה.

עוֹרַרְתָּ נִצְחֲךָ עָלָיו בְּנֶדֶד שְׁנַת   לַיְלָה.
פּוּרָה תִדְרוֹךְ לְשׁוֹמֵר מַה   מִלַּיְלָה.
צָרַח כַּשּׁוֹמֵר וְשָׂח אָתָא בֹקֶר וְגַם   לַיְלָה.
וַיְהִי בַּחֲצִי הַלַּיְלָה.

קָרֵב יוֹם אֲשֶׁר הוּא לֹא יוֹם וְלֹא   לַיְלָה.
רָם הוֹדַע כִּי לְךָ הַיּוֹם אַף לְךָ   הַלַּיְלָה.
שׁוֹמְרִים הַפְקֵד לְעִירְךָ כָּל הַיּוֹם וְכָל   הַלַּיְלָה.
תָּאִיר כְּאוֹר יוֹם חֶשְׁכַּת   לַיְלָה.
וַיְהִי בַּחֲצִי הַלַּיְלָה.

Yisrael (Yaakov) fought with an angel
  and overcame him by   night.
      It came to pass at midnight.
Egypt's firstborn You crushed at   midnight.
Their host they found not upon arising at   night.
The army of the prince of Charoshes (Sisera)
  You swept away with stars of the   night.
      It came to pass at midnight.
The blasphemer (Sancheriv) planned to
  raise his hand against Jerusalem —
  but You withered his corpses by   night.
Bel was overturned with its pedestal,
  in the darkness of   night.
To the man of Your delights (Daniel)
  was revealed the mystery of the visions of   night.
      It came to pass at midnight.
He (Belshazzar) who caroused from the holy vessels
  was killed that very   night.
From the lions' den was rescued he (Daniel)
  who interpreted the "terrors" of the   night.
The Agagite (Haman) nursed hatred
  and wrote decrees at   night.
      It came to pass at midnight.
You began Your triumph over him when You
  disturbed (Achashveirosh's) sleep at   night.
Trample the winepress to help those who ask the
  watchman, "What of the long   night?"
He will shout, like a watchman, and say:
  "Morning shall come after   night."
      It came to pass at midnight.
Hasten the day (of Mashiach),
  that is neither day nor   night.
Most High — make known that Yours are day and
                                            night.

Appoint guards for Your city,
  all the day and all the   night.
Brighten like the light of day the darkness of   night.
      It came to pass at midnight.

On the first night continue on page 246.

Outside Eretz Yisrael, the following *piyut* is recited on the second night of Pesach. *Minchas Asher* writes that the refrain, "And you shall say: This is the feast of Pesach," should not be said at the conclusion of the *piyut*. *Yaavetz* writes that it should not even be recited at the conclusion of every stanza, but only once at the beginning of the *piyut*.

This piyut is from the Yotzros of Shabbos HaGadol.
It was written by R' Eliezer HaKalir.

וּבְכֵן וַאֲמַרְתֶּם זֶבַח פֶּסַח:

אֹמֶץ גְּבוּרוֹתֶיךָ הִפְלֵאתָ   בַּפֶּסַח.

בְּרֹאשׁ כָּל מוֹעֲדוֹת נִשֵּׂאתָ   פֶּסַח.

גִּלִּיתָ לְאֶזְרָחִי חֲצוֹת לֵיל   פֶּסַח.

וַאֲמַרְתֶּם זֶבַח פֶּסַח.

דְּלָתָיו דָּפַקְתָּ כְּחֹם הַיּוֹם   בַּפֶּסַח.

הִסְעִיד נוֹצְצִים עֻגוֹת מַצּוֹת   בַּפֶּסַח.

וְאֶל הַבָּקָר רָץ זֵכֶר לְשׁוֹר עֵרֶךְ   פֶּסַח.

וַאֲמַרְתֶּם זֶבַח פֶּסַח.

זוֹעֲמוּ סְדוֹמִים וְלוֹהֲטוּ בָּאֵשׁ   בַּפֶּסַח.

חֻלַּץ לוֹט מֵהֶם וּמַצּוֹת אָפָה בְּקֵץ   פֶּסַח.

טִאטֵאתָ אַדְמַת מוֹף וְנוֹף בְּעָבְרְךָ   בַּפֶּסַח.

וַאֲמַרְתֶּם זֶבַח פֶּסַח.

יָהּ רֹאשׁ כָּל אוֹן מָחַצְתָּ בְּלֵיל שִׁמּוּר   פֶּסַח.

כַּבִּיר עַל בֵּן בְּכוֹר פָּסַחְתָּ בְּדַם   פֶּסַח.

לְבִלְתִּי תֵּת מַשְׁחִית לָבֹא בִּפְתָחַי   בַּפֶּסַח.

וַאֲמַרְתֶּם זֶבַח פֶּסַח.

מְסֻגֶּרֶת סֻגָּרָה בְּעִתּוֹתֵי   פֶּסַח.

נִשְׁמְדָה מִדְיָן בִּצְלִיל שְׂעוֹרֵי עֹמֶר   פֶּסַח.

שֹׂרְפוּ מִשְׁמַנֵּי פּוּל וְלוּד בִּיקַד יְקוֹד   פֶּסַח.

On the first night continue on page 246.

Outside Eretz Yisrael, the following *piyut* is recited on the second night of Pesach. *Minchas Asher* writes that the refrain, "And you shall say: This is the feast of Pesach," should not be said at the conclusion of the *piyut*. *Yaavetz* writes that it should not even be recited at the conclusion of every stanza, but only once at the beginning of the *piyut*.

This piyut is from the Yotzros of Shabbos HaGadol.
It was written by R' Eliezer HaKalir.

And you shall say: This is the feast of Pesach.

You displayed wondrously Your mighty powers
on Pesach.

Above all festivals You elevated   Pesach.
To the Oriental (Avraham) You revealed
   the future midnight   of Pesach.
      And you shall say: This is the feast of Pesach.
At his door You knocked in the heat of the day
on Pesach;

He satiated the angels with matzah-cakes   on Pesach.
And he ran to the herd —
   symbolic of the sacrificial feast   of Pesach.
      And you shall say: This is the feast of Pesach.
The Sodomites provoked (God)
   and were devoured by fire   on Pesach;
Lot was withdrawn from them —
   he had baked matzos at the time   of Pesach.
You swept clean the soil of Mof and Nof (in Egypt)
   when You passed through   on Pesach.
      And you shall say: This is the feast of Pesach.
God, You crushed every firstborn of On (in Egypt)
   on the watchful night   of Pesach.
But Master — Your own firstborn,
   You skipped by merit of the blood   of Pesach,
Not to allow the Destroyer to enter my doors   on Pesach.
      And you shall say: This is the feast of Pesach.
The beleaguered (Yericho) was besieged   on Pesach.
Midyan was destroyed with a barley cake,
   from the Omer   of Pesach.
The mighty nobles of Pul and Lud (Assyria) were
   consumed in a great conflagration   on Pesach.

וַאֲמַרְתֶּם זֶבַח פֶּסַח.

עוֹד הַיּוֹם בְּנֹב לַעֲמוֹד עַד גָּעָה עוֹנַת פֶּסַח.

פַּס יָד כָּתְבָה לְקַעֲקֵעַ צוּל בַּפֶּסַח.

צָפֹה הַצָּפִית עָרוֹךְ הַשֻּׁלְחָן בַּפֶּסַח.

וַאֲמַרְתֶּם זֶבַח פֶּסַח.

קָהָל כִּנְּסָה הֲדַסָּה צוֹם לְשַׁלֵּשׁ בַּפֶּסַח.

רֹאשׁ מִבֵּית רָשָׁע מָחַצְתָּ בְּעֵץ חֲמִשִּׁים בַּפֶּסַח.

שְׁתֵּי אֵלֶּה רֶגַע תָּבִיא לְעוּצִית בַּפֶּסַח.

תָּעֹז יָדְךָ וְתָרוּם יְמִינְךָ כְּלֵיל הִתְקַדֶּשׁ חַג פֶּסַח.

וַאֲמַרְתֶּם זֶבַח פֶּסַח.

Tashbatz Katan (99) writes that the Maharam of Rothenburg was accustomed to say the following piyut. Its authorship is uncertain, but Iyun Tefillah suggests that it was written by R' Eliezer HaKalir.

On both nights continue here:

כִּי לוֹ נָאֶה, כִּי לוֹ יָאֶה:

אַדִּיר בִּמְלוּכָה, **בָּחוּר** כַּהֲלָכָה, **גְּדוּדָיו** יֹאמְרוּ לוֹ, לְךָ וּלְךָ, לְךָ כִּי לְךָ, לְךָ אַף לְךָ, לְךָ יהוה הַמַּמְלָכָה, כִּי לוֹ נָאֶה, כִּי לוֹ יָאֶה.

דָּגוּל בִּמְלוּכָה, **הָדוּר** כַּהֲלָכָה, **וָתִיקָיו** יֹאמְרוּ לוֹ, לְךָ וּלְךָ, לְךָ כִּי לְךָ, לְךָ אַף לְךָ, לְךָ יהוה הַמַּמְלָכָה, כִּי לוֹ נָאֶה, כִּי לוֹ יָאֶה.

זַכַּאי בִּמְלוּכָה, **חָסִין** כַּהֲלָכָה, **טַפְסְרָיו** יֹאמְרוּ לוֹ, לְךָ וּלְךָ, לְךָ כִּי לְךָ, לְךָ אַף לְךָ, לְךָ יהוה הַמַּמְלָכָה, כִּי לוֹ נָאֶה, כִּי לוֹ יָאֶה.

And you shall say: This is the feast of Pesach.
He (Sancheriv) would have stood that day at Nob,
but for the advent   of Pesach.
A hand inscribed the destruction of Zul (Babylon)
                 on Pesach.
As the watch was set, and the royal table decked
                 on Pesach.

And you shall say: This is the feast of Pesach.
Hadassah (Esther) gathered a congregation
for a three-day fast   on Pesach.
You caused the head of the evil clan (Haman)
to be hanged on a fifty-cubit gallows   on Pesach.
Doubly, will You bring in an instant upon Utzis (Edom)
                 on Pesach.
Let Your hand be strong, and Your right arm exalted,
as on that night when You hallowed the festival
                 of Pesach.

And you shall say: This is the feast of Pesach.

*Tashbatz Katan (99) writes that the Maharam of Rothenburg
was accustomed to say the following piyut. Its authorship is uncertain,
but Iyun Tefillah suggests that it was written by R' Eliezer HaKalir.*

On both nights continue here:

To Him praise is due! To Him praise is fitting!

Mighty in majesty, perfectly distinguished, His companies of angels say to Him: Yours and only Yours; Yours, yes Yours; Yours, surely Yours; Yours, HASHEM, is the sovereignty. To Him praise is due! To Him praise is fitting!

Supreme in kingship, perfectly glorious, His faithful say to Him: Yours and only Yours; Yours, yes Yours; Yours, surely Yours; Yours, HASHEM, is the sovereignty. To Him praise is due! To Him praise is fitting!

Pure in kingship, perfectly mighty, His angels say to Him: Yours and only Yours; Yours, yes Yours; Yours, surely Yours; Yours, HASHEM, is the sovereignty. To Him praise is due! To Him praise is fitting!

יָחִיד בִּמְלוּכָה, **כַּבִּיר** כַּהֲלָכָה, **לִמּוּדָיו** יֹאמְרוּ לוֹ,
לְךָ וּלְךָ, לְךָ כִּי לְךָ, לְךָ אַף לְךָ, לְךָ יהוה הַמַּמְלָכָה,
כִּי לוֹ נָאֶה, כִּי לוֹ יָאֶה.

מֶלֶךְ (מוֹשֵׁל) בִּמְלוּכָה, **נוֹרָא** כַּהֲלָכָה, **סְבִיבָיו**
יֹאמְרוּ לוֹ, לְךָ וּלְךָ, לְךָ כִּי לְךָ, לְךָ אַף לְךָ, לְךָ יהוה
הַמַּמְלָכָה, כִּי לוֹ נָאֶה, כִּי לוֹ יָאֶה.

עָנָיו בִּמְלוּכָה, **פּוֹדֶה** כַּהֲלָכָה, **צַבָּאָיו** (צַדִּיקָיו)
יֹאמְרוּ לוֹ, לְךָ וּלְךָ, לְךָ כִּי לְךָ, לְךָ אַף לְךָ, לְךָ יהוה
הַמַּמְלָכָה, כִּי לוֹ נָאֶה, כִּי לוֹ יָאֶה.

קָדוֹשׁ בִּמְלוּכָה, **רַחוּם** כַּהֲלָכָה, **שִׁנְאַנָּיו** יֹאמְרוּ
לוֹ, לְךָ וּלְךָ, לְךָ כִּי לְךָ, לְךָ אַף לְךָ, לְךָ יהוה
הַמַּמְלָכָה, כִּי לוֹ נָאֶה, כִּי לוֹ יָאֶה.

תַּקִּיף בִּמְלוּכָה, **תּוֹמֵךְ** כַּהֲלָכָה, **תְּמִימָיו** יֹאמְרוּ
לוֹ, לְךָ וּלְךָ, לְךָ כִּי לְךָ, לְךָ אַף לְךָ, לְךָ יהוה
הַמַּמְלָכָה, כִּי לוֹ נָאֶה, כִּי לוֹ יָאֶה.

The following piyut of unknown authorship was first printed in the Prague Haggadah. It is mentioned among the customs of the Maharam of Rothenburg (see Magen Avraham 480).

אַדִּיר הוּא יִבְנֶה בֵיתוֹ בְּקָרוֹב, בִּמְהֵרָה, בִּמְהֵרָה,
בְּיָמֵינוּ בְּקָרוֹב. אֵל בְּנֵה, אֵל בְּנֵה, בְּנֵה
בֵיתְךָ בְּקָרוֹב.

אַדִּיר הוּא יִבְנֶה בֵיתוֹ בְּקָרוֹב
He is most mighty. May He soon rebuild His House

Many names were given to the site upon which the Beis Hamik-dash was built. *Chazal* tell us that each of the Avos gave it a different name: Avraham called it הַר, *mountain*, Yitzchak called it שָׂדֶה, *field*, and Yaakov called it בַּיִת, *house* (see *Pesachim* 88a, see also above p. 166).

Alone in kingship, perfectly omnipotent, His scholars say to Him: Yours and only Yours; Yours, yes Yours; Yours, surely Yours; Yours, HASHEM, is the sovereignty. To Him praise is due! To Him praise is fitting!

Majestic (commanding) in kingship, perfectly wondrous, His surrounding angels say to Him: Yours and only Yours; Yours, yes Yours; Yours, surely Yours; Yours, HASHEM, is the sovereignty. To Him praise is due! To Him praise is fitting!

Gentle in kingship, perfectly the Redeemer, His legions (His righteous ones) say to Him: Yours and only Yours; Yours, yes Yours; Yours, surely Yours; Yours, HASHEM, is the sovereignty. To Him praise is due! To Him praise is fitting!

Holy in kingship, perfectly merciful, His troops of angels say to Him: Yours and only Yours; Yours, yes Yours; Yours, surely Yours; Yours, HASHEM, is the sovereignty. To Him praise is due! To Him praise is fitting.

Almighty in kingship, perfectly sustaining, His perfect ones say to Him: Yours and only Yours; Yours, yes Yours; Yours, surely Yours; Yours, HASHEM, is the sovereignty. To Him praise is due! To Him praise is fitting!

The following piyut of unknown authorship was first printed in the Prague Haggadah. It is mentioned among the customs of the Maharam of Rothenburg (see Magen Avraham 480).

He is most mighty. May He soon rebuild His House, speedily, yes speedily, in our days, soon. God, rebuild, God, rebuild, rebuild Your House soon!

R' Aharon of Belz explains this based on a Midrash that states that Hashem created the world using His Name מַחֲנֶה, *Encampment*. Hashem created the spiritual preparation for the first wall of the Beis Hamikdash, endowing it with the power of His Name, מַחֲנֶה, which has a numerical value of 103.

בָּחוּר הוּא. גָּדוֹל הוּא. דָּגוּל הוּא. יִבְנֶה בֵּיתוֹ
בְּקָרוֹב, בִּמְהֵרָה, בִּמְהֵרָה, בְּיָמֵינוּ בְּקָרוֹב. אֵל בְּנֵה,
אֵל בְּנֵה, בְּנֵה בֵיתְךָ בְּקָרוֹב.

הָדוּר הוּא. וָתִיק הוּא. זַכַּאי הוּא. חָסִיד הוּא.
טָהוֹר הוּא. יָחִיד הוּא. כַּבִּיר הוּא. לָמוּד [לוֹחֵם]
הוּא. יִבְנֶה בֵּיתוֹ בְּקָרוֹב, בִּמְהֵרָה, בִּמְהֵרָה, בְּיָמֵינוּ
בְּקָרוֹב. אֵל בְּנֵה, אֵל בְּנֵה, בְּנֵה בֵיתְךָ בְּקָרוֹב.

מֶלֶךְ הוּא. נוֹרָא הוּא. סַגִּיב הוּא. עִזּוּז הוּא.
פּוֹדֶה הוּא. צַדִּיק הוּא. קָדוֹשׁ הוּא. רַחוּם הוּא. שַׁדַּי
הוּא. תַּקִּיף הוּא. יִבְנֶה בֵּיתוֹ בְּקָרוֹב, בִּמְהֵרָה,
בִּמְהֵרָה, בְּיָמֵינוּ בְּקָרוֹב. אֵל בְּנֵה, אֵל בְּנֵה, בְּנֵה
בֵיתְךָ בְּקָרוֹב.

A handwritten siddur from the year 5166 (1406)
states that the following piyut was found written on parchment
in the Beis Midrash of Rokei'ach. Its authorship is unknown.

אֶחָד מִי יוֹדֵעַ? אֶחָד אֲנִי יוֹדֵעַ. אֶחָד אֱלֹהֵינוּ
שֶׁבַּשָּׁמַיִם וּבָאָרֶץ.

שְׁנַיִם מִי יוֹדֵעַ? שְׁנַיִם אֲנִי יוֹדֵעַ. שְׁנֵי לֻחוֹת
הַבְּרִית, אֶחָד אֱלֹהֵינוּ שֶׁבַּשָּׁמַיִם וּבָאָרֶץ.

שְׁלֹשָׁה מִי יוֹדֵעַ? שְׁלֹשָׁה אֲנִי יוֹדֵעַ. שְׁלֹשָׁה
אָבוֹת, שְׁנֵי לֻחוֹת הַבְּרִית, אֶחָד אֱלֹהֵינוּ שֶׁבַּשָּׁמַיִם
וּבָאָרֶץ.

Avraham Avinu added another wall to the Beis Hamikdash, giving
it another 103, to equal the *gematria* of the word הַר (although the
word הַר only equals 205, another 1 is added for the word itself).
Yitzchak added a third wall, giving the Beis Hamikdash another 103,
to equal the *gematria* of the word שָׂדֶה (309). Yaakov added the final

He is distinguished, He is great, He is exalted. May He soon rebuild His House, speedily, yes speedily, in our days, soon. God, rebuild, God, rebuild, rebuild Your House soon!

He is all glorious, He is faithful, He is faultless, He is righteous. He is pure, He is unique, He is powerful, He is all-wise. May He soon rebuild His House, speedily, yes speedily, in our days, soon. God, rebuild, God, rebuild, rebuild Your House soon!

He is King, He is awesome, He is sublime, He is all-powerful, He is the Redeemer, He is the all-righteous. He is holy, He is compassionate, He is Almighty, He is omnipotent. May He soon rebuild His House, speedily, yes speedily, in our days, soon. God, rebuild, God, rebuild, rebuild Your House soon!

A handwritten siddur from the year 5166 (1406) states that the following piyut was found written on parchment in the Beis Midrash of Rokei'ach. Its authorship is unknown.

Who knows One? I know one: One is our God, in heaven and on earth.

Who knows two? I know two: two are the Tablets of the Covenant; One is our God, in heaven and on earth.

Who knows three? I know three: three are the Patriarchs; two are the Tablets of the Covenant; One is our God, in heaven and on earth.

---

wall, giving another 103, to equal the *gematria* of בַּיִת (412). The only thing now lacking was 103 for the roof, which Moshe Rabbeinu added through the 515 prayers he offered to be allowed entrance into Eretz Yisrael (515 is the *gematria* of וָאֶתְחַנַּן).

[R' Aharon told this explanation to R' Elchanan Wasserman, when they met at a summer resort, and R' Elchanan is said to have praised it highly.]

אַרְבַּע מִי יוֹדֵעַ? אַרְבַּע אֲנִי יוֹדֵעַ. אַרְבַּע אִמָּהוֹת,
שְׁלֹשָׁה אָבוֹת, שְׁנֵי לֻחוֹת הַבְּרִית, אֶחָד אֱלֹהֵינוּ
שֶׁבַּשָּׁמַיִם וּבָאָרֶץ.

חֲמִשָּׁה מִי יוֹדֵעַ? חֲמִשָּׁה אֲנִי יוֹדֵעַ. חֲמִשָּׁה חֻמְשֵׁי
תוֹרָה, אַרְבַּע אִמָּהוֹת, שְׁלֹשָׁה אָבוֹת, שְׁנֵי לֻחוֹת
הַבְּרִית, אֶחָד אֱלֹהֵינוּ שֶׁבַּשָּׁמַיִם וּבָאָרֶץ.

שִׁשָּׁה מִי יוֹדֵעַ? שִׁשָּׁה אֲנִי יוֹדֵעַ. שִׁשָּׁה סִדְרֵי
מִשְׁנָה, חֲמִשָּׁה חֻמְשֵׁי תוֹרָה, אַרְבַּע אִמָּהוֹת,
שְׁלֹשָׁה אָבוֹת, שְׁנֵי לֻחוֹת הַבְּרִית, אֶחָד אֱלֹהֵינוּ
שֶׁבַּשָּׁמַיִם וּבָאָרֶץ.

שִׁבְעָה מִי יוֹדֵעַ? שִׁבְעָה אֲנִי יוֹדֵעַ. שִׁבְעָה יְמֵי
שַׁבַּתָּא, שִׁשָּׁה סִדְרֵי מִשְׁנָה, חֲמִשָּׁה חֻמְשֵׁי תוֹרָה,
אַרְבַּע אִמָּהוֹת, שְׁלֹשָׁה אָבוֹת, שְׁנֵי לֻחוֹת הַבְּרִית,
אֶחָד אֱלֹהֵינוּ שֶׁבַּשָּׁמַיִם וּבָאָרֶץ.

שְׁמוֹנָה מִי יוֹדֵעַ? שְׁמוֹנָה אֲנִי יוֹדֵעַ. שְׁמוֹנָה יְמֵי
מִילָה, שִׁבְעָה יְמֵי שַׁבַּתָּא, שִׁשָּׁה סִדְרֵי מִשְׁנָה,
חֲמִשָּׁה חֻמְשֵׁי תוֹרָה, אַרְבַּע אִמָּהוֹת, שְׁלֹשָׁה
אָבוֹת, שְׁנֵי לֻחוֹת הַבְּרִית, אֶחָד אֱלֹהֵינוּ שֶׁבַּשָּׁמַיִם
וּבָאָרֶץ.

תִּשְׁעָה מִי יוֹדֵעַ? תִּשְׁעָה אֲנִי יוֹדֵעַ. תִּשְׁעָה יַרְחֵי
לֵדָה, שְׁמוֹנָה יְמֵי מִילָה, שִׁבְעָה יְמֵי שַׁבַּתָּא, שִׁשָּׁה
סִדְרֵי מִשְׁנָה, חֲמִשָּׁה חֻמְשֵׁי תוֹרָה, אַרְבַּע אִמָּהוֹת,
שְׁלֹשָׁה אָבוֹת, שְׁנֵי לֻחוֹת הַבְּרִית, אֶחָד אֱלֹהֵינוּ
שֶׁבַּשָּׁמַיִם וּבָאָרֶץ.

עֲשָׂרָה מִי יוֹדֵעַ? עֲשָׂרָה אֲנִי יוֹדֵעַ. עֲשָׂרָה
דִּבְּרַיָּא, תִּשְׁעָה יַרְחֵי לֵדָה, שְׁמוֹנָה יְמֵי מִילָה,

Who knows four? I know four: four are the Matriarchs; three are the Patriarchs; two are the Tablets of the Covenant; One is our God, in heaven and on earth.

Who knows five? I know five: five are the Books of the Torah; four are the Matriarchs; three are the Patriarchs; two are the Tablets of the Covenant; One is our God, in heaven and on earth.

Who knows six? I know six: six are the Orders of the Mishnah; five are the Books of the Torah; four are the Matriarchs; three are the Patriarchs; two are the Tablets of the Covenant; One is our God, in heaven and on earth.

Who knows seven? I know seven: seven are the days of the week; six are the Orders of the Mishnah; five are the Books of the Torah; four are the Matriarchs; three are the Patriarchs; two are the Tablets of the Covenant; One is our God, in heaven and on earth.

Who knows eight? I know eight: eight are the days of circumcision; seven are the days of the week; six are the Orders of the Mishnah; five are the Books of the Torah; four are the Matriarchs; three are the Patriarchs; two are the Tablets of the Covenant; One is our God, in heaven and on earth.

Who knows nine? I know nine: nine are the months of pregnancy; eight are the days of circumcision; seven are the days of the week; six are the Orders of the Mishnah; five are the Books of the Torah; four are the Matriarchs; three are the Patriarchs; two are the Tablets of the Covenant; One is our God, in heaven and on earth.

Who knows ten? I know ten: ten are the Ten Commandments; nine are the months of pregnancy; eight are the days of circumcision;

שִׁבְעָה יְמֵי שַׁבַּתָּא, שִׁשָּׁה סִדְרֵי מִשְׁנָה, חֲמִשָּׁה חֻמְשֵׁי תוֹרָה, אַרְבַּע אִמָּהוֹת, שְׁלֹשָׁה אָבוֹת, שְׁנֵי לֻחוֹת הַבְּרִית, אֶחָד אֱלֹהֵינוּ שֶׁבַּשָּׁמַיִם וּבָאָרֶץ.

אַחַד עָשָׂר מִי יוֹדֵעַ? אַחַד עָשָׂר אֲנִי יוֹדֵעַ. אַחַד עָשָׂר כּוֹכְבַיָּא, עֲשָׂרָה דִבְּרַיָּא, תִּשְׁעָה יַרְחֵי לֵדָה, שְׁמוֹנָה יְמֵי מִילָה, שִׁבְעָה יְמֵי שַׁבַּתָּא, שִׁשָּׁה סִדְרֵי מִשְׁנָה, חֲמִשָּׁה חֻמְשֵׁי תוֹרָה, אַרְבַּע אִמָּהוֹת, שְׁלֹשָׁה אָבוֹת, שְׁנֵי לֻחוֹת הַבְּרִית, אֶחָד אֱלֹהֵינוּ שֶׁבַּשָּׁמַיִם וּבָאָרֶץ.

שְׁנֵים עָשָׂר מִי יוֹדֵעַ? שְׁנֵים עָשָׂר אֲנִי יוֹדֵעַ. שְׁנֵים עָשָׂר שִׁבְטַיָּא, אַחַד עָשָׂר כּוֹכְבַיָּא, עֲשָׂרָה דִבְּרַיָּא, תִּשְׁעָה יַרְחֵי לֵדָה, שְׁמוֹנָה יְמֵי מִילָה, שִׁבְעָה יְמֵי שַׁבַּתָּא, שִׁשָּׁה סִדְרֵי מִשְׁנָה, חֲמִשָּׁה חֻמְשֵׁי תוֹרָה, אַרְבַּע אִמָּהוֹת, שְׁלֹשָׁה אָבוֹת, שְׁנֵי לֻחוֹת הַבְּרִית, אֶחָד אֱלֹהֵינוּ שֶׁבַּשָּׁמַיִם וּבָאָרֶץ.

שְׁלֹשָׁה עָשָׂר מִי יוֹדֵעַ? שְׁלֹשָׁה עָשָׂר אֲנִי יוֹדֵעַ. שְׁלֹשָׁה עָשָׂר מִדַּיָּא, שְׁנֵים עָשָׂר שִׁבְטַיָּא, אַחַד עָשָׂר כּוֹכְבַיָּא, עֲשָׂרָה דִבְּרַיָּא, תִּשְׁעָה יַרְחֵי לֵדָה, שְׁמוֹנָה יְמֵי מִילָה, שִׁבְעָה יְמֵי שַׁבַּתָּא, שִׁשָּׁה סִדְרֵי מִשְׁנָה, חֲמִשָּׁה חֻמְשֵׁי תוֹרָה, אַרְבַּע אִמָּהוֹת, שְׁלֹשָׁה אָבוֹת, שְׁנֵי לֻחוֹת הַבְּרִית, אֶחָד אֱלֹהֵינוּ שֶׁבַּשָּׁמַיִם וּבָאָרֶץ.

The following piyut is found in the Prague Haggadah and in
an ancient handwritten siddur attributed to the era of Rokei'ach.

חַד גַּדְיָא, חַד גַּדְיָא, דְּזַבִּין אַבָּא בִּתְרֵי זוּזֵי, חַד גַּדְיָא חַד גַּדְיָא.

seven are the days of the week; six are the Orders of the Mishnah; five are the Books of the Torah; four are the Matriarchs; three are the Patriarchs; two are the Tablets of the Covenant; One is our God, in heaven and on earth.

Who knows eleven? I know eleven: eleven are the stars (in Yosef's dream); ten are the Ten Commandments; nine are the months of pregnancy; eight are the days of circumcision; seven are the days of the week; six are the Orders of the Mishnah; five are the Books of the Torah; four are the Matriarchs; three are the Patriarchs; two are the Tablets of the Covenant; One is our God, in heaven and on earth.

Who knows twelve? I know twelve: twelve are the tribes; eleven are the stars (in Yosef's dream); ten are the Ten Commandments; nine are the months of pregnancy; eight are the days of circumcision; seven are the days of the week; six are the Orders of the Mishnah; five are the Books of the Torah; four are the Matriarchs; three are the Patriarchs; two are the Tablets of the Covenant; One is our God, in heaven and on earth.

Who knows thirteen? I know thirteen: thirteen are the attributes of God; twelve are the tribes; eleven are the stars (in Yosef's dream); ten are the Ten Commandments; nine are the months of pregnancy; eight are the days of circumcision; seven are the days of the week; six are the Orders of the Mishnah; five are the Books of the Torah; four are the Matriarchs; three are the Patriarchs; two are the Tablets of the Covenant; One is our God, in heaven and on earth.

The following piyut is found in the Prague Haggadah and in an ancient handwritten siddur attributed to the era of Rokei'ach.

A kid, a kid, that father bought for two *zuzim*, a kid, a kid.

וְאָתָא שׁוּנְרָא וְאָכְלָה לְגַדְיָא, דְּזַבִּין אַבָּא בִּתְרֵי זוּזֵי, חַד גַּדְיָא חַד גַּדְיָא.

וְאָתָא כַלְבָּא וְנָשַׁךְ לְשׁוּנְרָא, דְּאָכְלָה לְגַדְיָא, דְּזַבִּין אַבָּא בִּתְרֵי זוּזֵי, חַד גַּדְיָא חַד גַּדְיָא.

וְאָתָא חוּטְרָא וְהִכָּה לְכַלְבָּא, דְּנָשַׁךְ לְשׁוּנְרָא, דְּאָכְלָה לְגַדְיָא, דְּזַבִּין אַבָּא בִּתְרֵי זוּזֵי, חַד גַּדְיָא חַד גַּדְיָא.

וְאָתָא נוּרָא וְשָׂרַף לְחוּטְרָא, דְּהִכָּה לְכַלְבָּא, דְּנָשַׁךְ לְשׁוּנְרָא, דְּאָכְלָה לְגַדְיָא, דְּזַבִּין אַבָּא בִּתְרֵי זוּזֵי, חַד גַּדְיָא חַד גַּדְיָא.

וְאָתָא מַיָּא וְכָבָה לְנוּרָא, דְּשָׂרַף לְחוּטְרָא, דְּהִכָּה לְכַלְבָּא, דְּנָשַׁךְ לְשׁוּנְרָא, דְּאָכְלָה לְגַדְיָא, דְּזַבִּין אַבָּא בִּתְרֵי זוּזֵי, חַד גַּדְיָא חַד גַּדְיָא.

וְאָתָא תוֹרָא וְשָׁתָה לְמַיָּא, דְּכָבָה לְנוּרָא, דְּשָׂרַף לְחוּטְרָא, דְּהִכָּה לְכַלְבָּא, דְּנָשַׁךְ לְשׁוּנְרָא, דְּאָכְלָה לְגַדְיָא, דְּזַבִּין אַבָּא בִּתְרֵי זוּזֵי, חַד גַּדְיָא חַד גַּדְיָא.

חַד גַּדְיָא — A kid, a kid

The commentaries attempt to uncover the significance of this cryptic song. What relevance does the story of this goat have to the Seder night?

R' Naftali of Ropshitz quoted the Chozeh of Lublin as having said that this song is recited as a *segulah* to protect us from the *ayin hara* (evil eye) of the angels' jealousy. How is this so?

Chazal mention frequently that the angels are jealous of Hashem's affection for us. The Talmud tells us that when Hashem carved Yaakov's likeness into His Throne of Glory, the angels wanted to harm him (*Chullin* 91b, see *Rashi*).[1]

The Seder night is a time of tremendous holiness. Hashem gathers

---

1. See also *Gilyon HaShas* by R' Akiva Eiger on *Shabbos* 88a; *Minchas Asher* on *Sefer Bereishis, Parashas Vayeitzei*.

A cat then came and devoured the kid that father bought for two *zuzim*, a kid, a kid.

A dog then came and bit the cat, that devoured the kid that father bought for two *zuzim*, a kid, a kid.

A stick then came and beat the dog, that bit the cat, that devoured the kid that father bought for two *zuzim*, a kid, a kid.

A fire then came and burnt the stick, that beat the dog, that bit the cat, that devoured the kid that father bought for two *zuzim*, a kid, a kid.

Water then came and quenched the fire, that burnt the stick, that beat the dog, that bit the cat, that devoured the kid that father bought for two *zuzim*, a kid, a kid.

An ox then came and drank the water, that quenched the fire, that burnt the stick, that beat the dog, that bit the cat, that devoured the kid that father bought for two *zuzim*, a kid, a kid.

His Heavenly court to watch Bnei Yisrael praise Him for the miracles of Exodus. *Zohar* (*Raya Mehemna, Parashas Bo,* 180) states, "At this time, the Holy One, Blessed is He, gathers His court and says, 'Go and hear the stories of My praise that My children speak, as they rejoice in My redemption.'" At this holy time, we fear that the jealousy of the angels may be aroused.

How is this song a *segulah* for protection?

The kid goat in this song represents Bnei Yisrael, of whom the verse states, "Israel is [like] scattered sheep" (*Yirmiyah* 50:17). In this account of how the kid goat is attacked, and his assailants are subsequently attacked by even greater threats — all the way up to the Angel of Death — we are shown how the entire world follows a causative chain of events in which one nation devours the next, all surrounding the one little kid, Hashem's people. As such, this song is a lesson for all the nations — and for the angels as well — never to harm Hashem's cherished people.

→◦◦◦←

This song can also be interpreted as a message to the Jewish

וְאָתָא הַשּׁוֹחֵט וְשָׁחַט לְתוֹרָא, דְּשָׁתָא לְמַיָּא,
דְּכָבָה לְנוּרָא, דְּשָׂרַף לְחוּטְרָא, דְּהִכָּה לְכַלְבָּא,
דְּנָשַׁךְ לְשׁוּנְרָא, דְּאָכְלָה לְגַדְיָא, דְּזַבִּין אַבָּא בִּתְרֵי
זוּזֵי, חַד גַּדְיָא חַד גַּדְיָא.

וְאָתָא מַלְאַךְ הַמָּוֶת וְשָׁחַט לְשׁוֹחֵט, דְּשָׁחַט
לְתוֹרָא, דְּשָׁתָה לְמַיָּא, דְּכָבָה לְנוּרָא, דְּשָׂרַף
לְחוּטְרָא, דְּהִכָּה לְכַלְבָּא, דְּנָשַׁךְ לְשׁוּנְרָא, דְּאָכְלָה
לְגַדְיָא, דְּזַבִּין אַבָּא בִּתְרֵי זוּזֵי, חַד גַּדְיָא חַד גַּדְיָא.

וְאָתָא הַקָּדוֹשׁ בָּרוּךְ הוּא וְשָׁחַט לְמַלְאַךְ הַמָּוֶת,
דְּשָׁחַט לְשׁוֹחֵט, דְּשָׁחַט לְתוֹרָא, דְּשָׁתָה לְמַיָּא,
דְּכָבָה לְנוּרָא, דְּשָׂרַף לְחוּטְרָא, דְּהִכָּה לְכַלְבָּא,
דְּנָשַׁךְ לְשׁוּנְרָא, דְּאָכְלָה לְגַדְיָא, דְּזַבִּין אַבָּא בִּתְרֵי
זוּזֵי, חַד גַּדְיָא חַד גַּדְיָא.

Some stay up all night, reciting *Shir HaShirim* and other songs
and praises and occupying themselves with stories of the Exodus
and the laws of Pesach until sleep overtakes them.

---

people to follow the advice of *Chazal:* "Let a man never favor one of
his children over the others. For the sake of two coins worth of
expensive cloth (that Yaakov sewed onto Yosef's coat, thus inciting
the jealousy of his brothers), one event followed another and our
forefathers ultimately descended to Egypt" (*Shabbos* 10b, see *Rashi*).
The kid goat in this song symbolizes the Jewish people. The father
is Yaakov Avinu. The two *zuzim* for which he bought the goat
symbolize the two coins with which he favored Yosef. We sing this
song at the conclusion of the Pesach Seder in order to ingrain this
important message in our hearts. We realize that it was the strife
between us that caused our descent to Egypt, and we must make
every effort on this memorable night to encourage harmony and
love among our people.

In a similar vein, Rabbeinu Manoach (Commentary on the *Rambam, Hilchos Chametz U'Matzah* 8:2) writes that *karpas* symbolizes
the *kesones pasim* (striped coat) with which Yaakov favored Yosef.

A slaughterer then came and slaughtered the ox, that drank the water, that quenched the fire, that burnt the stick, that beat the dog, that bit the cat, that devoured the kid that father bought for two *zuzim*, a kid, a kid.

The angel of death then came and killed the slaughterer, who slaughtered the ox, that drank the water, that quenched the fire, that burnt the stick, that beat the dog, that bit the cat, that devoured the kid that father bought for two *zuzim*, a kid, a kid.

The Holy One, Blessed is He, then came and slew the angel of death, who killed the slaughterer, who slaughtered the ox, that drank the water, that quenched the fire, that burnt the stick, that beat the dog, that bit the cat, that devoured the kid that father bought for two *zuzim*, a kid, a kid.

> Some stay up all night, reciting *Shir HaShirim* and other songs and praises and occupying themselves with stories of the Exodus and the laws of Pesach until sleep overtakes them.

Alternatively, we can explain that the kid goat in this song represents the goats that Yaakov Avinu fed to his father Yitzchak, when he posed as Eisav to receive the blessings. For deceiving his father, Yaakov was punished *middah k'neged middah* (in an equal and appropriate measure), when his sons dipped Yosef's coat into goat's blood to substantiate their story, and deceived him into believing that Yosef had been killed.

As a result of the two goats that Yaakov Avinu fed his father, our forefathers eventually descended to Egypt. The kid goat mentioned twice at the end of each stanza represents the two goats that Yaakov fed Yitzchak. (The two goats were for the *Korban Pesach* and *Korban Chagigah* — see *Pirkei D'Rabbi Eliezer* Ch. 32; *Targum Yonasan*.) Alternatively, they represent the goat that Yaakov fed Yitzchak and the goat whose blood was used to deceive Yaakov.

This song is meant to remind us of the reason we descended to Egypt, and encourage us to cleanse ourselves of all deceptive practices.

שיר השירים / Song of Songs

Many recite שִׁיר הַשִּׁירִים, *Song of Songs*, after the Haggadah.

פרק א

א שִׁיר הַשִּׁירִים אֲשֶׁר לִשְׁלֹמֹה. ב יִשָּׁקֵנִי מִנְּשִׁיקוֹת פִּיהוּ, כִּי טוֹבִים דֹּדֶיךָ מִיָּיִן. ג לְרֵיחַ שְׁמָנֶיךָ טוֹבִים, שֶׁמֶן תּוּרַק שְׁמֶךָ, עַל כֵּן עֲלָמוֹת אֲהֵבוּךָ. ד מָשְׁכֵנִי אַחֲרֶיךָ נָּרוּצָה, הֱבִיאַנִי הַמֶּלֶךְ חֲדָרָיו, נָגִילָה וְנִשְׂמְחָה בָּךְ, נַזְכִּירָה דֹדֶיךָ מִיַּיִן, מֵישָׁרִים אֲהֵבוּךָ. ה שְׁחוֹרָה אֲנִי וְנָאוָה, בְּנוֹת יְרוּשָׁלָיִם, כְּאָהֳלֵי קֵדָר, כִּירִיעוֹת שְׁלֹמֹה. ו אַל תִּרְאֻנִי שֶׁאֲנִי שְׁחַרְחֹרֶת, שֶׁשְּׁזָפַתְנִי הַשָּׁמֶשׁ, בְּנֵי אִמִּי נִחֲרוּ בִי, שָׂמֻנִי נֹטֵרָה אֶת הַכְּרָמִים, כַּרְמִי שֶׁלִּי לֹא נָטָרְתִּי. ז הַגִּידָה לִּי, שֶׁאָהֲבָה נַפְשִׁי, אֵיכָה תִרְעֶה, אֵיכָה תַּרְבִּיץ בַּצָּהֳרָיִם, שַׁלָּמָה אֶהְיֶה כְּעֹטְיָה עַל עֶדְרֵי חֲבֵרֶיךָ. ח אִם לֹא תֵדְעִי לָךְ, הַיָּפָה בַּנָּשִׁים, צְאִי לָךְ בְּעִקְבֵי הַצֹּאן, וּרְעִי אֶת גְּדִיֹּתַיִךְ עַל מִשְׁכְּנוֹת הָרֹעִים. ט לְסֻסָתִי בְּרִכְבֵי פַרְעֹה דִּמִּיתִיךְ, רַעְיָתִי. י נָאווּ לְחָיַיִךְ בַּתֹּרִים, צַוָּארֵךְ בַּחֲרוּזִים. יא תּוֹרֵי זָהָב נַעֲשֶׂה לָּךְ, עִם נְקֻדּוֹת הַכָּסֶף. יב עַד שֶׁהַמֶּלֶךְ בִּמְסִבּוֹ, נִרְדִּי נָתַן רֵיחוֹ. יג צְרוֹר הַמֹּר דּוֹדִי לִי, בֵּין שָׁדַי יָלִין. יד אֶשְׁכֹּל הַכֹּפֶר דּוֹדִי לִי, בְּכַרְמֵי עֵין גֶּדִי. טו הִנָּךְ יָפָה, רַעְיָתִי, הִנָּךְ יָפָה, עֵינַיִךְ יוֹנִים. טז הִנְּךָ יָפֶה, דוֹדִי, אַף נָעִים, אַף עַרְשֵׂנוּ רַעֲנָנָה. יז קֹרוֹת בָּתֵּינוּ אֲרָזִים, רַהִיטֵנוּ בְּרוֹתִים.

פרק ב

א אֲנִי חֲבַצֶּלֶת הַשָּׁרוֹן, שׁוֹשַׁנַּת הָעֲמָקִים. ב כְּשׁוֹשַׁנָּה בֵּין הַחוֹחִים, כֵּן רַעְיָתִי בֵּין הַבָּנוֹת. ג כְּתַפּוּחַ בַּעֲצֵי הַיַּעַר, כֵּן דּוֹדִי בֵּין הַבָּנִים, בְּצִלּוֹ חִמַּדְתִּי וְיָשַׁבְתִּי, וּפִרְיוֹ מָתוֹק לְחִכִּי. ד הֱבִיאַנִי אֶל בֵּית הַיַּיִן, וְדִגְלוֹ עָלַי אַהֲבָה. ה סַמְּכוּנִי בָּאֲשִׁישׁוֹת, רַפְּדוּנִי בַּתַּפּוּחִים, כִּי חוֹלַת אַהֲבָה אָנִי. ו שְׂמֹאלוֹ תַּחַת לְרֹאשִׁי, וִימִינוֹ תְּחַבְּקֵנִי. ז הִשְׁבַּעְתִּי אֶתְכֶם, בְּנוֹת יְרוּשָׁלָיִם, בִּצְבָאוֹת אוֹ בְּאַיְלוֹת הַשָּׂדֶה, אִם תָּעִירוּ וְאִם תְּעוֹרְרוּ אֶת הָאַהֲבָה עַד

שֶׁתֶּחְפָּץ. ח קוֹל דּוֹדִי הִנֵּה זֶה בָּא, מְדַלֵּג עַל הֶהָרִים, מְקַפֵּץ עַל הַגְּבָעוֹת. ט דּוֹמֶה דוֹדִי לִצְבִי, אוֹ לְעֹפֶר הָאַיָּלִים, הִנֵּה זֶה עוֹמֵד אַחַר כָּתְלֵנוּ, מַשְׁגִּיחַ מִן הַחֲלֹּנוֹת, מֵצִיץ מִן הַחֲרַכִּים. י עָנָה דוֹדִי וְאָמַר לִי, קוּמִי לָךְ, רַעְיָתִי, יָפָתִי, וּלְכִי לָךְ. יא כִּי הִנֵּה הַסְּתָו עָבָר, הַגֶּשֶׁם חָלַף הָלַךְ לוֹ. יב הַנִּצָּנִים נִרְאוּ בָאָרֶץ, עֵת הַזָּמִיר הִגִּיעַ, וְקוֹל הַתּוֹר נִשְׁמַע בְּאַרְצֵנוּ. יג הַתְּאֵנָה חָנְטָה פַגֶּיהָ, וְהַגְּפָנִים סְמָדַר נָתְנוּ רֵיחַ, קוּמִי לָךְ, רַעְיָתִי, יָפָתִי, וּלְכִי לָךְ. יד יוֹנָתִי, בְּחַגְוֵי הַסֶּלַע, בְּסֵתֶר הַמַּדְרֵגָה, הַרְאִינִי אֶת מַרְאַיִךְ, הַשְׁמִיעִנִי אֶת קוֹלֵךְ, כִּי קוֹלֵךְ עָרֵב, וּמַרְאֵיךְ נָאוֶה. טו אֶחֱזוּ לָנוּ שֻׁעָלִים, שֻׁעָלִים קְטַנִּים, מְחַבְּלִים כְּרָמִים, וּכְרָמֵינוּ סְמָדַר. טז דּוֹדִי לִי, וַאֲנִי לוֹ, הָרֹעֶה בַּשּׁוֹשַׁנִּים. יז עַד שֶׁיָּפוּחַ הַיּוֹם, וְנָסוּ הַצְּלָלִים, סֹב דְּמֵה לְךָ, דוֹדִי, לִצְבִי אוֹ לְעֹפֶר הָאַיָּלִים, עַל הָרֵי בָתֶר.

פרק ג

א עַל מִשְׁכָּבִי בַּלֵּילוֹת בִּקַּשְׁתִּי אֵת שֶׁאָהֲבָה נַפְשִׁי, בִּקַּשְׁתִּיו וְלֹא מְצָאתִיו. ב אָקוּמָה נָּא וַאֲסוֹבְבָה בָעִיר, בַּשְּׁוָקִים וּבָרְחֹבוֹת, אֲבַקְשָׁה אֵת שֶׁאָהֲבָה נַפְשִׁי, בִּקַּשְׁתִּיו וְלֹא מְצָאתִיו. ג מְצָאוּנִי הַשֹּׁמְרִים הַסֹּבְבִים בָּעִיר, אֵת שֶׁאָהֲבָה נַפְשִׁי רְאִיתֶם. ד כִּמְעַט שֶׁעָבַרְתִּי מֵהֶם, עַד שֶׁמָּצָאתִי אֵת שֶׁאָהֲבָה נַפְשִׁי, אֲחַזְתִּיו וְלֹא אַרְפֶּנּוּ, עַד שֶׁהֲבֵיאתִיו אֶל בֵּית אִמִּי, וְאֶל חֶדֶר הוֹרָתִי. ה הִשְׁבַּעְתִּי אֶתְכֶם, בְּנוֹת יְרוּשָׁלַיִם, בִּצְבָאוֹת אוֹ בְּאַיְלוֹת הַשָּׂדֶה, אִם תָּעִירוּ וְאִם תְּעוֹרְרוּ אֶת הָאַהֲבָה עַד שֶׁתֶּחְפָּץ. ו מִי זֹאת עֹלָה מִן הַמִּדְבָּר, כְּתִימְרוֹת עָשָׁן, מְקֻטֶּרֶת מֹר וּלְבוֹנָה, מִכֹּל אַבְקַת רוֹכֵל. ז הִנֵּה מִטָּתוֹ שֶׁלִּשְׁלֹמֹה, שִׁשִּׁים גִּבֹּרִים סָבִיב לָהּ, מִגִּבֹּרֵי יִשְׂרָאֵל. ח כֻּלָּם אֲחֻזֵי חֶרֶב, מְלֻמְּדֵי

מִלְחָמָה, אִישׁ חַרְבּוֹ עַל יְרֵכוֹ, מִפַּחַד בַּלֵּילוֹת.
ט אַפִּרְיוֹן עָשָׂה לוֹ הַמֶּלֶךְ שְׁלֹמֹה מֵעֲצֵי הַלְּבָנוֹן.
י עַמּוּדָיו עָשָׂה כֶסֶף, רְפִידָתוֹ זָהָב, מֶרְכָּבוֹ אַרְגָּמָן,
תּוֹכוֹ רָצוּף אַהֲבָה מִבְּנוֹת יְרוּשָׁלָיִם. יא צְאֶינָה וּרְאֶינָה,
בְּנוֹת צִיּוֹן, בַּמֶּלֶךְ שְׁלֹמֹה, בָּעֲטָרָה שֶׁעִטְּרָה לוֹ אִמּוֹ,
בְּיוֹם חֲתֻנָּתוֹ, וּבְיוֹם שִׂמְחַת לִבּוֹ.

פרק ד

א הִנָּךְ יָפָה, רַעְיָתִי, הִנָּךְ יָפָה, עֵינַיִךְ יוֹנִים, מִבַּעַד
לְצַמָּתֵךְ, שַׂעְרֵךְ כְּעֵדֶר הָעִזִּים, שֶׁגָּלְשׁוּ מֵהַר גִּלְעָד.
ב שִׁנַּיִךְ כְּעֵדֶר הַקְּצוּבוֹת שֶׁעָלוּ מִן הָרַחְצָה, שֶׁכֻּלָּם
מַתְאִימוֹת, וְשַׁכֻּלָה אֵין בָּהֶם. ג כְּחוּט הַשָּׁנִי שִׂפְתוֹתַיִךְ,
וּמִדְבָּרֵךְ נָאוֶה, כְּפֶלַח הָרִמּוֹן רַקָּתֵךְ, מִבַּעַד לְצַמָּתֵךְ.
ד כְּמִגְדַּל דָּוִיד צַוָּארֵךְ, בָּנוּי לְתַלְפִּיּוֹת, אֶלֶף הַמָּגֵן
תָּלוּי עָלָיו, כֹּל שִׁלְטֵי הַגִּבֹּרִים. ה שְׁנֵי שָׁדַיִךְ כִּשְׁנֵי
עֳפָרִים, תְּאוֹמֵי צְבִיָּה, הָרֹעִים בַּשּׁוֹשַׁנִּים. ו עַד שֶׁיָּפוּחַ
הַיּוֹם, וְנָסוּ הַצְּלָלִים, אֵלֶךְ לִי אֶל הַר הַמּוֹר, וְאֶל
גִּבְעַת הַלְּבוֹנָה. ז כֻּלָּךְ יָפָה, רַעְיָתִי, וּמוּם אֵין בָּךְ.
ח אִתִּי מִלְּבָנוֹן, כַּלָּה, אִתִּי מִלְּבָנוֹן תָּבוֹאִי, תָּשׁוּרִי
מֵרֹאשׁ אֲמָנָה, מֵרֹאשׁ שְׂנִיר וְחֶרְמוֹן, מִמְּעֹנוֹת
אֲרָיוֹת, מֵהַרְרֵי נְמֵרִים. ט לִבַּבְתִּנִי, אֲחֹתִי כַלָּה,
לִבַּבְתִּנִי בְּאַחַת מֵעֵינַיִךְ, בְּאַחַד עֲנָק מִצַּוְּרֹנָיִךְ. י מַה
יָּפוּ דֹדַיִךְ, אֲחֹתִי כַלָּה, מַה טֹּבוּ דֹדַיִךְ מִיַּיִן, וְרֵיחַ
שְׁמָנַיִךְ מִכָּל בְּשָׂמִים. יא נֹפֶת תִּטֹּפְנָה שִׂפְתוֹתַיִךְ,
כַּלָּה, דְּבַשׁ וְחָלָב תַּחַת לְשׁוֹנֵךְ, וְרֵיחַ שַׂלְמֹתַיִךְ כְּרֵיחַ
לְבָנוֹן. יב גַּן נָעוּל אֲחֹתִי כַלָּה, גַּל נָעוּל, מַעְיָן חָתוּם.
יג שְׁלָחַיִךְ פַּרְדֵּס רִמּוֹנִים, עִם פְּרִי מְגָדִים, כְּפָרִים עִם
נְרָדִים. יד נֵרְדְּ וְכַרְכֹּם, קָנֶה וְקִנָּמוֹן, עִם כָּל עֲצֵי לְבוֹנָה,
מֹר וַאֲהָלוֹת, עִם כָּל רָאשֵׁי בְשָׂמִים. טו מַעְיַן גַּנִּים, בְּאֵר
מַיִם חַיִּים, וְנֹזְלִים מִן לְבָנוֹן. טז עוּרִי צָפוֹן, וּבוֹאִי תֵימָן,

הֵפִיחוּ גַנִּי, יִזְּלוּ בְשָׂמָיו, יָבֹא דוֹדִי לְגַנּוֹ, וְיֹאכַל פְּרִי מְגָדָיו.

פרק ה

א בָּאתִי לְגַנִּי, אֲחֹתִי כַלָּה, אָרִיתִי מוֹרִי עִם בְּשָׂמִי, אָכַלְתִּי יַעְרִי עִם דִּבְשִׁי, שָׁתִיתִי יֵינִי עִם חֲלָבִי, אִכְלוּ רֵעִים, שְׁתוּ וְשִׁכְרוּ דּוֹדִים. ב אֲנִי יְשֵׁנָה וְלִבִּי עֵר, קוֹל דּוֹדִי דוֹפֵק, פִּתְחִי לִי, אֲחֹתִי, רַעְיָתִי, יוֹנָתִי, תַמָּתִי, שֶׁרֹּאשִׁי נִמְלָא טָל, קְוֻצּוֹתַי רְסִיסֵי לָיְלָה. ג פָּשַׁטְתִּי אֶת כֻּתָּנְתִּי, אֵיכָכָה אֶלְבָּשֶׁנָּה, רָחַצְתִּי אֶת רַגְלַי, אֵיכָכָה אֲטַנְּפֵם. ד דּוֹדִי שָׁלַח יָדוֹ מִן הַחֹר, וּמֵעַי הָמוּ עָלָיו. ה קַמְתִּי אֲנִי לִפְתֹּחַ לְדוֹדִי, וְיָדַי נָטְפוּ מוֹר, וְאֶצְבְּעֹתַי מוֹר עֹבֵר, עַל כַּפּוֹת הַמַּנְעוּל. ו פָּתַחְתִּי אֲנִי לְדוֹדִי, וְדוֹדִי חָמַק עָבָר, נַפְשִׁי יָצְאָה בְדַבְּרוֹ, בִּקַּשְׁתִּיהוּ וְלֹא מְצָאתִיהוּ, קְרָאתִיו וְלֹא עָנָנִי. ז מְצָאֻנִי הַשֹּׁמְרִים הַסֹּבְבִים בָּעִיר, הִכּוּנִי פְצָעוּנִי, נָשְׂאוּ אֶת רְדִידִי מֵעָלַי שֹׁמְרֵי הַחֹמוֹת. ח הִשְׁבַּעְתִּי אֶתְכֶם, בְּנוֹת יְרוּשָׁלָיִם, אִם תִּמְצְאוּ אֶת דּוֹדִי, מַה תַּגִּידוּ לוֹ שֶׁחוֹלַת אַהֲבָה אָנִי. ט מַה דּוֹדֵךְ מִדּוֹד, הַיָּפָה בַּנָּשִׁים, מַה דּוֹדֵךְ מִדּוֹד, שֶׁכָּכָה הִשְׁבַּעְתָּנוּ. י דּוֹדִי צַח וְאָדוֹם, דָּגוּל מֵרְבָבָה. יא רֹאשׁוֹ כֶּתֶם פָּז, קְוֻצּוֹתָיו תַּלְתַּלִּים, שְׁחֹרוֹת כָּעוֹרֵב. יב עֵינָיו כְּיוֹנִים עַל אֲפִיקֵי מָיִם, רֹחֲצוֹת בֶּחָלָב, יֹשְׁבוֹת עַל מִלֵּאת. יג לְחָיָו כַּעֲרוּגַת הַבֹּשֶׂם, מִגְדְּלוֹת מֶרְקָחִים, שִׂפְתוֹתָיו שׁוֹשַׁנִּים, נֹטְפוֹת מוֹר עֹבֵר. יד יָדָיו גְּלִילֵי זָהָב, מְמֻלָּאִים בַּתַּרְשִׁישׁ, מֵעָיו עֶשֶׁת שֵׁן, מְעֻלֶּפֶת סַפִּירִים. טו שׁוֹקָיו עַמּוּדֵי שֵׁשׁ, מְיֻסָּדִים עַל אַדְנֵי פָז, מַרְאֵהוּ כַּלְּבָנוֹן, בָּחוּר כָּאֲרָזִים. טז חִכּוֹ מַמְתַקִּים, וְכֻלּוֹ מַחֲמַדִּים, זֶה דוֹדִי וְזֶה רֵעִי, בְּנוֹת יְרוּשָׁלָיִם.

פרק ו

א אָנָה הָלַךְ דּוֹדֵךְ, הַיָּפָה בַּנָּשִׁים, אָנָה פָּנָה

דוֹדֵךְ, וּנְבַקְשֶׁנּוּ עִמָּךְ. ב דּוֹדִי יָרַד לְגַנּוֹ, לַעֲרֻגוֹת הַבֹּשֶׂם, לִרְעוֹת בַּגַּנִּים וְלִלְקֹט שׁוֹשַׁנִּים. ג אֲנִי לְדוֹדִי, וְדוֹדִי לִי, הָרוֹעֶה בַּשּׁוֹשַׁנִּים. ד יָפָה אַתְּ רַעְיָתִי כְּתִרְצָה, נָאוָה כִּירוּשָׁלָיִם, אֲיֻמָּה כַּנִּדְגָּלוֹת. ה הָסֵבִּי עֵינַיִךְ מִנֶּגְדִּי, שֶׁהֵם הִרְהִיבֻנִי, שַׂעְרֵךְ כְּעֵדֶר הָעִזִּים, שֶׁגָּלְשׁוּ מִן הַגִּלְעָד. ו שִׁנַּיִךְ כְּעֵדֶר הָרְחֵלִים, שֶׁעָלוּ מִן הָרַחְצָה, שֶׁכֻּלָּם מַתְאִימוֹת, וְשַׁכֻּלָה אֵין בָּהֶם. ז כְּפֶלַח הָרִמּוֹן רַקָּתֵךְ, מִבַּעַד לְצַמָּתֵךְ. ח שִׁשִּׁים הֵמָּה מְלָכוֹת, וּשְׁמֹנִים פִּילַגְשִׁים, וַעֲלָמוֹת אֵין מִסְפָּר. ט אַחַת הִיא יוֹנָתִי תַמָּתִי, אַחַת הִיא לְאִמָּהּ, בָּרָה הִיא לְיוֹלַדְתָּהּ, רָאוּהָ בָנוֹת וַיְאַשְּׁרוּהָ, מְלָכוֹת וּפִילַגְשִׁים, וַיְהַלְלוּהָ. י מִי זֹאת הַנִּשְׁקָפָה כְּמוֹ שָׁחַר, יָפָה כַלְּבָנָה, בָּרָה כַּחַמָּה, אֲיֻמָּה כַּנִּדְגָּלוֹת. יא אֶל גִּנַּת אֱגוֹז יָרַדְתִּי לִרְאוֹת בְּאִבֵּי הַנָּחַל, לִרְאוֹת הֲפָרְחָה הַגֶּפֶן, הֵנֵצוּ הָרִמֹּנִים. יב לֹא יָדַעְתִּי, נַפְשִׁי שָׂמַתְנִי, מַרְכְּבוֹת עַמִּי נָדִיב.

פרק ז

א שׁוּבִי שׁוּבִי, הַשּׁוּלַמִּית, שׁוּבִי שׁוּבִי וְנֶחֱזֶה בָךְ, מַה תֶּחֱזוּ בַּשּׁוּלַמִּית, כִּמְחֹלַת הַמַּחֲנָיִם. ב מַה יָּפוּ פְעָמַיִךְ בַּנְּעָלִים, בַּת נָדִיב, חַמּוּקֵי יְרֵכַיִךְ כְּמוֹ חֲלָאִים, מַעֲשֵׂה יְדֵי אָמָּן. ג שָׁרְרֵךְ אַגַּן הַסַּהַר, אַל יֶחְסַר הַמָּזֶג, בִּטְנֵךְ עֲרֵמַת חִטִּים, סוּגָה בַּשּׁוֹשַׁנִּים. ד שְׁנֵי שָׁדַיִךְ כִּשְׁנֵי עֳפָרִים, תָּאֳמֵי צְבִיָּה. ה צַוָּארֵךְ כְּמִגְדַּל הַשֵּׁן, עֵינַיִךְ בְּרֵכוֹת בְּחֶשְׁבּוֹן, עַל שַׁעַר בַּת רַבִּים, אַפֵּךְ כְּמִגְדַּל הַלְּבָנוֹן, צוֹפֶה פְּנֵי דַמָּשֶׂק. ו רֹאשֵׁךְ עָלַיִךְ כַּכַּרְמֶל, וְדַלַּת רֹאשֵׁךְ כָּאַרְגָּמָן, מֶלֶךְ אָסוּר בָּרְהָטִים. ז מַה יָּפִית וּמַה נָּעַמְתְּ, אַהֲבָה בַּתַּעֲנוּגִים. ח זֹאת קוֹמָתֵךְ דָּמְתָה לְתָמָר, וְשָׁדַיִךְ לְאַשְׁכֹּלוֹת. ט אָמַרְתִּי, אֶעֱלֶה בְתָמָר, אֹחֲזָה בְּסַנְסִנָּיו, וְיִהְיוּ נָא שָׁדַיִךְ כְּאֶשְׁכְּלוֹת הַגֶּפֶן, וְרֵיחַ אַפֵּךְ כַּתַּפּוּחִים. י וְחִכֵּךְ כְּיֵין הַטּוֹב, הוֹלֵךְ

לְדוֹדִי לְמֵישָׁרִים, דּוֹבֵב שִׂפְתֵי יְשֵׁנִים. יא אֲנִי לְדוֹדִי, וְעָלַי תְּשׁוּקָתוֹ. יב לְכָה דוֹדִי, נֵצֵא הַשָּׂדֶה, נָלִינָה בַּכְּפָרִים. יג נַשְׁכִּימָה לַכְּרָמִים, נִרְאֶה אִם פָּרְחָה הַגֶּפֶן, פִּתַּח הַסְּמָדַר, הֵנֵצוּ הָרִמּוֹנִים, שָׁם אֶתֵּן אֶת דֹּדַי לָךְ. יד הַדּוּדָאִים נָתְנוּ רֵיחַ, וְעַל פְּתָחֵינוּ כָּל מְגָדִים, חֲדָשִׁים גַּם יְשָׁנִים, דּוֹדִי, צָפַנְתִּי לָךְ.

פרק ח

א מִי יִתֶּנְךָ כְּאָח לִי, יוֹנֵק שְׁדֵי אִמִּי, אֶמְצָאֲךָ בַחוּץ אֶשָּׁקְךָ, גַּם לֹא יָבֻזוּ לִי. ב אֶנְהָגֲךָ, אֲבִיאֲךָ אֶל בֵּית אִמִּי, תְּלַמְּדֵנִי, אַשְׁקְךָ מִיַּיִן הָרֶקַח, מֵעֲסִיס רִמֹּנִי. ג שְׂמֹאלוֹ תַּחַת רֹאשִׁי, וִימִינוֹ תְּחַבְּקֵנִי. ד הִשְׁבַּעְתִּי אֶתְכֶם, בְּנוֹת יְרוּשָׁלָיִם, מַה תָּעִירוּ וּמַה תְּעֹרְרוּ אֶת הָאַהֲבָה עַד שֶׁתֶּחְפָּץ. ה מִי זֹאת עֹלָה מִן הַמִּדְבָּר, מִתְרַפֶּקֶת עַל דּוֹדָהּ, תַּחַת הַתַּפּוּחַ עוֹרַרְתִּיךָ, שָׁמָּה חִבְּלַתְךָ אִמֶּךָ, שָׁמָּה חִבְּלָה יְלָדַתְךָ. ו שִׂימֵנִי כַחוֹתָם עַל לִבֶּךָ, כַּחוֹתָם עַל זְרוֹעֶךָ, כִּי עַזָּה כַמָּוֶת אַהֲבָה, קָשָׁה כִשְׁאוֹל קִנְאָה, רְשָׁפֶיהָ רִשְׁפֵּי אֵשׁ, שַׁלְהֶבֶתְיָה. ז מַיִם רַבִּים לֹא יוּכְלוּ לְכַבּוֹת אֶת הָאַהֲבָה, וּנְהָרוֹת לֹא יִשְׁטְפוּהָ, אִם יִתֵּן אִישׁ אֶת כָּל הוֹן בֵּיתוֹ בָּאַהֲבָה, בּוֹז יָבוּזוּ לוֹ. ח אָחוֹת לָנוּ קְטַנָּה, וְשָׁדַיִם אֵין לָהּ, מַה נַּעֲשֶׂה לַאֲחוֹתֵנוּ בַּיּוֹם שֶׁיְּדֻבַּר בָּהּ. ט אִם חוֹמָה הִיא, נִבְנֶה עָלֶיהָ טִירַת כָּסֶף, וְאִם דֶּלֶת הִיא, נָצוּר עָלֶיהָ לוּחַ אָרֶז. י אֲנִי חוֹמָה, וְשָׁדַי כַּמִּגְדָּלוֹת, אָז הָיִיתִי בְעֵינָיו כְּמוֹצְאֵת שָׁלוֹם. יא כֶּרֶם הָיָה לִשְׁלֹמֹה בְּבַעַל הָמוֹן, נָתַן אֶת הַכֶּרֶם לַנֹּטְרִים, אִישׁ יָבִא בְּפִרְיוֹ אֶלֶף כָּסֶף. יב כַּרְמִי שֶׁלִּי לְפָנָי, הָאֶלֶף לְךָ שְׁלֹמֹה, וּמָאתַיִם לְנֹטְרִים אֶת פִּרְיוֹ. יג הַיּוֹשֶׁבֶת בַּגַּנִּים, חֲבֵרִים מַקְשִׁיבִים לְקוֹלֵךְ, הַשְׁמִיעִנִי. יד בְּרַח דּוֹדִי, וּדְמֵה לְךָ לִצְבִי, אוֹ לְעֹפֶר הָאַיָּלִים, עַל הָרֵי בְשָׂמִים.

REFLECTIONS AND INSIGHTS ON THE THEMES AND LAWS OF PESACH

∽ THE MITZVAH TO RELATE THE STORY OF THE EXODUS

∽ THE MIRACLES IN OUR LIVES

∽ THE REDEMPTION OF OUR SOULS

∽ THE STATUTES OF PESACH AND PARAH ADUMAH

∽ SMOKING CIGARETTES ON PESACH: A HALACHIC DISCUSSION

◈§ The Mitzvah to Relate the Story of the Exodus

מצות עשה של תורה לספר בניסים ונפלאות שנעשו לאבותינו
במצרים בליל חמשה עשר של ניסן שנאמר 'זכור את היום
הזה אשר יצאתם ממצרים' כמו שנאמר 'זכור את יום השבת.'
ומנין שבליל חמשה עשר תלמוד לומר 'והגדת לבנך ביום
ההוא לאמר בעבור זה' בשעה שיש מצה ומרור מונחים לפניך.

*The Torah commands us to tell of the miracles and
wonders that were performed for our forefathers in
Egypt on the night of the fifteenth of Nissan, as it is
written, "Remember this day on which you left
Egypt." This is similar to the verse, "Remember the
day of Shabbos." How do we know that this mitzvah
is performed on the night of the fifteenth of Nissan?
Because it is written, "And you shall tell your son on
this day, saying, 'For the sake of this [the mitzvos of
the Seder night], Hashem performed for me miracles." This mitzvah must be performed when matzah
and maror are set before us.*

(Rambam, Hilchos Chametz U'Matzah 7:1).

From the verse, "Remember this day on which you left Egypt"
(*Shemos* 13:3), we see only that we are commanded to remember
the Exodus. It would appear that it is sufficient to remember it in our
minds. Yet *Rambam* learns from here that there is a positive commandment to *tell* the story of the miracles. How did he discern from
the verse that we are to verbally recall the Exodus?

Furthermore, what did *Rambam* wish to teach us by comparing
the mitzvah of remembering the Exodus to the mitzvah of remembering Shabbos?

Ohr Samei'ach suggests that we must remember the Exodus over
a cup of wine on the Seder night, just as we must remember
Shabbos over a cup of wine. Although this is halachically true, it
does not seem to be *Rambam*'s intent. Drinking wine for *Kiddush*
and for the four cups of the Seder is only a Rabbinic mitzvah.
Rambam is not detailing the Rabbinic mitzvos of the Seder night in
this section, but presenting the Torah obligation of recalling the
Exodus.

Minchas Chinuch (Mitzvah 21) raises another question. It is a mitzvah to remember the Exodus every night of the year, as the Talmud learns from the verse, "In order that you may remember the day you left Egypt *all* the days of your life" (*Devarim* 16:3). The seemingly superfluous word, "all," teaches us that we must remember the Exodus not only during the day, but also at night.[1] Why does the Torah specifically instruct us to remember the Exodus on the Seder night, if we are commanded to remember it every night of the year?

Minchas Chinuch answers that throughout the year, it is sufficient to recall the Exodus to ourselves. On the Seder night, we must tell the story to others, as the verse states, "You will tell your son on that day" (*Shemos* 13:8). If one sits alone at the Seder and has no one to tell, he must suffice with recalling the Exodus to himself, as he does throughout the year.

If that is the case, however, *Rambam* should have quoted as the verse, "You shall tell your son" the source for this mitzvah. From the verse he quotes, "Remember this day" (*Shemos* 13:3), we learn no more than the mitzvah to remember the Exodus every night of the year. Pressed for an answer to explain *Rambam's* words, *Minchas Chinuch* concludes that the mitzvah to recall the Exodus every night is not explicit in the Torah, but is derived from the extra word "all." The mitzvah to recall the Exodus on the Seder night *is* explicit. When a person makes an oath (*shevuah*) to refrain from an explicit mitzvah, the oath is invalid. Thus, *Rambam* learns from the verse, "Remember this day," that whereas an oath not to recall the Exodus would be valid throughout the year, it is invalid on the Seder night.

In my humble opinion, it seems unlikely that the only distinction between recalling the Exodus on the Seder night and recalling the Exodus every night is in regard to the improbable case of a person who makes an oath not to fulfill this mitzvah.

Distinctions Between the Two Mitzvos

I would like to suggest that the difference between the mitzvah to recount the story of the Exodus on the night of Pesach differs from the daily obligation to recall the Exodus is not limited to instances in which we sit and tell our children or others gathered at our table the story of the Exodus. Even if we sit alone and ask and answer the questions ourselves, there are several distinctions between the

1. *Berachos* 12b, according to Ben Zoma, whose opinion is accepted in halachah. See *Rambam, Hilchos Krias Shema* 1:3.

mitzvah of remembering the Exodus throughout the year, and the mitzvah of verbally relating it on the Seder night:

1. Throughout the year, any mention of the Exodus is sufficient. By simply saying, "In remembrance of the Exodus," as we do during Friday night Kiddush, one fulfills his obligation. On the Seder night, the mitzvah to tell the story of the Exodus entails providing details, as people generally do when telling a story. One does not fulfill his obligation by simply recalling that there was an Exodus; he must describe how it occurred. As *Rambam* writes, we must tell of the miracles and wonders our forefathers experienced.[1]

    Magen Avraham (67:1) and *Chasam Sofer* argue over whether one fulfills the mitzvah of remembering the Exodus by reciting *Az Yashir* the Song at Sea, which describes the splitting of the Yam Suf. *Chasam Sofer* insists that this is insufficient, since one must recall the events of the Exodus, when we were freed from Egyptian servitude. Although *Chasam Sofer* seems correct in his assertion that *Az Yashir* is insufficient (and indeed, *Rambam*'s text of the Haggadah omits the miracles of the Yam Suf), the splitting of the Yam Suf was still among the miracles of the Exodus, and represents an important detail of the story. Therefore, it is part of the mitzvah. Once we have fulfilled the primary mitzvah of describing the Exodus, it is praiseworthy to go on to describe the splitting of the Yam Suf, as our Sages tell us, "The more one tells about the Exodus, the more he is praiseworthy."

2. Most mitzvos involving speech are fulfilled even if one speaks so softly that he cannot hear his own words.[2] According to some opinions, it is even sufficient to contemplate the words without speaking them aloud. (This opinion is rejected in halachah.[3]) Yet on the Seder night, when telling the story of the Exodus, we must speak loudly enough for others to hear, as the verse states, "You shall tell your son." Even if one conducts his Seder alone, and tells the story to himself, he must speak loudly enough that others could have heard, had they been present.[4] Otherwise, it

---

1. This distinction is offered by *Maharam Shick* (Mitzvah 21); *Panim Yafos (Parashas Bo* s.v. *Veyeish l'faresh*); and *Chayei Adam* (130:11), who writes, "In addition to the mitzvah to recall the Exodus, on the Seder night we must describe the event."

2. See *Shulchan Aruch* O.C. 62:3 regarding *Shema*, in accordance with the opinion of R' Yehudah in *Berachos* 15a.

3. See *Bei'ur Halachah* 62:4 s.v. *Yatza*.

4. R' Shlomo Kluger (gloss on *Shulchan Aruch* O.C. 474; *Ha'Alef Lecha Shlomo*, appendix to O.C. 40) challenges the *Pri Megadim* (M.Z. 1 and introduction to the

is not considered a fulfillment of the mitzvah to tell the story of the Exodus.[6]

The *Poskim* do not seem to address this distinction, although it has significant practical relevance. Often, the head of the family reads the Haggadah aloud, while the rest of the family reads along quietly. They do not intend to fulfill their obligation through his recital, but through their own quiet reading. However, according to what we have discussed above, they do not fulfill their obligation unless they can hear themselves speak.[7]

3. On the Seder night, we must emphasize that Hashem freed us from Egypt in a miraculous way. If it seems from our description that Hashem freed us in a natural way, we do not fulfill our obligation. The miracles of the Exodus must be emphasized because they are a central pillar of our faith. *Ramban*[8] writes that by contemplating the revealed miracles of the Exodus, we take notice of the hidden miracles that constantly occur to every Jew. Accordingly, *Rambam* states that on the Seder night we must tell

---

laws of *Shema*), who holds that contemplating the story of the Exodus is sufficient.

6. A similar question is raised regarding *Megillah* reading on Purim. *Beis Yosef* (O.C. 689) notes an apparent contradiction in *Rambam*. On the one hand, *Rambam* rules that when saying *Shema* (or performing other mitzvos that involve speech), one need not hear his words. On the other hand, he rules that a deaf person may not read *Megillah* for others — since he is exempt, for he is unable to fulfill the mitzvah, he cannot read for others who are obligated. Why is he unable to fulfill the mitzvah? According to *Rambam*'s own opinion, he should be able to fulfill the mitzvah by reading *Megillah*, even if he cannot hear it. To resolve this contradiction, *Beis Yosef* concludes that due to the mitzvah of *pirsumei nisa* (publicizing the miracle), one must read the *Megillah* loudly enough to hear. Presumably, the same is true about publicizing the miracles of the Exodus on the Seder night.

7. Some *Poskim* contend that it is best for the head of the household to read the Haggadah alone, and the rest of the family to remain silent and fulfill their obligation through the principle of *shomei'a k'oneh* — hearing is like responding. It is a greater honor for the mitzvah when many people fulfill it together, rather than each person fulfill it by himself (see *Shulchan Aruch HaRav* 427:22, 473:24). This was the custom of the Vilna Gaon (see *Maaseh Rav*). On the other hand, *Aruch HaShulchan* (473:20) writes that now that the Haggadah has been translated, women and children often read along in a language they understand, while the head of the household reads in Hebrew.

8. *Shemos* 13:16: "From the great and revealed miracles, we come to recognize the hidden miracles, the belief in which forms the foundation for the entire Torah. A person has no portion in the Torah of Moshe Rabbeinu unless he believes that all occurrences are miraculous, and do not follow the natural order of the world. This applies to the Jewish people as a whole, and to each Jew individually. When we perform mitzvos, we are rewarded with success, and when we sin we are punished — everything depends upon Hashem's decree."

of the miracles and wonders our forefathers experienced. The rest of the year, it is sufficient to recall that He redeemed us from Egypt, without making any mention of the miracles.

4. The rest of the year, we need only recall that Hashem redeemed us from Egypt, but we need not make any mention of the date on which this occurred. On the Seder night, we must recall that on this very night, Hashem redeemed us from Egypt. This distinction is apparent from the verses. On all other nights, we fulfill the verse, "In order that you may remember the day you left Egypt." On the Seder night, we fulfill the verse, "Remember *this day* on which you left Egypt."

We can now explain why *Rambam* compared the mitzvah of recalling the Exodus on the Seder night to the mitzvah of Kiddush on Shabbos. On Shabbos we must remember that on this very day, Hashem rested from the work of Creation. Similarly, on the Seder night we remember that on this very night, Hashem redeemed us from Egypt.[1]

Further examination leads us to the conclusion that this distinction is in fact a central theme of the Seder night. Our children ask, "Why is this night different from all other nights?" We answer, "We were slaves to Pharaoh in Egypt, but Hashem, our God, took us out from there" — i.e., on this night Hashem took us out, and therefore this night is different from all others.

---

1. This point is supported by the wording of the Midrash, "The Holy One, Blessed be He, said to Moshe Remember the miracles I performed for you in Egypt, and remember the day on which you left, as the verse states, 'Remember this day'" (*Shemos Rabbah* 19:7). *Rambam* continues, "According to the child's level wisdom of the child, his father teach him If he is young or slow, his father should say, 'We were slaves and *on this night* Hashem redeemed us.'" This implies that we must recall that the Exodus occurred on this very night. Perhaps this is also *Rambam*'s intention when he writes (ibid. 6), "In each generation one must view himself as if he had personally left Egypt *now*." Not just in this generation, but on this very night. However, in *Rambam*'s Haggadah he does not stress that the Exodus occurred on the Seder night.

R' Chaim Soloveitchik of Brisk is quoted as having interpreted *Rambam*'s statement, "The Torah commands us to tell of the miracles and wonders that were performed for our forefathers in Egypt on the night of the fifteenth of Nissan," to mean that we must tell how the miracles occurred on the fifteenth (see *Sefer Zikaron: Eish Tamid*). It seems to me, however, that R' Chaim must have been misquoted, since it is obvious that this is not *Rambam*'s intent. Rather, *Rambam* means to say that we must tell on the fifteenth of Nissan of the miracles that Hashem performed. This is evident from *Rambam*'s continuation, "From where do we know that this mitzvah is performed on the night of the fifteenth of Nissan?" to which *Rambam* answers, "This exclamation must be made when matzah and maror are set before us."

The Brisker Rav[1] said in the name of his father, R' Chaim, that there are three conditions of the mitzvah to relate the story of the Exodus on the Seder night that do not apply on all other nights:

(1) On the Seder night, we must discuss the Exodus in the manner of question and answer.[2]

(2) We must begin by describing the lowly state to which we had fallen, and conclude by praising Hashem for having uplifted us.[3]

(3) We must explain the reason for the mitzvos of *Korban Pesach*, matzah and maror.[4]

In my opinion, R' Chaim did not intend to distinguish between the mitzvah to relate the story of the Exodus on the Seder night and the mitzvah to remember it on all other nights. Rather, he meant to establish certain requirements for telling the story of the Exodus on the Seder night. Yet these requirements are only Rabbinic.[5] According to Torah law, it is sufficient just to describe the miracles of the Exodus, "each person according to the eloquence of his tongue," as *Rambam* himself writes (*Sefer HaMitzvos*, Positive Commandment 157). The four distinctions we presented above are still necessary to explain the intrinsic difference between the Torah obligation of relating the Exodus on the Seder night, and the obligation to remember it throughout the year.

---

1. Cited in *Eimek HaBerachah: Inyanei Haggadah*.

2. See *Pesachim* 116a.

3. Ibid.

4. Ibid.

5. This is certainly true regarding R' Chaim's first two conditions. The source of his third condition is the subject of a dispute between the *Rishonim*. *Tosafos* (*Pesachim* 116a) seems to view it as a Torah obligation. *Shibolei HaLeket* sources it to the verse, "And you shall tell your son on that day, saying, 'It is because of this [the mitzvos of the Seder night] that Hashem acted on my behalf when I left Egypt'" (*Shemos* 13:8).

According to *Ran*, however, Rabban Gamliel's teaching that whoever neglects to explain the significance of *Korban Pesach*, matzah and maror does not fulfill his obligation (*Pesachim* 116a), means that he does not properly fulfill his obligation according to Rabbinic law. His Torah obligation is still fulfilled.

Rambam seems to contradict himself in this matter. In one place he seems to imply that according to Torah law we must mention *Korban Pesach*, matzah and maror (*Hilchos Chametz U'Matzah* 7:5). He learns this from the verse, "You shall say, 'It is a Pesach offering to Hashem'" (*Shemos* 12:27). Elsewhere he writes that according to Torah law it is enough for each person to describe the Exodus, "according to the eloquence of his tongue" (*Sefer HaMitzvos*, Positive Commandment 157).

Learning the Laws of Pesach in Place of Relating the Story

The Brisker Rav suggested that by studying the laws of Pesach, we fulfill the requirement to tell the story of the Exodus on the Seder night. He proves this from *Tosefta*, where we find that Rabban Gamliel and the Sages remained awake for the entire Seder night, studying the laws of Pesach.[1] This is also apparent from *Tur* (O.C. 481), who writes: "We are obligated to delve into the laws of Pesach and the story of the Exodus, describing the miracles Hashem performed for our forefathers, until we are overcome by sleep." *Shulchan Aruch* (481:2) writes the same.

It is not enough, however, to learn the laws of Pesach, and place the story of the Exodus aside. A person who does so does not fulfill the mitzvos of "Remember this day on which you left Egypt" and "You shall tell your son on this day."

Rather, once a person has fulfilled the basic mitzvah of relating the story of the Exodus, he fulfills an additional mitzvah by also discussing the laws of Pesach, since they are relevant to the story. This is included in our Sages' teaching, "The more one tells about the Exodus, the more he is praiseworthy" (*Rambam, Hilchos Chametz U'Matzah* 7:1).

We find a similar concept discussed by the *Rishonim*. *Sifra* rules that we must remember the deeds of Amalek by recalling them aloud. *Raavad* and the *Rash* of Shantz write that by studying the laws of *Megillah*, we fulfill this obligation. Similarly, whereas *Sifra* requires us to remember the punishment of Miriam by recalling it aloud, the *Rishonim* write that we fulfill this mitzvah by study the laws of *tzaraas*.

Clearly, one cannot suffice with learning the laws of *Megillah* and *tzaraas* and ignore the episodes of Amalek's attack and Miriam's punishment. Rather, after having mentioned these episodes, one fulfills the mitzvah further by learning the relevant laws.

---

1. *Tosefta, Pesachim* 10:8. However, the Vilna Gaon edited the *Tosefta*, and replaced "the laws of Pesach," with "the story of the Exodus." Accordingly, there is no proof from here for the Brisker Rav's thesis. See commentary section, p. 15.

☙ The Miracles in Our Lives

"There are several commandments that serve as reminders of the Exodus, testifying before all future generations of the great miracles that occurred, so that we will not forget them.

"From the awesome, obvious miracles, we become aware of the hidden miracles. Recognizing all the miracles in our lives is the foundation of the entire Torah.

"Man has no portion in the Torah of Moshe Rabbeinu unless he believes that all the events of his life are miraculous. Nothing is due to nature or coincidence."
(*Ramban, Parashas Bo*)

The Miracles of Nature

Ramban's insight helps us understand the true purpose of the miracles of the Exodus. Those miracles not only served Bnei Yisrael at that time, they also demonstrated for all generations that even things that appear to be "natural" are, in fact, indications of Divine Providence. *Everything* is miraculous. Indeed, our Sages (*Bereishis Rabbah* 14:9) teach that we must thank Hashem for every breath we take, for each breath is a miracle.

On Purim and Chanukah, we thank Hashem for the "*nissim v'niflaos*" — miracles and wonders — that He performs. What is the real meaning of the word *nes* (literally, miracle)? People often assume that miracles and wonders are one and the same. They understand that a miracle must be an extraordinary occurrence, outside the boundaries of what we call nature. Is this truly so?

The word *nes* also means "flag" or "banner," as we find in the verse, "You will see when the banner (*nes*) is hoisted up upon the mountains" (*Yeshayah* 18:3). In *Shemoneh Esrei* we also say, "Raise the banner (*nes*) to gather our exiles."

The two meanings of the word *nes* — miracle and banner — go hand in hand. When a country conquers a territory, it raises its banner or flag to show its dominance, since a banner symbolizes sovereignty. Similarly, miracles serve as banners to signal Hashem's Sovereignty over Creation. As *Ramban* teaches, the great miracles help us realize that everything that occurs to us is miraculous.

In the laws of Chanukah, *Rema* rules that if one forgot to recite *Al Hanissim* in its proper place in *Bircas HaMazon*, he should recite it at the end of *Bircas HaMazon*, with the introduction, "May the Merciful One perform for us miracles and wonders, as He performed for our forefathers." The commentaries note that this prayer seems to contradict the Mishnah that states: "If someone's wife is pregnant and he prays that she should give birth to a boy, that is an empty prayer" (*Berachos* 54a). The Talmud explains that we are not meant to pray for miracles.[1] Why, then, do we pray on Chanukah that Hashem perform for us miracles and wonders?

According to what we have explained, we may only pray for those miracles that serve the purpose of demonstrating Hashem's Sovereignty over the world. The miracles of Chanukah and Purim, which were performed for our forefathers in the days of Mattisyahu and in the days of Mordechai and Esther, were of this variety. Through these miracles, Hashem's Name was sanctified. It is certainly a great mitzvah to pray that Hashem's Name be sanctified again in our own generation. Indeed, the entire purpose of our existence is to sanctify Hashem's Name.

In contrast, miracles that do not publicize Hashem's Sovereignty do not achieve this purpose. What benefit would there be if a female fetus miraculously turned into a male? Would this sanctify Hashem's Name? Would anyone even realize what had happened, and be amazed and inspired by it? Certainly not. Therefore, this is a meaningless miracle, the type of miracle for which we should not pray.

The Talmud (*Shabbos* 53b) tells the story of a man whose wife died, leaving him with an infant child for whom he could not afford to hire a nursemaid. A miracle occurred, and he was given the ability to nurse his child. Regarding this, R' Yosef said, "See how great was this man that such a miracle was performed for him."

"Just the opposite," answered Abaye. "How lowly was this man that nature was distorted for him."

Tosafos Yeshanim questions Abaye's response, citing a Midrash that the same miracle occurred for Mordechai, who was able to nurse the orphaned Esther when she was a baby. Perhaps we can explain that the miracle of Mordechai's nursing Esther was different, since the bond between them eventually served to sanctify Hashem's Name. Years later, Esther faithfully heeded Mordechai's directions, endangering her own life to rescue the Jewish nation.

---

1. *Berachos* 60a. See *Yeshuos Yaakov* §2.

Great miracles were then performed, allowing the Jews to defeat their enemies, and resulting in a sanctification of Hashem's Name. In this case, the course of nature was not distorted for Mordechai's benefit. It was altered to serve as a banner to publicize Hashem's providence.

The story is told of a child who asked his father after the Pesach Seder why the splitting of the Yam Suf (Sea of Reeds) is considered such a great miracle. "Hashem created the Yam Suf," the child reasoned. "Surely He has no difficulty splitting it. Why do we consider this so amazing?"

The father explained by means of a parable. Once there was a skilled sculptor, who fashioned a marble statue of a horse that was perfectly lifelike. He put his statue in the public square, so that all who passed by could see it and marvel at his skill. He then stood at the side to see how people would react.

To his great chagrin, no one even noticed his handiwork. People passed by the statue and continued on without pausing to admire his masterpiece.

The sculptor returned home and shared his disappointment with his family, who tried their best to console him. "Do not feel bad," they said. "Your statue is so lifelike that no one could even distinguish it from a real horse. Do you think busy people have time to stop and admire horses and donkeys?"

"What should I do?" he asked. "Should I make an imperfect replica, so that people will notice that it is not real? I would not demean my art in such a way."

The sculptor's family then advised him to cut the horse in half and leave the two halves near each other in the public square. People would pass by and be amazed to see a live horse cut in two, but still standing on its feet. Upon closer inspection they would realize that it was not a real horse at all, but a perfect replica.

The same was true of the splitting of the Yam Suf. If we would perceive the beauty and wondrousness of Hashem's world, we would have had no need for this miracle.

The prophet Yeshayah said, "Raise your eyes on high and see Who created these [things]! He brings forth their legions by number; He calls to each of them by name; by the abundance of His power and by vigor of His strength, not one is missing" (*Yeshayah* 40:26). Similarly, King David said, "When I behold Your heavens, the work of Your fingers, the moon and the stars that You have set in place, [I think,] "What is frail man that You should remember him?" (*Psalms* 8:5).

Rambam (*Hilchos Yesodei HaTorah* 2:5) writes, "What is the path to love and awe of the Creator? When a person contemplates Hashem's wondrous deeds and creations, he will surely see the infinite wisdom within them and become filled with love of Hashem and a strong desire to praise Him and to know His Name."

Over time, we grow so accustomed to Hashem's everyday wonders that we simply take them for granted. Our eyes and hearts become so used to the miracles we see around us that we no longer recognize them as miracles. They all seem so commonplace.

To cure us of this malady and shake us out of our stupor, Hashem occasionally performs open miracles. He split the Yam Suf before our eyes to remind us that the sea's normal existence is just as miraculous as its splitting. Open miracles make us aware of the hidden miracles and Divine Providence that we encounter in each and every facet of our lives, in all places, and at all times. This heightened awareness spurs us to offer profound thanks to Hashem for all of the seemingly "natural" kindnesses He bestows upon us, down to every breath He allows us to take.

Yeshayah prophesized that during the days of Mashiach, "The earth will be as filled with knowledge of Hashem *as water covering the sea*" (*Yeshayah* 11:9). The Yam Suf had to be split miraculously in order to reveal Hashem's presence. When Mashiach comes, Hashem's presence will be equally manifest in the natural state of the sea, when it is filled with water. There will no longer be a need to draw inspiration from the splitting of the sea.

Just as we must uncover Hashem's presence in the general course of nature, we must also discover Him in every minute detail of our lives. We should not only turn to Him in times of trouble, or when we stand by the crossroads of weighty decisions. We must also turn to Him in prayer and gratitude for each and every breath. Rabbeinu Yonah writes in his commentary on *Mishlei*:

"Trust in Hashem with all your heart. In all your ways know Him." (*Mishlei* 3:5, 6). Before you perform any action, remember Hashem, and direct your hope toward Him with faith that He will grant you success. Place upon your heart the sincere recognition that your success is not in your own hands.

The second verse, "In all your ways know Him," adds to the first. Some people trust Hashem in a general sense, believing that everything is ordained by Heaven. They realize that their success depends on Hashem, and not on their own prowess or the favors of others. However, they do not apply this faith to the minute details of their lives, to look toward Him to help them in all their endeavors.

Therefore, the second verse tells us, "In all your ways know Him."

R' Nachman of Breslov *zt"l* would instruct his followers to daven to Hashem in their own words, as a child turns to his mother for help.

The Talmud (*Berachos* 4b) tells us that if a person prays *Shemoneh Esrei* immediately after completing the blessing of *Go'al Yisrael*, he is assured of a place in the World to Come. Why is this considered a worthy accomplishment, deserving of such a great reward?

Rabbeinu Yonah explains:

When we pray immediately after recalling the Exodus, we show that we have full trust in Hashem that He will hear our prayers, just as He heard the prayers of our forefathers in Egypt; otherwise we would not bother praying. The Midrash (*Shemos Rabbah, Parashas Bo*) states that when Bnei Yisrael saw the miracles and wonders that the Creator did for them, they learned to trust Him, as the verse says, "Israel saw the great hand that Hashem inflicted upon Egypt and they had faith in Hashem" (*Shemos* 14:31).

When we recall the Redemption, in which our forefathers trusted Hashem and He rescued them, and immediately afterward begin to pray, it shows that we trust that Hashem will answer our prayers, as He answered the prayers of our forefathers. In reward for this demonstration of faith in Hashem, we are granted a place in the World to Come.

We see that trusting Hashem and praying for His help in every small detail of our lives is the foundation of our faith. We are obligated to cultivate this outlook within our hearts, as the prophet Yirmiyah said, "Accursed is the man who trusts in people ... and turns his heart away from Hashem" (*Yirmiyah* 17:5), and, in contrast, "Blessed is the man who trusts in Hashem" (ibid. 7).

When a person makes every effort to strengthen his trust in Hashem, He is granted Divine assistance; as the *Rambam* writes in his open letter to the Yemenite Jewish community, "Hashem implanted faith in the nature of the Jewish soul."

When we contemplate the miracles that Hashem performs for our people, we receive a Heavenly gift of love and fear of Hashem. Our faith and trust in Him are strengthened, and we are inspired to devote ourselves lovingly to His service. Rabbeinu Yonah writes that the whole purpose of the Exodus was for Bnei Yisrael to accept upon themselves the yoke of Hashem's service, as the verse says, "For they are My servants, whom I have taken out of the land of Egypt" (*Vayikra* 25:42). This is another reason that the blessing of *Go'al Yisrael* must be immediately followed by *Shemoneh Esrei*. After recalling how Hashem liberated us from Egypt, we resolve to serve Him with prayer, as the Talmud (*Taanis* 2a) says, "Prayer is the service of the heart."

The commentaries note an apparent contradiction in the *Rambam*.[1] In *Yad HaChazakah* (*Hil. Shema* 1:3), the *Rambam* rules like Ben Zoma (*Berachos* 12b), who holds that one must recall the Exodus each day and night. But *Rambam* does not record this obligation in his lists of the 613 mitzvos — *Sefer Hamitzvos* and *Minyan Hamitzvos*. Why?

Perhaps the Rambam held that remembering the Exodus is not one of the 613 mitzvos. Rather, it is included in the mitzvah to recite the *Shema* each morning and evening. When we say *Shema*, we accept upon ourselves the yoke of Hashem's service. To enable ourselves to dedicate ourselves to Him fully, we first recall the great miracles He performed for us, when He rescued our forefathers from slavery in Egypt. Therefore, *Rambam* mentions this obligation only in the context of the laws of *Shema*.

Torah Inspires Love of Hashem

In two different places, the *Rambam* offers advice as to how a person can become inspired to love Hashem. In *Hilchos Yesodei HaTorah* (2:5), he writes:

What is the path to love and awe of the Creator? When a person contemplates Hashem's wondrous deeds and creations, he will surely see infinite wisdom within them and become filled with love of Hashem and a strong desire to praise Him and to know His Name.

Elsewhere (*Sefer Hamitzvos* 3), the *Rambam* writes that love of Hashem can be attained by toiling in Torah study:

We are commanded to love Him. This means that we must consider and contemplate His mitzvos, His words and His deeds until we understand them, and enjoy this understanding with the greatest possible enjoyment. This is the love of Hashem of which we are commanded.

These two paths lead to two different kinds of love for Hashem. The love that comes from learning His teachings and contemplating His wisdom is the love of the mind. The love that comes from contemplating His wondrous deeds and creations is the love of the heart, of which the *Rambam* writes:

What is the proper love for Hashem? One should love Him with such a great, overwhelming passion that his soul is bound with the

---

1. See *Tzelach* on *Berachos*, and *Ohr Samei'ach*.

love of Hashem, and He is entirely consumed with it, as if he is lovesick and can think only of the subject of his desire when he lies down and wakes up, when he eats and when he drinks. Our love for Hashem should be even greater than this, such that we are entirely absorbed with thoughts only for Him, as we are commanded, "You must love Hashem your God with all your heart and all your soul." This is as King Shlomo said, "My soul aches with love for You." The entire *Shir HaShirim* is a parable for this love (*Hilchos Teshuvah* 10:3).

We see the love for Hashem described as a passionate, emotional love, which burns in the hearts of His servants until they are sick with love for Him.

It is interesting to note that regarding the intellectual love that comes about through studying Torah, the *Rambam* writes, "This is the love of Hashem of which we are commanded," and he includes this form of love of Hashem in his *Sefer Hamitzvos*, which lists the 613 commandments.

The *Rambam* refers to the passionate, emotional love that emanates from contemplating the wonders of Creation as "the *proper* love for Hashem," implying that it is not absolutely mandatory. He describes this love in *Hilchos Yesodei HaTorah*, which details not only the obligatory commandments, but also to methods of character perfection.

The *Rishonim* offer two explanations of the mitzvah to accept upon ourselves the yoke of Hashem's service while reciting *Shema*. According to *Sefer HaChinuch* (Mitzvah 417), this mitzvah entails recognizing and believing in Hashem's Oneness: "*Hashem Echad*." According to *Abudraham* (in his commentary to *Shacharis*), the mitzvah entails subjugating ourselves to His service and resolving to fulfill all of His commandments: "*Hashem Elokeinu*," He is our God, Whom we must obey.

It seems that both opinions are correct, and they complement each other. We must believe that Hashem is *Elokeinu*, our God, Who chose us from all the nations and made us into His special servants. We must also believe that He is *Echad*, the one God, Who has no peer or rival and rules alone over all Creation.

We come to recognize Hashem in His role of *Elokeinu*, the God of Israel, by toiling in the study of Torah, which was granted to our people as an inheritance, and in which no other nation has any part. Through this, we foster in our minds the intellectual love to which the Rambam refers in *Sefer Hamitzvos*.

We come to recognize Hashem in His role of *Echad*, the One God, by contemplating the awesome beauty of Creation, through which

He displays His infinite wisdom. Through this, we foster in our hearts the passionate love of which the *Rambam* wrote in *Hilchos Yesodei HaTorah*.

The blessings recited before *Shema* in the morning correspond to these two ideas. In the first blessing, *Yotzeir Hameoros*, we praise Hashem for the wonders of Creation — specifically, for the sun that rises each morning. This corresponds to Hashem's role as *Echad*, the One God of all Creation, toward whom we direct our emotional love.

In the second blessing, *Ahavah Rabbah*, we thank Hashem for granting us the Torah, and we pray for His help in studying and understanding it.[1] This corresponds to Hashem's role as *Elokeinu*, the God of Israel Who chose us from among the nations and granted us His Torah, and toward Whom we direct our intellectual love.

On a deeper level, my *rebbe*, the Klausenberger Rebbe *zt"l*, would say that someone who merits to toil in Torah with all his might can achieve the pinnacle of closeness to Hashem, and he then has no need to contemplate the wonders of Creation to recognize Hashem's greatness. Accordingly, the Klausenberger Rav *zt"l* explained the Mishnah, "One who walks on the road while reviewing his Torah lesson, and interrupts his studies to say, 'How beautiful is this tree! How beautiful is this plowed field!' is liable for his life" (*Pirkei Avos* 3:9). Since he is a Torah scholar, he need not be inspired by the beautiful tree or field to recognize Hashem's greatness. Instead, he should draw his inspiration from the Torah.

The Natural and the Supernatural

Akeidas Yitzchak[2] writes that before Adam sinned, the world was guided along a supernatural path. All Creation was devoted to fulfilling man's needs, to enable him to dedicate himself to serving Hashem without distraction. Our Sages tell us that the angels would roast meat and filter wine for Adam (*Sanhedrin* 59b).[3] The earth sprouted only those trees and plants that were beneficial for him. After Adam's sin, he was cursed that the earth would sprout thorns and thistles. Since man distanced himself from his true purpose of serving Hashem, all Creation distanced itself correspondingly from its true purpose of serving man. For this reason, man is called an

---

1. See *Berachos* 9b.

2. *Parashas Noach*, Shaar 12, Maamar Niggun Olam.

3. In a similar vein, *Zohar* states that if not for his sin, Adam would have ruled over the angels (*Zohar Chadash* 14).

"*olam katan,*" a microcosmic world. The entire world acts in response to his deeds.

This principle was true not only of Adam, but also of all subsequent generations. The deeds of man influence the course of Creation, since everything was created for him (*Shabbos* 30b).[1] *Ramban* (*Vayikra* 26:6, 11) writes:

When Bnei Yisrael fulfilled Hashem's mitzvos, Eretz Yisrael was as perfect as the world before Adam's sin, and no animal or insect ever harmed anyone. When Bnei Yisrael serve Hashem perfectly, they are not guided along the path of nature at all — not in regard to their bodies or their land, and not in regard to the community or the individual. Their bread and water is blessed, and no disease ever befalls them. They have no need of doctors or therapeutic practices, as it says "I, Hashem, am your healer."

This principle is expressed in the Mishnah (*Kiddushin* 82a):

R' Shimon ben Elazar said: Have you ever seen a beast or bird plying a trade? They find their livelihood without worry. If they, who were created to serve me, can find their livelihood without worry, then certainly I, who was created to serve Hashem, should be able to do so. Yet my own wicked deeds have cut off my source of livelihood.

We see from here that if not for man's sins, he would receive his livelihood without any worry or hassle, just as the animals do.

Not only is man's livelihood influenced by his actions, but all that happens in the world is influenced, as well. Regarding this, the Mishnah (*Pirkei Avos* 5:1) says, "Why was the world created with ten utterances? To punish the wicked who destroy the world that was created with ten utterances and to give ample reward to the righteous who sustain the world that was created with ten utterances."

Man's deeds have the power to uplift Creation, or to send it crashing down. Man can support the earth, or destroy it.

This is true not only of mankind as a whole, but even of the individual. When a person attains perfection in the service of Hashem, having ascended to the heights of holiness and purity, the entire world is subjugated to his will — since he fulfills the will of his Creator.

Countless *tzaddikim* throughout the generations merited having miracles performed on their behalf. For instance, the Talmud (*Berachos* 34b) describes at length the wonders performed by R' Chanina ben Dosa. In more recent generations, as well, there have been

---

1. See *Moreh Nevuchim* 3:25.

tzaddikim in whose merit open miracles were performed for the benefit of Klal Yisrael. Why, then, did Abaye call the man who nursed his daughter "lowly" for distorting nature, rather than praising him,[1] just as these *tzaddikim* are praised for the miracles that came about through them?

The reason is that these *tzaddikim* did not distort nature at all. On the contrary; the true nature of the world, and the original purpose for which it was created, was to bow to the will of *tzaddikim*. For this reason, Mordechai was not considered lowly for nursing Esther. The man of whom Abaye spoke was considered lowly because he had no great merit for this miracle to be performed for him. It was therefore considered a distortion of nature.

Our Sages tell us that the Exodus was performed not by an angel, but by Hashem Himself. Since Bnei Yisrael were not worthy at that point of having nature bend to perform their will, Hashem had to bend it for them.

We find in the Talmud (*Taanis* 24a) that R' Yose of Yukras told his son, "Since you troubled your Creator [with prayer] to make the fig tree produce fruit before its time, you will be gathered before your time." We learn from here that any disruption of the course of Creation is overseen by Hashem, not by angels. Since R' Yose's son was not worthy of this miracle, it was considered outside the normal course of Creation, and Hashem had to personally oversee it. Similarly, Hashem Himself performed the miracles of the Exodus.

Sound and Vision

The revelation of Hashem's miracles changes the outlook of those who see them, granting them an entirely different perspective on the world, and enabling them to perceive amazing things to which they previously had been blind. For example, when Bnei Yisrael received the Torah on Mount Sinai, they "saw" Hashem's voice (*Shemos* 20:15). Our Sages explain that they could see the sounds, and hear the sights (*Mechilta, Parashas Yisro*).

Hashem granted us five senses to collect information about what transpires around us, and use this information to nourish our minds. Of all the senses, there is none as descriptive as sight. Although the other senses often deceive, once a person has seen something with his own eyes, he has no doubt at all of its veracity. This is true in a general sense, for the majority of mankind. Hence the adage, "Seeing is believing."

---

1. See p. 10.

Bnei Yisrael, however, value the tradition we have received from our forefathers over our own sense of sight. For example, we cannot see Hashem, yet we are so certain of His existence that the Rambam writes, "Everything that exists in heaven and earth, and all that is between them, have no existence other than what they draw from the ultimate truth of His own existence" (*Hilchos Yesodei HaTorah* 1:1).

What is man if not the breath of life that Hashem has blown into his lungs? This breath of life, the immortal soul, cannot be seen. Nor can we see the angels that constantly circle the world, doing Hashem's bidding. Yet we have no question at all of their existence, for we rely on the tradition we received in an unbroken chain from generation to generation. For this reason, *Ramban* (*Devarim* 4:9) and *Sefer HaChinuch* (Introduction) write that our faith is founded not on what we perceive with our own eyes, but on the tradition we have received from our forefathers.

When Bnei Yisrael stood at Mount Sinai, we were elevated to an exalted level at which we could "see the sounds." This means that we could accept the words of our parents and teachers and believe them completely, as though we had seen those things ourselves. We could "hear the sights" — i.e., the visible, physical world became so distant from our thoughts that it was as though we had only heard about it, and had never seen it with our own eyes.[1]

With this insight, we can explain an interesting episode in the Talmud (*Bava Basra* 75a):

R' Yochanan taught that in the future, Hashem will take gems thirty cubits tall and thirty cubits wide, and carve an opening ten cubits wide and twenty cubits tall, and stand them by the gates of Jerusalem.

One of his students mocked this teaching, scoffing, "Today no gem is even as big as a bird's egg, and in the future such giant gems will be found?"

Later, this student was traveling by boat when he saw in the Heavens a vision of angels carving the giant gems that R' Yochanan had described.

"Who are these for?" he asked.

"In the future, Hashem will stand these gems by the gates of Jerusalem," the angels told him.

The student then returned to R' Yochanan and said, "Teach, *rebbi*, teach. I have seen exactly what you described."

---

1. See *Meshech Chochmah, Parashas Chukas* and *Maor Einayim, Parashas Beshalach.*

"Empty one!" R' Yochanan scolded him. "Had you not seen it, you would not have believed. You mock the words of the Sages." R' Yochanan then set his eyes upon him, and turned him into a pile of bones.

Why did R' Yochanan scold the student only after he returned to verify his teacher's words with his own testimony? Why did he not turn the student into a pile of bones when the student first challenged his teachings?

When the student returned to R' Yochanan, amazed by the sight he had seen, he showed that he valued the vision of his own eyes over the tradition he heard from his rebbi, who based his teachings on verses from the Torah. That is what angered R' Yochanan. The student had obviously attained a lofty spiritual level, having been able to converse with angels. Accordingly, he should have been able to "see the voice" of R' Yochanan, accepting his Torah teachings as though he had seen them with his own eyes.

The punishment of being transformed into a pile of bones was *middah k'neged middah* — in equal and appropriate measure to his sin. In outward appearance, the human body is no more than a collection of bones held together by flesh and sinews. The body comes to life because it has an invisible soul within it. Since the student valued only what was visible to his eyes, he was transformed into a lifeless pile of bones — all that is visible of man. Thus, R' Yochanan called him "*reika*," empty one, as if to say, "Are you empty of the holy soul, which you cannot see? Just as you believe in the existence of your own soul, you should believe my words."

R' Yochanan endeavored to instill in his students the faith that there is no absolute truth except what we learn from the Torah. For example:

R' Yochanan taught, "Yaakov Avinu never died."

"Then why did they eulogize, embalm and bury him?" asked his peers.

R' Yochanan answered, "I learned this from the verse, 'Do not fear, My servant Yaakov, the word of Hashem, and do not be afraid, Yisrael; for behold, I am saving you from distant places, and your descendants from the land of their captivity" (*Yirmiyah* 30:10). The verse equates Yaakov to his descendants. Just as his descendants live on, so he does (*Taanis* 5b).

Although Yaakov Avinu appeared to have died, and was even embalmed by the Egyptians, R' Yochanan taught that we must not heed the vision of our own eyes, but rather the truth as it is expressed by the Torah.

The Talmud (*Berachos* 58a) records the following episode:

Rav Sheishes was blind. When everyone went to greet the king, he went with them. A Sadducee taunted him, saying, "Why does the broken bucket go to the river?" [Just as it cannot draw water from the river, so too you cannot see the king.]

"Come and I will show you that I can see the king better than you can," answered Rav Sheishes.

When the first contingent of the king's men passed before the spectators, there was a great roar of applause. "The king has come," the Sadducee told Rav Sheishes.

"He has not come yet," said Rav Sheishes.

When the second contingent passed, there was again a great uproar. "Now the king has come," the Sadducee said.

"He has not come yet," answered Rav Sheishes again.

When the third contingent passed, there was silence. "Surely, now the king has come," said Rav Sheishes.

"How did you know?" asked the Sadducee.

Rav Sheishes explained, "The kingdom of mortal men parallels the kingdom of Heaven, of which it is said, 'Go out and stand on the mountain before Hashem. And behold, Hashem passed by him. Before Hashem, there was a great and mighty wind, which uprooted mountains and crumbled stones — but Hashem was not in the storm wind. After the storm wind there was a great noise — but Hashem was not in the noise. After the noise there was a fire — but Hashem was not in the fire. After the fire there was a faint voice" (*I Kings* 19:12).

When the king came, Rav Sheishes recited a blessing, "Blessed are You, Hashem, Who shared His honor with flesh and blood."

The Sadducee exclaimed, "You recite a blessing over something you cannot see!"

What was the fate of the Sadducee? Some opinions say that his peers gouged his eyes out. Others say that Rav Sheishes set his eyes on him and turned him into a pile of bones.

This passage follows the same principle that R' Yochanan taught his students. Our perception of the truth should not be determined by what our eyes see, but by what our ears perceive. Rav Sheishes, who could not see at all, was more aware than the Sadducee not only of what occurs in Heaven above, but even of the mundane occurrences of this lower world. When the Sadducee obstinately refused to concede that he perceived less than Rav Sheishes, going so far as to mock Rav Sheishes for reciting a blessing over what he could not see, he was punished *middah k'neged middah*, either by having his eyes gouged out or by being transformed into a pile of bones like R' Yochanan's student.

With this we can understand Adam's response to Hashem after he sinned, "I heard the sound of You in the garden, and I was afraid because I am naked" (*Bereishis* 3:10). Adam was afraid because he realized that he was no longer able to "see" Hashem's voice, only to hear it. In the future, however, we will once again be able to see Hashem's voice, as the verse says, "The glory of Hashem will be revealed, and all flesh together will *see* that the mouth of Hashem has spoken" (*Yeshayah* 40:5). We pray for this in the *Kedushah* of *Mussaf*: "In His mercy, He will let us hear a second time, *before the eyes* of all living things."

Perhaps it is for this reason that in commanding us to remember the giving of the Torah, the Torah states, "Beware for yourself and greatly beware for your soul, lest you forget the words that *your eyes have beheld*" (*Devarim* 4:9). Regarding the mitzvos to remember other events, such as the Exodus, no mention is made of sounds being seen, since this phenomenon was exclusive to the giving of the Torah.

Everything Hashem Does Is for the Best

Upon contemplating the miracles of the Exodus, we learn another important lesson: to recognize that everything Hashem does, even that which appears disastrous, is nothing but a veiled manifestation of His lovingkindness. Hashem shook the very foundations of the world and brought upon the Egyptians the most horrendous plagues imaginable. Yet all this was for the good of His beloved children, to rescue us from slavery.

In this aspect as well, the miracles served as a banner to publicize that Hashem's attribute of strict justice is actually another aspect of his mercy. Although we do not always merit seeing the kindness inherent in all of His ways, we must firmly believe that, "Everything the Merciful One does is for the best" (*Berachos* 60b).

When a person feels that he has been struck by Hashem's attribute of justice, he must work on himself until he can see and feel Hashem's mercy hidden behind the misfortune. Commenting on the verse, "You are children to Hashem, your God — you shall not cut yourselves and you shall not make a bald spot between your eyes for a dead person" (*Devarim* 14:1), *Ibn Ezra* writes:

You must realize that you are Hashem's children, and He loves you more than a father loves his children. Do not cut yourselves in grief over your suffering, since everything Hashem does is for the best. If you cannot understand this, just like a small child cannot understand his father's decisions, you must trust Him like a child trusts his father.

The story is told of a person who came to the Maggid of Mezeritch *zt"l* for advice how to fulfill our Sages' counsel that we must bless Hashem for the bad things, just as we bless him for the good (*Berachos* 54a). The Maggid suggested that he search the Beis *Midrash* for R' Zusha of Anipoli, who could best answer this question. The man found R' Zusha, sitting in tattered rags, toiling in Torah study. The poverty and hardship that engulfed him were clearly evident. When the man asked R' Zusha his question, R' Zusha answered that there must have been some mistake. "I cannot possibly understand why the Maggid sent you to me. I have never suffered misfortune in my life, and therefore I can't teach you to bless Hashem sincerely for the bad things that happen to you."

This was the outlook of the Sages of the Talmud. The Talmud (*Berachos* 34b) tells the story of R' Chanina ben Dosa, who went to study Torah from R' Yochanan ben Zakkai. When he arrived, R' Yochanan asked him to daven for his son who was sick. R' Chanina placed his head between his knees and prayed for mercy until the child recovered. R' Yochanan then said, "Had Ben Zakkai stuck his head between his knees all day long, he would not have been answered."

"Is Chanina greater than you?" asked his wife.

"No," answered R' Yochanan, "but he is like a servant before the King, while I am like a minister before the King."

Kedushas Levi (*Parashas Chukas*) explains that a king's ministers play a role in his decisions, and understand the reason for his decrees. His servants, on the other hand, are not involved in his decisions, and do not understand the reasons behind them. R' Yochanan ben Zakkai was like Hashem's minister, and understood how everything Hashem does is pure mercy and kindness. Since he understood the reason for Hashem's decrees, his prayers that Hashem may rescind them were not wholehearted.

R' Chanina ben Dosa was like a servant before Hashem. When he saw suffering befall the Jewish people, he was shaken to the core. He could not understand or come to terms with it, so he prayed with all his heart that Hashem rescind the harsh decree. (This was the root of R' Chanina's soul, and the purpose for which he was sent to this world: to pray on behalf of the Jewish people, and rescind seemingly harsh decrees.)

Like R' Yochanan ben Zakkai, R' Akiva was also a minister before the king, who understood the wisdom behind Hashem's seemingly harsh decrees. Whenever hardship would befall him, he would say, "Everything the Merciful One does is for the best" (*Berachos* 60b). *Talmud Yerushalmi* states that even when R' Akiva was arrested by the Romans and led to his execution, he laughed, for he recognized that this, too, was for the best.[1]

Not only in his own suffering did R' Akiva see the good, but even in the suffering of his mentor, R' Eliezer ben Hyrkanos. The Talmud (*Sanhedrin* 101a) relates the following story:

Once, R' Eliezer fell ill and his students came to visit him. "Hashem's anger against me is fierce," he told them. The students began to cry, and R' Akiva began to laugh.

"Why are you laughing?" they asked him.

"Why are you crying?" he responded.

"A *Sefer Torah* like our *rebbi* is suffering. Should we not cry?" they said.

"For this very reason I laugh," he told them. "All the years that I have known our *rebbi*, his wine has never turned to vinegar, his flax crop has never rotted, his oil has never fermented, and his honey has never spoiled. I worried that perhaps he might have received his reward in this world. Now that I see that he, too, suffers in this world, I am relieved to know that he will receive his reward in the World to Come. Therefore I rejoice."

A similar incident occurred in which the ill R' Eliezer was visited by four Sages: R' Tarfon, R' Yehoshua, R' Elazar ben Azaryah, and R' Akiva. The first three Sages spoke, comparing R' Eliezer to a raindrop, to the sun, and to a father and mother. R' Akiva then spoke, and said, "Suffering is beloved." Of all of these words, R' Akiva's were the most comforting to R' Eliezer.

R' Akiva could see the hidden good even in the exile of the Jewish people and the destruction of the Beis Hamikdash. The Talmud (*Makkos* 24b) relates another story:

Rabban Gamliel, R' Elazar ben Azaryah, R' Yehoshua, and R' Akiva were walking along the road, and they could hear the tumultuous sound of the House of Rome from a distance of one hundred and twenty *mil*. The Sages began to cry, and R' Akiva laughed.

"Why are you laughing?" they asked him.

"Why are you crying?" he responded.

"These *Kushiyim* worship abominations and sacrifice to idols, yet they dwell in peace and security, while the house that was the footstool of Hashem was consumed by fire. Should we not cry?"

---

1. Cited by *Tosafos*, Sotah 31.

"For this very reason I laugh," he told them. "If such is the portion of those who violate the will of Hashem, how much greater will be the portion of those who fulfill his will."

Another time they ascended to Jerusalem. When they arrived at the Temple Mount, they saw a fox coming out of the place where the Holy of Holies had once stood. The Sages began to cry, and R' Akiva laughed.

"Why are you laughing?" they asked him.

"Why are you crying?" he responded.

"The place about which it is written, 'An alien who approaches shall die,' is now frequented by foxes. Should we not cry?"

"For this very reason I laugh. Uriah prophesized, 'Thus, Zion will be plowed like a field,' whereas Yirmiyah prophesized, 'Old men and women will yet sit in the streets of Jerusalem.' Now that the prophecy of Uriah has been fulfilled, I am certain that Yirmiyah's prophecy will also be fulfilled."

"Akiva, you have consoled us," they said.

Here again we see R' Akiva in his role as a "minister before Hashem," who understood the deep wisdom behind Hashem's seemingly harsh judgments. He could see the light hidden within the darkness, and the good hidden within the evil, not only in his own suffering, but also in the suffering of his entire nation. He could see the dawn of redemption breaking forth from the dark night of exile.[1]

When Hashem instructed Moshe Rabbeinu to lead Bnei Yisrael out of Egypt, Moshe demurred. "Please send through whomever You will send," he said (*Shemos* 4:13). The Midrash (*Osiyos d'Rabbi Akiva* 90) explains that he referred to R' Akiva. This fascinating Midrash requires further study. Hashem showed Moshe Rabbeinu the Torah leaders of all future generations: the judges, kings, prophets, the Men of the Great Assembly and their students, the first of the *Tannaim*. Among them all, Moshe could find no one he deemed worthy of being the instrument of Bnei Yisrael's redemption except for R' Akiva. The Talmud (*Menachos* 29b) also says that upon seeing a prophetic vision of R' Akiva, Moshe was amazed that Hashem decided to grant the Torah through him, and not through R' Akiva. Why?

---

1. We should not misinterpret R' Akiva's remarks as being indicative of a lighthearted, almost flippant personality. Upon reading the verse, "Her husband has revoked them (her vows), and Hashem will forgive her (*Bamidbar* 30:13)," R' Akiva began to cry, at the implication of how much we are dependent on Hashem's forgiveness for our sins. Like all the Sages of the Talmud, R' Akiva's words and deeds were based on deep contemplation of the manner of serving Hashem that was appropriate for him, based on the source of his soul in Heaven. R' Yisrael Salanter *zt"l* discusses this at length in *Ohr Yisrael* Ch. 28.

After beseeching Hashem to forgive Bnei Yisrael for the sin of the Golden Calf, Moshe asked Hashem, "Make Your way known to me" (*Shemos* 33:13). The Talmud (*Berachos* 7a) explains that he asked Hashem why sometimes the righteous suffer, while the wicked prosper. What is the relevance of this request to the sin of the Golden Calf?

At the birth of the Jewish nation, when we were first drawn close to Hashem's service, we erred in the heinous sin of idolatry. Hashem showed Moshe all the suffering we were destined to endure throughout the generations, as part of our punishment for the Golden Calf. Moshe saw that the righteous would suffer, and the wicked would prosper. He also saw all future generations and their leaders. He saw R' Akiva in his unshakeable optimism, laughing at the sight of a fox in the Holy of Holies and at the sound of Rome's prosperity, and responding to all of his misfortunes with a sincere exclamation of, "All that the Merciful One does is for the best." Moshe then thought that R' Akiva should surely be the one to lead Bnei Yisrael through their most difficult times.

When Moshe asked to understand Hashem's ways, Hashem said, "You may see My back, but My face may not be seen." The Talmud (*Menachos* 35b) explains that Hashem showed Moshe the knot of His *tefillin*, tied at the back of His neck, so to speak. The letters of Hashem's Name, שַׁדָּ-י, are inscribed on the *tefillin* — the *shin* on the box of the head, the *dalet* on the knot behind the neck, and the *yud* on the knot of the hand.

Our Sages offer two explanations of the significance of this Name: "I was the One Who said to My world, '*Dai!*' — enough [ordering it to cease its expansion]" (*Chagigah* 12a); and "The entire world is not enough (*dai*) to contain My Godliness" (*Bereishis Rabbah* 46:3).[1]

In the first explanation, the Name שַׁדָּ-י is used as a reference to constraint (*tzimtzum*), which represents the Divine Attribute of Justice. In the second explanation, it refers to unlimited expansion, representing the Divine Attribute of Mercy. This teaches us that these two attributes are inseparably intertwined. Even Hashem's harsh judgments stem from His infinite mercy. This is one of the foundations of our faith, as *Tiferes Shlomo* (Commentary on the Holidays — Succos) explains the verse, "To proclaim Your kindness in the morning, and Your faith in the nights" (*Psalms* 92:3):

The real test of a person's faith is at night, when the light of Hashem's kindness is hidden, and it seems as though harsh judgment has engulfed the world. *Succah* and matzah both serve as

---

1. See *Sfas Emes, Parashas Va'eira*.

remembrances of the Exodus, to remind us that Hashem will eventually redeem us from our suffering, just as He redeemed our forefathers. Therefore their primary obligation is at night, when our faith is tested.

The Midrash says that when R' Yishmael the Kohen Gadol was executed, the angels cried, "Master of the universe! Is this the reward for studying Your Torah?"

"If you are not silent, I will return the entire world to *tohu vavohu*," Hashem answered.[1]

Regarding the beginning of Creation, the verse states, "The earth was *tohu vavohu*" (*Bereishis* 1:2). *Ramban* explains that *tohu vavohu* are the two elemental building blocks from which the entire world was created. Why did Hashem threaten to return the world to its fundamental elements? If He had no need for the world, He could have returned it to utter nothingness. This can be explained by means of a parable I once heard.

Once there was a man who gave a piece of fabric to a tailor, and asked him to sew a garment from it. When the garment was finished, the man measured it and noticed that it seemed smaller than the amount of fabric he had given the tailor. The man demanded the remaining fabric from the tailor, and accused him of theft when he failed to produce it.

The innocent tailor then told his customer, "You know nothing about sewing, and you cannot possibly understand how fabric is transformed into a beautiful garment. If you want to see where all your missing fabric went, let us take a pair of scissors and cut up your garment. Then I will unfold all the pieces and you will see that every last inch of the fabric is accounted for. If you do not wish to see your garment destroyed, then hold your peace."

Hashem gave the same response to His angels. Only Hashem can understand why events play themselves out as they do, because only He sees everything. In order to explain it to others, the world would have to be destroyed, and He could then show us how each event fits perfectly into the grand picture.

When Iyov complained about his suffering, Hashem told him, "Where were you when I laid the earth's foundation? Tell, if you know understanding! Who set its dimensions? — if you know — or who stretched a [surveyor's] line over it? Into what are its bases sunken, or who laid its cornerstone?" (*Iyov* 38:4-6). Only if Hashem were to cause the entire world to revert to its original building blocks could we possibly understand the wisdom of His plan.

---

1. Midrash "*Eilah Ezkarah*," and in the *piyut* recited as part of Yom Kippur *Mussaf*.

"Perfect is His work, for all His paths are justice; a God of faith without iniquity, righteous and fair is He" (*Devarim* 32:4-5). All that Hashem does for us is motivated by His infinite mercy and loving-kindness, although we cannot always understand it.

I heard from my *rebbi*, the Klausenberger Rebbe *zt"l*, that this is the reason we place our hand over our eyes when reciting *Shema*. "Hashem" is the Name of Mercy, and "*Elokim*" is the Name of Justice. Sometimes our eyes trick us, and it seems as if His justice is unmerciful. Therefore, we cover our eyes and say, "*Hashem Elokeinu, Hashem Echad*," affirming that His Mercy and Justice are One and inseparable, even though we cannot always see how this is true.

In the introduction to *Teshuvos Kol Aryeh*, the author explains the verse, "Have no fear of descending to Egypt, for I shall establish you as a great nation there. I shall descend with you to Egypt, and I shall also surely bring you up; and Yosef shall place his hand on your eyes" (*Bereishis* 46:3-4). Yaakov was afraid to descend to the spiritual wasteland of Egypt, so Hashem assured him that although it appeared as if the move to Egypt was a terrible descent for them and a harsh decree from Hashem, he would eventually see that it was in fact an ascent. There, Yaakov's family would be able to bring rectification to the world, and thus merit great holiness.

Hashem encouraged Yaakov to learn from the example of Yosef, who was thrown into a snake pit, sold into slavery, and imprisoned in Egypt. All this seemed to be a terrible misfortune. Yet in the end it was revealed that Yosef's descent was necessary, for this allowed him to provide for his family and for the entire world in the years of famine that were to come.

Hashem told Yaakov, "Yosef shall place his hand on your eyes." This signified the recitation of *Shema*, in which we cover our eyes and affirm our trust in Hashem's mercy, despite any misleading appearances that seem to contradict it. Yosef's own descent to Egypt, and the good that eventually came out of it, was the greatest proof of this. This is why *Zohar* comments that this verse is "the secret of *Kerias Shema*."

Chasam Sofer explains the verse, "You will see My back, but My face (*panim*) may not be seen" (*Shemos* 33:23), to mean that we cannot see the innermost (*penimiyus*) kindness of Hashem, which is hidden behind a veil of strict justice. Only in retrospect can we perceive the kindness that was performed us.

In the Days to Come, when the gates of wisdom will swing open and the entire world will be filled with knowledge of Hashem, we will finally rejoice with the understanding of how the suffering and misfortune we endured in this world was all a manifestation of Hashem's mercy and kindness. King David compares our suffering in this world to the farmer who cries as he plants his seeds. When his crops have grown, he will rejoice as he gathers his produce (*Psalms* 126).

During the exile, we carry a heavy burden, as we sow the seeds of holiness, and see no benefit from them. After the redemption, we will harvest the benefit of all our suffering. Then, our suffering will seem as though it had all been nothing but a bad dream.

The Midrash (*Yalkut Shimoni*, *Psalms* 628) comments on the verse, "Do not rejoice over me, my enemy, for though I fell, I will rise! Though I sit in the darkness, Hashem is a light unto me!" (*Michah* 7:8): Had *Klal Yisrael* not fallen, we could never have risen. Had we not sat in darkness, we could never have experienced the light of Hashem.

The roots of redemption are buried deep within the exile. In the future, we will be able to see clearly how our every fall was an instrument for ascent. In the *Kinnos* for Tishah B'Av we mourn, "For Zion and her cities, like a woman in her birth pangs." The misfortunes we endure in exile are like birth pangs, heralding the wondrous new life that is about to be born.

The verse states, "On that day Hashem will be One and His Name will be One" (*Zechariah* 14:9). The Talmud (*Pesachim* 50a) asks: What is the meaning of this verse? Is His Name not One today? The Talmud goes on to explain that in this world, we recite the blessing, "Blessed is the Truthful Judge" over misfortune, and "Blessed is He Who is good and does good," over joyous events. In the World to Come, however, we will recite only, "Blessed is He Who is good and does good."

The commentaries note that the Talmud does not distinguish between the events of this world and those of the World to Come, and does not state that there will be no misfortune in the World to Come. Rather, the Talmud distinguishes between the way blessings are recited in this world and how they are recited in the next world. In the World to Come, we will recite, "Blessed is He Who is good and does good," over the misfortunes we suffered in this world. "Then our mouths will be filled with laughter" (*Psalms* 126:2) as we look back at all the apparent misfortunes we suffered in this world and realize that they were all events worthy of rejoice, worthy of the blessing, "Blessed is He Who is good and does good."

Our Sages tell us (*Yalkut, Yirmiyah* 312) that just as *Klal Yisrael* was stricken with a double blow — as the verse says, "She has received double for all her sins from the hand of Hashem" (*Yeshayah* 40:2) — we will be comforted with a double consolation, as the verse says, "Comfort, comfort My people," (ibid. 40:1). The double blow of our affliction consists of the actual suffering we have endured, and also the mistaken impression that Hashem has abandoned us in our misery.

Rashi (*Bereishis* 37:25) states that although the Ishmaelite caravans usually carried foul-smelling tar, the caravan to which Yosef was sold carried fragrant spices. The *mussar* masters explain that this was a sign from Heaven to Yosef that even in his suffering, Hashem was with him, protecting him and ensuring that he would not suffer one iota more than necessary.

The Jewish people have suffered through thousands of years of our exile, through the valley of tears, suffering unspeakable hardships, without the slightest sign of Heavenly favor to console us. This is the double blow of our affliction; not only do we suffer, but we see no sign of Hashem taking pity on us. In the future, however, we will merit a double consolation. Hashem will bring an end to all our suffering, and we will merit seeing an era of pure joy and tranquility, in which we will realize retroactively that Hashem's watchful eye had never left us, and His kindness had never forsaken us for even one moment.

Our Sages tell us that all the holidays will ultimately be annulled, except for Purim.[1] The miracle of Purim was different from the miracles for which the other holidays were founded. The other miracles, such as those of the Exodus, were open revelations of Hashem's glory, transcending the laws of nature. In the future, all existence will be raised to a plane above the boundaries of nature. Miracles will no longer be necessary to reveal the Divine Presence. We will then experience an era that will be entirely Yom Tov, forever. The holidays that we celebrate now will therefore have no special significance.

Purim, in contrast, does not commemorate a miracle that transcended nature. Rather, the "natural miracle" of Purim demonstrated how Hashem's presence is evident even in harsh judgments, such as that of Haman. Haman's decree was turned against him, and he and his sons were hanged while the Jewish people celebrated.

The other holidays are named after the miracles of our salvation: Pesach commemorates Hashem passing over our houses to spare us from the Plague of the Firstborn; Succos commemorates the Clouds of Glory that protected us in the desert; and Chanukah commemor-

---

1. See *Yotzros* for *Parashas Zachor.*

ates the inauguration of the altar after it was liberated by the Maccabees. Purim, in contrast, was not named after the salvation, but after the danger that threatened us. Purim means "lottery," in memory of the lots Haman threw to decide when to annihilate the Jews.

Bnei Yissaschar explains that the name "Purim" shows that even the harsh decrees are ultimately revealed as the keys to our salvation. Purim will never be annulled, because it will serve as an eternal remembrance that the suffering we endured in exile was a manifestation of Hashem's hidden kindness, which served as the key to our ultimate Redemption.

The Talmud (*Chullin* 139b) searches for an allusion in the Torah to Esther, and finds the verse, "I will surely have concealed (*haster astir*) My face" (*Devarim* 31:18) The miracles of *Megillas Esther* serve as an important message for the generations challenged by adversity, when it seems as though Hashem conceals Himself from us.

On Purim, we do not recite Hallel. The Talmud (*Megillah* 14b) tells us that reading *Megillas Esther* takes the place of reciting Hallel. But even a person who does not hear the *Megillah* on Purim does not recite Hallel.[1] Why? Because just as the miracles of this day were hidden, so too, our expression of thanksgiving is hidden.

The Midrash (*Midrash Talpios, Achashveirosh*) tells us that Haman planned to hang Mordechai at the time when the *Shema* is recited. Perhaps this idea was planted in Haman's head to teach us that all of his evil plans ultimately led to our benefit. What first appeared as an expression of Hashem's strict justice was later revealed to be pure mercy. This is the secret of *Kerias Shema*, as we quoted above from the *Zohar*.

This also explains our Sages' teaching that Haman was hanged during Pesach (*Megillah* 15a), because the miracles of Purim displayed an important tenet of our faith and trust in Hashem, serving as a continuation of the lessons of faith learned from the Exodus.

The Talmud (*Beitzah* 25a) states:

It was taught in the name of R' Meir: Why was the Torah given to Bnei Yisrael? Because they are brazen.

It was taught in the name of R' Yishmael: "From His right hand he presented the fiery Torah to them" (*Devarim* 33:2). Hashem said, "They are worthy of receiving a fiery Torah."

Rashi explains that because we are brazen, we were given a fiery Torah, in the hopes that by studying it, our brazenness would be tempered, and our hearts subdued. The commentaries note that this

---

1. *Meiri* holds that in such a case, Hallel should be recited.

seems to imply that we were given the Torah not due to our unique greatness, but to alleviate us of our unique deficiency. This is difficult to understand, since the *Kuzari* (1:95) writes that the Jewish people are the greatest of all nations.

According to what we have explained above, we can offer a different interpretation of the Talmud. The Jewish people were chosen to receive the Torah because we are brazen enough to remain loyal to our ideals even amidst the harshest and darkest periods of exile.

The Ramban comments that the verse, "From His right hand he presented the fiery Torah to them," teaches us how Hashem's justice and mercy are one. His right hand signifies His loving mercy, as our Sages teach (*Sotah* 47a): "The right hand draws close, and the left pushes away." Hashem's fire represents His Attribute of Justice. The fiery Torah was given from Hashem's right hand, only to the Jewish people, who can recognize Hashem's mercy even in our most difficult times.

Faith and Trust When Hashem's Kindness Is Hidden

Through the most bitter periods of exile, when Hashem's countenance is hidden from us, we have found the strength to cling to our *emunah* and await Hashem's salvation with faith and trust. The Talmud (*Avodah Zarah* 18a) relates that R' Chanina ben Teradyon was found gathering groups of students together and publicly teaching them Torah, while holding a *Sefer Torah* on his lap. The Romans seized him, wrapped him in his *Sefer Torah*, surrounded him with bundles of dry vines, and set him on fire. They placed wet sponges of wool next to his heart as he burned, so that he would die slowly and painfully.

"Rebbi, what do you see?" his students asked.

"I see the parchment of the *Sefer Torah* burning, and its letters ascending into the air," he said.

Tosafos questions why his students assumed that he saw anything extraordinary. Perhaps we can explain that they did not mean to ask what he saw with his physical eyes. They meant to ask what he saw with the "eyes" of his wisdom. Klal Yisrael at that time was enduring unspeakable hardship and destruction. The harsh decrees of the wicked Romans had crushed their spirits and brought them to the verge of despair. Worst of all, they now witnessed the execution of the Rebbi who had supported them throughout their most difficult trials. "What do you see, Rebbi?" they asked. "Can you see any hope for us in our bitter plight? What will become of us, after we are left like a flock without a shepherd?"

R' Chanina ben Teradyon consoled them, urging them not to fear the death of his physical body. The wicked Romans could do what they wished with the bodies of Bnei Yisrael, but they could never harm our immortal souls. Our bodies are like the parchment on which a *Sefer Torah* is written, and our souls are like the letters. When the bodies are burned, the souls ascend unharmed to Heaven. At the time that Hashem deems fit, the letters will return to this world to settle on a different parchment. The souls of the Sages will return to teach Torah again, for Hashem has assured us that the holy Torah will never be forgotten from Bnei Yisrael.

This outlook, which pierced through the veils of nature and transcended human reasoning, led to the downfall of the Roman Empire (*Tosafos, Avodah Zarah* 2b). In the merit of Bnei Yisrael's sacrifice for Torah, even in times of pain and darkness, the Divine Presence will be revealed in the world, and we will finally be redeemed.

When the second Beis Hamikdash was built, its gates were made of copper. Later, all of the gates were replaced with golden gates, except for the Gates of Nikanor, which were left in place, due to the miracle that occurred to them (*Yoma* 38a).

Miracles in the Beis Hamikdash were no great novelty. The Mishnah (*Avos* 5:5) lists ten miracles that regularly occurred there. Elsewhere, the Talmud (*Menachos* 86b) states that sunlight was not necessary to illuminate the Beis Hamikdash, since a miraculous light emanated from it. Furthermore, the Holy Ark did not take up any space in the Holy of Holies (*Megillah* 10b). These and many other miracles were constantly occurring in the Beis Hamikdash. What, then, was the uniqueness of the Gates of Nikanor?

Nikanor made two gates in Egypt, to be transported to Eretz Yisrael by boat. While at sea, a storm hit, and giant waves threatened to sink the ship. To lighten the load, the sailors took all the heavy cargo and threw it overboard. They threw one of Nikanor's gates overboard, but the storm still did not subside. The sailors then prepared to throw the other gate overboard, but Nikanor clung tightly to it and said, "If you throw it overboard, you must throw me with it." Immediately, the storm ceased.

Nikanor grieved over the lost gate, until they arrived at the port of Akko and found that the gate had become lodged beneath the boat, and was carried along with them to Eretz Yisrael. (According to another opinion, it was swallowed by a giant sea creature and disgorged on the shore of Akko.)

Nikanor's had no right to ask the sailors to risk their lives by keeping the heavy gate on board. Nor did he demand it. In what appeared to be a suicidal request, he asked to be thrown overboard with the gate, although he would gain nothing from drowning together with his gate.

This teaches us an important lesson. When waves of darkness and oppression threaten to engulf our people, some segments of our nation would have us lighten our load by throwing overboard the proverbial gates of the Beis Hamikdash: our dedication to Torah and mitzvos. When such a threat looms over us, we must cling with all our might to our ideals, even if it means sacrificing our lives. To serve as an eternal reminder of Nikanor's sacrifice and the miracle he experienced as a result, his gates remained in the Beis Hamikdash when all the others were replaced.

Our generation faces a challenge similar to Nikanor's. We also had two gates through which we entered into Hashem's service: the gate of Torah and the gate of *avodah*. The gate of *avodah* was lost — for the most part — with the destruction of the Beis Hamikdash. Therefore, we must cling with all our might to the gate of Torah study, sacrificing ourselves with love, joy, and determination. In the merit of our sacrifice, we will merit to see the second gate returned to us, with the fulfillment of Yeshayah's prophecy, "The glory of Hashem will be revealed, and all flesh together will see that the mouth of Hashem has spoken" (*Yeshayah* 40:5).

↝ The Redemption of Our Souls

I.

The mitzvah of remembering the Exodus has the unique ability to propel our souls to the loftiest spiritual heights. R' Naftali of Ropshitz *zt"l* explained the passage in Shabbos *Kiddush,* תְּחִלָּה לְמִקְרָאֵי קֹדֶשׁ זֵכֶר לִיצִיאַת מִצְרָיִם, *the prologue to the holy convocations, a memorial of the Exodus from Egypt,* to mean that that the first and foremost call that inspires a person to grow in holiness is the remembrance of Exodus.

The miracles of the Exodus serve to strengthen our *emunah* and *bitachon* (faith and trust) in Hashem. The Talmud (*Berachos* 4b) tells us that if a person prays *Shemoneh Esrei* immediately after completing the blessing of *Go'al Yisrael,* he is guaranteed a place in the World to Come. Rabbeinu Yonah explains that *Go'al Yisrael* describes the miracles our forefathers witnessed when Hashem rescued them from Egypt. Through these miracles, they learned to trust Him, as the verse (*Shemos* 14:31) says, "Israel saw the great hand that Hashem inflicted upon Egypt ... ; and they had faith in Hashem."

When we begin to pray immediately after recalling the Redemption — in which our forefathers trusted Hashem, and He rescued them — this shows that we trust Hashem to answer our prayers, as He answered theirs.

The Chazon Ish authored a treatise on the subject of *emunah* and *bitachon,* in which he defines both at length. Many misinterpret his opinion as contrary to the opinion espoused by Chassidic sources.

The Chazon Ish (*Emunah U'Bitachon,* 2) writes that when a person finds himself in a difficult situation and says confidently, "Hashem will help," he may well be fooling himself. How can he be sure that Hashem will rescue him from his plight? There is a Judge in Heaven who metes out justice for all of man's actions; perhaps his difficult situation was brought upon him as a punishment for his sins. Hashem does not always rescue a person just because he trusts in Him. We say in the *Selichos* supplications, "*Perhaps* He will pity a poor and impoverished nation; *perhaps* He will show mercy." One must have faith that Hashem *can* help, but on what basis can a person assume that Hashem will indeed help?

In contrast, *Toldos Yaakov Yosef* (*Parashas Mikeitz*), quotes the Baal Shem Tov's explanation of the verse (*Psalms* 32:10), "One who trusts in Hashem, kindness surrounds him," as follows: If a person's trust in Hashem is perfect, he is surrounded by angels who guard his every step against misfortune.

Elsewhere (*Keser Shem Tov*), the Baal Shem Tov is quoted as saying that even if a Heavenly decree has been pronounced upon a person, his trust in Hashem will protect him.

At first glance, the opinions of the Chazon Ish and the Baal Shem Tov seem to be contradictory. This is not necessarily so, however.

R' Chaim of Volozhin writes in *Nefesh HaChaim* (3:12) that in times of trouble, a person should concentrate on Hashem's absolute power, recognizing that there is no force that can help or harm him except for Hashem's Will. If he fully acknowledges this truth, nothing in the world will be able to harm him.

The Chazon Ish would certainly not argue against the words of R' Chaim of Volozhin, who based his teachings upon those of his mentor, the Vilna Gaon. The Chazon Ish himself writes (*Emunah U'Bitachon* 2:7), "If a person trusts Hashem, a Divine spirit rests upon him, and a spirit of might accompanies him, assuring him that Hashem will surely help. This is as King David said (*Psalms* 27:3), 'Though an army would besiege me, my heart would not fear; though war would arise against me, in this I trust.'"

The Chazon Ish proceeds to explain that this Divine protection depends on the sincerity of a person's trust. When the Chassidic masters and R' Chaim of Volozhin taught that trust in Hashem will guard a person from harm, they spoke of a person who trusts in Hashem with every fiber of his being.[1]

Nevertheless, there remains a subtle distinction between the two schools of thought. According to the Chazon Ish, a person's *bitachon* protects him only in proportion to his spiritual level. His *bitachon* must reflect who he is.

According to the Chassidic masters, however, Divine protection depends solely on the sincerity of the person's *bitachon*, regardless of whether he is worthy. The Midrash seems to support this position. On the verse, "One who trusts in Hashem is surrounded by kindness," the Midrash (*Yalkut, Psalms* 32:10) states that even if a

---

1. See *Radak* on *Psalms* 116:10; *Emunah U'Bitachon* by *Ramban*, end of Ch. 1.

wicked person trusts in Hashem, he will be surrounded by His kindness.[1]

Many people profess to believe in Hashem and in the miracles of the Exodus. However, we find it difficult to apply this faith to the hardships of our personal lives, such as lack of livelihood, health problems, and so on. But these hardships are the true test of a person's faith.

Rabbeinu Yonah's words teach us how to apply our faith to our own lives, as well. When we think about the miracles of the Exodus and realize how very relevant they are to us, we are inspired to pray with sincere faith and trust in Hashem. Our faith becomes more than mere philosophy. It becomes an integral part of our lives, as we place our personal burdens in Hashem's hands with full confidence that He will help us.

II.

Our Sages tell us that in every generation, we must view ourselves as if we personally left Egypt. This means that the lessons of the Exodus must become part of our personal lives.

R' Yisrael of Ruzhin taught in *Knesses Yisrael* that the search for chametz is performed only at night because night represents exile, when we wage war against our evil inclination, but cannot fully conquer it. The chametz is destroyed in the morning after the search. Likewise, only when the dawn of Mashiach breaks will we finally be able to eradicate the evil inclination from the world.

The message in this idea is that the search for and destruction of chametz is not just a mechanical chore, but is symbolic of the search for and destruction of evil in our hearts.

Radvaz[2] cites *Tosafos'* question why we are so much more stringent with chametz than with any other forbidden food. (For instance, there is no prohibition against owning non-kosher meat. Only chametz must be searched for and destroyed.) He explains that chametz is more severe because it represents idolatry and the evil inclination.

Indeed, there is a broad parallel between chametz and idolatry. For example, these are the only two prohibitions where we find the concept of *bitul* — nullification — after which the forbidden substance becomes permitted. When they cannot be nullified, they must both be destroyed by fire. And neither may be kept in a Jew's

---

1. See also *Sefer Ha'Ikarim* 4:46.
2. *Teshuvos Radvaz* vol. 3, 546.

possession. All these points of comparison support the assertion of the *Radvaz* that the search for and destruction of chametz parallels the destruction of idolatry and the evil inclination.

The same is true with all the mitzvos of Pesach. Our ancestors' liberation from their Egyptian servitude represents our own liberation from the bonds of our evil inclination, each and every year.

The Baal Shem Tov explains the verse (*Psalms* 69:19), "Draw near to my soul, redeem it," to mean that every person has the power to draw redemption closer by freeing his own soul from the bonds of the evil inclination. In every person's life there is an element of exile, an enslavement of the soul to the base, animalistic tendencies of the body. When a person struggles against these tendencies, raising his soul to ever higher planes of holiness, he redeems his own soul, and thereby hastens the ultimate Redemption of Israel.

Ramban calls *Sefer Shemos* "The Book of Exile and Redemption." *Sefer Shemos* begins with the story of our ancestors' subjugation in Egypt, and proceeds to describe their miraculous Redemption. The story of the Redemption seems to conclude with *Parashas Beshalach*. In the next seven *parshiyos*, *Sefer Shemos* describes the giving of the Torah and how Bnei Yisrael built and inaugurated the Mishkan in the desert. *Ramban* explains that these *parshiyos* are also part of the story of the Redemption. Bnei Yisrael were not considered truly redeemed until they had returned to the exalted spiritual level of the Patriarchs.

The concluding verse in *Sefer Shemos* (40:38) states, "For the cloud of Hashem would be on the Mishkan by day, and fire would be on it by night, before the eyes of all of the House of Israel throughout their journeys." The Divine Presence had returned to rest upon them, as it had rested in the tents of the Patriarchs. (Elsewhere, *Ramban* writes that the entire purpose of the Mishkan was to allow the Divine Presence, which had appeared to Bnei Yisrael on Mount Sinai, to accompany them in all their journeys.)

Just as the redemption of the individual involves a spiritual redemption, the Redemption of our nation also has two aspects — a physical liberation from suffering, and a spiritual liberation from the evil inclination.

Sfas Emes explains that this is the distinction between *Yetzias Mitzrayim* and *Kerias Yam Suf* (the splitting of the Red Sea). At the conclusion of the Ten Plagues, we experienced a physical liberation, and were allowed to leave Egypt, the land of our affliction. However, our spiritual liberation did not occur until *Kerias Yam Suf*, when even a simple servant girl saw a prophetic revelation greater than what the prophet Yechezkel saw (*Mechilta, Parashas Beshalach*). This was the culmination of the Redemption. (According to the Ramban cited above, our spiritual redemption was still not complete until the Divine Presence rested on the Mishkan.)

We see that there are two aspects to redemption. When we celebrate Pesach, we must also remember to celebrate the spiritual aspect of the Redemption, and endeavor to free our own souls from the evil inclination.

III.

The three festivals — Pesach, Shavuos, and Succos — are all celebrated in commemoration of the Exodus. Each one represents a different aspect of the Redemption. On the first day of Pesach, we celebrate our physical liberation from Egypt. On the seventh day, we celebrate the spiritual redemption of *Kerias Yam Suf*. On Shavuos, we celebrate receiving the Torah, which was the ultimate purpose of the Redemption. On Succos, we commemorate the intermediate stage, our preparation to receive the Torah: "I caused Bnei Yisrael to dwell in booths (*succos*) when I took them from the land of Egypt" (*Vayikra* 23:43).

The Midrash says that when Hashem took Bnei Yisrael out of Egypt, we were on a dismal spiritual level. During our forty-nine-day trek to Mount Sinai, Hashem raised us from one level to the next, until we were worthy of receiving the Torah.

The three aspects of the redemption represent the three stages of a person's liberation from the evil inclination. King David said, "Turn from evil and do good" (*Psalms* 34:15). The first step of spiritual ascent is to turn away from evil and purify ourselves from sin. This is as the prophet Yeshayah instructed, "Wash yourselves, purify yourselves, remove the evil of your deeds" (*Yeshayah* 1:16). When a person is submerged in sin, he cannot rise to a lofty spiritual level. The Dubno Maggid offered a parable to explain this concept:

Once there was a simple villager who envied his acquaintances for their well-fitting, custom-made clothing. He had never worn anything better than a coarse, ill-fitting fur jacket that sat on his shoulders like a potato sack. He began to scrape together coins, putting aside all his spare money, until finally he had enough to purchase the finest suit in town. He took his bag of coins to the tailor and had himself measured. The tailor gave him a beautiful, elegant new coat, and told him to take it into a changing room to try it on. A few moments later the villager emerged, furious. "What kind of business is it to give me a coat like this? Do you think this fits me? I can't even get my arm through the sleeve!"

"My dear sir," the tailor responded, "maybe try taking off your old coat before you try on the new one."

Before a person can adopt a new lifestyle of Torah and mitzvos, he must abandon his lifestyle of sin. First we must turn away from evil, and only then can we do good. When we purify our souls from evil, we can begin to appreciate the joy of Torah and mitzvos.

However, between turning away from evil and doing good there is also an intermediate stage: preparing for the mitzvah. Before performing a mitzvah we must awaken in ourselves a longing for it, by contemplating its importance.

Sfas Emes (5634, *Haazinu*) writes that in some cases, preparation for a mitzvah is more important than the mitzvah itself. He cites the Midrash that refers to the first day of Succos as the first day of the new year's accounting of sins (*Midrash Rabbah* 23:1). On Yom Kippur we are forgiven for all our old sins, and between Yom Kippur and Succos we are too busy to sin, since we are preparing the *succah* and the Four Species. *Sfas Emes* notes that *preparing* for these mitzvos protects us from sin, whereas the mitzvos themselves do not. Therefore, the first day of Succos marks the beginning of our new accounting of sins.

Ritva (*Pesachim* 7b) offers two explanations why blessings are recited before, and not after, the performance of mitzvos. First, the blessing shows that one's intention in performing the mitzvah is to fulfill the will of Hashem. Second, a blessing is a service of the soul, while the performance of a mitzvah is a service of the body. It is proper that the service of the soul precede the service of the body. Here, again, we see the importance of preparing for a mitzvah.

When R' Akiva was executed, it was time to recite the *Shema*. As the Romans tore off his flesh with iron combs, he recited *Shema*, accepting upon himself the yoke of Hashem's service with love. His students were amazed at the extent of his self-sacrifice.

"My entire life I longed to fulfill the verse, 'You shall love Hashem …; with all your soul,' which means that we must sacrifice our lives for Him, if need be. Now that I have the opportunity, should I not fulfill it?" he explained (*Berachos* 61b).

Why were his students so surprised? Presumably, they were aware of this interpretation of the verse, having it heard it from R' Akiva before. Did they not expect their rebbi to practice what he taught?

Perhaps we can explain that the students knew that one must sacrifice his life for Hashem with love and joy, but they did not know how. *Talmud Yerushalmi* (*Berachos* 9:5, *Sotah* 5:5) adds that as R' Akiva's flesh was torn off, he laughed. The students could not understand how he had reached such a high level of self-sacrifice.

To this question, R' Akiva answered that he was not experiencing a momentary inspiration. He had spent his entire life preparing for this moment. Only after a lifetime of working on himself was he able to sacrifice his life with joy when the moment of trial arrived.

IV.

The holiday of Pesach is also marked by a tremendous amount of preparation. We must knead and bake the matzos with the express intention to fulfill the mitzvah. We may not eat a meal in the afternoon of Erev Pesach, so that we can eat matzah with an appetite and with enthusiasm. All this is done so that the taste of the matzah — and its positive influence — remain with us throughout the year.

As we begin the month of Nissan, the month of the Redemption, we prepare to relive the Exodus from Egypt. Why does the memory of the Exodus inspire such joy in us thousands of years after it occurred? The freedom we enjoyed then has since been lost, and we still suffer in this terrible exile. Two hundred years ago, *Bnei Yissaschar* wrote that our current exile, the exile of Edom, is much worse than the exile of Egypt. Since the time of the *Bnei Yissaschar* we have suffered through two centuries of hardship and bloodshed. Each new wave of suffering makes the trials that preceded it pale in comparison. In the past century we have endured what may have been the most difficult trial our nation has ever faced, when darkness covered the face of the earth and Hashem's loving countenance was hidden from us.

Nevertheless, even in our darkest and most difficult times we have celebrated Pesach, recalling the miracles of the Exodus. I often heard my father *shlita* tell of how he celebrated Pesach during the Holocaust together with the Sanzer Rebbe *zt"l* and a handful of Jews who kept the spark of Torah alive in their broken hearts. They endured great difficulty, and even risked their lives, to bake matzos for Pesach and rejoice together as the remembered the Exodus.

How can we understand this? What does the Exodus mean to us, now that the liberty we once enjoyed has been lost? R' Shaul Nathanson, the author of *Teshuvos Sho'eil U'Meishiv*, answered this question with a story:

Once there was a Jew who suffered from terrible poverty. It was not his lack of basic necessities that grieved him, however, as much as his inability to study Torah and to give his children a Torah education.

Hashem heard his prayers, and one day he discovered a buried treasure of great value. He took advantage of his good fortune and hired tutors to teach Torah to him and his children. From morning to night, he would devote himself entirely to Torah study, with no worldly burden to distract him.

Each year, on the anniversary of the day he found the treasure, he would invite his family and friends to celebrate together with him as he hosted a festive banquet in honor of the occasion.

The years passed, and the wheel of fortune again turned against him. He lost all his money, and was reduced to abject poverty. When the anniversary of his finding the treasure came, his family and friends were surprised to receive an invitation to join him again in his celebration. They came to his house and shared with him a meager meal of dry bread and water — the most he could afford.

"Why do you celebrate the fortune you once had, now that you have lost it again?" they asked.

"True, we have lost our money," the man said, "but the Torah we have studied and the house we have built on the foundation of Torah are ours to enjoy forever. This is our greatest treasure, and no misfortune can ever deprive us of it."

The same is true of our own celebration on the anniversary of our Exodus from Egypt. "This is your sign that I have sent you: When you take the people out of Egypt, you will serve God on this mountain" (*Shemos* 3:12). After the Exodus from Egypt, we were led to Mount Sinai, where we received the Torah. The Torah accompanies us wherever we may travel. From Sinai to Eretz Yisrael, and from there into exile; from Babylon to Europe, and even into the inferno that consumed European Jewry, Hashem and His Torah are always with us. The Torah we received as a result of the Exodus is our eternal possession. It is the primary cause for our rejoicing as we celebrate the holiday of Pesach.

❧ The Statutes of Pesach and Parah Adumah

King David prayed, "May my heart be perfect in Your statutes" (*Psalms* 119:80). The Midrash explains that this refers to two statutes: Pesach, of which it is written (*Shemos* 12:43), "This is the statute of the *Korban Pesach*"; and *Parah Adumah*, the red heifer, of which it is written, "This is the statute of the Torah" (*Bamidbar* 19:2). Why did King David pray that his heart be sincere in the fulfillment of these two mitzvos? What is the relationship between them?

Perhaps the Midrash did not intend to compare the two mitzvos, but to highlight the contrast between them. We are commanded to inquire and examine each aspect of the *Korban Pesach*. We encourage our children to ask question after question and to delve into its every nuance. Even the simple son asks, "What is this?", and we open the discussion for the son who does not know how to ask, to arouse his curiosity.

The mitzvah of *Parah Adumah* is just the opposite. King Solomon, the wisest of all men, said about this mitzvah, "I thought I could become wise, but it is beyond me" (*Koheles* 7:23). We cannot understand the *Parah Adumah*. It is a decree of the King, and we are forbidden to question it (*Rashi, Bamidbar* 19:2).

King David saw that sometimes we are forbidden to question, and sometimes we are required to do so. He prayed that Hashem help him balance the pursuit of wisdom with unquestioning acceptance of Hashem's will, and apply each one appropriately.

When are we supposed to ask and examine, and when are we supposed to humbly accept?

We learn the answer to this question from Avraham Avinu. After Avraham bound his son Yitzchak as a sacrifice and lifted a knife to slaughter him, an angel called out to him and instructed him not to harm his son.

Rashi (*Bereishis* 22:12) notes that Avraham then questioned Hashem's instructions. "First You told me, 'Through Yitzchak will offspring be considered yours.' Then You told me, 'Take your son ...

and bring him up as an offering.' Now You tell me, 'Do not stretch out your hand against the child.' "

Why did Avraham wait until after he was told not to harm Yitzchak to tell Hashem that the command to sacrifice Yitzchak seemed to contradict Hashem's promise that Yitzchak would continue his lineage? Why did he not ask Hashem immediately after he received the command?

As long as Avraham Avinu had an obligation to fulfill, he asked no questions. Hashem commanded him to offer Yitzchak as a sacrifice, and Avraham hastened to comply, voicing no misgivings. After Hashem told Avraham not to harm Yitzchak, he no longer had any obligation to fulfill. Only then did he ask, in order to fully understand Hashem's command.

The Talmud (*Shabbos* 88a) says that when Bnei Yisrael declared, "We will do and we will listen," angels descended to place two crowns on the head of every Jew, one for "We will do" and one for "We will listen." Apparently, we were rewarded on two counts: for agreeing to comply without even waiting to hear what our orders would be, and for then asking to listen and understand the reason for these orders. One crown represented unquestioning obedience, corresponding to the "statute of the *Parah Adumah.*" The other crown represented our desire to understand the wisdom behind the mitzvos, corresponding to the "statute of the *Korban Pesach.*"

Throughout the year, we engage extensively in the statutes of the *Parah Adumah,* performing Hashem's will without asking for any explanation. On the night of Pesach, we delve into the statutes of the *Korban Pesach,* in order to understand the meaning of this night to the best of our ability.

⤷ Smoking Cigarettes on Pesach

Disclaimer: Medical research has proven that smoking is dangerous. It is therefore forbidden to smoke, since the Torah commands us (Devarim 4:15), "You shall greatly beware for your souls."[1]

In previous generations, smoking on Yom Tov was permitted by many authorities. Today, however, this leniency does not apply. The Talmud stipulates that one may only transfer fire on Yom Tov for a purpose that is "shaveh l'chol nefesh" — *equally enjoyed by all people.[2] Since most people today do not smoke, smoking on Yom Tov is absolutely forbidden. The following discussion revolves solely around the issue of whether or not the prohibition against owning or enjoying chametz applies to cigarettes.*

Q: Tobacco manufacturers steep their products in chametz-based alcohol during production. Are cigarettes considered chametz? May one own or use tobacco products during Pesach?

A: Many years ago, the *Magen Avraham*[3] forbade tobacco snuff that was steeped in chametz alcohol, but his opinion was refuted by *Beis Meir*. Since then, a halachic debate has ensued, with many of the greatest *Poskim* supporting the *Magen Avraham*[4] and others arguing against him.[5]

Those who are lenient base their opinions on the general rule that any chametz that has become inedible even to dogs is no longer considered chametz, and it may be owned and used on Pesach.[6]

---

1. See *Berachos* 32b.
2. *Kesubos* 7a. See *Mishnah Berurah* 511 §1, 21; *Beur Halachah* ibid. 4, s.v. *Ein osin mugmar*.
3. O.C. 467 §10.
4. *Shulchan Aruch HaRav* §24; *Chok Yaakov* §22; *Mishnah Berurah* §33.
5. *Mor U'Ketzia*, end of 442. He cites that his father, the Chacham Tzvi, was also lenient in this matter, and he writes that the opinion of the *Magen Avraham* is "baffling."
6. *Shulchan Aruch* 442:2.

Once the chametz-based alcohol has been absorbed into the tobacco, it is no longer edible to dogs. Therefore, these *Poskim* permit it.

The *Magen Avraham* certainly agrees with this general rule, since it is clearly stated in the Talmud[1] and *Shulchan Aruch*.[2] What, then, is the point of contention in this debate? Perhaps the *Magen Avraham* understood that chametz becomes permitted only when it is *spoiled* to the extent that it is inedible even to dogs. Some kinds of chametz are inedible to dogs not because they are spoiled, but simply because they are not fit for a dog's diet. These kinds of chametz are clearly forbidden. For example, grain-based alcohol is considered chametz by Torah law,[3] even though it is not edible to dogs. Perhaps the *Magen Avraham* understood that the same is true of alcohol absorbed by tobacco. The alcohol itself is edible; it is just inaccessible, since it has been mixed with inedible tobacco. Therefore, the *Magen Avraham* forbade the tobacco snuff that was popular in his times. Other *Poskim* argue that since the alcohol cannot be eaten or drunk in its present state, it is not considered chametz.

The production process for tobacco has since developed so much that tobacco today is hardly comparable to the tobacco produced in the time of the *Magen Avraham*. Today, the chametz chemicals used to flavor tobacco are inedible even before they are mixed into the tobacco. Therefore, even the *Magen Avraham* would agree that our tobacco is considered inedible even to dogs, and is therefore permitted.

Ach'shivei — **Inedible Substances Treated as Edible**

Although it is permitted to own chametz that is inedible even to dogs, it is still forbidden to eat it, based on the principle of *Ach'shivei*.[4] This is a general principle that applies to many different areas of halachah.[5] Simply stated, *Ach'shivei* means that even when the Torah does not ascribe value to a certain food or action, it still recognizes that an individual might value them. In regard to chametz, *Ach'shivei* means that the Torah does not consider inedible foods to be chametz, but if a person decides to eat them, he clearly values them. In such a case, the Torah would recognize that this

---

1. *Pesachim* 45b.

2. Ibid.

3. *Mishnah Berurah* 442 §4.

4. Ibid. §21.

5. See also *Shabbos* 90b (regarding the *shiurim* for carrying on Shabbos); *Shabbos* 144a, *Beur Halachah* O.C. 320:1 s.v. *Mutar l'sochtan* (regarding squeezing fruits on Shabbos); *Bava Metzia* 87b (regarding *terumos* and *maasros*).

person considers the food to be edible, and it would therefore be forbidden for him.

Some contemporary *Poskim* apply this principle to smoking cigarettes that contain chametz. Just as it is forbidden to eat or drink inedible chametz because by doing so a person shows that he considers it edible, similarly, they contend, it is forbidden to smoke inedible chametz. In my opinion, this argument is entirely incorrect. Smoking is not comparable to drinking. Although several proofs have been cited to the contrary, they are all refutable.

The first proof cited is from *Mishnah Berurah*, who forbids smoking from a *tuten* (water pipe) on Tishah B'Av.[1] The contemporary *Poskim* who prohibit smoking understood that this is because smoking is comparable to drinking. This is clearly not *Mishnah Berurah*'s intention. *Mishnah Berurah* writes that if a person is addicted to smoking, he may smoke in private on Tishah B'Av in the afternoon. If it were true that smoking is comparable to drinking, there would be no room for such a leniency, just as there is no room to permit a ravenously hungry person to eat in private on Tishah B'Av afternoon.

Rather, we must explain that in those days people did not casually smoke water pipes as they smoke cigarettes today. Smoking a water pipe was considered a form of recreation, which detracts from the somber spirit of Tishah B'Av. In any case, most *Poskim* do permit smoking on fast days.[2] Clearly, therefore, there is no proof from here that smoking is comparable to drinking.

The second proof cited is from *Magen Avraham*,[3] who discusses whether a blessing should be made over smoking. On one hand, *Magen Avraham* compares smoking to smelling fragrant aromas, over which a blessing is recited. On the other hand, he compares it to food that is tasted and then spat out, over which no blessing is recited. These *Poskim* misunderstood the *Magen Avraham* to mean that smoking might be comparable to eating or drinking. However, it seems obvious that *Magen Avraham* only intended to compare smoking to eating in one particular regard: that perhaps exhaling the smoke is like spitting out food, which exempts it from a blessing.[4]

Even if we would concede that *Magen Avraham* questions

---

1. *Mishnah Berurah* 555 §8.

2. See *Mor U'Ketzia* 210; *Teshuvos Beis David*, O.C. 143; *Teshuvos Har HaCarmel* 19; *Machaneh Chaim* vol. 3, O.C. 43.

3. 210 §9.

4. See *Mishnah Berurah* (ibid. §17), who rules that no blessing is recited over smoking. *Ksav Sofer* (O.C. 24) writes that when R' Mordechai Bennett would smoke, he would first recite *shehakol* over food or drink, with the intention that his

whether smoking is a form of eating or drinking, the principle of *Ach'shivei* would still not apply. *Ach'shivei* in this context means that by eating the "inedible" food, one shows that he considers it edible, and therefore the prohibition against eating chametz applies. If one just tastes it and spits it out, however — as is the case with cigarette smoke — this does not show it to be edible.

Furthermore, *Ach'shivei* only applies if chametz is the principal ingredient of the food. This is not so in our case, where the principal ingredient is the tobacco, and the chametz alcohol is only one of many additives used to enhance the flavor.

Conclusion

Many of the greatest *Poskim* of recent generations permitted the use of tobacco flavored with chametz or non-kosher wine.[1] In our own generation, there is even greater reason to be lenient, since the chametz additives are rendered inedible even before they are mixed into the tobacco. Therefore, if a person wishes to be stringent, he may, but there is no basis to issue a general ban against cigarettes on Pesach.

---

blessing also exempt his smoking. *Ksav Sofer* concludes that the prevalent custom is not to follow this practice. Interestingly, R' Yitzchak of Kamarna writes that in theory, we should recite a blessing before smoking. However, we find no text for this blessing in the Gemara or *Rishonim*, and we are unable to devise a blessing on our own. The Baal Shem Tov, however, was endowed with Divine Inspiration, and he knew which blessing our Sages would have devised. Therefore, he did recite a blessing before he smoked.

1. See *Teshuvos Divrei Chaim* vol. 1, Y.D. 20; *Teshuvos Mahari Assad*, O.C. 156; *Minchas Yitzchak* vol. 5, 16 (regarding the issue of non-kosher animal fat in cigarettes).

This volume is part of
THE ARTSCROLL® SERIES
an ongoing project of
translations, commentaries and expositions on
Scripture, Mishnah, Talmud, Midrash, Halachah,
liturgy, history, the classic Rabbinic writings,
biographies and thought.

For a brochure of current publications
visit your local Hebrew bookseller
or contact the publisher:

Mesorah Publications, ltd

313 Regina Avenue
Rahway, New Jersey 07065
(718) 921-9000
www.artscroll.com